Green Policies and Practices

Proceedings of the International Conference on International Economic Cooperation and Integration (CIECI 2024)

This conference proceedings is for the International Conference on Green Policies and Practices: Catalyst or Pressure for Trade and Investment. The conference was organized on 22nd and 23rd November 2024 at University of Economics and Business, Vietnam National University – Hanoi. This conference was done in collaboration with Confab 360 Degree, India; Friedrich Naumann Foundation for Freedom in Vietnam (FNF), University of Adelaide (Australia); Sofia University (Bulgaria); Rangsit University (Thailand); Foreign Trade University (Vietnam), University of Economics and Law – VNU HCMC (Vietnam). The conference is the 12th in the series of annual Conferences on International Economic Cooperation and Integration (CIECI), initiated in 2013 by the VNU-UEB.

Assoc. Prof. Dr. Nguyen Anh Thu
Associate Professor Dr. Nguyen Anh Thu is the Vice Rector of University of Economics and Business, Vietnam National University - Hanoi. She leads the research and partnership development activities of the University. She received her Ph.D. in Economics in 2009 at Yokohama National University, Japan, specializing in International Development and had experiences in working for Ministry of Industry and Trade of Vietnam as the trade policy maker and other multinational companies before becoming a lecturer.

Dr. Anuj Kumar
Dr. Anuj Kumar is Head of Research at Rushford Business School, Switzerland. He is a Post-Doctoral Fellow in Malaysia, Honorary Research Fellow at INTI International University, Malaysia, Honorary Professor at the European Global Institute of Innovation & Technology, Malta, and Visiting Faculty at VNU University of Economics and Business, Vietnam. In addition, he serves as Editorial Head at Confab 360 Degree, India's first IAF-ISO certified company connecting global researchers through academic events and platforms.

Assoc. Prof. Dr. Vu Thanh Huong
Associate Professor Dr. Vu Thanh Huong is the Associate Dean of Faculty of International Business and Economics, University of Economics and Business, Vietnam National University - Hanoi VNU-UEB. She is a highly experienced lecturer and researcher with a master's degree in Natural Resource Economics and a doctor degree in International Economics. She has led and participated in many national and international projects related to international economics and published numerous articles, books and book chapters on international economics, trade, investment, global value chain and environment.

Green Policies and Practices

Proceedings of the International Conference on International Economic Cooperation and Integration (CIECI 2024)

Edited by

Assoc. Prof. Dr. Nguyen Anh Thu

Associate Professor, University of Economics and Business, Vietnam National University - Hanoi, Vietnam

thuna@vnu.edu.vn

Dr. Anuj Kumar

Head of Research, Rushford Business School, Switzerland; Research Fellow, INTI International University, Malaysia

profanuj15@gmail.com

Assoc. Prof. Dr. Vu Thanh Huong

Associate Professor, University of Economics and Business, Vietnam National University - Hanoi, Vietnam

huongvt@vnu.edu.vn

Routledge
Taylor & Francis Group

First edition published 2026
by Routledge
44 Park Square, Milton Park, Abingdon, Oxon, OX14 4RN

and by Routledge
605 Third Avenue, New York, NY 10158

Routledge is an imprint of the Taylor & Francis Group, an informa business

British Library Cataloguing-in-Publication Data
A catalogue record for this book is available from the British Library

ISBN: 9781041240785 (pbk)
ISBN: 9781041240723 (hbk)
ISBN: 9781003739982 (ebk)

DOI: 10.4324/9781003739982

Typeset in Times New Roman
by HBK Digital

Contents

List of Figures

List of Tables

Foreword

It gives us immense pleasure to present the proceedings of the International Conference on International Economic Cooperation and Integration (CIECI 2024), held on 22nd–23rd November 2024 at the University of Economics and Business, Vietnam National University, Hanoi.

The theme of the conference, “Green Policies and Practices: Catalyst or Pressure for Trade and Investment”, reflects one of the most pressing debates of our time: the balance between economic growth and environmental sustainability. As global trade and investment deepen, the urgency of integrating green standards into policies and practices has never been greater.

The conference has brought together distinguished academics, researchers, policymakers, industry leaders, and young scholars from across the world to deliberate on the theoretical, empirical, and practical dimensions of green policies and their impact on international economic integration. Their contributions not only enrich academic discourse but also provide practical insights to guide future strategies for sustainable trade and investment.

We extend our deepest gratitude to the partner institutions - VNU University of Economics and Business, Vietnam National University, Hanoi; Confab 360 Degree (India) ; Friedrich Naumann Foundation for Freedom in Vietnam (FNF), University of Adelaide (Australia); Sofia University (Bulgaria); Rangsit University (Thailand); Foreign Trade University (Vietnam), University of Economics and Law – VNU HCMC (Vietnam).

We hope these proceedings will serve as a valuable resource for academics, practitioners, and policymakers committed to fostering greener, more inclusive economic cooperation worldwide.

1 Elements of customers' trust in bank: a case study from Mumbai

Irvin Kaur[1,a] *and Nishikant Jha*[2,b]

[1]Research Scholar, Department of Banking and Finance, K.P.B. Hinduja College of Commerce, University of Mumbai, Maharashtra, India

[2]Vice Principal, Thakur College of Science and Commerce; Research Guide, University of Mumbai, Maharashtra, India

Abstract

Trust is a firm belief in someone that makes us rely on them. The public deposits money in banks, trusting that the banks will return it at a future date, making it important to understand the elements of customers' trust in banks. Prior studies have determined that several factors are important in determining confidence in banks: stability, shared values (value congruence), competence (ability/expertise), integrity (fairness, honesty), transparency (open and clear communication), and customer orientation (benevolence). This study also examines "management competency" as a potential predictor of bank customer trust. 208 individuals with bank accounts provided primary data via a standardized questionnaire. The data is analyzed using Cronbach's alpha, Spearman's rank correlation, Chi-square test, ordinal logistic regression, and generalized ordered logit model. The test result suggests that all components included in trust are significantly linked to the general idea of trust. The results of ordinal logistic regression indicate that the customer's trust in their bank is significantly influenced by client orientation, competence, integrity, transparency, stability and management competency. Shared value was found not to be a significant determinant of trust in the bank.

Keywords: Bank trust, Banking system, stability, stability, trust in bank

Introduction

In contemporary society, individuals, industries, and countries are all interdependent and cannot exist in isolation. They must count on each other to exist, which can solely be achieved by trusting one another. When we trust someone, we put our conviction in them to act in a specific way and fulfil their obligations. In all sorts of relationships, be they personal or professional, we can find trust to be their foundation. Banks are vital to any country's economy, but their form is highly delicate because of what they do by nature [6]. Customers and banks are mutually dependent; each one needs the other to exist [17]. Banks accept deposits and grant loans, but to perform this function, people must have faith in their bank. Sprague [18] stated that confidence in banks is exceedingly precarious, and a vulnerable bank is susceptible to damage from any rumors, whether substantiated or unsubstantiated.

While Rousseau et al. [13] stated that when we place our trust in someone, we enter a psychological state of accepting vulnerability where we have a positive expectation of the other person's intentions, Bertrand et al. noted that trust is a crucial mechanism that facilitates economic transactions and fosters favorable economic outcomes. Similarly, when we deposit our hard-earned money in the bank, we have positive expectations that it will be available for withdrawal at a future date. This paper focuses on the reasons/factors or elements that make it possible for customers to rely on the bank and enable them to trust the bank with all their savings, retirement funds, or funds for purchasing a house.

According to Ennew and Sekhon [7], financial institutions are becoming less trusted. Lack of faith in banks can lead to serious economic issues since depositors may withdraw their money, which might result in a bank run and the failure of even financially sound institutions [5]. A person will become less trustworthy if he has experienced harm in previous interactions [1]. Because it adds protection against negative events, consumers' faith in banks can help protect the financial system and protect it from bank runs [8]. Researching the elements that encourage or impact customers to trust the bank is crucial as a result.

[a]irvinkaur18@gmail.com, [b]drnishikantjha@gmail.com

DOI: 10.4324/9781003739982-1

Concepts and Literature

Using six variables from earlier research, this study attempts to investigate the following factors that influence consumers' institutional or interpersonal confidence in their bank:

- In the UK, Ennew and Sekhon [7] investigated the following factors as predictors of consumer trust: (a) competence; (b) honesty; (c) communication; (d) shared values; and (e) kindness.
- Schumann et al. [14] studied (a) ability, (b) benevolence, (c) predictability, and (d) integrity as determinants of trust for service providers.
- Sekhon et al. [16] investigated the following factors as drivers of trust: (a) competence and expertise; (b) consistency and integrity; (c) communication; (d) shared values; and (e) kindness and compassion.
- According to Van Esterik-Plasmeijer and van Raaji [20], these elements affect how much people in the Netherlands trust: (a) their service, (b) what they know, (c) their honesty, (d) their openness, (e) common principles and (f) their consistency.

Elements of trust

In addition to previous research, management competency will be assessed as a component of the factors that influence consumers' confidence in the financial institution. To measure association between all the seven parameters of trust: client orientation, competence, integrity, transparency, shared values, stability, and management competency a hypothesis is formulated:

H_0: There is no significant association between client orientation, competence, integrity, transparency, shared values, stability, and management competency with customers' trust in the bank

Client orientation or benevolence

In today's competitive market, a customer-centric approach is critical for survival, making proactive client orientation a must. Prioritizing customers' needs and interests before the organizational goals result in value creation, customer satisfaction, and loyalty [2]. Enhancing strong relationships builds trust among customers. Being honest about our weaknesses will increase credibility Tiwari and Deshpande [19], so warning customers of wrong decisions and thinking about them first will increase their trust in the bank.

H_0: There is no significant impact of client orientation on customer's trust in the bank

Competence or ability

Ability is a collection of characteristics, skills, and aptitudes that allow an individual or organization to make a difference in a particular profession [11]. The bank should be competent in knowing the financial needs of their customers and selecting the right product for them. Ability also involves perceived ability concerning skills, competence, and other characteristics; we will trust an institution more or less based on how competent we perceive it to be [15].

H_0: There is no significant impact of competence on customers' trust in the bank.

Integrity

Integrity implies acting in an honest manner and behaving ethically. Banks perform intermediation functions between multiple parties, so trust and integrity are essential for banks' existence [3]. Integrity is about the reliability of trust Butler [4], Banks should abide by the laws and regulations and treat their customers in a fair manner and only then will customers be able to trust the bank and rely on it.

H_0: There is no significant impact of integrity on customer trust in the bank.

Transparency or communication

Transparency entails forthrightness, openness, and honesty in communication. Transparency is essential to fostering interpersonal trust [9]. Incomplete information to customers can lead to erosion of trust in the institution. Customers require their bank to be open about all procedures that are followed, costs and risks associated with their product, and clear communication.

H_0: There is no significant impact of transparency on customer's trust in the bank.

Shared values or value convergence

Shared values are common values shared among people. The institutions function as a part of society and should in turn contribute to the society in the form of local activities, sponsorships, and creating a sustainable society. A strategic approach that helps businesses turn social challenges into economic opportunities is the creation of shared values. Solving societal problems will develop a close relationship with stakeholders [12].

H_0: There is no significant impact of shared values on customer's trust in the bank.

Stability

Stability refers to the ability of the institution to remain stable, solid, and in a sound financial state. As per Van Esterik-Plasmeijer and van Raaji [20], stability is a long-term aspect and generally depends on incomplete information possessed by the customer regarding his bank. A bank with stable and good financial health will be trusted by customers.

H_0: There is no significant impact of stability on customer's trust in the bank.

Management competency

Management competency refers to the skill, expertise, proficiency, and qualifications of the top management of the institution. Managers are obliged to be competent and can handle unforeseen circumstances with ease since they are responsible for giving directions to the entity [10].

H_0: There is no significant impact of management competency on customer's trust in the bank.

Research methodology

Sampling and data collection

Primary data of 208 respondents with bank accounts was collected from customers having a bank account in Mumbai through a structured questionnaire.

Design measurements and questionnaire

The survey had 29 questions, 24 of which measured the determinants of trust and five of which were demographic questions. Van Esterik-Plasmeijer and van Raaji's [20] research served as the basis for 21 of the questions, and three more were added to gauge managerial ability.

Research techniques

- Cronbach's alpha is applied to assure that the scale is reliable and to back up what was said during the assessment of constructs.
- Spearman's rank correlation is used to examine how strongly trust and its components are related.
- The relationship between trust and each of the seven components of trust is examined using the chi-square test.
- The link between trust (a dependent variable) and its determinants (an independent variable)—client orientation, competence, integrity, transparency, shared values, and managerial competency—is determined using ordinal logistic regression. To analyze the connection between stability (independent variable) and trust (dependent variable), we rely on the generalized ordered logit model.

Research tools

SPSS IBM is used as a tool for measuring Cronbach's alpha and Spearman's rank correlation as well as performing ordinal logistic regression. Python is used to perform generalized ordered logit model, and Chi-square test.

Data analysis and interpretation

According to Table 1.1, the overall Cronbach's alpha value for the trust-related factors was 0.874. None of the items have an alpha value higher than 0.874, which implies that the deletion of any item will not improve

Table 1.1 Reliability test (Cronbach's alpha Test).

Cronbach's alpha	N of Items
.874	7

Source: Author

Table 1.2 Spearman's rank correlation.

		T	CO	C	I	T	SV	S	MC
Trust in own bank	p(rho)	1.000	.294**	.193*	.284**	.228**	.105	.316**	.264**
Sig.	.	<.001	.005	<.001	<.001	.130	<.001	<.001	

Source: Author

Table 1.3 Chi-square test (trust and elements determining trust).

Determinants of Trust	Chi-square value	P value
Client Orientation	1153.8070	<0.01
Competence	1476.03544	<0.01
Integrity	1238.4970	<0.01
Transparency	1363.4778	<0.01
Shared Values	1451.7542	<0.01
Stability	767.6523	<0.01
Management Competency	1056.2033	<0.01

Source: Author

Table 1.4 Ordinal logistic regression (trust and client orientation).

Predictor	Estimate	Std. Error	Wald	df	Sig.	95% Confidence Interval	
						Lower	Upper
Client Orientation	.739	.183	16.386	1	<.001	.381	1.097

Source: Author

the alpha value. Also, when the values of each determinant are analyzed individually, all the values are above 0.70, proving that the scale is reliable.

Table 1.2 illustrates Spearman's rank correlation, where T= transparency, CO= Client Orientation, C=competency, I=integrity, T=transparency, SV=shared values, MC=management competency and S=stability. Results reveal a very strong positive relationship between trust and client orientation, integrity, transparency as well as management competency at a 1% significance value. Furthermore, at precisely a 5% significance level, competence and bank trust are positively correlated, whereas shared values show a positive but not statistically significant correlation.

H_1: There is a significant association between client orientation, competence, integrity, transparency, shared values, management competency, stability with customers' trust in the bank.

All the parameters of trust, i.e. client orientation, competence, integrity, transparency, shared values, stability, and management competency, have a p-value < 0.01, depicting a significant association between these parameters and trust as illustrated in Table 1.3.

H_2: There is a significant impact of Client orientation on customers' trust in the bank

Table 1.4 represents the ordinal logistic regression between trust and client orientation. The p-value of client orientation is 0.01 significant at 1%, i.e. 0.01 alpha value. Therefore, we show that client orientation has a considerable impact on customers' trust in the bank and reject the null hypothesis. Thus, focusing on the interests of clients will raise their degree of confidence in the bank.

H_3: Being competent plays a major role in how customers trust the bank.

Ordinal logistic regression between competence and trust in Table 1.5 returned a p-value that is lower than the 1% significance level. Because of this, we can reject the null hypothesis, meaning that skill, knowledge or competence plays a significant part in building consumer trust. That is why increasing a bank's skills and competencies is important for gaining and maintaining the trust of its clients.

H_4: There is a significant impact of Integrity on customer's trust in the bank

Table 1.6 highlights the fact that the p-value for the ordinal regression is 0.01 (lower than the 5% alpha value of 0.05) convinces us to accept the alternative (two-tailed) hypothesis, so we reject the null hypothesis that states integrity does not affect trust. Thus, if banks have high integrity the customers are more likely to trust the bank.

H_5: There is significant impact of transparency on customer's trust in the bank

Table 1.7 demonstrates a relationship between trust and transparency through ordinal logistic regression. The p-value of transparency is 0.01 P-value is less than 5% i.e. 0.05, so the null hypothesis is rejected indicating a significant impact of transparency on customers' trust in the bank at a 1% significance level. Therefore, if banks are clear in communication and provide transparent information to the customers, they will be inclined to put trust in the bank.

H_6: There is a significant impact of shared values on customer's trust in the bank.

Table 1.8 indicates that shared values only border on significance, as the p value is 0.087, compared to the alpha value of 0.05. The results imply that shared value might affect how much trust consumers put in the bank.

Table 1.5 Ordinal logistic regression (trust and competence).

Predictor	Estimate	Std Error	Wald	df	Sig.	95% CI	
						Lower	Upper
Competence	.700	.211	11.042	1	<.001	.287	1.113

Source: Author

Table 1.6 Ordinal logistic regression (trust and integrity).

Predictor	Estimate	Std Error	Wald	df	Sig.	95% CI	
						Lower	Upper
Integrity	1.316	.282	21.715	1	<.001	.763	1.870

Source: Author

Table 1.7 Ordinal logistic regression (trust and transparency).

Location	Estimate	Std. Error	Wald	df	Sig.	95% CI	
						Lower	Upper
Transparency	.866	.223	15.056	1	<.001	.428	1.303

Source: Author

Table 1.8 Ordinal logistic regression (trust and shared values).

Location	Estimate	Std. Error	Wald	df	Sig.	95% CI	
						Lower	Upper
Shared values	.332	.194	2.925	1	.087	–.048	.712

Source: Author

Table 1.9 Generalized ordered logit model: (trust and stability).

	Coef	std err	z	P>|z|	[0.025	0.975]
Stability	1.3904	0.285	4.877	0.00	0.832	1.949

Source: Author

Table 1.10 Ordinal logistic regression (Trust and management competency).

Location	Estimate	Std. Error	Wald	df		Sig.Lower	95% CI	
							Lower	Upper
Management competency	.945	.219	18.687	1	<.001		.517	1.374

Source: Author

H_7: There is a significant impact of stability on customer's trust in the bank.

There was a violation of the proportional odds assumption, which is essential for ordinal logistic regression ($p < 0.05$). Therefore, the impact of stability on consumers' confidence was examined using a generalized ordered logit model.

The generalized ordered logit model in Table 1.9 indicates a substantial correlation between stability and trust at the 1% significance level. The results demonstrate that customers would place a high value on a solid and sound bank. Customers will, however, lose faith in banks if they are having financial problems.

H_8: There is a significant impact of Management Competency on customer's trust in the bank.

Table 1.10 describes the relationship between managerial competency and trust from an ordinal logistic regression. The p-value for Management Competency is 0.01 which is less than 5% or 0.05. The null hypothesis is rejected because management skills strongly affect how much trust consumers have in the bank. Consequently, a bank will earn greater credibility and trust with customers if its management team is strong and has many years of experience.

Findings and Conclusion

This research demonstrated the relationship between elements of trust revealing that elements of trust: client orientation, competence, integrity, transparency, shared values, management competency, and stability, displayed a significant association with customers' trust in their bank but when testing the relationship client orientation, competence, integrity, transparency, management competency, and stability had an important effect on the extent of client confidence in the bank ($p < 0.01$) conversely the impact shared values had on trust was insignificant (p-value 0.087).

The findings of the study necessitate banks to focus on the needs and interests of their client, provide them with a clear and transparent picture, adhere to laws and regulations, and enhance the competency of their management through corporate training programs and refresher courses. Management is the one who gives direction to the company, effective guidance and proper direction play a great role in fostering customers' trust in the bank.

India ranked fourth in a Statista poll of 33 nations, demonstrating a strong degree of customer trust in banking, even though people in many areas of the world are losing faith in their banks. The results of this study are important because, even if confidence in financial institutions is declining globally, the present research on trust clients in Indian banks may provide useful information for other nations.

References

[1] Alesina, A., & La Ferrara, E. (2002). Who trusts others? *Journal of Public Economics*, 85(2), 207–234. https://doi.org/10.1016/S0047-2727(01)00084-6.

[2] Blocker, C. P., Flint, D. J., Myers, M. B., & Slater, S. F. (2010). Proactive customer orientation and its role for creating customer value in global markets. *Journal of the Academy of Marketing Science*, 39(2), 216–233. https://doi.org/10.1007/s11747-010-0202-9.

[3] Boatright, J. R. (2011). Trust and integrity in banking. *Ethical Perspectives*, 18(4), 473–489.

[4] Butler, T. (1991). Toward understanding and measuring conditions of trust: evolution of a conditions of trust inventory. *Journal of Management*, 17(3), 643–663. https://doi.org/10.1177/014920639101700307.

[5] Diamond, D. W., & Dybvig, P. H. (1983). Bank runs, deposit insurance, and liquidity. *Journal of Political Economy*, 91(3), 401–419. https://doi.org/10.1086/261155.

[6] Diamond, D. W., & Rajan, R. G. (2001). Liquidity risk, liquidity creation, and financial fragility: a theory of banking. *Journal of Political Economy*, 109(2), 287–327. https://doi.org/10.1086/319552.

[7] Ennew, C., & Sekhon, H. (2007). Measuring trust in financial services: the trust index. *Consumer Policy Review*, 17, 62–68.

[8] Kidron, A., & Kreis, Y. (2020). Listening to bank customers: the meaning of trust. *International Journal of Quality and Service Sciences*, 12(3), 355–370.

[9] Koohang, A., Paliszkiewicz, J., & Goluchowski, J. (2017). The impact of leadership on trust, knowledge management, and organizational performance: a research model. *Industrial Management and Data Systems*, 117(3), 521–537. https://doi.org/10.1108/IMDS-02-2016-0072.

[10] Maas, P., & Graf, A. (2004). Leadership by customers? new roles of service companies' customers. Zeitschrift für Personal forschung / German. *Journal of Human Resource Research*, 18(3), 329–344. https://doi.org/10.1177/239700220401800305.

[11] Mayer, R. C., Davis, J. H., & Schoorman, F. D. (1995). An integrative model of organizational trust. *Academy of Management Review*, 20(3), 709–734. https://doi.org/10.5465/amr.1995.9508080335.

[12] Menghwar, P., & Antonio, D. (2021). Creating shared value: a systematic review, synthesis and integrative perspective. *International Journal of Management Reviews*, 23(4), 466–485.

[13] Rousseau, D. M., Sitkin, S. B., Burt, R. S., & Camerer, C. (1998). Not so different after all: a cross-discipline view of trust. *Academy of Management Review*, 23(3), 393–404. https://doi.org/10.5465/amr.1998.926617.

[14] Schumann, J. H., Wünderlich, N. V., & Evanschitzky, H. (2010). Drivers of trust in relational service exchange: understanding the importance of cross-cultural differences. *Journal of Service Research*, 13(4), 453–468. https://doi.org/10.1177/1094670510368425.

[15] Svare, H., Gausdal, A. H., & Möllering, G. (2019). The function of ability, benevolence, and integrity-based trust in innovation networks. *Industry and Innovation*, 27(6), 585–604.

[16] Sekhon, H., Ennew, C., Kharouf, H., & Devlin, J. (2014). Trustworthiness and trust: influences and implications. *Journal of Marketing Management*, 30(3–4), 409–430. https://doi.org/10.1080/0267257X.2013.842609.

[17] Sheppard, B. H., & Sherman, D. M. (1998). The grammars of trust: a model and general implications. *Academy of Management Review*, 23(3), 422–437. https://doi.org/10.5465/amr.1998.926619.

[18] Sprague, I. H. (1986). Bailout: An Insider's Account of Bank Failures and Rescues. Washington, D.C.: Beard Books.

[19] Tiwari, A. K., & Deshpande, A. P. (2022). Relationship transparency–trust cycle: a matter of trust and competency for frontline managers. *Cardiometry*, 22, 476–484.

[20] Van Esterik-Plasmeijer, W. J., & Van Raaij, W. F. (2017). Banking system trust, bank trust, and bank loyalty. *International Journal of Bank Marketing*, 35(1), 97–111. https://doi.org/10.1108/IJBM-12-2015-0195.

2 Green bank: international practices and implications for Vietnam

Hoan Xuan Pham[1,a], *Hoa Thi Nguyen*[2,b] *and Tri Trong Chu*[3,c]

[1]Assistant Professor, International School, Vietnam National University, Vietnam

[2]JSC Bank for Investment and Development of Vietnam, Vietnam

[3]University of Economics and Business, Vietnam National University, Vietnam

Abstract

Economic activities conducted at the expense of the environment have resulted in climate change, a loss of natural resources and polluted air, water and land, all of which seriously harm human life. Consequently, nations everywhere are emphasising sustainable development as well as economic progress. By controlling capital, banks both support and shape the foundation of the economy. As such, they can impact other sectors and play an important part in reaching sustainable development goals. Building 'green banking' is an essential approach that addresses problems caused by climate change and supports the long-term growth of the economy, which many countries are introducing as their way of meeting their environmental responsibilities. However, in Vietnam, green banking has not been widely adopted. This paper uses existing studies, insights from other countries and existing green banking activities in Vietnam to suggest strategies for developing green banking in the country. Because of this, the State Bank of Vietnam must introduce policies for green banking, organise seminars and provide training to experts who can support commercial banks. Commercial banks can expand their green banking offerings, arrange eco-friendly credit practices and work on improving how much employees know about eco-friendly banking.

Keywords: Green bank, green finance, green growth, Vietnam

Introduction

Green Banking first appeared in the early 2000s. Still, it was not popular until recently, mainly due to the growing urgency of environmental protection in developing countries like Vietnam, which handled its environment at the cost of economic growth until recently. Studies on financial institutions/green banking, and sustainable development have been increasing in academic texts over the years. Until now, scientists have not reached a common explanation of what green banking is. The concept, topics and techniques of green banking are understood differently in different countries.

The State Bank in Vietnam is actively supporting the Government's policy for a green economy by hosting many events that promote green banking and updating the associated regulations. On August 7, 2018, the State Bank published Decision No.1604/QD-NHNN that approved the Project on creating green banking in Vietnam [6]. In particular, the State Bank asks credit institutions to make a "Green Banking Strategy Framework" based on their business strategy, the kinds of customers they target, the services they offer and the strengths and capacities of the banks. However, the project does not clearly define "green banking" or provide clear directions for following a green model, detailed tools for reviewing progress, and rules for labelling a bank as "Green."

That's why it is essential to examine the implementation of green banking at banks in developed and developing countries to design and build a solid framework for applying it in Vietnam. Analysis, evaluation and implicatión have supported the Green Banking Development Project with a clear path for the credit institution system to strengthen and reach its goals in Vietnam.

The paper aims to clarify what Green Banks do, explain how various nations set up their green banking and analyze how green banking exists in Vietnam today. Based on this analysis, the paper will provide important recommendations for growing green banking in Vietnam.

[a]pxhoan@vnu.edu.vn, [b]hoanguyen1796@gmail.com, [c]trict@vnu.edu.vn

DOI: 10.4324/9781003739982-2

Methodology

This study employs a qualitative research approach, primarily relying on a literature review and case study analysis to examine the development and implementation of green banking models globally and in Vietnam. The methodology consists of the following key components:

Literature review

Existing research related to green banking, sustainable finance and financial institutions' efforts to promote sustainability was carefully reviewed. The review used academic works, policy documents, regulatory schedules and industry standards from developed and developing nations. The study synthesizes definitions, conceptual frameworks, and strategic approaches to green banking, highlighting key trends and challenges in its adoption.

Case study analysis

The research utilizes a comparative case study approach, analyzing green banking practices in selected countries, including the United States, the United Kingdom, China, and India. These case studies provide insights into the different models of green banking, regulatory approaches, policy incentives, and strategic interventions implemented in each country. By examining both market-driven and government-led green banking initiatives, the study identifies best practices that may be applicable to Vietnam.

Analysis of Vietnam's green banking status

The study takes a look at what green banking looks like in Vietnam right now by analysing government legislation, banking laws and activities by financial institutions. Useful sources are reports by the State Bank of Vietnam (SBV), directives issued by relevant ministries and sustainable reports provided by large Vietnamese banks. It explores how Vietnamese banks are including environmental factors into their credit offering, banking activities and daily operations.

Policy implication development

Using analysis from literature and case study findings, the study introduces policy suggestions for the green banking sector in Vietnam. These recommendations are aimed at enhancing regulatory clarity, financial incentives, risk management frameworks, and capacity-building initiatives to facilitate the expansion of green banking practices.

Using both theoretical explanations and real case studies allowed me to investigate the way green banking functions in Vietnam's financial economy. The insights from this paper mean to support people at the top, in banking and with key influence in creating sound policies for sustainable finance and achieving goals set for Vietnam.

Literature Review

Green bank concept

The idea of green banking is divided into three key parts:

Level 1: Green Bank focuses solely on improving the environment and reducing carbon emissions. According to Meena [4], green banking encompasses financial activities that aim to lower overall carbon emissions by funding green technology projects and minimizing pollution. By engaging in green banking, banks carefully evaluate environmental risks in a project before approving a loan and help to strengthen green activities. ESCAP, in its 2012 report, says green banking includes ways for banks to support the environment and lower carbon emissions. This means motivating customers to choose sustainable products and services, factoring in environmental requirements for loan decisions, and providing special credits for businesses working to cut CO_2 emissions and build energy from renewable sources. Practising green banking will encourage banks and their customers to minimise their contribution to climate change. In Lalon [3] pointed out that an organisation may be called a green bank when its main activities help improve the environment.

Level 2: [10] suggest that green banking is essentially a form of social or responsible banking, as environmental and social problems are tied together. The terms used by Kaeufer [2] include calling "social banking" a financial system that overcomes modern issues and benefits society, nature and different cultures. Likewise, banks must make a strong commitment to sustainability by bringing corporate social responsibility (CSR) into their main systems.

Level 3: In the context of banking, green banking means working sustainably. Singh and Singh [5] write that green banking follows the same path as traditional banking, but it takes care of the environment and social matters too. For this reason, green banking has also been called ethical banking or sustainable banking. In 2010, Imeson & Sim A argued that green banking is similar to sustainable banking. Long-term sustainability for a bank can be reached if investment decisions relate financial gains to how consumers are treated, the way the economy develops, the comfort of society and the preservation of nature. As defined by [11], green banking applies sustainability concepts to every part of financial activity. The Global Alliance for Banking on Values [1] claims that a bank's basic principle should cover environmental, social and financial sustainability and it should also work for inclusion and transparency with its governance [1]. Sustainable development focuses on problems of the environment as well as social and economic issues.

In recent times, ESG has been used a lot, but its meaning isn't always clear. Overlapping elements between green banking, sustainable banking, and ESG have led to some confusion. Figure 2.1 shows a simplified framework for comprehending broad terms. According to [12], there are clear distinctions between green, sustainable and socio-environmental points of view:

UNEP reports that inclusive sustainable finance looks at social, environmental and economic matters, but green finance is limited to climate change and various environmental problems. It is clear from the relevant theories that the green banking concept is closely linked to sustainability and ESG. While the concept is still evolving, it broadly falls into two interpretations. In a narrow sense, green banks refer to financial institutions that finance activities specifically aimed at environmental improvement and carbon emission reduction. In a

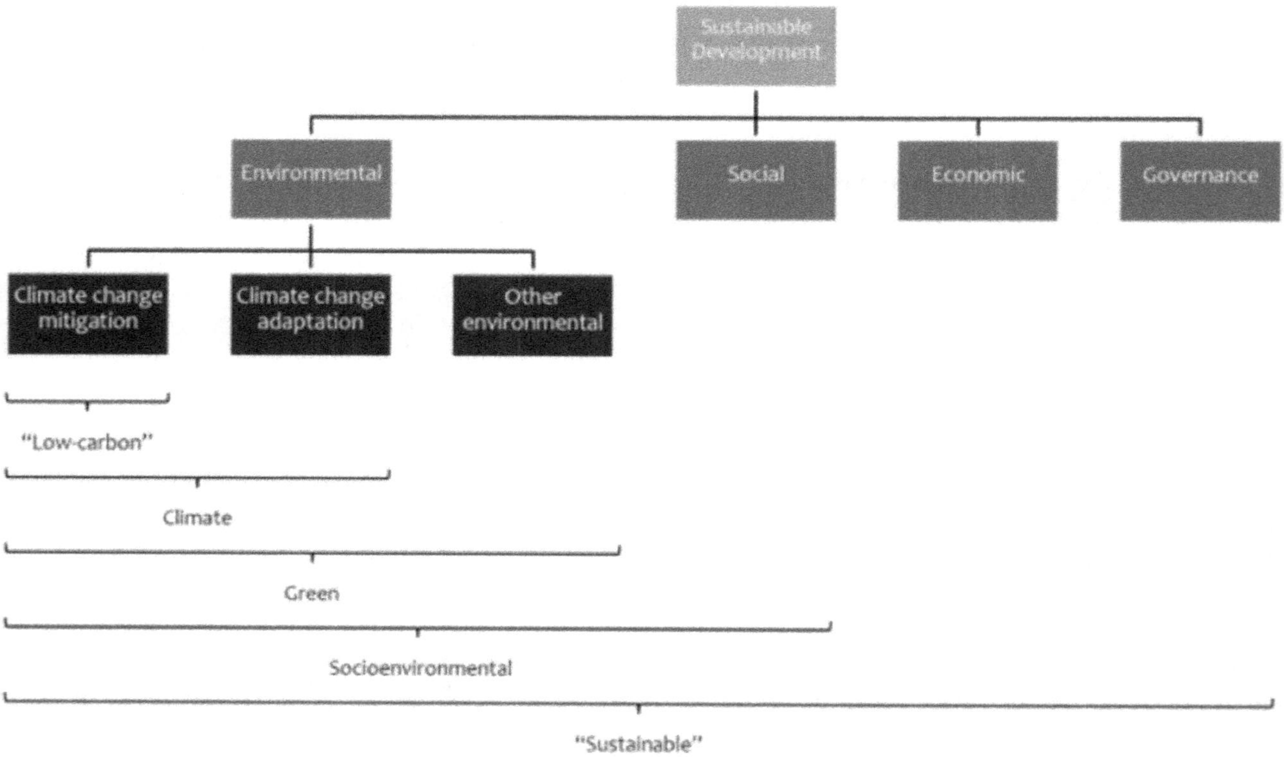

Figure 2.1 A simplified framework for comprehending broad terms
Source: UNEP, 2016

broader sense, green banks are sustainable banks that comprehensively integrate ESG practices into all aspects of their operations. Overall, banks contribute greatly to the sustainable world by supplying sustainable and particularly green, finance and incorporating ESG into their operations. This paper examines green banking and other aspects of finance that participate in reducing greenhouse gases and helping people resist the results of climate change. These projects are carried out to help achieve wider sustainable development such as benefiting the economy, supplying work opportunities and supporting equal rights for people of all genders. As a result, green banking greatly contributes to conserving the environment and improving social and economic situations.

Green bank model

This paper has studied the approaches of Kaeufer [2] on the Green Banking - Responsible Banking development model, Weber [8] describes the sustainable banking model, Yip and Bocken [9] approach through 08 aspects of sustainable business operations, Tan & Tsionas [7] step-by-step modular strategy for different phrases of integration. In general, except for Yip & Bocken [9], the remaining authors mention the approach to develop green/sustainable banking in each stage or implementation level, starting from not implementing only for compliance purposes to comprehensive integration into business operations and promoting a strategic and proactive sustainable ecosystem. It further explains what basic aspects should be incorporated at every point and the way to go forward to the next step. Elemental challenges like risk management, interaction between parties and accountability and transparency are not specifically covered at the strategic stage.

Kaeufer [2]

Kaeufer [2] introduced a Green Bank model with five levels (see Table 2.1), as follows:

Weber [8]

Weber outlines a four-stage sustainability model (See Table 2.2) for banks as follows:

Tan and Tsionas [7].

Table 2.3 shows the five levels of classification for sustainable banking that Tan and Tsionas [7] outlined as follows:

Table 2.1 Kaeufer's Green Bank model [2].

Level 1	Level 2	Level 3	Level 4	Level 5
Banks engage in supplementary activities such as sponsoring environmentally focused events. These actions are mostly symbolic and do not significantly alter banking operations.	Banks introduce standalone green products and services. However, these offerings represent only a minor portion of the bank's overall portfolio and are often driven by public relations rather than a strategic commitment to sustainability.	At this stage, banks systematically integrate environmental considerations into their core business activities. The organizational structure is designed to support green banking principles across four key dimensions: people, processes, principles, and objectives.	The initiative for strategic ecosystem balance extends green banking beyond individual businesses to include networks, alliances, community dialogues, and broader ecosystems. This approach aims to achieve sustainability across social, environmental, and financial dimensions	The initiative for a balanced ecosystem involves green banking activities that resemble those at Level 4 but are executed intentionally and intentionally. Unlike the strategic outreach initiatives at Level 4, which address external changes, this initiative focuses on actively and purposefully implementing green banking practices

Source: Author

Table 2.2 Weber's green bank model [8].

Stage 1	Stage 2	Stage 3	Stage 4
integration for compliance purposes	Banks begin offering sustainable financial products, integrating environmental considerations into risk management, and adopting internal resource efficiency measures.	banks incorporate social responsibility by going beyond regulatory requirements in their corporate social responsibility (CSR) initiatives. They actively promote measures that contribute to the improvement of social, cultural, and environmental issues.	describes a sustainable bank where all principles of sustainable development are fully integrated into the core business operations. The board of directors is gender-balanced, with both women and men represented, and compensation practices are transparent. Banks at this stage ensure transparency, gender-balanced leadership, and comprehensive sustainability reporting.

Source: Author

Table 2.3 Tan and Tsionas's green bank model [7].

Level 1	Level 2	Level 3	Level 4	Level 5
Banks participate in superficial environmental activities, such as sponsorships and public campaigns, without substantive green banking initiatives.	Banks introduce isolated green products, but these remain peripheral to their main business model.	Sustainability principles are integrated into banking processes, influencing the bank's core financial products and services.	The strategic ecosystem innovation phase, where banks work beyond individual transactions and adopt sustainability at an industry-wide level.	Banks drive intentional ecosystem transformation, prioritizing environmental and social sustainability at a systemic level.

Source: Author

Yip and Bocken [9]

Yip and Bocken propose eight sustainable business model archetypes for banks, offering diverse strategies rather than a linear approach. The first archetype aims to enhance material and energy efficiency through digitization, reducing costs and environmental impact. The second improves business resilience by delivering digital services that are fast, convenient, and eco-friendly. The third promotes sufficiency by accurately assessing customer needs, preventing over-lending, and moral hazards. The fourth emphasizes stakeholder engagement for long-term social and environmental benefits. The fifth encourages inclusive value creation through responsible lending. The sixth advocates for reuse, delivering socially and environmentally responsible services. The seventh incorporates sustainability into lending to reduce risks, and the eighth focuses on providing sustainable investment products like crowdfunding and impact investing.

International Experiences

Green banking has received more global notice because financial institutions are key to making economies more sustainable. Different countries have gone about green banking in various ways, as developed places often rely on things like markets and personal choice. In contrast, developing nations tend to make rules and give out incentives handed down from the government. This section looks at green banking practices in the United States, the United Kingdom, China and India to guide Vietnam on useful policies, issues and best courses of action.

United States

The US Government recognizes that green and sustainable banking will become inevitable. As a result, the Government has helped support initiatives to boost green banking and green activities by creating special legal policies. Not only do US regulations protect the environment from polluting businesses, but they also require stakeholders to be responsible. This Act exempts lenders from any liability, but when lenders are involved to a certain extent in managing polluting projects, they must pay a sizable fine. In addition, CERCLA's strict regulations on environmental compensation also indirectly affect banks because if they must pay this amount, the cash flow to repay banks will also be affected. The US also develops standards to assess and rank banks' "green" performance, which are periodically published by the Federal Deposit Insurance Corporation (FDIC). The First Green Bank (FGB) was established in the US, representing the retail banking model. This bank was founded by a group of experienced and prestigious bankers in the state of Florida in 2009. In addition, the country started green banks in several states, including Connecticut Bank in 2011 and later New York in 2013.

The Coalition for Green Capital (CGC) was organised as a non-governmental body through the ICC Act of 2012 to unite green banks and green banking ideas. CGC is committed to helping accelerate clean energy adoption in established and emerging countries and the US in order to achieve a totally emission-free system. Developers, investors, service providers, NGOs, institutions, policymakers, and other actors interested in supporting and participating in green banking investments will be engaged through the Coalition. In 2014, CGC made a big splash in establishing the Green Bank Institute as a green banking research body, representing the production of green banking ideas by experts and leaders from more than half of the states across the US [13].

The American Green Bank Consortium, established as a project of the Coalition for Green Capital (CGC) in early 2019, functions as a hub for the expanding and evolving green banking sector in the United States. It facilitates knowledge exchange and provides various services to strengthen the green banking community. The consortium collaborates with capital providers, investors, lenders, foundations, and government agencies to develop integrated clean energy investment strategies that can be scaled nationwide through the Green Bank network. Additionally, it partners developers, technology firms, and other market participants to secure funding and implement innovative financing solutions for sustainable projects. In addition, the consortium collaborates with policymakers, NGOs and advocacy groups to advance Green Bank activities by helping to expand industry conversations, make new policies and distribute important information.

United Kingdom

In the UK, the main approach is for companies to publish climate-related risks according to the Task Force on Climate-Related Financial Disclosure (TCFD) [10]. By 2018, the UK's government was on board with TCFD, and it is still a voluntary movement [14].

Like the US, the UK also established a green bank called the UK Green Investment Bank (GIB), but unlike the US, which is a retail bank, the GIB represents the investment banking model, and the UK Government is the exclusive shareholder. The GIB was officially established in October 2012 as a national green bank incorporated under the Companies Act. By August 2017, the majority of GIB's shares were sold to the Macquarie Group, with a small stake retained by the Government.

The UK Government amended the Enterprise and Regulatory Reform Act 2013 to guarantee that GIB consistently maintains a "green purpose." As a result, GIB backs projects that improve the environment based on one of the five leading aspects of green impact: (1) Cutting down on greenhouse gases, (2) helping to use natural resources more efficiently, (3) saving or bettering our natural environment, (4) supporting biodiversity and (5) addressing environmental sustainability. GIB focuses its investments on four areas: offshore wind, waste and bioenergy, onshore renewable energy, and energy efficiency. The green purpose is the basis for GIB's investment decisions.

When GIB was sold to Macquarie, the Government allocated a "special shareholding" to Green Purpose Company Limited (GPC) (a UK Treasury company) to protect GIB's green purpose. The Green Purposes Company (GPC) plays a key role in the Green Investment Bank (GIB) governance structure. However, it does not participate in the daily operations or management of GIB, as these responsibilities are assigned to the Executive Board. The GIB Board of Directors (BOD) consists of 11 members, including seven non-executive directors and one shareholder representative director from the GPC. The Chairman of GIB is appointed by the Government's Department for Business, Innovation and Skills.

GIB also designed a monitoring framework to measure its performance against its set policy goals. Key indicators include a green index, mobilization rate, and portfolio profitability. In addition, to ensure transparent operations, GIB must conduct two main types of reports: monthly shareholder reports (on financial performance, capital allocation, operating costs, impact on the green economy, etc.) and annual reports to the public.

China

The development of green banking in China has experienced several important stages since 1995. That step was started when the People's Bank of China announced that banks were required to consider environmental factors when deciding to give credit. At this time, banks were first directly regulated about the environment.

Policies that encouraged the environment and green sectors were introduced in the early 2000s. The Circular on Environmental Protection Verification of Enterprises Applying for Listing (2003) and the Implementing the Scientific Outlook on Development and Enhancing Environmental Protection policy (2005) both urged banks to focus on greener investment.

Green banking policies in China are explained by the Green Credit policy. In 2007, the CBRC issued clear instructions on how the banking industry should manage energy efficiency and reduce emissions when making credit choices. As a result of the Green Credit Policy, capital for green projects has grown noticeably in China. However, one of the biggest difficulties in implementing this policy is the lack of a reliable assessment system for industries and facilities, causing environmental pollution to serve as a basis for banks to classify projects, especially when many polluting industries are also industries that bring high profits to many localities. It took China nearly five years from the beginning of the policy until it was able to develop a relatively detailed guide to implement this policy. Then in 2012, the Green Credit Guidelines were launched and in 2013, CBRC established its green credit system. Up to 21 large banks were required, under this method, to disclose their progress on green credit.

In 2016, the release of the Guidelines for Establishing the Green Financial System supported the growth of green credit policies among different ministries and regulatory agencies. They also introduced ways to financially reward banks such as providing access to lending tools and considering green factors in your analysis of the whole financial system. Using such comprehensive strategies has enabled China to lead in creating green banks.

Monetary policy instruments

Through its monetary policy, the People's Bank of China (PBoC) encourages the use of green finance. Mainly, this support works under the re-lending policy, helping banks grow their offering of green credit. First, under the Standing Lending Facility (SLF), the PBoC accepts green credit in prioritized sectors as collateral, enabling banks to secure short-term liquidity more easily. This mechanism ensures that financial institutions can continue funding environmentally sustainable projects without liquidity constraints. Second, under the Medium-Term Lending Facility (MLF), the PBoC accepts high-rated green bonds (AA and above) as collateral, allowing banks to access medium-term funding to support large-scale green projects. This initiative strengthens capital availability for sustainable investments, fostering long-term environmental and economic benefits. By integrating green finance into its monetary policy, the PBoC enhances liquidity access for green banking, incentivizing financial institutions to prioritize environmentally responsible lending and investment.

Since 2018, banks' green performance has been integrated into the PBoC's Macro Prudential Assessment (MPA). Under this framework, the interest rate on required reserves held at the PBoC may be adjusted based on the bank's green performance. In the MPA framework's "credit policy implementation" section, green performance is evaluated using both quantitative and qualitative standards. Specifically, 80% of the evaluation is based on quantitative variables, such as the proportion of green loans, while 20% is based on qualitative indicators, including whether the bank has issued green bonds.

Furthermore, China's government launched a measure to lower the risk rating for green assets, so banks are encouraged to invest more in green finance. As part of this, banks with a greater share of green loans are allowed to keep less money in reserve and can also more easily issue green bonds. CBIRC will use the non-performing loan (NPL) ratios as the basis for deciding if banks are providing enough green financing compared to loans that support other activities. By aligning regulatory policies with sustainability goals, this measure enhances financial institutions' willingness to support environmentally friendly projects while maintaining financial stability.

Bank instruments

Chinese banks are increasingly utilizing a wide array of green financial instruments, with their use expanding rapidly in recent years. Although detailed statistics on the proportion of each instrument are not available, their growing diversity is noteworthy. Specialized green tools, several forms of collateral, asset-backed securities and international credit lines fall under this range. This trend underscores green banking encompasses more than just green loans. It also bolsters the development of green bond markets and fosters international cooperation in green finance. The expansion of these diverse instruments highlights the evolution and broadening scope of green banking practices, reflecting a more integrated and comprehensive approach to supporting sustainable finance initiatives.

India

In India, green initiatives aimed at fostering environmental sustainability and benefiting local communities have been in place for over two decades. These initiatives have mostly focused on lending money to local economic development projects and providing loan programs for women. By introducing the "Green Channel Counter (GCC)" and the "No Queue Banking" system at more than 5,000 branches across the country, the State Bank of India (SBI) has been leading the way in green banking technologies since July 2010. These initiatives mark significant steps towards establishing a "green bank," where paperless transactions are prioritized to reduce environmental footprints. Indian banking and financial institutions have been progressively adopting green banking practices as part of their broader commitment to environmental stewardship. These practices illustrate a growing awareness of the need to incorporate environmental concerns into the day-to-day operations and financial decision-making processes.

SEBI introduced the requirement for the top 100 publicly listed companies to make a Business Responsibility Report (BRR) in 2012. Also, the Ministry of Corporate Affairs required businesses to follow the Corporate Social Responsibility (CSR) standards found in the Companies Act of 2013. In 2015, the Federation of Indian Chambers of Commerce & Industry (FICCI) introduced the National Voluntary Guidelines for Responsible Financing (NVGRF), which developed a structure for responsible and sustainable banking.

Because it values green finance, the Indian government is working to enhance the green bond market. With this plan, the capital market in India looks to increase investments in projects that create long-lasting environmental effects. In 2014, India's central bank enlarged the priority sector lending (PSL) list to include loans meant for small-scale renewable energy projects and water infrastructure. Banks using PSL guidelines must provide 40% of their financing to agriculture and SMEs to help promote investment in environmentally friendly projects.

Indian banks are both reducing their environmental impact and helping support sustainable projects by choosing green banking. Company leaders are involved in funding alternative energy schemes, lessening energy waste and boosting the use of eco-friendly technology. Through these measures, Indian banks are making significant contributions to reducing their environmental impact and promoting sustainable development within the financial sector.

Indian banks promote green banking through various initiatives. They offer Green Deposits with higher interest rates for online banking, Green Mortgages and Loans for renewable energy projects, and Green Credit Cards with rewards for eco-friendly spending. Green Reward Checking Accounts encourage paperless transactions, while Mobile Banking reduces paper use. Banks also implement Energy Efficiency Initiatives, invest in Renewable Energy, and adopt Paperless Banking. They follow Green Building Standards, participate in Carbon Offsetting Programs, and engage employees in sustainability efforts. Additionally, banks improve Transportation to reduce emissions, ensure Environmental Reporting, promote Green Supply Chain Management, and advocate for community conservation projects.

Green Bank in Vietnam

On March 2, 2015, Directive No. 03/CT-NHNN from the State Bank of Vietnam (SBV) was issued to support green credit and raise the standards for handling environmental and social issues in providing credit. The guidelines in Circular No. 36/2016/TT-NHNN (Article 4) mention that lending and borrowing should comply with environmental protection legal requirements and other relevant rules.

The State Bank of Vietnam has established a Green Project List that provides comprehensive guidelines for 44 domains, covers 21 economic sectors, and divides projects into six groups. The Green Banking Development Project in Vietnam was authorised on August 7, 2018, by the State Bank Governor's Decision No. 1604/QD-NHNN. The ruling lays out a plan for advancing green baning initiatives across the country. The Green Banking Development Project's primary goals include (i) raising banks' awareness of and commitment to fair practices for climate change and environmental protection, (ii) implementing green banking practices gradually, (iii) favouring loan provision for sustainable projects, (iv) promoting the use of clean energy and green products and services, and (v) attempting to enhance green growth and sustainable development in the nation. This initiative aims to embed environmental sustainability into the core of banking practices, ensuring that financial activities align with broader ecological and developmental goals. In Decision 1604, 05 levels of green banking referenced by the SBV are currently referring to Kaeufer's original research (details in section 3 above).

However, there are 02 differences compared to the original research: (i) In the original study, levels 1 and 2 were more negative than positive, with the author using the term "greenwashing" (a company exaggerating its environmental activities to improve its image) at level 1. And at level 2, developing isolated green products but constitute only a very small fraction of the overall portfolio and (possibly) in response to public opinion; (ii) In the original study, level 5 was explained more clearly by the author, meaning that green banking activities are carried out intentionally to address the challenges of the times. Vietnamese banks have focused more on green banking activities. However, the results mainly emphasize the growth of the credit scale for green industries/sectors and the development of some related products and services. Most of the implementation has only reached level 2 in the 05-level model according to the guidance of the State Bank in Project 1604. To reach level 3, banks will need more time, resources, and research on policies and strategies to implement green banking comprehensively in all aspects (governance, organization, processes, policies, ...) and each business activity of the bank.

The Prime Minister intends to complete the legislative framework in green credit and green banking by 2025, as per the Project on Restructuring the System of Credit Institutions in conjunction with Bad Debt Settlement for the 2021-2025 period (Decision No. 689/QD-TTg from June 8, 2022); Establish advantageous regulations and help lenders expand green finance for low-carbon sectors; Use 4.0 technology to establish non-cash payments in green banking.

The Environmental and Social Risk Assessment Handbook was created and published in 2017 by the State Bank of Vietnam in collaboration with the IFC. Chemicals, construction, agriculture, infrastructure, food processing, energy, textiles, mining of mineral and non-metallic goods, petroleum, and waste treatment are the 10 industries covered in this guidebook. It shows ways to lower these risks across pertinent industries and offers advice to businesses and credit institutions on how to handle environmental and social issues that result from issuing loans. Circular No. 17/2022/TT-NHNN, which will take effect in June 2023, mandates that credit institutions and overseas bank branches adhere to environmental risk management standards, according to the State Bank of Vietnam's Deputy Governor. By highlighting the role that credit institutions play in sustainable development and environmental preservation, circulars promote green banking. According to SBV statistics from 2024, all Vietnamese commercial banks finished internal rules and environmental risk assessments for lending decisions by the end of 2023. Additionally, 17 commercial banks established specialist divisions to supervise social and environmental risk management.

In 2023, Vietnamese commercial banks have embraced digitalization to support green banking and reduce paper use. For instance, ACB saved 204 tons of paper by digitizing processes like Green Transactions, while HDBank cut paper usage by 26.12% through mobile and internet banking, using eKYC and customer analysis systems. MB digitized 90% of its products via the MBBank App, minimizing paperwork. Vietcombank leveraged its core banking system to enhance service automation with platforms like VCB Digibank. Additionally, Vietnamese banks are seeking international cooperation for green projects. Agribank has participated in World Bank-sponsored environmental projects, Vietcombank secured a $300 million loan from Japanese banks, BIDV signed a $100 million SUNREF Green Credit agreement with the French Development Agency, and HDBank partnered with Proparco to finance renewable energy. VPBank received a $150 million loan from the IFC for environmental sectors, while Nam A Bank launched a 183 billion VND "Green Credit" initiative with the Global Climate Partnership Fund.

During 2017-2023, the system's green sector's credit balance grew by more than 22% each year. On March 31, 2024, 47 credit institutions had recorded outstanding green credit loans of VND 636,964 billion which were about 4.5% of the total nationwide outstanding loans. Credit balances considered for environmental and social risks have been steadily growing and currently stand at VND 2.9 million billion, representing more than a fifth of outstanding loans in Vietnam. It reveals that green finance is steadily growing in Vietnamese banks. In addition, credit institutions wish to contribute to green banking by pushing for technology updates, building their own guidelines for being green and getting involved in environmental community activities [15].

International organizations and banks typically report on general ESG implementation without specifically focusing on green banking. This paper assesses green banking in Vietnam through ESG data. The World Wide Fund for Nature (WWF) publishes the Sustainable Banking Report annually, evaluating ESG integration in banks across six pillars: purpose, policy, process, people, product, and portfolio. Based on data from annual reports and websites, Vietnam ranks lowest among the eight Asian countries (Singapore, Indonesia, Japan, Korea, Malaysia, Philippines, Thailand, and Vietnam) in all six pillars.

Conclusion and implications for Vietnam

Conclusion

In the cases discussed and in the State Bank of Vietnam's Project on promoting green banking in Vietnam (Decision No. 1604/QD-NHNN), there are no specific words defining or describing "green banking," and no exact standards are defined to identify "green" banks. Currently, there are no financial institutions in Vietnam that meet all the requirements to be called a Green Bank. Rather, lots of banks are adopting green measures or handing out loans that fit with their pledge to help the environment. Though banks now take into account emissions, changes in surroundings, water resources and quality of life during their lending, it is only a small piece of the puzzle to build a true Green Bank. At present, such services are not very developed or used by most Vietnamese banks in their planning. Several problems make it hard for green banking to develop in Vietnam:

Despite efforts to examine and align with the government's regulations and guidelines, as well as directives from various ministries and local authorities on green growth, the existing legal framework remains vague and incomplete. Because regulations are not clearly defined, it is difficult for banks to successfully carry out green credit programs. Therefore, while environmental considerations are being acknowledged, the financial sector in Vietnam still has significant progress to make in transitioning towards a fully sustainable, green banking system.

Green financial products and services in Vietnam's banking sector are not yet diverse. Most offerings are loans from international organizations, which require compliance with their environmental standards. Globally popular green credit products such as those for renewable energy (geothermal, bioenergy, solar), energy-efficient products, and sustainable investments are largely unavailable in Vietnam. Besides, a few banks have divisions specifically designed to handle environmental and social problems or establish green credit. There are still no clear methods for judging environmental and social effects, and banks rely on varying and flawed tools for environmental risk assessment.

Many modern banking features are available in Vietnam, but not many people are using them. Less than half the population use internet banking, mobile banking, phone banking or any type of payment card here. Most people still pay taxes, bills, for healthcare and tuition using cash. Because many prefer cash, old payment methods are still used a lot which causes problems like inefficiency, more expenses and unused resources.

People in rural communities continue to keep cash, gold and valuable things in their homes. Many credit institutions in the region lack enough modern banking technology, so the overall modernization of banking is delayed. The process of greening banking activities is currently receiving limited support.

Implications for Vietnam

After reviewing the present situation and what some nations have accomplished, building green banking in Vietnam requires the banking industry to plan strategically, introducing actions and complete solutions supported by policies, along with encouraging coordination among ministries, branches and agencies and supplying banks with more financial resources and capabilities to assist in the implementation of green banking.

- Enhance and clarify the legal framework: Vietnam needs to establish a clear legal framework for green banking, including a specific definition of "green banking," criteria for assessment, and detailed guidelines on implementing this model. It could introduce standards for measuring the bank's commitment to the environment and arrange a monitoring program to check the bank's performance against its green-related targets, along the lines of those employed by US and UK. This would provide banks with a solid legal foundation to effectively carry out green credit activities.
- Provide financial incentives: The government could provide tax breaks for banks that invest in green projects, green bonds and environmentally positive initiatives, as is common in China. This might mean granting banks with lots of green credit an easier reserve requirement or reducing the risk measure for green loans.
- Encourage green investment: Ensuring that the State Bank of Vietnam, the Ministry of Finance and the Ministry of Natural Resources and Environment cooperate to build clear guidelines and reduce the need for extra papers for environmental projects. This collaboration would streamline project evaluations, ensuring faster approvals and credit appraisals.
- Raise awareness and build capacity: Educate the banking industry about green credit and handling environmental risk using training, workshops and working with international bodies to obtain and use additional financial resources.
- Integrate technology and digitization: Vietnamese banks should continue to digitize processes to reduce paper use, as seen in India's practices. Technological applications can help conserve resources and reduce negative environmental impacts.
- Diversify green credit products: It would be beneficial if the Bank expanded its green credit activities to cover projects in renewable energy, environmental construction and sustainable farming. India's experience shows that these products not only protect the environment but also contribute to green economic growth.
- Foster international cooperation: Vietnam should explore opportunities for global collaboration, learning from successful models like the US's Coalition for Green Capital. This would help attract more green financing and technical support for domestic banks.

References

[1] Global Alliance for Banking on Values. (2012). "Global Alliance for Banking on Values: Strong, straightforward and sustainable banking", (2012): 1–195. Retrieved from https://www.scribd.com/document/104997393/Strong-Straightforward-and-Sustainable-Banking

[2] Kaeufer. (2010). "Banking as a Vehicle for Socio-economic Development and Change: Case Studies of Socially Responsible and Green Banks". *Presencing Institute, Cambridge, MA*

[3] Lalon, R. M. (2015). Green banking: going green. *International Journal of Economics, Finance and Management Sciences*, 3(1), 34–42.

[4] Meena, R., & Research India Publications. (2013). Green banking: As initiative for sustainable development. *Global Journal of Management and Business Studies*, 3(10), 1181–1186. Retrieved from https://www.ripublication.com/gjmbs_spl/gjmbsv3n10_21.pdf (2025-05-23).

[5] Singh, H., & Singh, B. P. (2012). An effective and resourceful contribution of green banking towards sustainability. *International Journal of Advances in Engineering Science and Technology*, 1(2), 41–45.

[6] State Bank of Vietnam. (2018). Decision No. 1604/2018/QD-NHNN, dated on August 7, 2018. Retrieved from https://thuvienphapluat.vn/van-ban/Tien-te-Ngan-hang/Quyet-dinh-1604-QD-NHNN-2018-phe-duyet-De-an-phat-trien-ngan-hang-xanh-tai-Viet-Nam-411378.aspx

[7] Tan, Y., & Tsionas, M. G. (2020). Modeling sustainability efficiency in banking. *International Journal of Finance and Economics*, 27(3), 3754-3772. https:// doi. org/ 10. 1002/ ijfe. 2349

[8] Weber, O. (Ed.) (2016). Sustainable Banking: Managing the Social and Environmental Impact of Financial Institutions. University of Toronto Press. https://doi.org/10.3138/978144262932.

[9] Yip, A. W., & Bocken, N. M. (2018). Sustainable business model archetypes for the banking industry. Journal of Cleaner Production, 174, 150-169. https://doi.org/10.1016/j.jclepro.2017.10.190.

[10] Park, H., & Kim, J. D. (2020). Transition Towards Green Banking: Role of Financial Regulators and Financial Institutions. Asian Journal of Sustainability and Social Responsibility, 5(5). https://doi.org/10.1186/s41180-020-00034-3

[11] Institute for Development and Research in Banking Technology (2013). Green Banking for Indian Banking Sector. IDRBT. Retrieved from https://www.scribd.com/document/187258785/Green-Banking-Framework-2013

[12] UNEP (2016). Annual Report: Empowering people to protect the planet. UN Environment 2016 Annual Report.

[13] Ha, N. P. (2017). Demand-driven Propagation: Evidence from the Great Recession. Policy Research Working Paper, No.7456 World Bank. Retrieved from http://hdl.handle.net/10986/22869

[14] Task Force on Climate-Related Financial Disclosures. (2018). 2018 Status Report. Retrieved from https://assets.bbhub.io/company/sites/60/2020/10/FINAL-2018-TCFD-Status-Report-092518.pdf

[15] State Bank of Vietnam. (2024). Towards a Sustainable Future: Strengthening Vietnam – Korea Financial Cooperation. Retrieved from https://news.laodong.vn/kinh-doanh/viet-nam-va-han-quoc-tang-cuong-hop-tac-tai-chinh-1399427.ldo

3 Leveraging artificial intelligence to transform strategic performance measurement. a case for Ugandan NGOs

Edith Tendo Okello[a]

Student, Doctor of Business Administration, Rushford Business School, Switzerland

Abstract

This research paper focuses on the transformative potential of Artificial Intelligence (AI) in enhancing strategic performance measurement within Non-Governmental Organizations (NGOs) in Uganda. The problem addressed is the inefficiency and inadequacy of current performance measurement systems that hinder NGOs' effectiveness in measuring their performance, especially impact and delivering the social, environmental, and economic change they desire to. The study employs a cross-sectional qualitative methodology, reviewing over 70 relevant research papers and articles to identify the intersection of Artificial Intelligence and strategic performance measurement in the Ugandan context. Findings indicate that Artificial Intelligence can significantly improve data management, reporting, and the overall effectiveness of NGOs by enabling smarter Key Performance Indicators (KPIs) and facilitating real-time data analyzis. However, challenges such as limited technical infrastructure, data quality issues, and resistance to change currently impede the adoption of Artificial Intelligence technologies. The implications of this research suggest that NGOs must invest in training, infrastructure, and ethical considerations to fully leverage Artificial Intelligence's capabilities, ultimately enhancing their operational effectiveness and impact in addressing Uganda's pressing development challenges.

Keywords: Artificial intelligence, impact data management, non-government organisations, reporting, strategic performance measurement (SPM)

Introduction

Historically, the focus on performance within non-profit organizations has evolved significantly since World War II, driven by criticisms regarding professionalism and the ability to meet performance targets [2]. In subsequent years, many non-profit organisations were set up, thanks to people's interest and the acknowledgement by authorities of their work in serving communities. Traditionally, performance assessment used output as a main indicator, but nowadays we are placing greater importance on outcomes. As a result, organisations now turn to process-based means that rely on measures aside from only finances to demonstrate their effectiveness.

In Uganda and other developing countries, Non-Government Organizations assist a great deal with serious social, environmental, and economic challenges [3]. There are approximately 14,000 NGOs registered in Uganda. These entities supplement the government in delivering services and implementing development policies. However, many Ugandan NGOs grapple with inefficiencies in program implementation, resource allocation, and performance evaluation, which hinder their effectiveness and impact. Another challenge is poor accountability due to inadequate performance measurement systems, which hinder transparency, impact assessment, and learning from past experiences, ultimately compromising their ability to demonstrate effectiveness.

The emergence of Artificial Intelligence offers a transformative opportunity to improve operational efficiency and strategic decision-making, particularly in facilitating strategic performance measurement, especially impact measurement.

The research paper seeks to explore how the adoption of artificial intelligence-driven performance measurement systems can contribute to improved effectiveness and impact of Ugandan NGOs. This paper seeks to address the question: How can the incorporation of Artificial Intelligence tools improve strategic impact measurement in Ugandan non-profit organizations?

[a]edyth.okello@gmail.com

DOI: 10.4324/9781003739982-3

Literature review

Using AI tools to improve the effectiveness of strategic performance measurement in non-government organisations

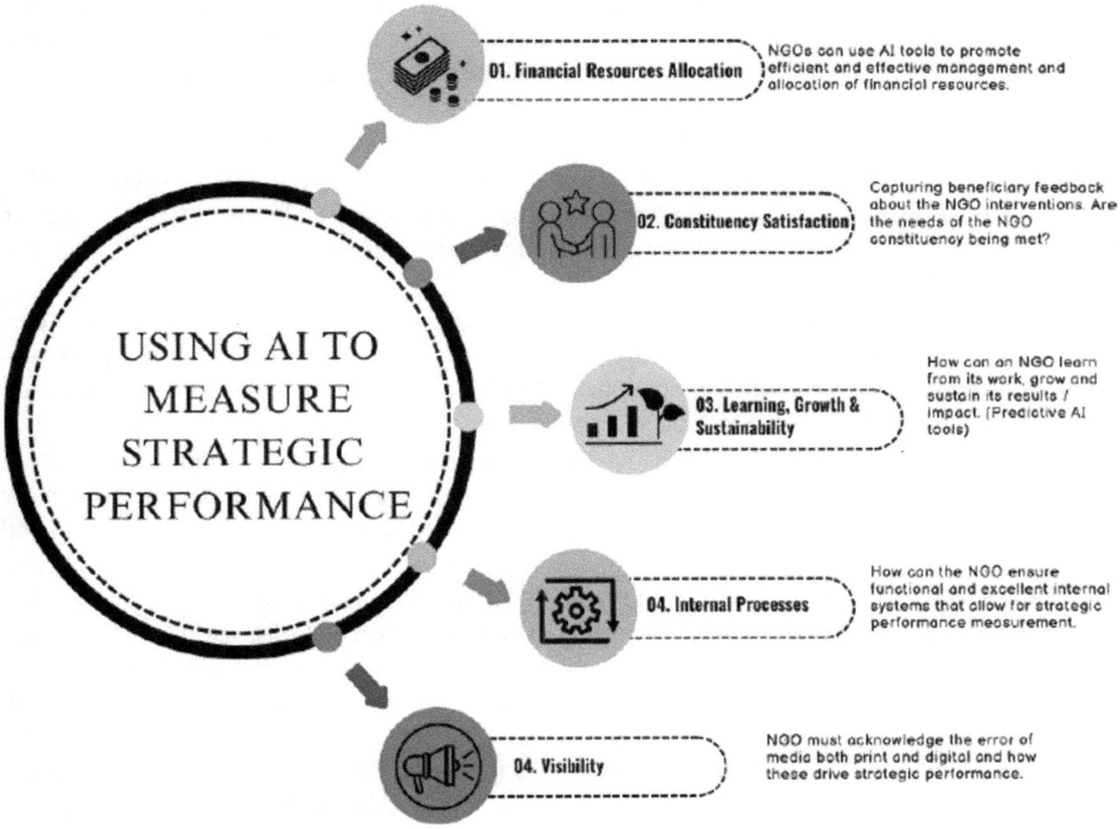

Figure 3.1 Measuring strategic performance

Note: Some Ideas for the diagram below were picked from David P. Norton of the Balanced Scorecard Collaborative

Source: Author

Understanding non-government organisations and their role in the development sector

Non-governmental organizations (NGOs) are private entities established for defined purposes or service objectives, frequently functioning inside the non-profit sector. According to the World Bank, they are characterized as private organizations that mitigate suffering, champion the underprivileged, safeguard the environment, provide social services, or implement community development projects. NGOs can range from large to small groups, operate locally or globally, and focus on a single problem or multiple themes. In the last decade, the number of NGOs has significantly increased, serving as advisors to governments, international agencies, and the United Nations.

NGOs are essential in tackling diverse social, environmental, and economic challenges globally, including in Uganda [1]. These organizations strive to maximize their impact, and as such, they must develop and implement effective performance measurement systems that align with their strategic objectives. Nonetheless, despite the critical importance of the NGO sector, this business is often impeded by considerable inefficiencies in program implementation, resource allocation, and impact assessment. These inefficiencies are not only logistical challenges; they represent a core barrier to achieving the optimal social impact that these organizations may realize.

Uganda is home to over 14,000 registered non-governmental organizations (NGOs) as of 2021, with several operating in the humanitarian sector to address issues such as poverty, health, and education. Approximately, 21.4% of Ugandans live in abject poverty according to the Uganda Bureau of Statistics, and the country ranks

159th out of 189 countries on the Human Development Index. These statistics underscore the critical need for effective humanitarian interventions and the importance of measuring their impact.

The increasing need for strategic performance measurement for non-government organisations

Performance measurement is a systematic process used to assess the advancement made towards predetermined goals. Strategic performance measurement (SPM) is a powerful approach that helps organizations align their strategic goals with day-to-day operations and monitor progress effective as detailed in figure 3.1 (Author, 2025).. According to Thapa [4], Given the increasing expectations and trust of many stakeholders in non-profit organizations, it is evident that performance must be systematically evaluated and assessed on a tangible basis. Various initiatives have been undertaken to meet the requirements of diverse stakeholders and society. Diverse assessment methodologies have been developed and evaluated to gauge the efficacy of non-profit organizations. Insufficient performance measures not only undervalue but also distort the organization's contributions [5].

Wright [7] several strategic performance frameworks on cascade.app. These include McKinsey's Strategic Horizons, founded on three principles: maintaining and defending core business, cultivating developing ventures, and establishing authentically novel enterprises. Then, the Value Disciplines focused on product leadership, operational excellence, and customer intimacy. Another framework is the stakeholder theory, which lists various business stakeholders, such as employees, customers, the community, shareholders and society at large. The timeless Balanced Scorecard is built on the premise that your business strategy should be equally divided into 4 quadrants financial, customer, internal business process and learning & growth, among several other frameworks.

In Uganda, the application and adaptation of the above and other performance measurement frameworks face unique challenges, including limited resources, varying stakeholder expectations, and socio-economic factors. The incorporation of artificial intelligence into the voluntary sector provides a revolutionary chance to surmount these obstacles, providing the possibility to improve both operational efficiency and overall effectiveness.

A report by the Uganda National NGO Forum [6] highlighted that only 35% of NGOs in Uganda have a robust performance measurement system in place. Therefore, identifying and implementing effective strategic performance measurement strategies tailored to the Ugandan context is crucial for enhancing the impact and efficiency of humanitarian not-for-profit organizations operating in the country.

The advancing digital space and how non-government organisations can leverage it, specifically artificial intelligence, to improve strategic performance measurement

Although not at the rapid pace that many assume, artificial intelligence is transforming the business environment. Artificial Intelligence is presently impacting decisions across various issues. Nevertheless, concepts such as fully automated customer service are not distant prospects. Technologies that facilitate Artificial Intelligence, including substantial processing power, data storage, and development platforms, are advancing rapidly and becoming increasingly accessible. Non-governmental organizations seem well-positioned to leverage Artificial Intelligence. It is anticipated that within the next decade, Artificial Intelligence will enhance the global economy by $13 trillion.

The charity industry is undergoing a transformation resulting from artificial intelligence, which provides creative ways to improve effectiveness, impact, and transparency. Charities can increase donor engagement, manage resources more wisely, and carry out their missions more successfully by utilizing Artificial Intelligence. Artificial Intelligence tools have the capacity to accurately and swiftly analyze large volumes of data and yield insightful information that can enable NGOs to make wise and informed decisions. For example, donor data can be processed by Artificial Intelligence-powered analytics platforms to spot patterns and forecast future donations. This makes it possible for charities to more successfully customize their fundraising plans. Programs like Google Analytics and IBM Watson Analytics use Artificial Intelligence to provide predictive analytics and data visualisation, helping charities see their impact.

Research Methodology

I employed a cross-sectional qualitative approach to review Artificial Intelligence utilization, tools and strategic performance measurement in totality. This allowed me to read widely about AI, emerging technologies and how these can support performance measurement strategies in NGOs in Uganda. I designed a template to collect data from relevant articles, which included the field of research, Objectives of that research, methodology, key findings, any Artificial Intelligence tools/systems examined, context prioritizing papers about the developing world, NGOs and Uganda, Implications, challenges, research gaps and limitations.

I conducted a thorough search from Research Gate, Google Scholar, and other relevant sites and read over 70 research papers, blogs, and articles. Papers included in this research included the research paper keywords. They addressed the intersection of Artificial Intelligence tools and strategic performance measurement, in the context of Uganda or other developing nations, and were published in 4 or fewer years in recognized academic journals, peer-reviewed journal articles, conference papers, reputable academic publications, and NGO sites. These papers reflect the most current advancements and trends in Artificial Intelligence and strategic performance measurement. Other major considerations were the methodological quality of the studies, substantial data and insights or case studies with contextual relevance to Uganda's NGOs. To ensure a focused, relevant, and academically rigorous literature review, several research papers were excluded on the basis of topics being irrelevant, outdated (5 years and above), non-peer-reviewed sources, lack of empirical evidence, irrelevant geographical scope, language barriers, duplicate studies, and papers with minimal citation impact.

I categorised all the articles, papers, and blogs and used thematic analysis to identify 4 common themes from which I deduced my discussion in the next subsection. The themes created are Artificial Intelligence and Ugandan Context, innovations Artificial Intelligence could bring to strategic performance measurement, Artificial Intelligence tools available for Non-Government Organisations in Uganda, and limitations and challenges in Ugandan NGOs.

Examples of NGOs driving SPM and impact using Artificial Intelligence tools in Uganda

Outbox Uganda operates a program titled Civic Technology and Data, wherein organizations collaborate on civic technology initiatives to illustrate the capacity of digital tools to enhance accountability, civic engagement, and transparency. The Artificial Intelligence tools they have developed include Code Africa, Manifesto Tracker, and Pimaa. The Women of Uganda Network is developing an artificial intelligence chat bot on their website to furnish information regarding online gender-based violence for survivors.

The Women of Uganda Network (WOUGNET) is creating an artificial intelligence chatbot on its website to offer information regarding online gender-based violence for survivors. Viamo, a global leader in mobile engagement, is committed to linking businesses and governments with individuals in low-connectivity settings and is collaborating with civil society organizations to bridge the digital divide and interact with marginalized populations. The "Ask Viamo Anything" tool provides easy access to the latest information across Zambia by means of basic mobile phones. Technologies are applied to build special resources for learning and advocating digital literacy among individuals and in online groups.

Discussion

Defining artificial intelligence and the Ugandan context

As Mutembesa of Makerere Artificial Intelligence lab explains, Artificial Intelligence describes many tools designed to let machines behave like people. There are sizable efforts in Uganda to use artificial intelligence in areas such as health, farming and official matters. With partners such as Sunbird AI, the government demonstrates how it wants to use Artificial Intelligence for the good of the public. FAIR Forward is designed to prepare workers for the next era of AI and improve understanding of artificial intelligence while helping plan the country's move to digital transformation through initiatives such as Digital Uganda Vision and the National ICT Innovation Hub.

Understanding the evaluation of strategy in non-government organisations and the potential benefits of artificial intelligence for the sector

When talking about performance measurement approaches, it is clear that many theorists analyse whether they really work and in which situations. Many traditional management techniques, such as Total Quality Management (TQM), Benchmarking and the Balanced Scorecard, are widely adopted but commonly criticised for not being applicable to today's complex organisations. Even though TQM helped organisations improve and focused on stakeholders in the past, it has come under criticism for not identifying specific challenges and the causes in a company's operations. This critique shows that using a single modelling system for planning, management, and evaluation is not enough, because each process has its own needs. Hence, weak terminology and its application can cause confusion and problems in managing how the organisation works.

As a result, Performance Prism and Results-Based Management (RBM) are being introduced to give a better picture of performance. This multidimensional approach came from the Performance Prism, which Neely designed to show that performance should consider stakeholder opinions and the different factors within a business. Furthermore, RBM works by weaving together strategic planning and monitoring results to guarantee both good performance and accountability. Nonetheless, it is challenging to put these frameworks into practice. Performance measurement techniques have their limitations, which can lead practitioners to understand only a part of how the organisation really works. For this reason, systems for measuring performance must be revisited and improved over time to fit the constantly changing environment of organisations. In addition, though the Logical Framework is used widely in development work, it has been questioned because its method can be too rigid and fails to represent the complexity of such projects. Often, the model assumes causes and effects, yet this doesn't match the way actual development efforts are carried out in varying and unexpected situations. This approach reflects a growing awareness in performance measurement that flexible systems focusing on processes are needed to meet the demands of real-life situations. In response to these issues, many are now seeking to combine proven elements from performance measurement systems to create more useful and effective solutions for the organisation. The goal of evolving performance measurement approaches is to develop ways that not only track performance but also support important changes and improvement for an organisation.

Artificial Intelligence has the potential to revolutionize strategic performance measurement in non-profit work. In fact, foundations and organizations are funding charity work that utilizes Artificial Intelligence for social good, such as a $25 million grant to 15 non-profit projects from Google.org addressing Sustainable Development Goals and the Vaccine Confidence Fund's first program that uses chatbots and machine learning to boost vaccine confidence through social media. This is evidence of the potential of Artificial Intelligence in resource monilization and allocation in the NGO world.

Artificial Intelligence-enabling technologies are becoming critical in impact data management and reporting, including substantial processing power, data storage, and development platforms that are rapidly advancing and becoming increasingly accessible.

NGOs can use Artificial Intelligence tools to design and measure smarter Key Performance Indicators. KPIs serve as benchmarks to evaluate progress on a wide range of organizational objectives. Artificial Intelligence can support data-gathering techniques and analytics. These tools can support prioritization of what KPIs measure rather than how they are measured.

Artificial intelligence tools available for strategic performance measurement in non-government organisations in Uganda

Canva is a graphic design platform that offers tools for generating social media graphics, presentations, promotional products, and websites. Canva offers a complimentary premium package to groups registered as non-profit entities. It has user-friendly features.

Microsoft 365 Copilot is a platform that aids organizations in data analysis, goal development, identification of key performance indicators (KPIs), and predictive analytics. They may produce detailed reports, establish SMART objectives, monitor progress, and utilize historical data to predict future patterns, facilitating proactive decision-making and strategic modifications. Microsoft provides a grant of 365 to non-governmental organizations for a maximum of nine users.

Bonterra: "We provide the software that supports the mission, offering the tools and technology necessary to effect change and transform the world." Our tools enable your team to increase fundraising, enhance matching, expand granting, and attain more success with ease and efficiency. According to their website, Bonterra is software designed for the most social benefit.

Problems and limits that may hinder Ugandan NGOs from using AI systems for their strategy measurement

While Artificial intelligence helps a lot in performance measurement and data analytics, using these tools is not always without problems. Knowing what artificial intelligence technologies can and cannot do is important for NGOs to see how they can maximise their benefits from these systems.

Many NGOs find it challenging to deliver reliable data because of inconsistent data collection and limited knowledge in data management. The problem is made worse because there are not enough servers and cloud services to use advanced tools in Artificial Intelligence. Further barriers to the NGO sector using digital technology are limited internet access, pricey data plans, challenging cultural issues, and fears about data privacy. Not having enough technicians is stopping the effective implementation of Artificial Intelligence. Not enough people with the necessary skills may exist to build, implement and support Artificial Intelligence solutions. Low computer knowledge among NGO workers and beneficiaries, along with tight budgets, keeps Artificial Intelligence solutions out of reach.

Artificial intelligence tools do not fully understand personal and human stories. That is why the human touch remains crucial. Because the non-profit sector is based on connecting people and showing sensitivity, it's even more important to be careful and make sure there is balance. Some of the major risks around artificial intelligence include ethical concerns; oftentimes artificial intelligence tools have been built with biases. Thus, these biases are sent out with every use of these technologies. Not only can built-in biases hurt people, but they also change how people respond and analyze things. Additionally, because artificial intelligence is opaque, it is hard to fully understand how it makes decisions. There are concerns about who gains from Artificial Intelligence responses because these tools are not value-free.

What should NGOs do to prepare and be part of the AI era?

The successful adoption and implementation of artificial intelligence hinge on several factors, including a locally trained workforce capable of developing these solutions, adequate infrastructural capacity to manage the computational demands of algorithm training, representative datasets, governmental support and regulation to ensure the equitable use of these technologies, and independent civil institutions and policymakers that protect against detrimental applications while promoting responsibility and accountability. The use of technology in various sectors is fast growing and advancing. This calls for NGOs to reimagine and position themselves for now and the future. NGOs must understand what the future will look like for them and, in fact, determine or influence how it will look. A case in point, Apple computers seemed to have had the home technology needed by users in the late 90s. However, as a technology revolution swept around, the founder realized that these computers could become so many technologies in one, thus introducing various software to elevate the home computer. The visionary founder went on to invent other gadgets that would further meet the market demands, like being profitable and mobile, etc, because that is what the future looked like.

To successfully adopt Artificial Intelligence, NGOs should start by understanding its capabilities and identifying specific tasks it can perform. Focus on small-scale prototypes to evaluate AI ideas without allocating significant resources. Develop internal competencies by allocating resources, providing staff training, and partnering with Artificial Intelligence specialists. Utilize established Artificial Intelligence tools and platforms like TensorFlow, PyTorch, and scikit-learn. Data collection and quality assurance are crucial for accurate Artificial Intelligence models. Consider ethics and transparency by ensuring Artificial Intelligence solutions align with your organization's values and mission. Running pilot projects and learning from them can assist you in testing and improving AI projects. Work together with software companies, research organisations, and universities to move forward with your studies of artificial intelligence. Identify and recognise little achievements as you go, and be ready to adjust to new information. When adopting AI, people must continue to learn, talk about ethics and take part in their community. If organisations include these various components, they can use Artificial Intelligence most productively for society's benefit.

Conclusion

With AI incorporated, non-government organisations are using new tools to measure and enhance their work effectiveness. AI helps organisations handle data from various sources. This allows results to be tracked better and helps with more flexible and rapid choices. Organisations can pick better strategies and allocate resources by relying on Artificial Intelligence and predictive analytics to notice both usual patterns and any changes.

Performance evaluation with Artificial Intelligence helps companies establish a flexible culture that always seeks to improve. Because these technologies develop further, organisations are able to set reasonable targets and watch their development in real time. This leads to a culture where people are held responsible and support innovation. More people need to know about the important work these charities do. In addition to advocacy, we need responsible policy-makers and the appropriate setting for these innovations to turn into prototypes. In addition, artificial intelligence helps businesses measure their results better and adjust their actions in a way that promotes their long-term success and advancement.

References

[1] Banks, N., Hulme, D., & Edwards, M. (2015). NGOs, states, and donors revisited: still too close for comfort? *World Development*, 66(1), 707–718. https://doi.org/10.1016/j.worlddev.2014.09.028.

[2] Larsson, J., & Kinnunen, J. (2008). *Performance measurement in nonprofits: Much to be gained or a waste of resources?* (No. 2008:18). Luleå University of Technology. Available at https://www.diva-portal.org/smash/get/diva2:141869/FULLTEXT01.Pdf. Accessed on 19th May 2025.

[3] Ministry of Internal Affairs - Republic of Uganda. (2010). *The national NGO policy: Strengthening partnership for development*. The National Bureau for Non-Governmental Organizations. Available at https://www.ngobureau.go.ug/sites/default/files/laws_regulations/2021/04/National%20NGO%20Policy,%202010.pdf. Accessed on 19th May 2025.

[4] Thapa, M. S. (2019). Measuring performance of non-government organizations: A comparative study of AMDA Nepal and General Welfare Pratisthan (GWP). *JMC Research Journal*, 3(1). Available at https://www.nepjol.info/index.php/JMCRJ/article/download/43076/32678/126271. Accessed on 20th May 2025.

[5] Treinta, F. T., Moura, L. F., Cestari, J. M. A. P., de Lima, E. P., Deschamps, F., & da Costa, S. E. G. (2020). Design and implementation factors for performance measurement in non-profit organizations: A literature review. *Frontiers in Psychology, 11*. Available at https://doi.org/10.3389/fpsyg.2020.01799. Accessed on 20th May 2025.

[6] Uganda National NGO Forum. (2020). *UNNGOF annual report 2020*. Available at https://ngoforum.or.ug/downloads/unngof-2020-annual-report/. Accessed on 20th May 2025.

[7] Wright, T. (2024, January 17). *5 of the best strategy frameworks for your organization*. Cascade. Available at https://www.cascade.app/blog/best-strategy-frameworks. Accessed on 21st May 2025.

4 Managing global digital nomad software teams: leadership and management

Rupayan Choudhury[1,a] *and Anuj Kumar*[2,b]

[1]Student of Doctorate of Business Administration with Specialization in General Management, Rushford Business School, Maihofstrasse, Lucerne, Switzerland

[2]Rushford Business School, Maihofstrasse, Lucerne, Switzerland

Abstract

This research examines how software companies are changing their work culture due to having teams in different parts of the world. It analyses the strategies managers take to motivate, support and unify mobile workforces in other cultures and nations. By reviewing the literature and speaking with stakeholders in five remote-friendly companies, the research reveals which factors influence a company's management strategy for remote and hybrid teams. According to the study, the COVID-19 pandemic has greatly influenced the increasing use of flexible work environments. The study also investigates how government rules, laws regarding work and technological progress affect the ongoing nature of digital nomadism. With digital nomads growing in importance to global economies, the research points out that challenges and implications of remote work must be addressed for the growth and management of organizations worldwide.

Keywords: Borderless mobile workforce, digital nomads, leadership, management, remote workforce, software development

Introduction

Since the start of the pandemic, the idea of remote work becoming the standard has been up and down. Existing large companies have embraced a new model known as "work from anywhere," meaning employees can decide after the pandemic if they'd like to continue working remotely. Before the pandemic, many digital nomads had been working entirely remotely for a long time. Now may just be the perfect chance for you to understand the subject more completely. Because workplaces are changing rapidly, companies in software development are recognized as driving the shift to global and mobile teams. A revolution is happening in the way work takes place due to the emergence of digital nomads, those who use technology to work from anywhere they choose. Due to the trend toward borderless work, companies now deal with diverse groups of people from different locations who test traditional management approaches. Organizing such a staff comes with unique problems. While those in conventional jobs usually work in the office and are closely watched, digital nomads operate on their own, sometimes operating in different countries and time zones.

Therefore, organizations developing software need to use new styles of management to support and coordinate their remote workers. Today's software sector faces unique challenges, as successfully collaborating, thinking creatively and achieving high productivity play important roles. The pandemic greatly increased the speed with which many companies moved to a remote workforce. While this development has provided extra flexibility and more skilled workers, it has pointed out problems in older management methods. This research targets the question of how the main strategic approaches are adapting to suit work that is mobile and not tied to specific countries. The main aim of the study is to learn how companies manage their digital nomads and how these methods are changing the future of work. The study will analyze what is known and done in the industry about the management issues and advantages of remote working.

Literature Review

Remote working: an introduction and outcome

[a]rupayan111@gmail.com, [b]anuj.kumar@rushford.ch

DOI: 10.4324/9781003739982-4

Adoption of remote work

Remote work is known to be an ongoing model that keeps changing. Sometimes called telecommuting or working from home, it quickly developed from a small practice to one many people now use, mainly in the knowledge economy. New technologies and tools for communication now make it possible for employees to do their work remotely [8]. While more companies were bringing in remote work prior to the pandemic, COVID-19 made it happen nearly instantly for many organizations, requiring them to switch to remote or hybrid systems.

How remote work became popular in the software industry

Because software development happens mainly online, remote work fits well in the sector. Working together from different countries and zones is simpler now with cloud technologies, version control and agile project management tools. This sector has especially benefited from the flexibility of remote work, so businesses in the industry can connect with talented people worldwide [1]. There are unique advantages to remote work for both employees and employers. It leads to employees enjoying more freedom, greater independence and better ability to separate work from personal life. By eliminating the need for commuting, remote work allows workers to reclaim valuable time, reduce stress, and tailor their working environment to personal preferences. For companies, remote work presents opportunities to lower overhead costs, particularly in terms of office space, utilities, and maintenance, while also broadening access to a more diverse talent pool [6].

Remote work challenges

Even with its positives, remote work involves several problems that everyone needs to manage. One of the most commonly cited challenges is communication. In the traditional and conventional office settings, impromptu conversations and face-to-face interactions have been often seen to foster collaboration and encourage quick problem solving. In remote work settings, however, teams rely heavily on digital communication platforms like Zoom, Slack, Microsoft Teams, etc, which can sometimes hinder real-time collaboration, particularly when working across different time zones [18]. Having employees separated from their peers is another major challenge. Being far from the office can make workers feel outside the team and its culture. This isolation can contribute to feelings of loneliness and reduced engagement, making it imperative for managers to actively foster a sense of community and inclusion in virtual environments. Furthermore, remote work requires strong discipline and time management skills. Blurring lines between professional and personal life can lead to overwork and burnout, as remote employees may find it difficult to "switch off" when their home becomes their office [13].

Technological innovations supporting remote work

The success of remote work relies heavily on the integration of various technologies that facilitate communication, collaboration, and productivity [25]. Key technologies include:

Cloud-based collaboration tools

Real-time communication and smooth document sharing are made possible by technologies like Microsoft 365 and Google Workspace.

Project management platforms

Tools, which may also be called platforms, such as Jira, Trello, and Asana, help teams stay aligned on goals, timelines, and deliverables.

Communication platforms

Tools such as Slack, Zoom, and Microsoft Teams enable instant messaging, video conferencing, and file sharing, maintaining connectivity despite physical separation.

Trends shaping remote work

Hybrid models are probably what the future of remote work will look like, so workers may work from home or attend work on-site. Many companies have adopted "remote-first" or "hybrid" models, where remote work is encouraged. However, office spaces are still available for employees who prefer in-person interaction or need access to resources that might not be available at home. As remote work continues to evolve, new challenges and opportunities will emerge, particularly in areas like cybersecurity, data privacy, and the management of distributed teams [10]. For companies to remain competitive, it will be crucial to adopt flexible, adaptive management strategies that accommodate the preferences and needs of remote employees while leveraging the benefits of a globalized, borderless workforce [16].

Leadership and management in remote teams

Because more organizations are moving to remote work, especially in software development, new approaches to leadership and management are needed to handle the needs of a workforce that is often in many places at once. Leading remote teams requires a departure from traditional in-office leadership practices and emphasizes flexibility, communication, and trust. In the context of managing digital nomads - professionals who operate independently across global locations - effective leadership is crucial to ensuring team cohesion, maintaining productivity, and fostering engagement [9]. Figure 4.2 shows types of leadership in remote teams.

Transformational leadership in remote working

Leading remotely often works best with a transformational method. People with this type of leadership inspire staff by explaining their vision, encouraging them, and always focusing on what's ahead [15]. Special attention to autonomy, creativity and personal improvement is a key point in how transformational leaders deal with digital nomad teams.

For remote teams, especially in the software industry, transformational leadership:

- Give your team the ability to decide what and how to do things, share creative ideas, and keep moving forward without being supervised all the time.
- Promoting an aim that unites everyone, no matter their place in the world. Not having direct meetings means everyone needs to know and accept the mission clearly to feel connected to the company's goals.
- Encouraging adaptability and responsiveness, which are essential traits for digital nomads who often navigate different time zones, work environments, and cultural norms.

Servant leadership: building trust and engagement

This type of leadership believes that putting team members and stakeholders ahead of the leader is the main priority. The term was popularized by Robert K. Greenleaf in his 1970 essay "The Servant as Leader," emphasizing that true leadership emerges from a desire to help and empower others. Canavesi and Minelli [4] Servant leaders transform the traditional view of leadership by focusing on service and empowerment. This approach not only supports individual growth but also drives overall organizational success, making it particularly relevant in today's collaborative remote work environments.

Key aspects of servant leadership when working remotely are:

Supporting team members' well-being

Working remotely may result in being disconnected and overworked if your job and personal time start to mix. By being servant leaders, managers pay attention to their team's mental and emotional health and give them support to organize work and personal life.

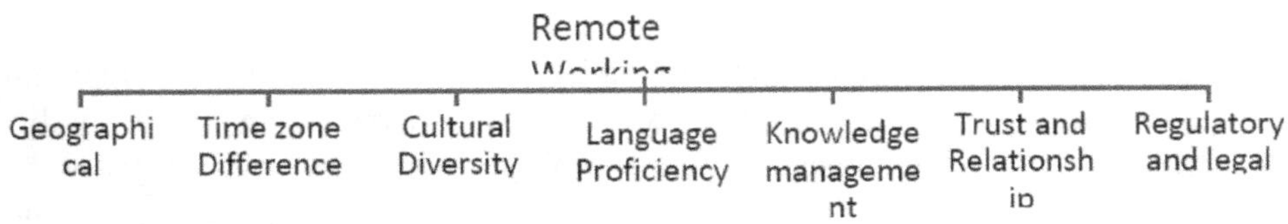

Figure 4.1 Remote working factors
Source: Author

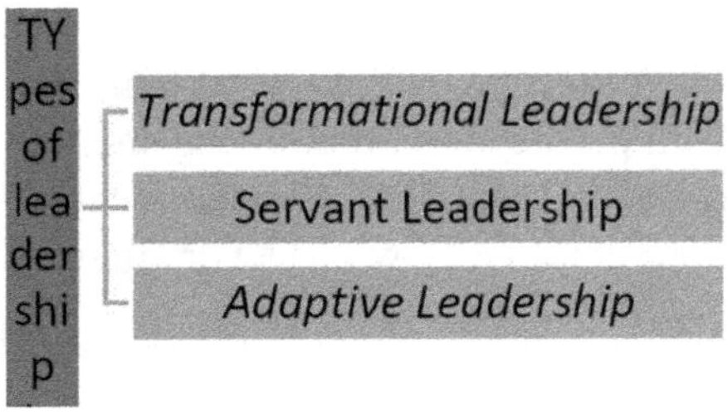

Figure 4.2 Types of leadership in remote teams
Source: Author

Developing individuals
Servant leaders take a proactive approach to the professional development of their team. In a remote setting, this might involve offering virtual training, mentorship, and opportunities for up-skilling.

Facilitating communication
Servant leaders take action to organize and improve communication with others. They set up the tools and help needed so that team members can work effectively together, no matter what their location. This means outlining when you expect to be reachable, meeting virtually, and providing feedback to avoid problems in digital communication.

Adaptive leadership: navigating uncertainty in a remote environment
Due to the way remote work is changing now, post-COVID-19, leaders must be adaptable and resilient. Adaptive leadership means being flexible, solving problems as they come up and being innovative, all of which are vital for leading digital nomads [12].

In practice, adaptive leaders in remote environments:

- Respond to changing circumstances: Remote work environments are often fluid, with team members working from different countries and dealing with local disruptions (e.g., internet outages, personal commitments, time zone issues). Adaptive leaders are responsive to these challenges and adjust expectations or processes as needed.
- Encourage experimentation and innovation: With remote teams, adaptive leaders foster a culture where employees are encouraged to try new approaches in product development or workflow management. This agility is vital for software development teams that must iterate quickly in response to changing client or market needs.
- Facilitate continuous learning: Adaptive leaders invest in their teams' ongoing education and development, especially in the use of new technologies and tools. Digital nomads frequently rely on cloud-based collaboration tools such as Slack, Jira, Google workspace etc. Hence, continuous learning ensures that they remain proficient and can adapt to any new systems or methods of working.

Challenges of leadership in remote work
Leading remote teams, particularly digital nomads, presents unique challenges that require specific management strategies:

- Communication barriers: To facilitate and foster better communication, leaders of software development companies that have digital nomad employees must eliminate communication barriers that arise from different time zones, cultural differences, and dependency on digital communication platforms. Without the informal and spontaneous interactions which are quite common in traditional workplaces, leaders should focus on establishing structured communication practices while allowing flexibility for asynchronous work [19].

- Building trust: Trust is one of the most important and key fundamental components of successful remote work. Leaders will have to establish trust not only by encouraging transparency and accountability but also by trusting employees to manage their own schedules and deliverables. For digital nomads, who work independently and often without direct supervision, this trust from their leaders on them is essential for maintaining motivation and performance.
- Engagement and motivation: Keeping remote employees engaged can be challenging when they are disconnected from the in-person interactions of an office environment. It is important for leaders to boost motivation by noticing achievements, giving team members feedback and supporting community among the team through online activities [22].

Research Methodology

This work employs a qualitative approach to study how software development companies lead digital nomad teams even when they are not in the same office. Reviewing sources from academia and from within the industry is the key step in forming the structure of this research. Semi-structured interviews with managers and team members from five leading remote work software companies formed the main way data was collected. One of the contributing companies works in a hybrid remote model, while the other four companies have a fully mobile workforce. The interviews gave useful information about the problems and methods involved in the management of remote and mobile employees. Thematic analysis was used on the interview data to find common themes and patterns in how management is done and the challenges involved. The literature review was combined with the data collected, adding more insight into how work culture is evolving. Ethical considerations were paramount throughout the study. Participants were informed of the research objectives and provided informed consent. Confidentiality was ensured by anonymizing all responses and securing data. The fact that the sample is quite small limits how much we can generalize from the study. Moreover, highlighting software development does not guarantee that the findings will apply to all industries.

Results and Discussions

Important factors affecting remote working
Countries' traditional borders have a range of effects on software development companies' global work teams, mainly related to remote work.

Geographical distance
The physical separation between teams located in different countries has been witnessed to lead to challenges in communication, coordination, and collaboration [11]. The distance has been found to be a factor complicating interactions among team members who may be working on the same project but are situated in different time zones and locations and thus separated by a large geographical distance.

Time zone differences
Time zone differences are a factor that led to challenges in coordination and internal communication among team members. It highlights that as the time zone span increases, the overlap of working hours decreases, which can reduce the overall synchronicity of communication. This makes it very difficult for teams to collaborate effectively, potentially impacting project outcomes. Miller [17]. Because of differences in time zones, communication and project completion are often delayed. Teams may struggle to find overlapping working hours for meetings, which can also hinder timely decision-making [3].

Cultural diversity
Each country has its own cultural norms, languages, and practices, which can lead to misunderstandings and miscommunication among team members [20]. Our society is known for being diverse culturally, and this tends to modify teamwork, and the methods teams use to complete tasks.

Language proficiency
Language barriers can impede effective communication, especially in teams where members speak different native languages. This can lead to a loss of communication richness and difficulties in understanding project requirements.

Knowledge management
Managing knowledge across geographically dispersed teams can be challenging, as information may come from various sources and needs to be shared effectively among all team members [26].

Trust and relationship building
Building trust and social ties among team members can be more difficult when they are separated by geographical borders. Building relationships is often more difficult in a remote work situation, as face-to-face meetings are not always possible.

Regulatory and legal issues
Every country has their own regulations regarding labor laws, data protection, and intellectual property, which can complicate the management of a global workforce [14]. Figure 4.1 shows remote working factors.

Key management strategies for remote teams
In addition to leadership styles, certain management strategies are crucial for managing digital nomad teams effectively:

Goal setting and performance metrics
Clear goals and performance metrics are critical in a remote environment with little direct oversight. Managers must set clear expectations, timelines, and deliverables to ensure alignment and accountability.

Virtual team building
Building a cohesive team culture in a remote setting requires deliberate efforts. Managers can foster team cohesion by organizing regular virtual meetings, informal chats, or even online team-building activities. This helps digital nomads feel connected to the organization and reduces feelings of isolation.

Regular feedback and check-ins
For teams that work apart, it's important to provide feedback all the time. Leaders should put in place regular one-on-one meetings to talk about advancements, look over any hurdles and supply helpful remarks. This system allows digital nomads to work through early problems and feel secure in their work, so they are not likely to disengage [24].

Leveraging technology for collaboration
Managing teams in different locations requires relying on helpful collaboration technology. Staying productive and united during remote work can be made easy by using platforms for project management (e.g., Jira, Trello), team communication (e.g., Slack, Zoom) and sharing documents (e.g., Google Drive, Microsoft 365).

Role of governmental policies and labor laws in shaping the viability and sustainability of digital nomadism
Because many now work and travel in many countries, governments and authority figures have started rethinking labor regulations to make them more suitable for this group of workers. Nowadays, professionals are increasingly choosing to live and work across borders. In such a scenario, the role of government policies and labor regulations become increasingly critical in shaping the viability and sustainability of digital nomadism [2].

Digital nomad visas and immigration policies

One of the key areas where government policies directly put a significant impact on digital nomadism is through the creation of digital nomad visas. These visas are specifically designed for remote workers who wish to live in a country temporarily while working for a company based elsewhere. Several countries, including Estonia, Spain, Croatia, Barbados, and Portugal, have introduced digital nomad visa programs to attract skilled workers to boost local economies without adding to the domestic labor market [23].

- Attracting talent: By offering special visa programs, governments can attract high-earning, skilled professionals who contribute to the economy through local spending, thus fostering economic growth of the country of residency of the digital nomad.
- Regulating stays: These visas typically offer flexible residency periods, allowing digital nomads to stay for extended periods (often six months to a year or longer) without needing traditional work permits or employment contracts with local companies. In some countries like Spain the digital nomad visas are also granted for a period of up to 3 or even 5 years.

The creation of such visas signals a shift in immigration policies, as governments recognize the potential of remote workers to contribute to local economies without taking jobs from the local population. These policies are instrumental in making digital nomadism a viable and sustainable option for professionals worldwide.

Taxation and social security

Another significant aspect of government policies shaping digital nomadism is taxation and social security. Many digital nomads run into problems with taxes when they move to new countries to work for companies in other countries. The ambiguity surrounding tax residency and social security contributions can deter individuals from fully embracing the digital nomad lifestyle [21].

- Tax residency rules: Normally, a country establishes tax residency by looking at how many days someone is physically present in the country. Most digital nomads can be taxed by two regions if they do not handle their residency correctly in various places.
- Double taxation treaties: Some countries deal with this problem by forming double taxation treaties that make sure people are taxed only once on the same earnings. However, the lack of uniformity across jurisdictions complicates this issue, and digital nomads must be vigilant in understanding local tax law [7].
- Social security: Another challenge is the contribution to social security systems. For digital nomads not tied to a particular country for employment, questions arise about where (or whether) they should contribute to social security. In some cases, nomads may be required to contribute to both their home country and host country social security systems, adding to the financial burden of remote work.

Governments that wish to encourage digital nomadism must develop clear and simplified tax and social security frameworks. Policies that allow digital nomads to pay taxes without incurring excessive penalties or burdens will promote the sustainability of the nomad lifestyle while ensuring that governments can still collect revenue from this group.

Labor laws and worker protections

The legal status of digital nomads from the context of labor laws is a key factor that determines the long-term viability of this lifestyle. In many cases, digital nomads work as independent contractors or freelancers, which can leave them outside the protection of traditional labor laws that cover full-time employees [5].

- Worker classification: The classification of remote workers as either employees or independent contractors has significant implications for benefits such as healthcare, unemployment insurance, and pension contributions. Digital nomads who work as freelancers or contractors may not be entitled to these benefits, which can create long-term security risks, particularly in cases of illness or economic downturns.

- Remote work regulations: Some countries have started to introduce specific regulations concerning remote work to provide legal protection for employees working from abroad. These laws address issues such as working hours, occupational safety, and data privacy in remote settings. However, the transnational nature of digital nomadism complicates the enforcement of such regulations.

Governments of the countries that support digital nomadism will have to consider the introduction of policies that protect nomads without imposing overly restrictive labor laws. This may include creating specialized regulations that provide digital nomads with access to essential protections while respecting their autonomy and flexibility.

Conclusions

The increasing number of digital nomads has transformed the software industry management, so leaders must adjust their ways of directing remote and mixed teams. This research emphasizes the importance of leadership styles like transformational and adaptive leadership, which prioritize trust, communication, and employee well-being. While digital nomadism offers access to global talent and operational flexibility, it also poses challenges such as time zone coordination, team cohesion, and communication gaps. Overcoming these requires clear goal setting, regular feedback, and leveraging technology for virtual collaboration.

The study also highlights the role of supportive government policies, such as digital nomad visas and updated labor laws, in sustaining remote work environments. As hybrid work models gain traction, businesses embracing agile management practices will thrive in a digital-first economy. Because of these insights, organizations can overcome obstacles, use management approaches wisely and take advantage of digital nomadism to ensure their long-term achievements.

References

[1] Balan, B. V. I. (2001). Impact of sudden increase in remote work on agile software engineering processes and productivity. (Doctoral dissertation, TechnischeUniversität Wien).

[2] Bednorz, J. (2024). Working from anywhere? work from here! Approaches to attract digital nomads. *Annals of Tourism Research*, 105, 103715. https://doi.org/10.1016/j.annals.2023.103715.

[3] Begel, A. (2008). Effecting change: Coordination in large-scale software development. In Proceedings of the 2008 International Workshop on Cooperative and Human Aspects of Software Engineering (CHASE '08), (pp. 17–20). https://doi.org/10.1145/1370114.1370119.

[4] Canavesi, A., & Minelli, E. (2022). Servant leadership and employee engagement: a qualitative study. *Employee Responsibilities and Rights Journal*, 34(4), 413–435.

[5] Collins, D., & Robinson, B. (2023). The digital nomad and the emergence of global labour mobility. In Research Handbook on Digital Trade, (pp. 329–343). Edward Elgar Publishing.

[6] Conchuir, E. O., Holmstrom, H., Agerfalk, P. J., & Fitzgerald, B. (2006). Exploring the assumed benefits of global software development. In 2006 IEEE International Conference on Global Software Engineering (ICGSE'06), (pp. 159–168). https://doi.org/10.1109/ICGSE.2006.261229.

[7] Costas, C. F., & Dohotar, C. (2021). Taxation of digital nomads. *Cluj tax FJ*, 77–78.

[8] Felstead, A. (2022). Remote Working: A Research Overview. Routledge.

[9] Gandrita, D., Gandrita, A., & Rosado, D. P. (2022). Overcoming remote leadership challenges: lessons learned from COVID-19. *Journal of Business and Management Studies*, 4(4), 170–183.

[10] He, X., Meng, X., Wang, Y., & Wang, Z. (2022). The impact of COVID-19 on various aspects of remote work software and future development. In 2022 7th International Conference on Financial Innovation and Economic Development (ICFIED 2022), (pp. 2761–2767). Atlantis Press.

[11] Kahya, M. D., & Seneler, Ç. (2018). Geographical distance challenges in distributed agile software development: case study of a global company. In 2018 3rd International Conference on Computer Science and Engineering (UBMK), (pp. 78–83).

[12] Kaniuk, I. (2022). Application of adaptive leadership practices to promote employee commitment in transition to remote work. (Doctoral dissertation, Vilniaus Universitetas).

[13] Karki, S. B. (2023). Impact of remote work on productivity of software developers and its challenges. https://www.theseus.fi/handle/10024/803162

[14] Leite, L., dos Santos, D. R., & Almeida, F. (2022). The impact of general data protection regulation on software engineering practices. *Information and Computer Security*, 30(1), 79–96.

[15] Loyless, L. H. (2023). Competence in virtual communication: remote transformational leadership. *Public Administration Review*, 83(3), 702–709.

[16] Maher, A. (2014). Leading remote and virtual teams: a real challenge for leaders and entrepreneurs. In European Conference on Management, Leadership, and Governance, (pp. 160–166).

[17] Miller, G. (2014). Effective collaboration amongst globally dispersed teams. (Doctoral dissertation). National College of Ireland, Dublin.

[18] Müller, K., Koch, C., Riehle, D., Stops, M., & Harutyunyan, N. (2023). Challenges of working from home in software development during COVID-19 lockdowns. *ACM Transactions on Software Engineering and Methodology*, 32(5), 1–41.

[19] Nikbakhsh, N. (2022). Assessing the impact of authentic leadership and conflict management on the performance of remote-working employees: The example of software/online platform development companies. *Unpublished master's thesis. Tallinn University of Technology.*

[20] Patel, D., Lawson-Johnson, C., & Patel, S. (2009). The effect of cultural differences on software development. In 5th Annual International Conference on Computing and ICT Research (ICCIR 2009), (pp. 250–263).

[21] Pignatari, L. T. (2023). The taxation of 'digital nomads' and the '3 W's': between tax challenges and heavenly beaches. *Intertax*, 51(5), 384–396.

[22] Saaron-Juhanson, P. (2019). The best practices of effective remote leadership in an information and communication technology company. (Master's thesis). Tallinn University of Technology. TalTech Library Digital Collection. https://digikogu.taltech.ee/et/Item/d7e14162-bc6f-4a8b-a438-6e0648eefac6.

[23] Sánchez-Vergara, J. I., Orel, M., & Capdevila, I. (2023). "Home office is the here and now." digital nomad visa systems and remote work-focused leisure policies. *World Leisure Journal*, 65(2), 236–255.

[24] Sharma, A. (2018). Managing remote teams in organisations: best practices for effective collaboration and communication. *Psychology and Education*, 55(1), 167–173.

[25] Urbaniec, M., Małkowska, A., & Włodarkiewicz-Klimek, H. (2022). The impact of technological developments on remote working: insights from the polish managers' perspective. *Sustainability*, 14(1), 552. https://doi.org/10.3390/su14010552.

[26] Zahedi, M., Shahin, M., & Babar, M. A. (2016). A systematic review of knowledge sharing challenges and practices in global software development. *International Journal of Information Management*, 36(6), 995–1019.

5 Market orientation of Indian micro-entrepreneurs

Monalisha Dutta[1,a] *and Ayekpam Ibemcha Chanu*[2,b]

[1]Research scholar, Department of Commerce, Bodoland University, Assam, India

[2]Professor, Department of Commerce, Bodoland University, Assam, India

Abstract

The growing intensity of competition necessitates firms devise strategies directed towards meeting the needs of the market. This exercise is especially important for the micro enterprises, which suffer from a multitude of issues like financial irregularities, a semi-skilled labor force, competition from the larger counterparts, etc. As a result, market orientation is key in supporting the effective operations of these companies. This work assesses how market-oriented the Bell Metal Industry of Assam is as an MSME listed by the Government of India. The study brings together and analyzes information gathered from the main sources. Researchers applied several chosen variables in the MKTOR Scale to measure market orientation. According to the report, most of the artisans had a medium degree of being market-focused. Regardless of how long they have been practicing, artisans are equally devoted to market orientation.

Keywords: Bell metal industry, market orientation, micro enterprise, MKTOR

Introduction

India has come a long way from being one of the developing nations to one of the five largest economies of the world. This feat can be attributed to a large extent to the role played by its domestic market in fostering its economic growth. This has been possible because of its nature of being a labor surplus and a vast domestic market-based economy [5]. The domestic market of India is dominated by the huge base of micro enterprises. Since they operate mostly in rural areas and follow practices specific to those areas, they help create local jobs, giving people less reason to move to big cities. Further, the financial, infrastructural and regulatory requirements of these enterprises are less in comparison to the larger ones, making it possible for individuals with innovative ideas to start such enterprises. Micro enterprises are the fertile grounds of ideas, innovation, and mobilization of local resources.

As per the MSME Report of 2023-24, the Micro Sector, with an estimated total of 630.52 lakh enterprises, provides employment to 97% of the MSME sector workforce; thereby absorbing people with different skill sets and enabling them to earn a decent standard of living. In the year 1998, the Ministry of Micro, Small and Medium Enterprises, Government of India, adopted the Cluster Development approach to provide several forms of financial assistance, capacity building, and infrastructural facilities to the identified clusters. A cluster is a group of enterprises (particularly in the micro sector) formed into consideration the conditions namely: (i) located within a specified geographical area, (ii) engaged in producing similar or complementary products, (iii) similar usage of technology and marketing strategies (iv) communication among members of the cluster (v) similar opportunities and threats. Many traditional and hereditary-based micro enterprises were brought under this cluster development approach in an attempt to revive them.

In the context of Assam, though entrepreneurship is at its infancy stage, with a number of government assistance, the entrepreneurial landscape in this region has shown somewhat promising results. This region has always been the focal point of trade relationships with parties from other states as well as from abroad. This is mainly because of the presence of natural resources, the warmth and hospitality of its people, and the attitude of its entrepreneurs in holding its cultural identity. Among the different MSME clusters that continue to fulfil the varied needs of the market, the Bell Metal Cluster has been engaged in producing different products which form a part and parcel of the Assamese community over several decades. It has been mentioned in various chronicles that the Bell Metal industry existed in Assam from the 7th Century A.D. Initially confined

[a]monalishadutta58@gmail.com, [b]ibemchac6@gmail.com

DOI: 10.4324/9781003739982-5

only to Sarthrebari, over time a few artisans migrated to Hajo, another culturally rich town of Assam, and started practicing the craft from there. However, at present, this industry is confined only to Sarthebari and its neighbouring villages. An important feature of the craft form is that the artisans produce it manually using traditional practices learnt by them from their elder generations.

The data on the number of MSME shutdowns available on the Udhyam Registration Portal launched by the Ministry of MSME in 2020 shows that a considerable number of MSMEs are shut down all over the country, severely impacting the employment level. However, within the Bell Metal Industry, the situation is reversed. As shown in Table 5.1, the number of bell metals increased from 2014 to 2024, and the last ten years have seen a 22% rise in bell metal units.

Micro enterprises also suffer from certain disadvantages; a major problem is the competition they have to face from their larger counterparts. Large organizations with a good financial background have the propensity to spend a huge capital outlay on the adoption of different tactics to attract customers. In the era of globalization, competition arises not only from the domestic players but from the international field as well, so the only option left for the micro enterprises is to study their market in a lucid way and design strategies to help them create and satisfy customers. By observing the market dynamics, micro enterprises are in a position to customize their offers as per the needs of the customers and in the process create a niche for themselves. The more diligently they perform this activity, the more profitable they will be and the longer their sustenance will be. For this reason, market orientation is essential for the success of these companies. Market orientation involves firms focusing on both the internal and external factors that influence their functioning and that lead to their enhanced performance [12].

Statement of the problem

Data from 2024 in India shows that the Gini Coefficient fell in rural and urban regions, showing that income inequalities are becoming less common [13]. Meanwhile, compared to the other states, Punjab, Gujarat, Tamil Nadu, and Maharashtra are doing very well economically. However, Bihar, Odisha, and Jharkhand are still lagging [7]. In addition, the highest shares of MSMEs are found in Uttar Pradesh, West Bengal, Tamil Nadu, Maharashtra and Karnataka. In contrast, no states from the Northeastern Region could find a spot in the top ten [14]. What is the reason behind this? What deters Assam, the largest state from the Northeast, from finding a place among the top 10 contributing states? In the context of Bell Metal Industry, even if there is an increase in the number of units over the last ten years, it must face stiff competition from different substitutes and manufactures from other regions like Bankura, Murshidabad, Kerala, etc. (Field Survey) restricting its use only to some important occasions like marriage, funeral, religious gatherings, etc. among people in general. Why is it so? Shouldn't the artisans be able to know more about who buys their goods? There is a need to see at what level of market orientation the bell metal artisans stand. Also, since the craft form has been handed down for decades Choudhury [3], can we find any distinction in market awareness among artisans from different generations? The present study aims to answer these questions.

Review of Literature

Shivani et al [11] have examined links between entrepreneurial success and different socio-cultural variables. By collecting data from 200 entrepreneurs of Ranchi, the study found that the risk-taking propensity of the entrepreneurs is very low. Additionally, other than religion and family structure, factors related to caste and

Table 5.1 Increase in the number of bell metal units (2014-2024).

Year	Number of units	Percentage Increase (%)
2014	303	-
2024	370	22

Source: Directorate of Economics and Statistics, Barpeta 2014 and Field Survey, 2024.

family assistance play a big role in determining how well a business does. According to Nag and Das [9], the success of Indian micro entrepreneurs is judged by how highly they possess socio-cultural and practical skills such as education, prior work, communication, and leadership. Analysis of the questionnaires from 101 micro entrepreneurs in Jharkhand showed that entrepreneurs with higher education, outstanding communication, and great leadership skills tend to be more successful.

While the role of entrepreneurs' experience is not significant, Kansal and Bansal [6] emphasize that market orientation matters a lot for the success of small businesses. The link between market orientation and performance is greater for manufacturers than service providers. Abshar and Septrizola [1] and Barinta et al. (2022) found a positive link between market orientation and the performance of small and medium enterprises from several countries. Begum [2] has found that the industrialized process followed in other places has resulted in lowering the cost of the bell metal products, but the originality of the items produced in the bell metal industry of Sarthebari is desired by many people, often stimulating them to pay more to acquire those products. However, to ensure profitability, a balanced approach toward traditional craftsmanship and modern production techniques is required on the part of the artisans.

Research gap

The works reviewed have examined the impact of different socio-cultural factors on the success of the micro entrepreneurs Shivani et al. [11], Nag and Das [9], the influence of skill related factors on the entrepreneurial success Nag and Das [9], the positive impact of market orientation on the performance of SMEs Kansal and Bansal [6], Barinta et al., 2022; Abshar and Septrizola, [1] and the uniqueness that the bell metal products of Sarthebari holds in terms of their originality [2]. However, no study has been encountered that has measured the level of market orientation of the bell metal artisans, which is an important determinant to ensure long-term survival of the cottage-based industry in the era of cut-throat competition. So, the present study aims to fill this gap.

Objective of the study

This study seeks to ascertain to what extent the bell metal artisans of Assam are market-oriented.

Hypothesis:

Ho1: It does not seem that bell metal artisans of different generations differ much in their level of market orientation.

Research Methodology

The present study reports on a descriptive type of research. The data used is from primary and secondary sources. A structured interview schedule was used to collect primary data from the President of Assam Konhar Shilpi Sangha, Sarthebari, and 50 Master Bell Metal Artisans. For our secondary data, we consulted multiple journals and the MSME Report, 2023-24. An index is put together to assess the degree to which the artisans are oriented toward markets.

The total number of variables considered for Customer Orientation: 6

The total number of variables considered for Competitor Orientation: 4

The total number of variables considered for Interfunctional Coordination: 5

Total variables considered: 15

Results and Discussions

The Market Orientation of the Bell Metal Artisans

Researchers commonly agree on using two different instruments to calculate the extent of market orientation. MKTOR was the first developed by Narver and Slater [10], and MARKOR was later developed by Kohli et al. [8]. The present study applies the variables put forward by the developers of MKTOR to check the market orientation of artisans. According to Narver and Slater [10], the starting point for MKTOR is that an organization should always provide quality customer value. Accordingly, they identified three important dimensions:

1. **Customer orientation:** It involves carefully studying the expressed and latent needs of the current and prospective customers and providing them with valuable propositions.
2. **Competitor orientation:** It involves carefully tracking the strengths, weaknesses, strategies and capabilities of the present and future competitors and accordingly devising strategies to ward them off.
3. **Inter functional coordination:** It involves the unifying efforts of people across different functions and departments in providing superior customer value.

The level of market orientation is determined using the mean and standard deviation. The results show that the overall level of market orientation has a mean of 13.12 and a standard deviation of 1.10. So, the high level of market orientation is mean + standard deviation i.e. 13.12 + 1.10 = 14.22 (i.e. 14 and above); low level of market orientation is mean - standard deviation i.e. 13.12 – 1.10 = 12.02 (i.e. 12 and below); and the value in between is the medium level of orientation. Table 5.2 indicates the classification of the Level of Market Orientation.

Table 5.3 shows the level to which Bell artisans act with a market orientation. Results show that 26 percent of the artisans have a high level of market orientation, demonstrating their high motivation to adjust to what the market requires. Besides, 34 percent of the businesses have low market orientation, so they move forward traditionally, rarely considering what's happening in the market.

So, it can be derived from the findings that the highest share of artisans (40%) has a medium level of market orientation, i.e., they portray a moderate behavior towards working in a coordinated manner in comprehending

Table 5.2 Classification of the level of market orientation.

Level of market orientation	Score
High	Above 14
Medium	13
Low	Up to 12

Source: Author

Table 5.3 Level of market orientation of the bell metal artisans.

Level of market orientation	Count	%
High	13	26
Medium	20	40
Low	17	34
Total	50	100

Source: Field survey

Table 5.4 Distribution of artisans according to the generation to which they belong.

Sl. No.	Generation	Count	Percentage
1	1st	8	16
2	2nd	22	44
3	3rd and above	20	40
Total		50	100

Source: Field Survey

Table 5.5 Result of the normality test.

Tests of normality							
	Generation	Kolmogorov-Smirnov[a]			Shapiro-Wilk		
		Statistic	df	Sig.	Statistic	df	Sig.
MO	1st	.391	8	.001	.641	8	.000
2md		.293	22	.000	.740	22	.000
	3rd and above	.279	20	.000	.807	20	.001
a. Lilliefors significance correction							
Total		50	100	Total		50	100

Source: Field survey

Table 5.6 Kruskal-Wallis test result.

Kruskal-Wallis Test Result	
	MO
Chi-Square	1.693
df	2
Asymp. Sig.	.429

a. Kruskal Wallis test
b. Grouping variable: Generation
Source: Field survey

their customers and competitors and devising appropriate strategies to provide value propositions to the market. Table 5.4 indicates the distribution of artisans according to the generation to which they belong.

Among our respondents, 44% were part of the 2nd generation, and 40% belong to the 3rd or higher. 18% of all artisans are the first in their family to practice their craft. The findings suggest that the Sarthebari families carry the bell metal industry forward, as Choudhury [3] also points out.

Hypothesis testing

Normality test was conducted on the parameters of generation of the artisans (in terms of carrying on this profession. Table 5.5 reflects that the data does not conform to normal distribution.

As seen in Table 5.6, the values given by the Kruskal-Wallis test for Ho1 are $p = 0.429$ and $0.429 > 0.05$. With the significance level set at 5%, the present study supports Ho1: Bell Metal artisans do not show significant variances in their market orientation depending on what generation they belong to. There is no difference in the market orientation of artisans according to the different generations in which they exist.

Conclusion

The micro sector has been an important focal area of all government interventions in a developing country like India. This is because it has the potential to preserve the cultural heritage of the different regions, create jobs as well as contribute to economic growth. Nevertheless, the sustenance of these enterprises depends to a large extent on their ability to focus on the key strategic areas such as customers and competitors and deliver superior value to the market. In other words, they need to adjust themselves according to the changed business environment. It is vital for the long-term success of Assam's bell metal industry that businesses in the MSME Cluster respond to changes in the market [4]. This means artisans should be guided toward a market-oriented way of thinking. From the analysis, it was clear that the highest percentage of artisans had a medium-level market orientation, so even though they stick to their traditional ways, they are eager to adapt to market demand. In addition, the research found that artisans from different generations all have about the same level of market orientation. So, a holistic approach is required on the part of policymakers, different social groups, and the academic community to impart necessary education to the artisans to help them comprehend their market and devise effective strategies to provide value propositions. In this way, our future generations will be able to celebrate the glory that our ancestors have left for us.

References

[1] Abshar, D., & Septrizola, W. (2023). The influence of entrepreneurial orientation and market orientation on SME business performance. *Marketing Management Studies*, 3(1), 90–99.

[2] Begum, D. N. (2025). An analysis of economic viability of bell metal production in Sarthebari. *Metallurgical and Materials Engineering*, 31(1), 486–490.

[3] Choudhury, D. B. (2020). Efficacy of traditional marketing strategy of bell metal handicraft of Assam. *Indian Journal of Applied Research*, 10(4), 36–39.

[4] Chutia, L. J., & Sarma, M. K. (2017). Native tradition and changing market dynamics: the future sustainability of Hajo and Sarthebari metal crafts. *The Chitrolekha Journal on Art and Design*, 1(2), 1–21.

[5] Das, K. (2011). Indian micro and small enterprises in a changing policy environment. In Das, K. (Ed.), Micro and Small Enterprises in India: The Era of Reforms, (pp. 3–23). New Delhi: Routledge.

[6] Kansal, P., & Bansal, J. (2018). The impact of market orientation on the performance of MSMEs: a cross-sectional analysis of manufacturing and service firms in India. *IUP Journal of Business Strategies*, 15(4), 57–75.

[7] Kapoor, A. (2023, December 22). India's Developmental Challenge: Resolving Regional Disparities. *Financial Express: Read to Lead.*

[8] Kohli, A. K., Jaworski, B. J., & Kumar, A. (1993). MARKOR: a measure of market orientation. *Journal of Marketing Research*, 30(4), 467–477.

[9] Nag, D., & Das, N. (2014). Impact of sociocultural & skill-related factors for success of micro entrepreneurs. In Twelfth AIMS International Conference on Management, (pp. 406–410).

[10] Narver, J. C., & Slater, S. F. (1990). The effect of a market orientation on business profitability. *Journal of Marketing*, 54(4), 20–35.

[11] Shivani, S., Mukherjee, S. K., & Sharan, R. (2006). Socio-cultural influences on Indian entrepreneurs: the need for appropriate structural interventions. *Journal of Asian Economics*, 17, 5–13.

[12] Tomaskova, E. (2007). The current models of market orientation. *European Research Studies*, 11(Special Issue 3-4), 81–88.

[13] Kishore, R., & Jha, A. (2024, June 8). India logs fall in inequality between 2011-12 and 2022-23, says govt report. *Hindustan Times*.

[14] Ministry of MSME (2024). MSME Annual Report 2023–24. Government of India.

[15] Barinta, D. D., Aisjah, S., & Susilowati, C. (2022). Entrepreneurial orientation and Market Orientation as drivers of Micro Small and Medium Enterprises (MSMEs') Performance. *Journal of Business and Management Review*, 3(8), 548–562.

6 Microsoft goes carbon neutral - case study for Vietnamese tech giants

Quang Minh Le[a]
Faculty of International Business and Economics, VNU-University of Economics and Business, Hanoi, Vietnam

Abstract

Sustainable development is not solely the responsibility of governments but also a strategic imperative for multinational corporations, particularly tech giants consuming natural resources at an alarming rate. Although tech's share of net global emissions is relatively small, it has the potential to contribute up to a 15% reduction in global emissions by 2030. Tech companies, which dominate the world's wealthiest businesses, have a significant influence on the daily habits of billions of people. They possess expertise in rapidly expanding technological and organizational innovations, which often serve as inspiration for others to adopt. This case study focuses on Microsoft's ambitious pledge to achieve the goal of net-zero emissions by 2030, analyzing the implications and potential lessons for emerging Vietnamese tech companies. The research will examine how Microsoft integrates sustainability goals into its core strategy, while assessing the feasibility and challenges of adopting similar measures within the Vietnamese context. A critical question is whether Microsoft's efforts extend to manufacturing facilities in developing countries or remain confined to its US headquarters. The objective of the study is to provide insights about the role of tech corporations in fostering a sustainable future and key considerations for Vietnamese businesses as they navigate the balance between economic growth and environmental responsibility.

Keywords: Business strategy, carbon neutral, corporate environmental responsibility, developing countries, Microsoft, sustainable development, tech corporation, Vietnam

Introduction

The concept of sustainability is currently confronted with a multitude of obstacles, among which climate change emerges as a paramount concern for a fundamental reconsideration of our energy production and consumption practices. According to United Nations data, the year 2024 was the hottest on record, with global average temperatures exceeding 1.55 degrees Celsius above pre-industrial levels. It has become a recurring pattern that subsequent years surpass previous ones in terms of recorded temperatures. Therefore, it is anticipated that upcoming years will likely break the record set in 2024. Severe weather precipitated catastrophic heat waves, droughts, starvation, wildfires, typhoons, and floods with alarming regularity. The present experience of climate change has been unprecedented, and with the ongoing warming of the Earth, we will persistently observe and experience the adverse consequences on ecosystems and societies worldwide. Nevertheless, notwithstanding economic challenges, sustainability projects have the potential to provide quick ROI for enterprises and the environment, so generating additional motivations for taking action. The use of digital innovation can enable firms to decrease energy consumption, minimize travel, optimize resource utilization, and make data-driven decisions, thus contributing to cost and emission reduction.

Microsoft has been strongly committed to achieve carbon negativity by 2030, attaining zero trash generation and positive water consumption, and compensating for all greenhouse gas emissions produced since its inception by 2050. The corporation is allocating resources towards renewable energy, advocating for sustainability throughout the supply chain, and mitigating the carbon footprint of its products. Inclusive and fair access to clean energy benefits society. In response to the pressing nature of the sustainability issue, this organization has adopted a holistic strategy to tackle it. Through the promotion of sustainability and the utilization of digital innovation to facilitate advancement, Microsoft is actively contributing to the establishment of a more sustainable future for all individuals.

Microsoft, one of the world's powerful technologies corrporations, has made it a corporate policy to make "social investments" in the United States. In other nations where the company does business, there are still

[a]lqminh@vnu.edu.vn

DOI: 10.4324/9781003739982-6

opinions that Microsoft currently does not really have measures to reduce carbon emissions, especially in developing countries, and in 2022 while achieving its overall business by 18%, this corporate only reduced its planet-warming emissions 0.5%. Besides, Vietnam's large technology corporations can learn a lot from Microsoft's policies.

Literature Review

The well-known concepts of "corporate citizenship" and "corporate social and environmental responsibility" are well-established within the literature of business administration. Caroll [3] states that many leaders and organizational theorists accept that the profound and extensive changes occurring in society have had numerous repercussions on corporate organizations. An expanding corpus of literature in the business industry emphasizes that a growing number of corporate managers are recognizing the necessity to fulfill societal needs that extend beyond their primary economic role [2, 15, 16, 5].

Researchers, educators, and professionals have engaged in an ongoing discussion regarding the appropriate extent of corporate social responsibility. Friedman [7] had stated one of the most notable perspectives that emphasizes the social responsibility of any business. According to this perspective, the primary social responsibility of any business endeavor is to optimally deploy its resources and undertake activities to maximize profits, as long as it functions without making any deceit or fraud within the boundaries of fair and transparent competition, according to Wheelen et al. [20] and counterparts, Friedman's perspective can be summarized as follows: when a businessperson takes responsible actions such as reducing product prices to prevent inflation, investing in pollution reduction, or hiring long-term unemployed individuals, they are utilizing the shareholders' funds for the benefit of society as a whole.

While this perspective continued to be widely accepted in business literature, it eventually faced competition from alternative viewpoints that gained traction. For instance, [22] would not fully endorse this perspective. Carroll's perspective broadened the scope of company responsibility to encompass more than just economic obligations. Carroll asserts that managers of commercial organizations bear four distinct responsibilities: economic, legal, ethical, and discretionary. First and foremost, Carroll categorized economic activities as essential or necessary tasks. In order to fulfill their financial obligations to creditors and shareholders, businesses are required to generate valuable commodities and services for society.

Next, there are the legal activities, which consist of obligatory actions that management must undertake in accordance with government laws. Subsequently, there are the ethical activities, often known as 'should do' activities, which include adhering to the commonly accepted norms of behavior of a society. Finally, there are certain optional actions that an organization may choose to engage in. Corporations willingly undertake these commitments, which include philanthropic contributions, training and re-training for the long-term unemployed, and the provision of day care centres. Another author, Frost [8] contended that firms bear dual responsibilities, both commercial and social. Commercial responsibilities encompass effectively managing a business, generating financial gains, and meeting the expectations of shareholders. Conversely, social responsibilities encompass assuming obligations as a participant in the community and society by participating in endeavors that extend beyond financial gain, like environmental safeguarding, employee care, social problem handling, and ethical trade ethical conduction [12].

Similar to the ongoing discussion on the extent of businesses' social responsibility actions, there are also notable debates on whether firms could be permitted to engage in social duties or not. Davis [6] collated multiple perspectives supporting and opposing corporate social responsibility.

In his 1977 publication, Davis put out multiple arguments supporting the implementation of social responsibility initiatives. Here, we address some of these arguments. The text states that a company that is highly responsive to the requirements of its community will ultimately have a more favorable society in which to operate its business. It is further asserted that a superior region creates a more favorable business environment. Furthermore, given the current emphasis on social goals among the general public, a company that desires to cultivate a positive public perception must demonstrate its commitment to supporting these social goals. An exemplary public image can enhance a firm's ability to attract a larger consumer base, recruit superior staff, and reap several other advantages. Furthermore, it is imperative for enterprises to uphold the socio-cultural standards. Businesspeople adhere to the same cultural limitations as any other member of society. If society is currently transitioning towards social responsibility norms, businesspeople should likewise adhere to these norms. Furthermore, proponents argue that given the track record of numerous institutions in effectively addressing social issues and the widespread disillusionment with their failures, it is worth considering the option of entrusting the responsibility to businesses and allowing them to have a stab at it. Furthermore, proponents claim that corporations possess tremendous resources that could effectively address social issues, so society should leverage these resources.

Davis [6] consolidated multiple arguments opposing the notion of firms engaging in social duties. Firstly, there is an argument that engaging in social activities can be expensive. If firms are compelled to assume social responsibilities, these supplementary expenses may lead to the economic ineffectiveness of the business. Furthermore, numerous entrepreneurs may lack awareness and expertise to fulfill their social obligations. They may also lack the necessary philosophical and emotional qualifications for the job. Furthermore, it is contended that engagement in social objectives could weaken the focus of businesses on economic efficiency. Furthermore, it is argued that businesses already possess an ample amount of societal influence, and therefore, society should refrain from implementing any measures that will further augment their power. If a firm engages in both social and economic activities, it could lead to an excessive consolidation of power. Finally, there is a contention that businesspeople lack a direct obligation to the public. Hence, it would be imprudent to assign them obligations in areas where they are not held liable.

Regardless of the specific topics being debated, it is a fact that firms worldwide are actively engaging in social responsibility initiatives. Businesses are endeavoring to transcend a purely economic perspective of their activities. The business world's acknowledgment of social responsibility issues can be attributed to the legitimacy theory, a widely recognized concept. This idea posits that organizations consistently strive to be recognized as conforming to the established rules and standards of their societies. In other words, they want to ensure that their actions are viewed by external bodies as being legal and moral [23]. By engaging in social responsibility initiatives, often voluntarily, organizations actively strive to gain acceptance and recognition in society. Companies now recognize that prioritizing social responsibility is not merely an unproductive expense or burden, but rather a way to improve their reputation and credibility among stakeholders. In fact, the success or even survival of a company may depend heavily on it [11].

The corporate social responsibility concept has gained enormous traction in various economies in recent days. Consequently, the corporations have implemented many initiatives that encompass several levels of activity impacting corporate governance, supply chain management, employee relationships and customer connections, environmental management, community involvement, and critical business operations. Corporate responsibility encompasses all facets of a company's operations. According to Skinner and Ivancevich [17], customers, some specific interest groups, and the public are conscious of the influence that businesses have on society. They expect companies to go beyond simply pursuing profits and instead fulfill their social responsibilities. As a result, most managers now consider social responsibility to be an obligatory aspect of conducting business. Additionally, it is noted that business organizations exert influence on consumers, employees, the environment, and investors in the company.

Research Methodology

Case study is a term that is quite familiar to many scholars. This method is quite popularly used by university lecturers in teaching activities because it is intuitive, vivid, and easy to understand. The training fields that often use this method include business administration, management science, and leadership studies. This method is classified as a group of qualitative research methods, not only in economics but also widely applied in social sciences. The core content of this method is to help clarify one or more decisions; implementation processes in organizations to answer questions such as: why these decisions are made, how these decisions are implemented in practice, and what are the results of this implementation process? [24]. The above understanding refers to case studies of decisions of the case study research method and are also popular case studies when using this method. However, this method is not limited to the process of decision-making but also studies individual behavior, organizational behavior, implementation processes, implementation programs, or even events.

Based on Robert Yin's [21] ideology, a case study is better since it is an empirical investigation that enables a detailed examination of a contemporary phenomenon, particularly when there is no clear distinction between the phenomenon and the boundary. There are specific situations in which the case study method becomes highly suitable within scientific research.

To find a suitable research method, the researcher must rely on the research objectives, including general and specific objectives, followed by research problems. In general, there is no general answer to when to use the case study method, but in summary, this method will be more suitable if the research falls into the following three situations:

First, the research problem will be "how" or "why"; the research problem will require explanation and implementation process rather than answering the question "what" or "when". For example, the research problem is: "Why do technology corporations have strategies to be carbon neutral?" In this case, the case study method will clarify the case of one (or more) technological corporations, then provide the causes and scientific evidence

- Next, the researcher cannot manage or have an impact on research issues or events.
- Finally, the research focuses on issues and events that are happening in reality, or in other words, practice. This practical research makes case study research different from research using other methods in scientific research.

Because this method originates from practice, the researcher will have to utilize a strategy to make his/her research results persuasive. That is, he/she will have to use many different evidence sources (for example, documentation, interviews, observations, etc.) along with relevant data. This is the interesting point of this method, but it is also a challenge for researchers in terms of collecting data.

Theoretical Framework

Corporate social responsibility

Corporate social responsibility (CSR), is described by McWilliams and Siegel [14] as: "Actions that further the needs or goals of stakeholder groups or the larger social collective beyond the interests of the firm or what is required by law." CSR is defined as acts that go beyond a company's legal responsibilities and are aimed at benefiting interest groups and the public. CSR has attracted huge scholarly interest from researchers in several fields [1]. It is the most commonly employed term in academic literature to denote the concept of promoting sustainability and enhancing societal well-being [4]. According to Stobierski [18], the publications of CSR reports by public corporations have increased from 20% to 90%. As reported by the Global Sustainable Investment Alliance (GSIA) [9], the total value of the investments made in sustainable assets has exceeded US$30 trillion in 2022. Since CSR is a crucial business activity supported by governments and government-associated agencies, research in this area is on the rise, enriching the existing literature [19].

The CSR is a concept emphasizing the need for business professionals to consider the economic and social consequences of their business decisions so that their operations result in positive outcomes for society and the economy. The term becomes crucial as it disciplines a firm's ethical behavior. The proponents of this approach contend that the business corporations should recognize their moral obligations to society and admit their contributions to them that has facilitated their achievements.

Noblesse oblige is a French expression denoting the moral obligation for individuals of privileged social status to exhibit honorable and philanthropic conduct [10]. In a corporate environment, it refers to the act of exhibiting kind and generous behavior, which is considered the duty of prosperous businesses. Many businesspeople have long acknowledged the importance of corporations contributing to society. As a result, there is a significant and respected tradition of corporations investing in social endeavors to improve the well-being of the communit groups they operate in [13].

Carbon neutral

Carbon neutral indicates the reduction of CO_2 emissions from manufacturing and transportation activities through activities such as carbon removal or carbon offsetting. In other words, the purpose of carbon-neutral activities is to create no carbon footprint.

In order for a product to achieve Carbon Neutral certification, it is necessary to take the following steps:

- Calculate your product's Carbon Footprint
- Develop an action plan to reduce CO_2 emissions
- Carbon credits to neutralize CO_2 emissions
- Execute a CO_2 emissions reduction plan to maintain carbon-neutral certification

Achieving carbon neutrality requires a comprehensive approach that includes measuring, reducing, and offsetting emissions in addition to setting targets. To achieve this, businesses need to identify emissions sources and quantify production emissions. Once emissions have been measured, businesses can develop a plan to reduce emissions. This may involve investing in renewable energy, using energy-saving technology, optimizing supply chains, and reducing waste. However, an inevitable trend, achieving Carbon reconciliation, is not simple. From investment capital in production technology, renewable energy, or tree planting, to the determination of business leaders. Most importantly, carbon neutrality will be easier to implement if more businesses participate. Carbon neutrality plays a huge role in humanity's sustainable development journey because it will allow us to quickly reduce CO_2 emissions and help bring many social and community benefits.

Carbon neutrality is a new way of internationally recognized method for people to be more responsible to the environment regarding the inevitable daily life of CO_2 emissions as well as in production and business activities.

In Vietnam, according to Decree 06, manufacturing enterprises on the designated list have begun to carry out periodic inventories of greenhouse gas emissions from this year. After that, the period from 2026 to 2030 will begin to reduce greenhouse gas emissions according to the quota allocated to businesses by the Ministry of Natural Resources and Environment.

Each business will be limited to no more than a permitted level of emissions. However, if emissions are excessive, businesses still have the option to buy carbon credits. Vietnam is expected to operate a pilot carbon credit exchange by 2025 before officially operating in 2028. With such a legal corridor, carbon-neutral production will no longer just be a trend but mandatory.

Carbon offsets

Carbon offsetting is a mechanism that allows individuals, businesses and organizations to take responsibility for their greenhouse gas (GHG) emissions by investing in projects that reduce or eliminate a certain amount of emissions equivalent from the atmosphere.

When an entity releases carbon dioxide (CO_2) or other greenhouse gases into the atmosphere through activities such as energy consumption, transportation, or industrial processes, it contributes to climate change. Carbon offsetting offers a way to reduce these emissions by funding projects that help reduce or offset overall carbon emissions

This carbon offsetting concept can take many different forms, such as renewable energy projects (for example: solar power plants or wind farms), afforestation and reforestation efforts, methane gas recovery and utilization projects, improving energy efficiency, etc. These projects are designed to reduce emissions at the source or remove existing emissions from the atmosphere through carbon sequestration.

Renewable energy

Renewable energy refers to energy generated from naturally replenishing sources such as wind, water, sunlight, tides, etc. Since these sources are clean and continuously available, they are sustainable. The main principle is to extract a portion of this energy from the consistently available natural phenomenon and apply it to technological functions. Despite being a new source, it is widely used everywhere. It has the potential to efficiently replace traditionally predominant resources in four essential areas: heating water, generating power, fueling motors, and powering independent systems in rural areas.

Using renewable energy brings many benefits to people and the environment. For instance,

First, reduce the use of fossil resources: Renewable energy has contributed to reducing human dependence on fossil resources such as coal, oil, and gas, which allows people to maintain resources for future generations.

Second, it is increasing the diversity of energy sources used: Renewable energy has increased the diversity of energy supplies. This not only reduces the risk of energy shortages due to dependence on a single energy source, but also helps reduce the price of energy sources.

Third, reduce gas and carbon emissions into the environment: Renewable energy such as wind and solar energy does not produce CO_2 or other gasses that cause the greenhouse effect. Therefore, renewable energy contributes to reducing environmental pollution and climate change.

Fourth, renewable energy has created job opportunities and promoted economic development: The development of the renewable energy industry has created many job opportunities for many people. In particular, this development also helps the economy move towards green, clean, safe, and sustainable.

Case Study Analysis "Microsoft goes Carbon Neutral"

Overview of microsoft

Microsoft is a well-known American multinational company headquartered at Redmond in, Washington. The corporation develops licenses, builds, and provides support for multiple software products and services in computing and innovation. This corporation was initiated by Bill Gates and Paul Allen on 4th of April, 1975. Initially, Microsoft intended to build and market BASIC interpreters for the microcomputer, Altair 8800.

Key stages of development

1. The 1970s–The beginning:
   - In 1975, Microsoft was born with the goal of developing software for personal computers.
   - In 1980, Microsoft developed the MS-DOS operating system for IBM computers, marking a major turning point in the company's trajectory.
2. The 1980s–Breakthrough with Windows:
   - In 1985, Microsoft had the launch of Windows 1.0, its first graphical user interface operating system.
   - Windows quickly gained popularity, establishing Microsoft as a dominant player in the market.
3. The 1990s–Dominance and controversy:
   - In 1995, Microsoft released Windows 95, which was met with widespread acclaim and generated enormous revenue.
   - The company also faced legal challenges regarding antitrust issues and was investigated by the U.S. government.
4. The 2000s–Innovation and expansion:
   - Microsoft expanded into new areas such as gaming (Xbox) and online services (MSN, Hotmail).
   - The launch of Windows XP in 2001 received positive feedback from users.
5. The 2010s–Transformation to cloud computing:
   - Under the leadership of CEO Satya Nadella (since 2014), Microsoft shifted its focus to cloud computing with Azure.
   - The company also strengthened its development of services like Office 365 and Teams.
6. Present–Continuous innovation:
   - Microsoft continues to invest in artificial intelligence, virtual reality, and other emerging technologies.
   - The company now operates across various sectors, from software and hardware to cloud computing services.

Main developments

At the beginning of 2020, Microsoft made a stunning statement - the world's largest software company pledged to be carbon neutral by 2030 and eliminate all the CO_2 it has emitted since its founding in 1975 by 2050. Microsoft started its carbon neutrality strategy in 2012, mainly through initiatives like funding carbon dioxide absorption projects, including forest conservation efforts. The company has outlined a series of additional measures to reach its more ambitious goal of becoming carbon negative by 2030. Within the initiatives, the firm has a major commitment to incorporate a 100% electric-powered vehicle fleet by 20230 and also to drive all its facilities with renewable energy. The challenges look big, particularly associated with the energy needs of Microsoft's global server farms facilitating the Azure cloud computing platform. Hence, huge investments are required in renewable energy resources to combat the energy demands of the company efficiently.

In addition, Microsoft has taken huge efforts to lower carbon emissions through establishing innovation funds for about 1 billion USD that encourage the development of advanced technologies associated with it. The company has done several investments involved in carbon capturing such as absorbing atmospheric carbon by improving soil's capacity, widening reforestation projects, and finding innovative solutions to extract carbon present in the air and store that underground. Interestingly, Microsoft has enabled Azure users to track their emissions linked to their cloud computing usage through sustainability computing; thus, promoting transparency. The company's environmental sustainability report includes information related to the progression of these goals every year.

Moreover, Microsoft has indulged in educating its suppliers, partners, and customers about the importance of adopting sustainable practices recognizing their vital part of collaboration to address climate change. The company has also imposed an internal carbon fee across its business units to make them accountable for the emissions from their activities. Furthermore, teams would get fee incentives for reduced carbon footprint, which could be invested in sustainable solutions. However, Microsoft has been criticized for its recent agreements with major oil and gas companies like Exxon Mobil and Chevron. Several critics, including some employees working in Microsoft, contend that the firm should end their collaboration with any company that does not exhibit a transparent commitment to sustainability.

Nevertheless, Microsoft's carbon neutrality plan represents a significant step forward in corporate environmental responsibility. By aiming to remove more carbon from the atmosphere than it emits, the company is making a measurable impact in the fight against climate change. This initiative not only underscores

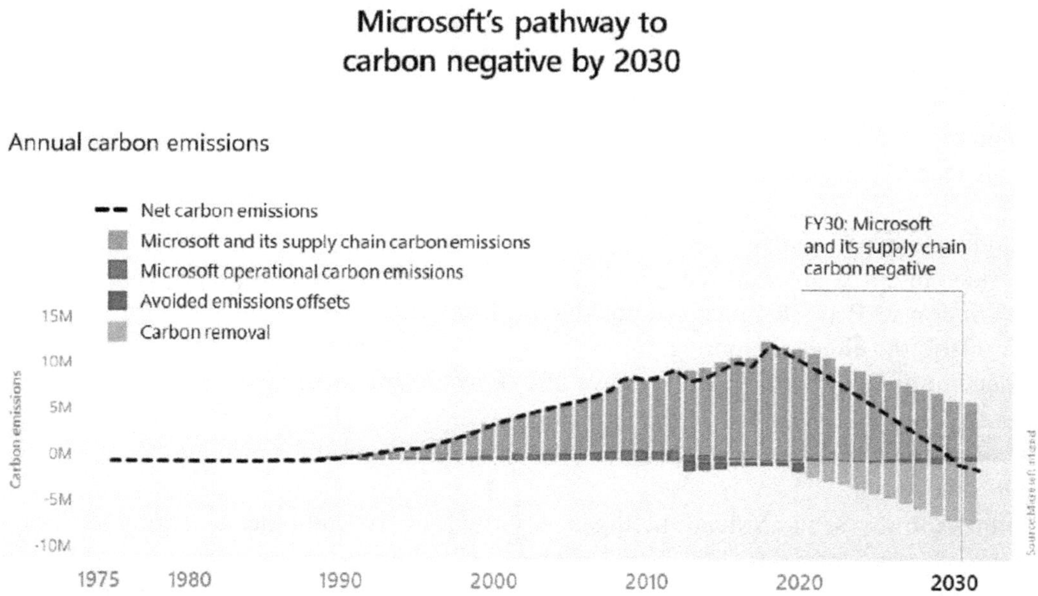

Figure 6.1 Microsoft's pathway to carbon negative by 2030
Source: Microsoft's 2022 Environmental Sustainability Report

Microsoft's dedication to sustainability but also sets an example for other organizations to follow. Moreover, its investments in carbon removal technologies have the potential to create new economic opportunities and drive innovation, fostering a sustainable technology ecosystem that extends beyond the corporation's own operations.

Microsoft's approach exemplifies its commitment to environmental stewardship. Through ambitious goals and actionable strategies, the company is paving the way for a more sustainable future. As technology continues to shape our world, it is encouraging to see a global leader like Microsoft taking proactive steps to address climate change. By pursuing its carbon-negative vision, Microsoft is not only minimizing its own environmental impact but also inspiring others to join the global effort to combat climate change. Figure 6.1 indicates Microsoft's pathway to carbon negative by 2030.

The driving force behind microsoft's carbon neutral commitment

The first motivation comes from subjective reasons, stemming from understanding the company's own responsibility and influence in contributing a small part to improving the world's climate. In 2020, following Microsoft's announcement to achieve the goal of carbon negativity by 2030 and then to remove all the CO_2 it has emitted since its founding by the year of 2050, the Corporation's President Brad Smith emphasized the ethical and moral responsibility of a global corporation like Microsoft to implement such a critical transformative policy. He emphasized that: *"The scientific consensus is clear. The world confronts an urgent carbon problem. The carbon in our atmosphere has created a blanket of gas that traps heat and is changing the world's climate. Already, the planet's temperature has risen by 1 degree centigrade. If we don't curb emissions, and temperatures continue to climb, science tells us that the results will be catastrophic.*

While the world will need to reach net zero, those of us who can afford to move faster and go further should do so. That's why today we are announcing an ambitious goal and a new plan to reduce and ultimately remove Microsoft's carbon footprint."

Another motivation comes from objective factors, as analysts remark that corporations such as Microsoft are progressively experiencing hard pressure from their stakeholders to manage emissions. An increasing proportion of investors, as well as a significant number of consumers and employees, are seeking improvements. Responding to Microsoft's initiatives, Dickon Pinner, the worldwide leader of McKinsey & Co.'s sustainability practice, observed that, "Sooner or later, regulators will react, and capital will react, so it is just

Our commitment	Our progress
Reducing direct emissions We will reduce our Scope 1 and 2 emissions to near zero by increasing energy efficiency, decarbonization, and reaching 100 percent renewable energy by 2025.	**Net zero Scope 1 and 2 emissions** Our Scope 1 and 2[1] emissions remained proportional with business growth in FY22.[2] More than 95 percent of our Scope 2 emissions were reduced by renewable energy from power purchase agreements (PPAs), green tariff programs, and unbundled renewable energy certificates.
Reducing value chain emissions By 2030, we will reduce our Scope 3 emissions by more than half from a 2020 baseline.	**Scope 3 emissions increased by 0.5 percent** Our value chain or Scope 3 emissions increased slightly at 0.5 percent, despite a 25 percent increase in purchased goods and services due to business growth. This result was driven by improvements in our operations, telemetry-based measurement, renewable energy investments, sustainable aviation fuel purchases, and procurement of unbundled renewable energy certificates (RECs).[3]
Replacing with 100/100/0 carbon-free energy By 2030, 100 percent of our electricity consumption will be matched by zero carbon energy purchases 100 percent of the time.	**13.5 GW of carbon-free energy** In FY22, we signed new Power Purchase Agreements (PPAs) around the globe, bringing our total portfolio of carbon-free energy to over 13.5 GW, including more than 135 projects in 16 countries.
Removing the rest of our emissions By 2030, Microsoft will remove more carbon than it emits. By 2050, we will remove an amount of carbon equivalent to all our historical emissions.	**Over 1.4M metric tons of carbon removal** We contracted 1,443,981 metric tons of carbon removal in FY22. We also made first-of-their-kind multi-year forward offtake commitments to carbon removal, which we view as the model for scaling the industry

Figure 6.2 Microsoft's carbon neutrality commitment progress tracker
Source: Microsoft's 2022 Environmental Sustainability Report

a good business decision if you have some confidence where this is heading." In other terms, Pinner asserts that Microsoft is proactively anticipating the unavoidable by implementing such measures, and that this is a commendable corporate approach.

Additionally, the carbon neutrality milestone achieved by Microsoft establishes a novel benchmark for corporate environmental accountability. Through deliberate extraction of a greater amount of carbon dioxide (CO_2) from the atmosphere than it releases, the corporation is actively contributing to the concrete efforts in combating climate change. This endeavour not only showcases Microsoft's dedication to sustainability but also motivates other corporations to engage in similar practices.

Microsoft's carbon neutrality progress update

To achieve its ambitious goal of becoming carbon negative by 2030 and removing from the atmosphere an amount of CO_2 equivalent to the total amount the company has emitted directly or indirectly through electricity use since its founding in 1975 by 2050, Microsoft has developed and implemented a closely monitored strategy. The company also tracks and reports on its progress annually. Figure 6.2 indicates Microsoft's carbon neutrality commitment progress tracker.

To facilitate effective waste management and carbon neutrality efforts, Microsoft categorizes its waste into three main areas/scopes

- Area/Scopes 1: Direct emissions created by a company's activities
- Area/Scopes 2: Indirect emissions from a company's activities
- Area/Scopes 3: Indirect emissions from all other activities up and down the value chain

In fiscal year 2022, Microsoft purchased and retired 1.44 million metric tons of carbon to achieve its annual carbon neutrality commitment. The amount of carbon retired every year indicates credits that are canceled in the corresponding year and will be canceled in the upcoming or later years.

In Figure 6.3, the column heights for sections A represent the amount of carbon Microsoft emitted each year. The column heights for sections B and C in the figure represent the amount of emissions avoided by reducing

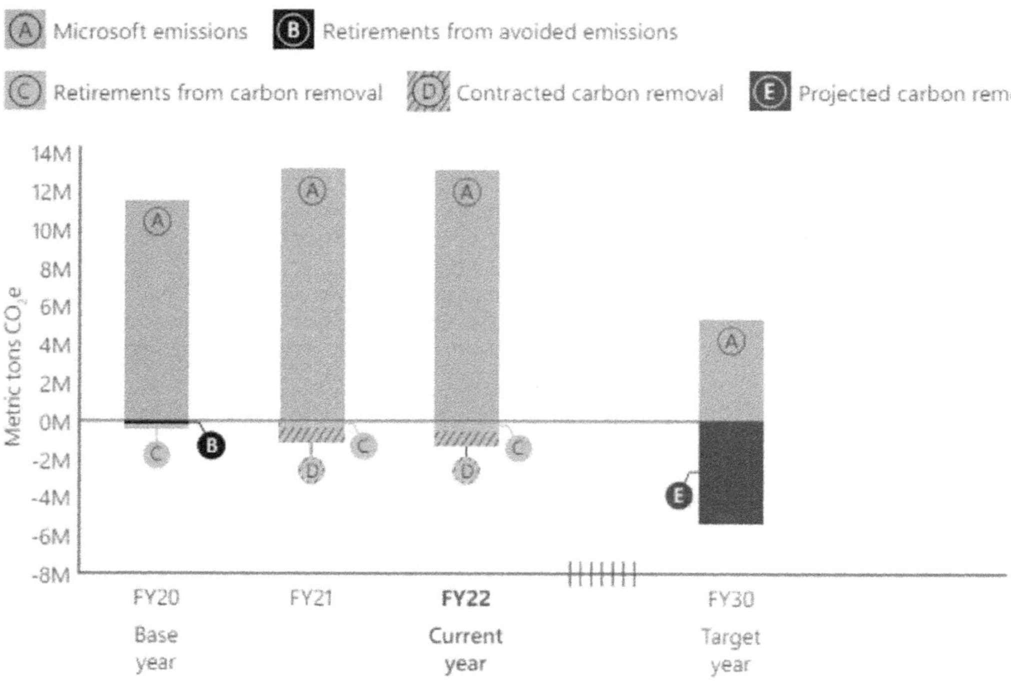

Figure 6.3 Microsoft's annual progress towards carbon negativity by 2030
Source: Microsoft's 2022 Environmental Sustainability Report

or replacing them and the amount of carbon removed from the environment or from fossil fuel emissions, respectively. The column height for section D represents the amount of carbon removed from the environment according to estimates of contracts and projects that Microsoft has signed. Finally, the column height for section E represents the amount of carbon that will be removed from the environment and neutralized with Microsoft's emissions by the 2030 target when carbon removal projects are implemented.

Assessing Microsoft's Actions from Various Perspectives

Friedman's viewpoint

Friedman, an economist and Nobel laureate, contended that the primary social obligation of a business is increase profit while complying with legal frameworks. He dismissed the idea that business firms should engage in social initiatives beyond what is legally required, viewing such actions as unnecessary for operational efficiency. For example, he contended that enhancing working conditions beyond legal standards or what is essential for employee productivity would diminish profits, making it unsuitable practice. Friedman believed that a company's focus should remain on profit maximization, as this directly benefits its shareholders. If shareholders wished to allocate their returns toward social causes, that decision rested with them, not the company's management.

However, Friedman's perspective faced significant criticism, with detractors arguing that his stance falters under closer scrutiny, particularly in micro-level contexts. While his theory might appear valid in international business settings, where varying governance systems and cultural norms create ambiguous regulations, it struggles to address ethical dilemmas. For instance, in developing countries where laws permit orphan or child labor, a multinational corporation might legally maximize productivity by employing children. Yet, such practices are widely regarded as unethical, conflicting with universal principles of morality and human rights. Similarly, in regions lacking pollution control regulations, a company could legally avoid investing in environmental safeguards to protect profit margins. However, ethical standards would deem it unacceptable to release harmful pollutants into rivers or emit toxic gases into the air, as these actions harm local communities and degrade global commons like the atmosphere and oceans, which are vital to all humanity.

Critics further highlight that the narrow focus of Friedman on profit does not have a wider scope to include the broader environmental and societal consequences of corporate activities. For example, pollution not only affects local ecosystems but also contributes to global challenges such as climate change and ocean degradation. These issues transcend national boundaries, emphasizing the need for businesses to adopt ethical practices that align with global sustainability goals, even when local laws do not mandate them. Thus, while Friedman's arguments emphasize shareholder interests, they fail to account for the ethical responsibility's businesses have toward society and the planet. This critique underscores the growing recognition that corporate success must be evaluated by the impact made by the firms on society and the environment, and not just financially.

Thus, from Friedman's perspective, Microsoft's intention to neutralize carbon becomes questionable when its efforts to reduce emissions require significant investment: building renewable energy infrastructure, developing carbon capture technology, and investing in carbon removal projects. These investments might affect the company's profitability in the short term. Friedman's theory suggests that environmental issues should be addressed by the government, not by companies. Microsoft is ahead of the government in this matter, which could be costly and unnecessary.

However, Microsoft's case also illustrates why becoming a carbon-negative company might align with shareholders' interests, even from Friedman's viewpoint:

Prevention: Investors are increasingly concerned about the sustainability of companies. By proactively minimizing emissions, Microsoft can attract investors interested in environmental, social, and governance factors.

Anticipating future regulations: Governments worldwide might enact stricter laws on emissions in the future. By proactively reducing emissions now, Microsoft can avoid the costly compliance expenses later.

New business opportunities: Investing in low-carbon technology can create new business opportunities for Microsoft. For example, the company can sell carbon capture technology to other companies.

In summary, Friedman's theory may suggest that Microsoft's decision goes against the short-term interests of shareholders. However, there are also reasons to believe that becoming a carbon-negative company could benefit shareholders in the long run.

The viewpoint of "right theories"

Emerging in the 20th century, rights-based theories recognize that individuals possess inherent rights and freedom that extend beyond boundaries and cultural differences across nations. These fundamental entitlements define a baseline for moral conduct, generally acceptable. A widely accepted interpretation of a basic right describes it as taking precedence over, or "trumping," collective interests. For instance, the right to freedom of self-expression is considered a fundamental right that outweighs most collective interests, except in cases were overriding concerns, such as maintaining civil harmony or ethical consensus, come into play. Moral philosophers contend that human rights serve as a foundational guide for managers when making ethically sound decisions. Specifically, they should avoid actions that infringe upon these rights.

Within the context of rights theories, certain individuals or organizations bear the responsibility to deliver compensations or offerings that safeguard others' rights. These duties are not limited to moral agents - entities capable of ethical decision-making, such as governments or corporations- but extend to anyone or any group capable of upholding these principles.

Microsoft's resolution to become carbon-negative portrays its responsible attitude to future generations. Climate change poses serious threats to the health and well-being of future generations, and by taking proactive measures to minimize carbon emissions, Microsoft is fulfilling its obligation to protect these rights.

Ethical theories often emphasize the concept of stewardship, including responsibly managing and safeguarding resources for the benefit of all. The investments made by Microsoft in renewable energy, carbon sequestration projects, and technological innovations demonstrate its commitment to being a responsible environmental steward.

As a pioneer in the technology industry, the company has the influence and resources to effect positive change. By setting ambitious sustainability goals and investing in carbon reduction projects, Microsoft exemplifies good corporate citizenship and fulfills its obligation to contribute positively to society.

Microsoft's commitment is tracked through its annual Environmental Sustainability Report, and providing tools like sustainability calculators for its customers enhances transparency and accountability. This ensures that all stakeholders know their company's impact on the environment and its efforts to mitigate it, in line with principles of ethical conduct.

In summary, Microsoft's determination to move towards carbon zero can be appraised ethically from the perspective of "rights theories," as it goes in line with the principles of responsibility, environmental stewardship, corporate citizenship, and transparency in addressing the urgent issue of climate change.

How do Vietnamese Technology Giants Learn from Microsoft's Carbon Neutral Strategy?

First and foremost, attaining net-zero emissions is of utmost importance for the future of every technological company and cannot be achieved as a secondary endeavor. Sustainability initiatives achieve greater success when they are fully incorporated into all aspects of the firm, beginning with a common vision for the future and encompassing a strategic plan that promotes accountability and mitigates risks. Incorporating sustainability into the comprehensive operating strategy of the organization establishes essential procedures to consistently enhance and adjust in order to achieve net-zero emissions objectives. It is crucial to develop a strategy that is in line with the organization's fundamental principles and business practices. For all organizational endeavors, Vietnamese IT giants should depend on the Leadership Model, which clearly states fundamental principles and establishes their culture and mission. This model will be the primary focus as it will construct their sustainability plan and is essential for accomplishing our aims.

With an overarching strategy in place, organizations can jump into the planning phase - for Vietnamese tech giants, that means taking the following steps:

Step 1: Vietnam's leading technology companies need to set achievable and measurable goals in the immediate future towards sustainable development.

To develop sustainably, or more specifically, in this case, reduce CO_2 emissions, Vietnamese technology companies first need to have specific goals. Businesses need to have time to research (possibly in collaboration with domestic and foreign research agencies) to determine specific, achievable, and measurable goals. It is important to consider sustainable development as a core strategy, rather than slogans. Enterprises need to review their entire business and production processes (data), then choose a sustainable development framework (this framework is the metrics) to determine their goals. For example, Vietnamese technology enterprises can choose the blueprint to execute Vietnam's sustainable development goals to 2030 (according to the decision of the Prime Minister) to create a standard framework (goals) for themselves. From that framework, enterprises will have to change their production and business activities. For example, in the near future, Vietnamese enterprises will start measuring CO_2 emissions from 2025, from which specific goals will be determined by the end of the fiscal year 2050:

- Achieve net-zero emissions in their operations
- Attain 50% renewable energy
- 20% energy reduction

Step 2: It is necessary to have a reasonable roadmap for implementing the strategy

Once the goals have been determined, Vietnamese enterprises need to come up with a reasonable roadmap for implementation, It will be very difficult to implement a sustainable strategy in a short time, even Microsoft needs more than 10 years to achieve initial results. The sustainable development strategy will probably have to be divided into strategies for each period, and for a small strategy, there must be a start date, monitoring during the implementation process, and an endpoint. The roadmap needs to remind us of the goal of 55% renewable energy consumption and 10% energy reduction by 2030 to keep them on track.

Step 3: It is necessary to align other goals with the main strategy

Having gained a clear understanding of their organizational goals and timeline, it is now crucial for Vietnamese IT giants to shift their attention towards implementing and realizing these objectives. Which specific strategies will they implement to achieve their objective?

For instance, they may devise multiple strategies to preserve energy and enhance the efficiency of their operations, encompassing both straightforward measures and large-scale conservation initiatives across the entire firm. These measures include enhancing maintenance schedules, converting our vehicle fleet and operations to electricity, installing renewable energy systems on-site, collaborating with environmentally friendly utility suppliers, and strategically procuring verified offsets to offset any remaining emissions.

Step 4. Need to develop a tracking system

In order to assure the successful implementation of their sustainability initiatives, it is crucial to establish effective monitoring and measurement mechanisms. Whether by utilizing current tracking systems or developing new ones, it is important to remember the principle: "If you cannot measure it, you cannot manage it" when it comes to their sustainability endeavors. As an illustration, they have the capability to establish resilient data management and analytics systems that can monitor their energy consumption and emissions output for the upcoming twenty years.

Step 5. Review progress and optimize

After Vietnamese tech firms implement their sustainability policies, their work is not finished. Companies should evaluate their progress and make necessary adjustments to their strategy. Consistently consult your strategic plan to verify that your project remains aligned with the established objectives.

Additionally, it is crucial to effectively convey updates to staff, customers, and investors. This serves to illustrate the organization's dedication to openness and encourages important stakeholders to maintain their support for the sustainability effort.

Vietnamese IT giants can communicate their sustainability initiatives through many channels, including our yearly CSR report, annual updates for shareholders, adherence to global norms and standards, participation in industry working groups, and regular internal communications.

Step 6. Collaborate on sustainability strategies across the industry

Although it is crucial to have a sustainability effort that is in line with the specific objectives of a business, there is no need to tackle it alone. Environmental concerns present a favorable occasion for corporations to collaborate with reputable counterparts in the industry. Seek advice on your sustainability strategy from various sources to ensure a comprehensive understanding of the best practices and maximize your potential effect. This partnership will result in enhanced decision-making, streamlined operations, and favorable outcomes. By implementing a strategic planning approach in their sustainability initiatives, firms improve the success of their program. By dedicating the necessary effort to develop a comprehensive strategy that aligns with your fundamental principles, encompassing the establishment of objectives, a schedule, specific methods, measurable indicators, and continuous improvement, the industry and the environment will reap significant advantages.

Contributions and gaps

The study is highly valuable for Vietnamese academics, businesses, and policymakers, as the application of Microsoft's carbon-neutral strategy to the tech industry of this developing nation is a relatively underexplored area. Besides, the study examines and leverages Microsoft's potential to set a global benchmark in its CSR and environmental accountability, transitioning from a mere compliance state to an active progression towards eliminating its historical emissions. The article offers a nuanced understanding by evaluating Microsoft's approach using different standpoints, viz., rights-based ethical frameworks and Friedman's profit-maximisation stance. Moreover, the paper provides a concise roadmap for implementation, facilitated by its six-step, practical, and highly actionable strategies.

The significant gaps include the reliance on secondary data, signalling the absence of empirical validation. Future studies could include Microsoft's presence in Vietnam and could also include research that differentiates strategies based on digital maturity or business models. Another limitation of this study is the acceptance of Microsoft as the global model without determining the capacity constraints of the Vietnamese tech industry. This study can serve as a background for future research that fills all these identified gaps.

Conclusion

This study has illuminated Microsoft's commendable strides toward achieving net-zero emissions by 2030, showcasing a commitment that significantly surpasses international agreements. However, the research also underscores a critical knowledge gap: Microsoft has yet to articulate a concrete roadmap for attaining net-zero emissions in developing nations where it has investments, including Vietnam. This raises questions about the comprehensiveness and equity of the corporation's sustainability strategy.

Nevertheless, Microsoft's case study offers invaluable lessons for Vietnamese technology companies. In the context of Vietnam's pledge at COP26 to reach net-zero emissions by 2050, domestic tech firms must recognize their role in contributing to this collective goal. The study has outlined actionable steps that Vietnamese technology corporations can take to implement net-zero projects, ranging from measuring and managing carbon emissions to investing in renewable energy and green technologies.

However, it is undeniable that Vietnam, as a developing nation, faces resource constraints in its transition to net-zero. Therefore, in addition to the efforts of the government and businesses, support and collaboration from global technology corporations are imperative. Sharing knowledge, technology, and financial resources will play a crucial role in assisting Vietnam and other developing countries in achieving their sustainable development goals, while ensuring a green and prosperous future for all.

References

[1] Boubakri, N., El Ghoul, S., Guedhami, O., & Wang, H. (2021). Corporate social responsibility in emerging market economies: determinants, consequences, and future research directions. *Emerging Markets Review*, 46, 100758. Available from: https://doi.org/10.1016/j.ememar.2020.100758.

[2] Buehler, V. M., & Shetty, Y. K. (1977). Managerial response to social responsibility challenge. In Caroll, A. B. (Ed.), Managing Corporate Social Responsibility. Boston: Little, Brown and Company.

[3] Caroll, A. B. (1977). Corporate social responsibility: Its managerial impacts and implications. In Caroll, A. B. (Ed.), Managing Corporate Social Responsibility. Boston: Little, Brown and Company.

[4] Christensen, H. B., Hail, L., & Leuz, C. (2021). Mandatory CSR and sustainability reporting: economic analysis and literature review. *Review of Accounting Studies*, 26(3), 1176–1248.

[5] Committee of Economic Development (1971). Social Responsibilities of Business Corporations. New York: Committee of Economic Development.

[6] Davis, K. (1977). The case for and against business assumption of social responsibilities. In Caroll, A. B. (Ed.), Managing Corporate Social Responsibility. Boston: Little, Brown and Company.

[7] Friedman, M. (1970). The social responsibility of business is to increase its profits. *New York Times Magazine*, 9, 126–127.

[8] Frost, P. (2001). Corporate Social Responsibility. Virtual Alumni Summit. Melbourne: University of Melbourne.

[9] Global Sustainable Investment Alliance (GSIA) (2023). Global Sustainable Investment Review (GSIR). London: Global Sustainable Investment Alliance (GSIA).

[10] Hill, C. W. (2021). Global Business Today, (12th edn.). New York: McGraw Hill LLC.

[11] Holme, R., & Watts, P. (2000). Corporate Social Responsibility: Making Good Business Sense. Geneva: World Business Council for Sustainable Development.

[12] Hossain, D. M., & Chowdhury, J. A. (2010). Climate change and corporate environmental responsibility. *Middle East Journal of Business*, 7(2), 4–13.

[13] Ioannou, I., & Serafeim, G. (2012). What drives corporate social performance? the role of nation-level institutions. *Journal of International Business Studies*, 43(9), 834–864.

[14] McWilliams, A., & Siegel, D. (2001). Corporate social responsibility: a theory of the firm perspective. *Academy of Management Review*, 27(1), 117–127. Available from: https://doi.org/10.5465/AMR.2001.4011987.

[15] Monsen, J. (1974). The social attitudes of management. In McGuire, J. W. (Ed.), The Social Attitudes of Management. New Jersey: Prentice-Hall.

[16] Rockfeller, D. (1974). Creative Management in Banking. New York: McGraw-Hill.

[17] Skinner, S. J., & Ivancevich, J. M. (1992). Business for the 21st Century. Boston: Irwin.

[18] Stobierski, T. (2021). 14 eye-opening corporate social responsibility statistics. 15 June. Accessed June 01, 2024. https://online.hbs.edu/blog/post/corporate-social-responsibility-statistics

[19] United Nations Trade and Development (UNCTAD) (2022). The Global Sustainable Finance Observatory (GSFO). Geneva: UNCTAD.

[20] Wheelen, T., Hunger, J. D., & Rangarajan, K. (2004). Concepts in Strategic Management and Business Policy, (9th edn.), Pearson Education.

[21] Yin, R. K. (2003). Case Study Research: Design and Methods. New York: Sage Publications, Inc.

[22] Carroll, A. B. (1979). A Three-Dimensional Conceptual Model of Corporate Performance. *The Academy of Management Review*, 4(4), 497–505. https://doi.org/10.2307/257850.

[23] Deegan, C., & Unerman, J. (2006). *Financial Accounting Theory, European Edition*. London: McGraw-Hill.

[24] Schramm, Wilbur. 1971. *Notes on case studies of instructional media projects*. Working paper, Stanford: Stanford University

7 Overview of current stampede management practices in India; role of AI in stampede prevention

Patil, Yojana[a]

Master in Business Administration- Clinical Research, Rushford Business School, Switzerland

Abstract

Human stampedes have been acknowledged as a major risk anywhere in the world where people congregate in large numbers, including India. Stampede prevention is a crucial area of research to minimize potential harm to people, property, and the environment. Effective emergency management requires utilizing observable data and integrating available resources in a timely manner. Artificial intelligence (AI) is experiencing rapid growth within the realm of technology. Effective data processing and wise decision-making are under ever-growing pressure due to big data. Hence, while creating a stampede prevention plan within the big data framework, AI technologies are crucial. This review summarizes the current crowd (stampedes) management methods and offers insights into various technologies that can be used in conjunction with AI for stampede prevention. In conclusion, a multi-faceted AI-integrated approach is required for effective stampede management and prevention in India.

Keywords: Artificial intelligence, crowd management, information and communication technology, prevention, stampede management

Introduction

Stampede - definition and process

An act of mass impulse in which a group of individuals starts running together without any apparent direction or goal is called a stampede. The phrase "human stampede" often refers to an abrupt rush of a crowded, agitated, and divided population that is essentially diverse and complicated, leading to numerous injuries and fatalities mostly from suffocation and trampling [5].

As per crowd management guidelines by the National Disaster Management Authority (NDMA), [10], the stampede process is described as follows. The main reasons for crowd disasters/stampedes include structural failures (e.g., structure collapse of barricades, wire fences, etc.; narrow and very few entry/exits), human errors (e.g., closed/locked exits), and natural calamities (e.g., fire caused by lightning). These have occasionally been brought about by: 1) high attendance, 2) a performer's response to an event, or 3) inappropriate or poor planning. As a result, visitors either experience exhilaration or terror, which further contributes to crowding or evacuation, respectively. When this occurs, the FIST factors—the crowd force, the information (whether true or false) that affects the crowd, the physical space (including the chairs, seating areas, hallways, ramps, doors, lifts, etc.), and the time duration of the incident (rapid ingress or egress) have a significant impact on the outcome, resulting in either high desired velocity (accelerated movement) or overcrowding (high crowd density: a significant number of people per unit area). On occasion, this has led to stampede deaths (trampling, asphyxia, and crushing). Figure 7.1 displays the stampede process per crowd management guidelines by the NDMA.

Overview of stampedes in India

India has the most religions and the largest population in the world [15]. Most communities hold religious gatherings where a sizable crowd gathers in public or private areas. Indian cities are susceptible to crowd tragedies in venues like stadiums, music concerts, nightclubs, and retail malls because of the country's rapid urbanization and population development.

In July 2024, at a Satsang (religious congregation) in Hathras, Uttar Pradesh, over 120 people perished in a stampede. This was one of the tragic stampedes that occurred in several years during religious gatherings/

[a]dryojana.patil@hotmail.com

DOI: 10.4324/9781003739982-7

temples (see Figure 7.2). Information on stampede incidents in India has been gathered since 1996 by the National Crime Records Bureau (NCRB), a division of the Ministry of Home Affairs of the Indian government that is in charge of recording crimes and unexplained deaths across the nation. According to the data, between 1996 and 2022, there were over 3,935 stampede incidents registered nationwide, with religious festivals accounting for about 79% of stampedes in India [6].

Stampedes at religious gatherings in India significantly impact local communities [13]. Some of the major impacts include trauma and loss of loved ones; economic hardships due to deaths of primary breadwinners, the cost of funerals, medical expenses etc., erosion of trust in the ability of organizers to keep devotees safe; and loss of productive social and human capital of the country due to deaths of young children and women.

Artificial intelligence

Artificially intelligent computer systems are those that can do difficult activities that are normally performed by people, such as thinking, decision-making, producing, etc. There is no universally accepted definition of artificial intelligence due to the fact that AI technologies may accomplish a wide variety of activities and yield a diverse range of outcomes [9].

Generally speaking, the more basic idea of artificial intelligence (AI) includes giving a computer or system human-like senses, reasoning, behavior, and adaptability. Both machine learning (ML) and deep learning (DL) are subfields or branches of AI, with ML being a more general term that includes DL as well as other methods. Particularly when talking about big data, predictive analytics, and other subjects related to digital transformation, AI and ML are frequently used interchangeably. ML enables machines to learn on their own by extracting information from data. To learn from data, DL makes use of artificial neural networks, which are modeled after the human brain. The relationship between AI, ML, and DL is shown in Figure 7.3.

Machine learning, data analysis, and decision-making are made possible by AI algorithms, also known as ML and DL [8]. These algorithms can carry out operations like pattern recognition, natural language comprehension, problem solving, and decision making that normally require human intellect. It's crucial to emphasize the importance of using appropriate data for algorithm training in any discussion on AI algorithms. Depending on the job and technique, either labelled or unlabeled data can be used to train ML or DL algorithms. Both ML and DL may be used for tasks like natural language processing, audio recognition, and picture identification.

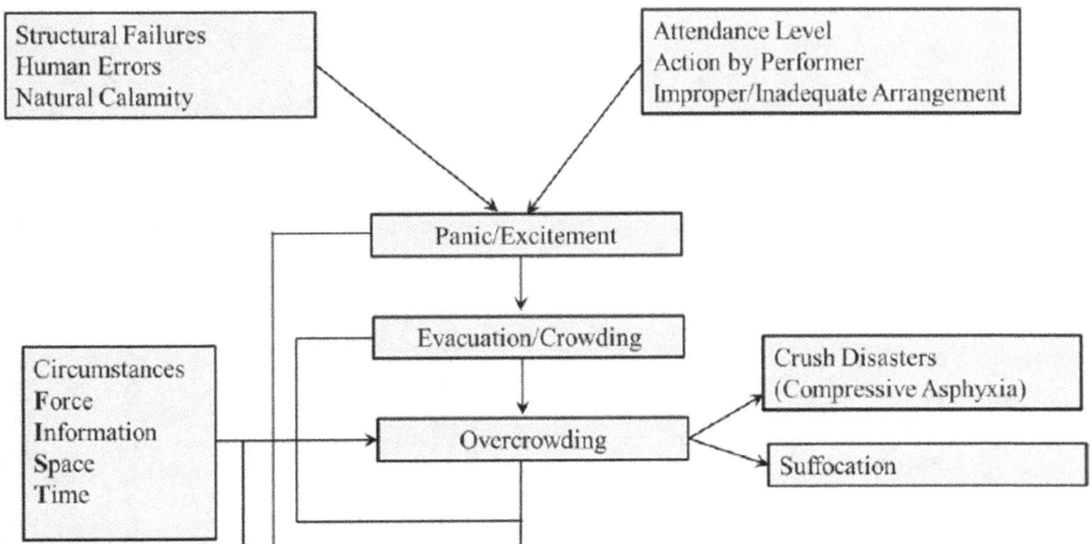

Figure 7.1 Stampede process [10]
Source: Author

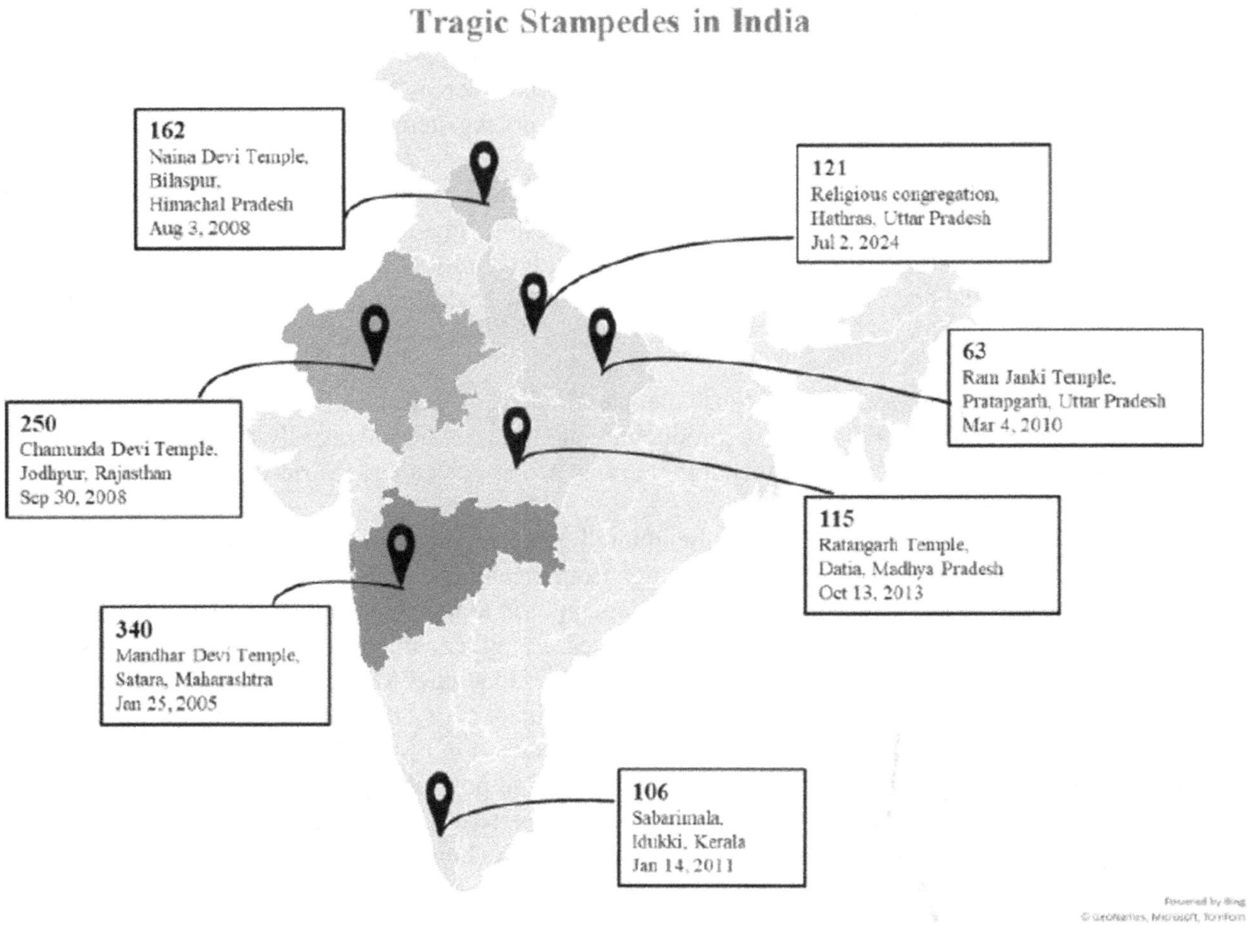

Figure 7.2 Tragic stampedes (>50 Deaths) in India at temple/religious gatherings since 2000 [3]
Source: Author

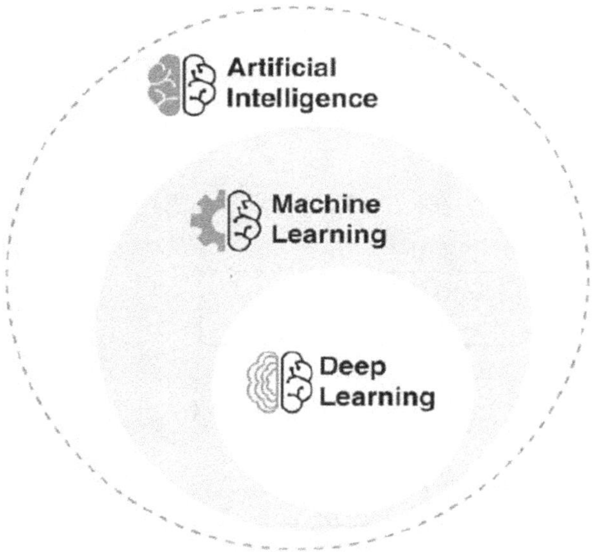

Figure 7.3 Artificial intelligence, machine learning, and deep learning fit together [9]
Source: Author

However, because DL can learn hierarchical data representations, it frequently performs better than classical ML in challenging pattern recognition tasks like object identification and picture categorization.

In general, AI refers to a machine's capacity to carry out certain cognitive tasks that are often associated with human brains [4]. Today, AI is a reality that is permeating everyday life and getting easier to use and more accessible. AI is starting to appear more frequently in the gadgets we use on a daily basis, such as home appliances, automobiles, and apps. More than that, AI also makes almost every other aspect of technology more approachable since it reduces barriers to human-machine communication.

Thus, AI-integrated technologies could play an essential role in stampede prevention and management in crowded places. In the following sections, we review and analyze current practices for stampede prevention and management in India and role of AI technologies for preventing stampedes and future challenges in implementation.

Objectives

- To learn about current practices for stampede management in India.
- To learn about the role of AI technologies in preventing stampedes and future challenges in their implementation.

Research Methods

Literature review methodology using online electronic databases was used to search for peer-reviewed literature for this paper. The databases used in the research were mainly Google Scholar. In addition, mass gathering events were identified from the online news, articles, reports, guidance documents, and blogs researched through various websites, while details on artificial intelligence were obtained from various online articles and websites. The search covered published articles between 2014 and 2024. The inclusion criteria for peer-reviewed journals included articles written in English that explored a form of correlation between artificial intelligence and crowd management, or other crowd technology and crowd management in conclusion. We screened 20 journal papers, of which nine were discussed in the review and met the inclusion criteria. Apart from the journal papers, two guidance documents from the Government of India and 3 websites for information on crowds/stampedes were reviewed and referred to in this paper.

Current stampede management practices in India

The Government of India's NDMA [10] rules for crowd control at events and large gathering locations are followed by India's existing stampede management procedures. This guideline offers valuable insights into the government's current strategy to stampede avoidance because it primarily focusses on the Crowd control Plan and the use of information and communication technology in crowd control.

Guidelines by the government of India

Crowd management plan

The NDMA created a "Suggestive Framework for Preparation of Crowd Management Plan for Events/Venues of Mass Gathering" in response to the frequent stampedes at places of mass gathering, including houses of worship, and the usually ad hoc reactions to such situations [10].

Guidelines for crowd control at large gathering locations recommend using a snake-line technique and continuously observing people to spot potential danger areas. Non-governmental organizations (NGOs) and civil defense might be involved in traffic management, people flow control, medical aid, cleanliness, and the mobilization of local resources in the event of a disaster by event/venue managers. Additionally, it is recommended that the administration handle all required clearances and make appropriate plans for the event's schedule, location, transportation, medical care, food, hygienic conditions, and emergency facilities.

The following are the different components of the crowd management strategy: 1) Long- and short-term capacity planning; 2) Crowd behavior understanding; 3) Crowd control; and 4) Stakeholder approach. An integrated method to crowd control that avoids stampedes is shown in Figure 7.4. Below is a thorough explanation of the crowd control plan and preparations needed for crowd arrival, event operation at the location, and crowd departure.

Recognizing the location, guests, and interested parties: It necessitates knowledge of 1) the type of event (religious, school/university, sports, music, or political), 2) the predicted crowd (age, gender, and financial groups), 3) the crowd intentions (societal, educational, spiritual, entertainment, financial, etc.), 4) the venue (place, topography of the area, temporal or permanent, open or closed), and 5) the role of other parties involved (NGOs, event venue neighbors, local managers, etc.).

Managing crowds entails the following: 1) Appropriate traffic control around locations for large gatherings. 2) An emergency escape route plan and a venue route map. 3) A barrier to regulate the flow of lines of people. 4) When there are long lines of people, the snake line method should be used. 5) Venue management and event planners should discourage ordinary admittance and have strategies in place for dealing with VIP guests.

Security and safety include the following: 1) The venue organizers should make sure that power is used appropriately and that fire extinguishers are used in accordance with safety regulations. 2) Using drones in the event of a huge crowd, and closed-circuit television (CCTV) cameras to keep an eye on people.

Communication: To interact with the masses, a public address system equipped with loudspeakers at every busy location is used.

Medical and emergency care: To manage post-disaster situations, medical first-aid rooms and emergency operation centers have to be established.

Event managers' role: Together with the local government and police, event planners and venue managers should create, carry out, evaluate, and update the disaster management plan.

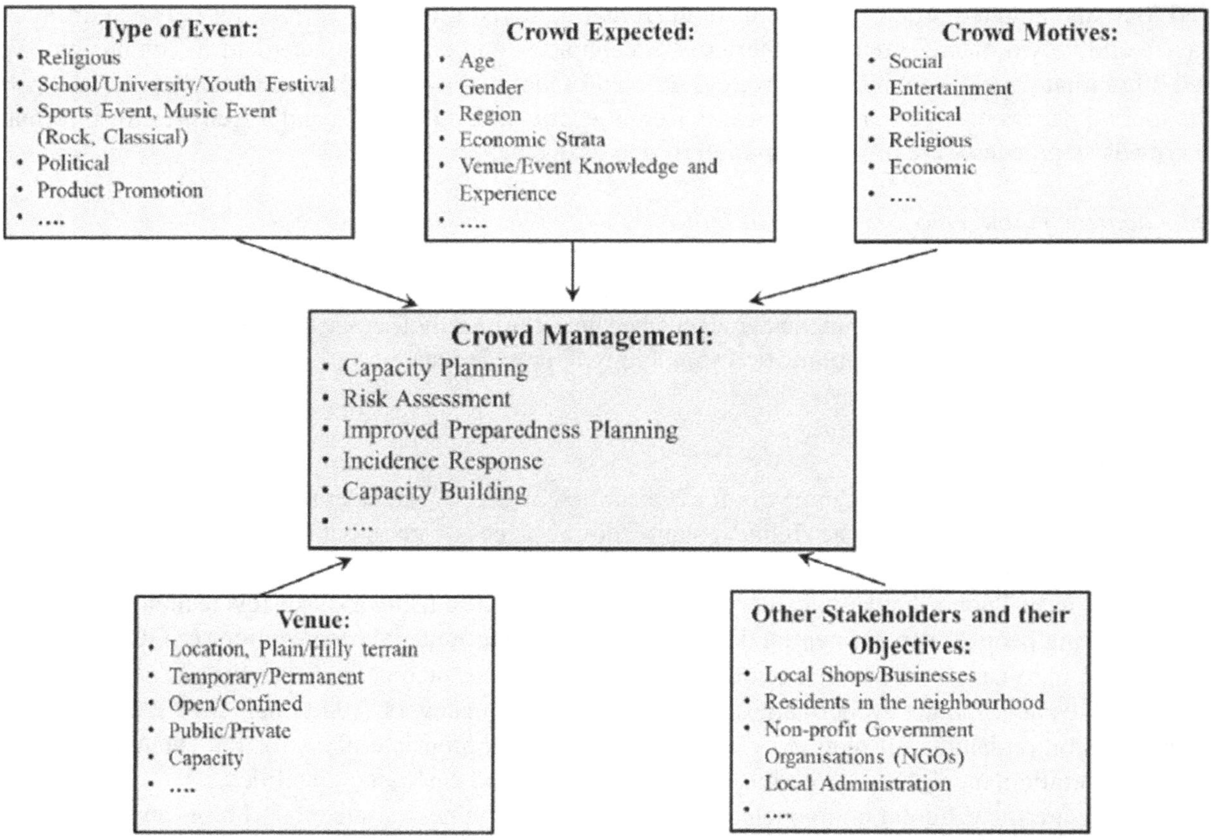

Figure 7.4 Integrated approach for crowd management [10]
Source: Author

Civil society role: In order to handle traffic, people movement, medical aid, sanitation, and the mobilization of local resources in the event of a crisis, event/venue management should collaborate with NGOs and civil defense.

Police role: Officers should actively assist in evaluating the location, conducting readiness inspections, and directing traffic and crowd flow.

The role of the media includes the following: 1) Educational: The media may inform the public of potential catastrophe risks, preventative measures, and how to be more prepared in the case of a disaster. 2) Critical: The media can assess disaster management plans critically and point out areas that need improvement.

Building capacity: To avert crowd tragedies, it is crucial to create capacity, run exercises, and periodically evaluate police and security personnel.

Information and communication technology

Enhancing information and communication technology (ICT) remains an integral aspect of crowd management worldwide. Figure 7.5 provides an overview of some of the most commonly used technologies and their usage in crowd management (stampede prevention and management) in India.

Literature Review

ICT models

To date, many ICT models have been developed for the detection and prevention of stampedes. Some studies have also been conducted using ICT models with machine learning and AI. A few examples are listed below:

ICT For Disaster Mitigation and Prevention	**ICT For Disaster Response and Relief**
Technology	*Technology*
• Geographic Information System, Remote Sensing	• Public Address system, SMS, UMS, Cell Broadcasting, Inter-operability of mobile service providers
• Radio, Television, Telephone	• Emergency lighting, alarms
• SMS, UMS, Cell Broadcasting, Internet/Social Media	• RFID Tags
• RFID	• Registration database software
• Space based sensors and Balloons	• Space based sensors and Balloons
Typical Usage	*Typical Usage*
• Early warning system, Potential Risks, Vulnerabilities	• To ensure rumours do not spread
• Registration of visitors, Virtual Queues, RFID	• Registering missing persons • Search and rescue
• Information dissemination	• Keeping track of relief organizations
• To regulate flow of visitors	• Insurance processing
• Prepositioning of resources	• Resource inventory management
Abbreviations: ICT = Information and Communication Technology; RFID = Radio Frequency Identification; SMS = Short Message Service; UNS = Unified Name Space.	

Figure 7.5 Use of information and communication technology in disaster management [10]
Source: Author

Verma and Mittal [16] proposed a real-time stampede detection system using computer vision (CCTV). This study presents a real-time technique for detecting stampedes in low to moderate population areas. The proposed method utilizes a feature vector based on optical flow entropy. A combination of a random forest with ten estimators and a support vector machine (SVM) was used to remove the necessity for thresholds. The entropy data's pertinent features provided good indications of the beginning of a stampede. To assess the method's accuracy and computing cost, it was evaluated on the UMN and PETS 2009 datasets and compared to existing methods. The results demonstrate that the proposed method produced more dependable outcomes without requiring a specific value. This achievement was made possible by the ability of ML models to adapt to changing conditions [16].

Kaur et al. [7] proposed using sensor-based techniques which are fundamental for the purpose of detecting stampedes during assemblages. Utilizing the SVM algorithm, data gathered from randomly assigned participants in crowded events using the LoRa communication protocol and wristband prototype were analyzed to determine the likelihood of a stampede. Study findings demonstrated that the prototype worked well to lessen the possibility of stampedes during public events, and gave event planners important knowledge to help ensure attendees' safety. To do this, the collected data were sent to the server node using an Inertial Measurement Unit (IMU), temperature, humidity, noise, and heartbeat sensors, and were analyzed. To forecast the likelihood of stampedes at public gatherings, server nodes continuously monitored activity using a trained ML model. The effectiveness of the proposed technique was demonstrated by experimental analysis using simulation and a developed prototype [7].

Shah and Kulkarni [12] proposed a stampede-detection and pilgrim tracking system using ICT. With the aid of image processing, a camera was used in this system to continuously monitor images and identify high-density crowds. The Global System for Mobile (GSM) system was used for base station communication. The Stampede Detection Unit used MATLAB software to analyze continuous image processing (every 10 seconds) and monitor the stampede scenario. If the number of people gathered in a particular area exceeded the threshold, an indication was sent via GSM to the Pilgrim unit, and an Advanced RISC Machine (ARM) microcontroller received a stampede warning via RS232 (Recommended Standard 232). Instead of using separate GSM and GPS modems, a single Global Positioning System (GPS)/GSM modem facilitated high-speed communication and provided the pilgrim's precise location. The ability to identify stampede conditions in advance allowed prompt action to prevent them, giving pilgrims a sense of security. GPS coordinates and the pilgrim's health parameters were sent in order to initiate continuous health status monitoring in addition to tracking and detecting stampedes. In the event of a medical emergency, the developed system's automatic monitoring of the pilgrim's physical conditions facilitated prompt access to medical assistance.

Crowd simulation models

One crucial area of study for stampede prevention is crowd simulation. A number of simulations have recently been developed to: 1) evaluate the capacity of the venue or holding area; 2) evaluate various crowd evacuation strategies; 3) evaluate and compare flow control strategies; 4) estimate evacuation time in the event of an emergency; and 5) estimate crowd density and force at entry and exit gates, barricades, etc. [10]. Here are some instances of research using crowd simulation models:

The increasing number of crowd-related events and fatalities that occur during the Hajj season particularly alarmed Saudi officials. The dynamics of the crowd at the Prophet's (PBUH) grave in the Holy Mosque of Madinah were examined by Al-Ahmadi et al. [2] when they were in the Ziara corridor during a continuous flow. With the crowd density kept below a safe level, the crowd flow rate was optimized using MassMotion, a pedestrian and crowd simulation program. To guarantee the safe and efficient operation of the visiting corridor, a strong regression model was created. According to the study's findings, crowds of more than 9200 people per hour and wait durations of more than 42 seconds in front of the Moajha (tomb) might cause a breakdown state. Decision makers and relevant authorities could use the study's findings to take prompt, appropriate corrective action to guarantee safe, orderly, and effective crowd control [2].

During Beijing Ditan's spring festival temple fair in Wang et al. [17] conducted the first crowd density danger early-warning study using mobile phone positioning technology. The method employed in this study was designed to make monitoring and alarm categorization of dense populations more feasible. It presented the correction coefficient for determining the state aggregation of pedestrians in time at the Ditan Temple Fair (2015) by comparing the measured data with the location data from mobile phones. The reasons for the evacuation delay time and the state of the Ditan crowd supervision were also disclosed by the numerical simulation study of the BaiTai evacuation model. This study's approach and conclusions can be used to forecast and provide an early warning to stop stampedes in crowded areas and ensure everyone's safety during evacuation.

Crowd behavior and policing strategies

Individuals who make up a crowd behave differently from one another. It is critical to comprehend the disposition, feelings, and traits of a crowd from a policing perspective. It is important to recognize and record instances of successful nonviolent crowd control policing. The police needed at a political rally would be different from that needed for the general public present at an accident scene or a fair. Further research must be conducted to understand when using force is advantageous, as well as when using psychological and persuasive control techniques would work well [10].

Gap in literature review

In India, organizers are not held legally accountable for any human catastrophes (such as stampedes) that occur at the event site or during the event itself. Nonetheless, a number of laws, rules, and sanctions, such the Disaster Management Act of 2005, help police and magistrates in their crowd control responsibilities. For Indian government officials and law enforcement organizations, enforcement and execution continue to be major obstacles.

The role of artificial intelligence

Crowd management is critical to public safety and efficient space utilization in areas with high pedestrian traffic, such as urban centers, sports stadiums, transportation hubs, and during large-scale events, including religious events and temple gatherings. The use of ML/AI can revolutionize crowd management by making it a more proactive, data-driven, and responsive practice, contributing significantly to public safety and efficient space management [14]. Traditional crowd management techniques often rely on manual surveillance and estimation, leading to real-time decision-making and risk mitigation challenges. The advent of ML/AI has introduced new opportunities to enhance crowd management strategies by utilizing these technologies for crowd density estimation, flow prediction, behavior analysis, and risk assessment. Suthar et al. [14] demonstrated that systems for crowd management that use ML can significantly increase the precision and effectiveness of crowd monitoring and control. These systems provide improved situational awareness, real-time analytics, and predictive capabilities, which help authorities make better decisions.

Advantages and disadvantages of artificial intelligence

To lessen the risk of stampedes, a variety of strategies have been put into place, including targeted crowd control techniques, enhanced framework, and pressure point marking (stairwells, points of entry and departure, etc.). Large gatherings demand extra caution because they present a risk of a catastrophic humanitarian crisis if crowd safety protocols are not followed. Manual crowd control is labor-intensive, heavily dependent on human intervention, and is more prone to human error. Hence, using AI technology for stampede prevention is advantageous. Figure 7.6 presents the key advantages and disadvantages of AI in general.

Successful implementation of AI at crowded religious events/pilgrims for stampede prevention

Case study at Hajj (2022), Kingdom of Saudi Arabia

The Hajj Ministry of Saudi Arabia has established an AI-based integrated system. The Kingdom of Saudi Arabia (KSA) was keen to employ AI techniques in carrying out its strategic plan, given the restricted number of pilgrims who would be permitted to complete the Hajj rituals under the extraordinary Coronavirus disease (COVID-19) conditions. Abalkhail and Sumiah [1] studied the KSA's experience managing crowds during the Hajj with AI to develop a model for comparable situations. The descriptive analytical method was used

Advantages	Disadvantages
• **Fewer errors**: AI can reduce the number of errors that human make, especially in repetitive tasks	• **Job loss:** AI can automate jobs previously performed by humans, leading to job displacement
• **Improved efficiency:** AI can perform tasks faster than humans, which can lead to increased productivity	• **Lack of creativity:** AI lacks the creativity and intuition that human possess, which limits its ability to perform certain tasks
• **Cost savings:** AI can automate tasks that would otherwise require human labour, which can lead to cost savings for businesses	• **Privacy concerns:** AI can be used to collect and analyse personal data, which raises privacy concerns
• **Improved accuracy:** AI can analyse substantial amounts of data and identify patterns that humans might miss, leading to more accurate predictions and decisions	• **Bias:** AI algorithms can be biased if they are trained on biased data or if they are designed with biased assumptions

Figure 7.6 Key advantages and disadvantages of artificial intelligence [4]
Source: Author

in this investigation. ArcGIS Pro 2.9.2 (desktop GIS application) was utilized to create maps associated with the research. A strategic analysis of the KSA's experience with crowd management was also conducted using SWOT analysis, which is a framework for identifying and analyzing an organization's strengths, weaknesses, opportunities, and threats, in connection to the studied topic. This paper claims that the KSA is now a leader in crowd management and a source of inspiration and reference due to its increasing usage of AI during the COVID-19 epidemic. The pilgrims were kept secure by taking all necessary safety measures, and no casualties were recorded [1].

Case study at Kumbh Mela (2019), Prayagraj, India

During the world's largest Kumbh Mela 2019 gathering in Prayagraj, India, Rajendran and Shankaran [11] demonstrated how L&T Smart World's AI-based crowd control system can successfully use an AI application in scenarios beyond human capabilities. The gathered information provided the basis for a framework for effective crowd control or evacuation strategies, which would lower the possibility of crowding and dangerous situations like stampedes. Deep learning is the solution to the problems of management and dense crowds. 23 crore pilgrims were kept safe throughout the 50-day Holy Kumbh Mela, demonstrating the effectiveness of the L&T Smart World crowd control analytics technology [11].

Discussion and Conclusion

The current practices for stampede management in India follow the NDMA crowd management guidelines and focus on planning for the event, understanding the event and its risk, initiating crowd management and control measures, command and control mechanisms, contingency planning, and documentation. But with a few exceptions, the major reason for stampedes at religious festivals in India continues to be "lack of planning" on the part of the organizer, which includes risk assessment, crowd management and control methods, resource management, and efficient stakeholder coordination. Lack of adoption and implementation of NDMA's crowd management guidelines, rapidly increasing population, greater tolerance of Indians for crowded places, and failure of governance and lack of accountability are the major limitations in implementing the current NDMA crowd management guidelines in India.

To guarantee safe crowd evacuation during emergencies, proactive management of large gatherings is essential. Due to insufficient services, poor crowd control, and poor planning, there are increased risks of a stampede. The planning of a mass gathering is based on the event's characteristics and the associated risk analysis. Before, during, or after an event, there is a plethora of potential risks that could arise, big or small, foreseeable or unforeseeable. Managing all these risks is difficult, especially in light of the few resources - trained staff, tools, supplies, services, and money that are available. To protect the safety of large gatherings, it is essential to identify and rank the highest risks.

The early phases of AI development present enormous opportunities, as they do for many other technologies. However, as with so many other scientific advances, technological advancements frequently occur far more quickly than the development of technology's ethical implications. Hence, while utilizing AI technology, ethical considerations (mainly data privacy) remain the biggest challenge apart from job loss, and lack of creativity. Accuracy is another major concern in the initial stages of technological development. AI can help identify false information; however, when flawed algorithms gather inaccurate data, it can also help disseminate false information. Numerous incidents of erroneous facial recognition technology have resulted in false arrests. Apart from these challenges, the need for large and diverse datasets, as well as system robustness and reliability faced in implementing these systems, remain key challenges.

Studies conducted using ICT models, AI, or ML have demonstrated dependable outcomes in real-time stampede detection. However, continued research and cooperation are needed to manage moral dilemmas and maximize system effectiveness in changing urban environments.

In conclusion, effective stampede management and prevention in India requires a multi-faceted AI-integrated approach. By integrating AI-driven technology, comprehensive legislation for stampedes, enhancing professional training, fostering community involvement, evaluating venue capacity, maintaining a public addressal system for crowd control, assessing crowd behavior management, strict penalties for effective compliance for all stakeholders, and implementing learnings from past stampede lessons and global best practices in crowd management, we can significantly manage to prevent stampedes. Ongoing assessment and modification of crowd management practices with forthcoming technologies are crucial for future success.

References

[1] Abalkhail, A., & Sumiah, A. (2022). Saudi Arabia's management of the Hajj season through artificial intelligence and sustainability. *Sustainability*, 14(21), 14142.

[2] Al-Ahmadi, H.M., Reza, I., Jamal, A., Alhalabi, W.S. and Assi, K.J. (2021). Preparedness for mass gatherings: a simulation-based framework for flow control and management using crowd monitoring data. *Arabian Journal for Science and Engineering*, 46(4), 1–13.

[3] IndiaToday. (2024). *Tragic Stampedes in India.* X [Online]. 03 July 2024. Available at: https://x.com/IndiaToday/status/1808436342499446933 (Accessed: 3 September 2025)

[4] Bressler, M., & Bressler, M. (2024). Artificial intelligence: increasing business profits at the cost of consumer privacy. *Journal of Strategic Innovation and Sustainability*, 19(1), 12.

[5] Chaturvedi, S. (2022). Training Module on Management of Crowd at Large Congregations. Delhi-110042: National Institute of Disaster Management (NIDM), Ministry of Home Affairs, Government of India.

[6] Kaloji, S. (2024). *Data: Over 3,000 Lives Lost in Stampedes between 2001 & 2022.* Factly. Available at: https://factly.in/data-over-3000-lives-lost-in-stampedes-between-2001-2022/ (Accessed: 3 September 2025)

[7] Kaur, K., Kumar, R., & Kumar, P. (2023) Early prediction of stampede in assemblage. In: *2023 8th International Conference on Intelligent Systems and Control (ISCON)*. IEEE, pp. 1–6.

[8] Kerner, S. M. and Tabsharani, F. (2024). *Types of AI algorithms and how they work.* Search Enterprise AI [Online]. 16 October 2024. Available at: https://www.techtarget.com/searchenterpriseai/tip/Types-of-AI-algorithms-and-how-they-work (Accessed: 3 September 2025).

[9] NASA. (2024). *What is Artificial Intelligence?* NASA [Online]. 13 May 2024. Available at: https://www.nasa.gov/what-is-artificial-intelligence/ (Accessed: 3 September 2025).

[10] NDMA (2014). Managing Crowds at Events and Venues of Mass Gathering - A Guide for State Government, Local Authorities, Administrators, and Organizers. New Delhi, India: National Disaster Management Authority (NDMA), Government of India.

[11] Rajendran, L. and Shankaran, R.S. (2021) Big data enabled real-time crowd surveillance using artificial intelligence and deep learning. In: *2021 International Conference on Artificial Intelligence in Information and Communication (ICAIIC)*, Jeju Island, Korea (South), 13–16 April 2021. IEEE, pp. 129–132.

[12] Shah, S., & Kulkarni, S. (2014). A review: monitoring and safety of pilgrims using stampede detection and pilgrim tracking. *IJRET: International Journal of Research in Engineering and Technology*, 4(4), 328–332.

[13] Shekhar, P. (2025). Stampede Disaster and its Management in India- Explained Pointwise. *ForumIAS Blog* [Online]. 30 January 2025. Available at: https://forumias.com/blog/stampede-disaster-and-its-management-in-india-explained-pointwise/ (Accessed: 3 September 2025).

[14] Suthar, M., Sharma, S., & Kumar, S. (2024). Current status and future directions for crowd management using machine learning. In 5th International Conference on Information Management & Machine Intelligence (ICIMMI'23), New York (NY), USA.

[15] Worldometer. (2025). Countries in the world by population (2025). *Worldometer* [Online]. Available at: https://www.worldometers.info/world-population/population-by-country/ (Accessed: 3 September 2025).

[16] Verma, U. & Mittal, U. (2023) Real time stampede detection system using computer vision. *SSRN Electronic Journal* [Online]. Available at: https://ssrn.com/abstract=4490376 (Accessed: 3 September 2025)

[17] Wang, J., Ding, Y. N., & Liu, D. D. (2015). The research on early warning of preventing the stampede on crowded places and evacuated technology. In International Forum on Energy, Environment Science and Materials (IFEESM 2015), (pp. 1544–1551).

8 Research on developing green tourism in Nha Trang using the two-wheel tourism model

Le Thi Kieu Anh[a] *and Duong Thanh Phuong*[b]

Thai Binh Duong University, 79 Mai Xuan Thuong, Nha Trang City, Khanh Hoa Province, Vietnam

Abstract

In Nha Trang, two-wheeled tourism has not received much attention and proper development from many businesses. However, there are many resources to develop this type of tourism. In particular, this type of tourism will promote the development of green tourism and green economy for the city, taking advantage of existing resources and creating jobs for many related subjects. The study uses a computational research method to understand the needs and behaviors of tourists towards two-wheeled services and proposes solutions to develop this service in a sustainable and environmentally friendly direction. Initial results show that tourists like the freedom and flexibility that two-wheeled vehicles bring but still face difficulties in traffic safety and a lack of information. The results of the study provide an important basis for policymakers and business administrators to develop environmentally friendly two-wheeled tourism services, while promoting the green economy in Nha Trang in particular and the country in general.

Keywords: Green economy, green tourism, two-wheeled tourism

Introduction

Nowadays, tourism has become an indispensable part of people's lives. More and more people want to experience unique trips and explore new places by using convenient, flexible, and easy means of transportation. Among these convenient means of transportation, two-wheeled vehicles, including motorbikes, bicycles, and electric bicycles, have become a popular and very popular type of transportation.

Two-wheeled vehicles are popular and commonly used in many countries; this trend is increasing in Southeast Asian countries. In the list of 10 countries with the highest rate of households using motorbikes in the world [22], Southeast Asia, including Thailand, Indonesia, Philippines, Malaysia, and Vietnam, are the countries that use two-wheeled vehicles in the majority. Thailand leads with 87% of households using motorbikes. Indonesia ranked 3rd with 85% of households using motorbikes, while Malaysia and the Philippines ranked 4th and 9th on the list. Vietnam ranked 2nd on this list with 86% of households using motorbikes. In particular, in recent years, consumers in these countries are switching from gasoline-powered two-wheelers to electric two-wheelers. According to Bloomberg NEF's estimates, annual electric vehicle sales in Southeast Asia will increase rapidly from 2024 to 2039. Figure 8.1 indicates the motorcycle consumption situation in Vietnam.

This is an extremely large vehicle resource for use in the green tourism industry in the future. Currently, in big cities in Vietnam, such as Ho Chi Minh City, Hanoi, traveling by two-wheelers is also increasingly popular and favored by tourists. Typical programs include: Journey to explore Saigon by Vespa, Hanoi City tour by motorbike, Street food tour by motorbike in Ho Chi Minh City... Steve Mueller shared that: "Traveling Ho Chi Minh City on a scooter is the best way, an authentic experience and also a way to understand more about the lives of the people here." Vietnam National Administration of Tourism [19]. Developing two-wheeled tourism in general and electric two-wheeled vehicles, by taking advantage of available resources, can generate revenue for the local community and contribute to the economic development of the region. This also brings new and attractive job opportunities, thereby promoting development and bringing benefits to the local community. According to the Ministry of Culture, Sports and Tourism, "Nature has endowed Nha Trang with excellent conditions for tourism development, namely Nha Trang Bay - one of the most beautiful bays in the world, warm weather all year round... This land also has many cultural sediments associated with the two cultures of Vietnam - Cham, unique festivals, diverse cuisine of coastal residents associated with gentle, hospitable

[a]anh.ltk@tbd.edu.vn, [b]duongthanhphuongqtkd20dh1@tbd.edu.vn

DOI: 10.4324/9781003739982-8

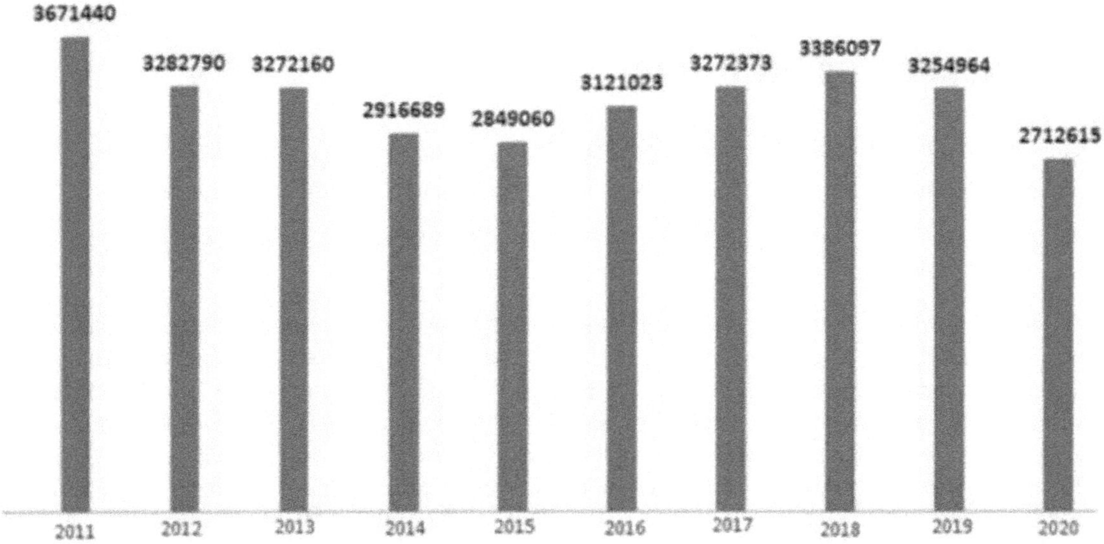

Figure 8.1 Motorcycle consumption situation in Vietnam
Source: Ngan [8]

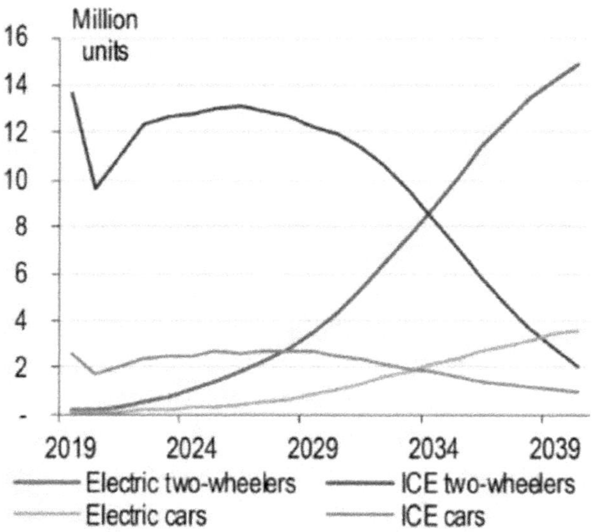

Figure 8.2 Estimated annual electric vehicle sales in Southeast Asia
Source: Binh Phuoc Provincial People's Committee [1]

people... World tourism experts assess that with its inherent potential, Nha Trang has all the advantages to become a world sea tourism center like Bali (Indonesia), Phuket (Thailand)" [20]. With such favorable conditions, the development of tourism by two-wheeled vehicles and electric two-wheeled vehicles in Nha Trang has not yet been widely applied. Figure 8.2 indicates estimated annual electric vehicle sales in Southeast Asia.

From there, the study aims to explore the demand for tourism services in two-wheeled vehicles and electric two-wheeled vehicles of tourists in Nha Trang using qualitative research methods. To discover criteria for building two-wheeled tourism products and services in general and electric two-wheeled tourism in particular. Creating a premise for policy makers and business managers to propose directions for developing this type of tourism.

Theoretical Basis of Research

Two-wheeled tourism is a form of travel where participants use motorcycles or bicycles as the primary mode of transportation during their trip. Participants in two-wheeled tourism must be capable of riding, self-driving, and taking responsibility for their own journey. Today, two-wheeled vehicles have become increasingly diverse and affordable, offering many alternatives for fuel sources. Tourists can choose vehicles powered by gasoline, electric batteries, or even bicycles. This has made this type of tourism more accessible.

According to [23], motorcycle tourism is defined based on three main characteristics: temporary travel, staying outside the home, and travel motive. Two-wheeled tourism encompasses all three of these components. The concept of temporary travel refers to traveling short distances for brief periods, requiring tourists to break their journey into several smaller segments. Motorcyclists may also need to stop frequently due to limited range and physical discomfort while riding. Staying outside the home can include moving away from one's usual residence and opting to sleep in tents or in hotels and inns along the journey. Meanwhile, the travel motive aspect refers to the reasons that motivate tourists to choose this mode of transportation when traveling.

It is important to note that motorcycle tourism differs from car tourism in that it involves a greater attachment to the vehicle itself, a higher likelihood of traveling in groups, and a greater emphasis on the journey's aspects rather than just the destination [21, 11]. Similarly, Pinch and Reimer [11] argue that two-wheeled tourism allows travelers a higher level of engagement in the riding experience.

Thus, it can be said that two-wheeled tourism can be classified as a subtype of self-driving tourism [12, 17]. In this understanding, the characteristics of self-driving tourism are similar to and related to two-wheeled tourism. For instance, the traveler is also responsible for controlling the vehicle, deciding on stops and breaks, choosing travel destinations, and determining travel times, as well as durations of stay at tourist spots or rest stops. In simple terms, two-wheeled tourism offers the most freedom to travelers.

Freedom is a key feature that provides an advantage in two-wheeled tourism. Prideaux and Carson [12] and Shih [16] once again emphasize the freedom and independence in the journey associated with this type of tourism. The freedom that two-wheeled tourism provides also allows tourists to move and disperse across various tourist locations rather than concentrating on a single destination at the same time, as is the case with group tourism. This dispersion enhances the spread of tourism in countries, especially in rural areas and remote regions, contributing to income for local residents in areas that do not have the potential for group tourism development.

Two-wheeled tourism offers significant advantages due to the flexibility and lightweight nature of this mode of transport. The lightweight and flexible characteristics enable two-wheeled travelers to easily access areas that are challenging to reach when traveling by car or large buses. Therefore, this form of travel is often prioritized for exploring new locations, experiencing local culture, and enjoying natural landscapes where public transportation systems are underdeveloped. Motorcycle tourism typically takes place on scenic roads with little traffic, allowing tourists to discover local landscapes and cultures. Motorcyclists often travel in groups to share experiences [18].

Motorcycles are a common and popular mode of transportation for the people of Vietnam. However, for foreign tourists, this mode can present many novel features, providing excitement and exhilaration. Due to the physical factors, skills, and choices involved in riding a motorcycle, Walker [21] suggests that it is often more beneficial to view motorcycling as a leisure phenomenon rather than merely mode of transportation. For foreign tourists, using a motorcycle for travel may not be the perfect choice, but participating in and using this mode certainly offers a valuable travel and entertainment experience.

Moreover, for those with little or no experience riding a motorcycle, taking a two-wheeled trip can evoke a sense of adventure and risk. In this context, there may be a connection between two-wheeled travel and the adventure tourism sector [3]. Enjoying the thrill of riding a motorcycle along challenging routes, especially for foreign tourists, can be a worthwhile experience. While most adventure tourism products in Vietnam and worldwide involve controlled risk experiences - that is, the sense of adventure is designed within high safety limits - two-wheeled tourism combines the freedom and flexibility of the journey with limitless adventure, potentially creating a unique type of travel. In this sense, motorcyclists are also adventure seekers, experiencing adventure tourism.

It is important to note that motorcycle tourism differs from car tourism in that it involves a greater attachment to the vehicle itself, a higher likelihood of group travel, and a greater emphasis on the journey's aspects rather than just the destination [21, 11]. Motorcyclists have a higher level of engagement in the riding experience [11].

Research Method

To address the research objectives, the research was conducted with the following research process:

Step 1: Overview of previous studies related to two-wheeled tourism
Step 2: Overview of the two-wheeled tourism situation in the world and in Vietnam
Step 3: Develop a structured questionnaire and identify interview subjects
Step 4: Conduct interviews
Step 5: Process results and discuss results

The research method used is a qualitative research method with two methods as follows: Document research method, and expert interview method. With the document research method used in steps 1 and 2 to evaluate the topic through theoretical and practical contexts. The expert interview method is used to explore the needs of two-wheeled tourism and two-wheeled electric tourism. Experts are identified as tourists experiencing tourism in Nha Trang. The experts were aged 20–40 years old, with experience of travelling to many destinations. The interviews lasted from 30–40 minutes and were conducted at prominent locations in Nha Trang, such as beaches and hotels. Data collection was stopped when similar opinions were repeated many times. The study conducted 22 interviews with 22 experts, and participant profiles are presented in Table 8.1.

Table 8.1 Survey subject information.

Name	Age	Occupation	Residence
Linh	20	Student	Ho Chi Minh City
Thảo	25	Supermarket employee	Daklak
Sáng	32	Teacher	Binh Duong
Quang	29	Delivery worker	Da Lat
Khải	22	Student	Ho Chi Minh City
Thư	32	Freelance	Ho Chi Minh City
Như	33	Bank	Hanoi
Thanh	40	Office	Hanoi
Thi	23	Office worker	Da Nang
Long	36	Business	Hanoi
KleT	20	Student	Ninh Thuan
Mai	28	Freelance	Hanoi
Thái	25	Supermarket employee	Binh Duong
Tiến	22	Coffee seller	Ho Chi Minh City
Hiếu	31	Doctor	Ho Chi Minh City
Thảo	28	Nurse	Ninh Thuận
Nam	27	Photographer	Ho Chi Minh City
Quyết	31	Chef	Ho Chi Minh City
Dũng	28	Road engineer	Hai Phong
Việt	26	Event	Ho Chi Minh City
Quyết	29	Office worker	Hanoi

Source: Author

Research Results

Reasons why tourists choose two-wheeled tourism services

Freedom

Tourists choose two-wheeled tourism services mainly because of their desire to move freely and control their time. This need comes from the desire to enjoy the scenery and be proactive in the trip without affecting others. As Khai shared, "I like to be free to move and explore beautiful scenery by motorbike. When traveling by motorbike, I feel free and proactive about time for my personal needs without fear of affecting others." This view is consistent with Shih [16] observation that more and more people are seeking freedom and independent experiences in tourism. This freedom also increases the dispersion of tourism to rural areas and less popular destinations.

Deep experience with nature

Many tourists choose two-wheel vehicles because they want to enjoy the beauty of nature throughout the trip. Ms. Thu said, "Traveling by motorbike helps me relax and have a new perspective on work." Traveling by two-wheel vehicles provides a more connected experience with the vehicle and the surrounding environment, facilitating group travel and focusing on the journey, not just the destination.

Minimize personal inconvenience

Some tourists choose two-wheel vehicles because they help minimize personal inconveniences, such as motion sickness. Thi shared: "I get very sick. Traveling by motorbike helps me explore destinations and avoid feeling motion sick." In addition, traditional forms of tourism, such as group tours or passenger vans, often lack flexibility, causing a feeling of being constrained and uncomfortable. Mr. Hieu said, "I don't like going on tours because I am constrained by time, which makes me lose comfort when traveling."

Learn and share

The need for culturally knowledgeable local guides is also an essential factor. Tourists want to interact with local people to understand the culture and lifestyle. Ms. Thu said, "When coming to a new city, finding someone who is knowledgeable and knows the destination well is very important to have a valuable experience."

Have a tour guide to support

Local guides bring many benefits, from introducing unique destinations to providing detailed information about local culture. Ms. Ma said, "Having a tour guide with you makes it much easier to find good restaurants and avoid getting lost." Tour guides not only save time but also enrich the travel experience. A survey in Lac Duong district, Lam Dong province, showed that the need for local guides is very high, with an average score of 4.33/5, proving that tourists are very interested in interacting with local culture through local people.

Tourists' demand for two-wheel tourism services

Demand for diversity in tourism service experiences

Diversity in products and services is a key factor influencing tourists' choice of destinations. Survey results show that tourists appreciate destinations that offer a variety of experiences. Mr. Long, a married man, shared: "I prioritize destinations that can meet the needs of the whole family, with a variety of services and activities." According to Nikjoo and Ketabi [10], pull factors (such as the sea and tourism resources) and push factors (such as the need to relax and explore) both play an important role in motivating tourists to seek diverse destinations.

Enjoying nature and emotions

Motorbike tourism is becoming increasingly popular, especially for tourists who love to connect with nature. Thanh shared: "I like freedom and want to experience many places with rich nature." Studies Scuttari [15], Frash et al. [5], Ramoa et al. [13], emphasize that the natural environment and excitement of the trip play an important role in creating a memorable experience. Traveling by motorbike provides a feeling of direct interaction with the surrounding environment, from the wind to the chirping of birds, creating a unique travel experience.

The need for local food experiences

Local cuisine is an important element in the travel experience, not only meeting physiological needs but also having deep cultural significance. Ms. Tien and Mr. Quyet shared: "Traveling by motorbike is suitable for exploring cuisine because motorbikes can access small, hard-to-reach eateries." Exploring local cuisine helps tourists better understand the culture and lifestyle of that land, and at the same time creates memorable memories. Reynolds [14] believes that cuisine not only satisfies the taste buds but also helps tourists feel the culture and people of the locality.

Need for flexibility in time

Flexibility in planning and experiencing travel is an important factor for people who often travel for work. Ms. Nhu shared: "I want to be free to explore without being constrained by a fixed tour schedule." Self-planning allows tourists to choose destinations and activities according to their interests, saving costs and providing more personalized experience. Mr. Long also said, "I want to be able to change plans and return early if needed, which is not allowed by traditional tours."

Need for safety

Although traveling by motorbike has many benefits, it also has many potential safety risks. Riding a motorbike requires high skills and concentration, especially in bad weather or difficult terrain. Linh shared: "Riding a motorbike can be risky, such as accidents on bad roads." Statistics from the Traffic Police Department show that the number of traffic accidents involving motorbikes remains high, especially in urban areas. Studies like Johnston et al. [7] indicate that motorbike riders are at a much higher risk of death than car riders.

The need for convenience in two-wheel travel

Travelling by motorbike can present challenges such as the effects of weather and carrying luggage. Bad weather can reduce comfort and affect travel plans, as Long shared: "The weather can be inconvenient and affect the trip." Carrying luggage is also difficult because motorbikes do not have a large storage space. "Traveling in a group by motorbike can be difficult to coordinate and manage," said Thai. In addition, motorbike maintenance and repair are also important issues, as Nam shared: "Finding a repair shop in remote areas can be difficult." Legality and compliance with traffic laws are other concerns, especially when traveling in groups.

To design an effective two-wheeled tourism service, it is necessary to pay attention to factors such as service diversity, flexibility in time, the ability to explore cuisine and nature, while ensuring safety and convenience. Two-wheeled tourism services should provide rich experiences, suitable for the needs of a variety of customers, from families and groups of friends to tourists who love freedom and exploration. By balancing these factors, two-wheeled tourism services can better meet customer needs and deliver memorable travel experiences.

Expectations about the price of two-wheel tourism products

Cost plays an important role in choosing tourism services, including two-wheeled services. Mr. Nam said that tourists often have a certain budget for the trip, for example, 3-4 million VND for a 3-day, 2-night backpacking trip. Research by Dellaert et al. [4], Nicolau and Mas [9] and Goossens [6] showed that price and service quality are decisive factors in choosing a destination, with Nicolau and Mas [9] emphasizing the influence of price and distance, and Goossens [6] emphasizing the combination of quality and price. Customers often look for a balance between price and quality, as in the case of Mr. Quyet, who is willing to spend about 20 million VND for a diverse experience. Students like Khai choose motorbikes to save costs, despite the safety risks. Therefore, tourism businesses should design service packages with flexible pricing policies, including discounts for children, family packages, and group deals to meet the diverse needs of customers.

Distribution channels in two-wheeled tourism services
Choosing a reliable distribution channel is an important factor in two-wheeled tourism services to ensure quality and customer satisfaction. Tourists are often hesitant when there is a lack of clear information about the tour program. Mr. Dung said, "I often rely on recommendations from acquaintances or travel agencies with good experience." Research shows that satisfaction and positive experiences influence the recommendation of a destination to others, with positive emotional characteristics and images playing an important role [2]. Mr. Viet said, "I often contact local friends to buy tours, showing the role of social networks and informal distribution channels." To build an effective distribution strategy, businesses should cooperate with reputable agents, invest in professional staff, connect with local hotel staff, and launch promotional campaigns in the local community. Diversifying distribution channels will improve sales efficiency and better meet customer needs.

Promotional activities in the two-wheel tourism model
In the tourism industry, promotional activities are key to attracting customers and promoting destinations. However, in an increasingly competitive environment, innovation in promotion is necessary to meet the increasing needs of tourists.

Promotion based on time factors
Time factors and the novelty of the destination greatly influence tourists' decisions. Mr. Thai shared: "Most of my friends like to travel and have flexible jobs. As long as there is a new, hot place, the whole group will schedule a trip." This emphasizes the importance of flexibility in terms of time and the attractiveness of new destinations.

Ms. Thao said, "If I don't go to the beach in the summer, it is a sin against Mother Nature. Seeing everyone doing it, I will do it too." This reflects the influence of crowd psychology and seasonal tourism trends. Mr. Long also shared: "The time when I travel with my family is summer because the weather is nice and the family has time. Natural places and the sea are the priority." This illustrates the connection between climate and destination choice, with destinations such as the sea attracting tourists in the summer, while mountainous areas attract those who love trekking and winter sports.

Promotion on social media platforms
Social media is a powerful tool in promoting tourism. TikTok and Facebook help create a "spread effect" through sharing images and videos of destinations. Mr. Sang shared: "Browsing Facebook and TikTok, I see beautiful videos about routes or happy moments, I send them to my lover to watch, if we can arrange it, we will go together." KOLs (Key Opinion Leaders) have a great influence on travel decisions, so businesses need to cooperate with them to build attractive marketing campaigns and increase brand awareness.

Personalizing the travel experience and being flexible in adjusting promotional plans are important. Businesses need to understand the needs and preferences of customers to provide appropriate services and monitor market trends to maintain attractiveness and competitiveness.

Conclusion

The study identified the main factors influencing tourists' choice of two-wheel tourism services in Nha Trang, including products and services, price, distribution, and accessibility. The results showed that tourists prioritized the experience of free exploration and connection with nature, consistent with previous studies Scutari [15], Frash et al. [5], Ramoa et al. [13]. Tourism Career Ladder Theory was found to be appropriate, with tourists increasingly planning and experiencing tourism at their own leisure. The increasing demand for two-wheel services, especially among young people, shows great potential for this model. However, the study was limited by the small sample size and only focused on Vietnamese tourists. For a more complete view, research with a larger sample and including international tourists is needed. Quantitative methods can support research and help design products that meet customer needs.

Recommendations

For authorities

It is necessary to establish clear policies on business conditions, safety standards, and the responsibilities of participants in two-wheeled tourism services. Develop service quality standards for suppliers, and invest in developing traffic infrastructure, parking lots, road signs, as well as related infrastructure such as rental, repair, and spare parts supply. Financial support policies, taxes, and loans should also be considered to support businesses in this tourism model. At the same time, authorities should strengthen inspection and supervision to ensure service quality and safety for tourists, towards a sustainable and effective development model.

For businesses

Tourism businesses need to focus on creating attractive promotional content, emphasizing the elements that tourists are looking for, such as exploring nature, experiencing local culture, and culinary specialties. Using attractive images and videos of local landscapes and activities will help create appeal. Businesses should design tours that suit the needs of customers, such as tours to explore coastal routes and learn about local culture. Pricing of products and services should be based on research on the price that customers are willing to pay, while considering operating costs and value. Businesses should also exploit effective distribution channels such as websites, travel applications, agents, retail outlets, and social networks to better reach customers.

Limitations of the study and future research directions

This study mainly focuses on surveying the needs of domestic customers for two-wheeled tourism services in Nha Trang. Due to cost and time constraints, the study only included domestic customers, ignoring international customers. Further studies can be expanded to include international customers, in order to build tourism products that are more suitable for their diverse needs. In addition to identifying product needs and design criteria, further studies can focus on surveying routes and destinations suitable for exploring nature, culture, cuisine, and architecture. This will help build attractive tour programs. Furthermore, the study should explore the development of technology applications to manage service quality and human resources more effectively. This study has laid the foundation for the development of two-wheeled tourism products and opened up new research directions to perfect and expand this product, meeting the needs of both domestic and international customers.

References

[1] Vietnam News Agency. (2024, October 20). Vietnam leads ASEAN in electric motorbike market growth. Vietnam News. Retrieved from https://vietnamnews.vn/

[2] Birley, S. (1985). Social networks and tourism: the role of word-of-mouth. *Journal of Travel Research*, 23(1), 5–10.

[3] Blackman, R. A., & Haworth, N. L. (2013). Tourist use of mopeds in Queensland. *Tourism Management*, 36, 580–589.

[4] Ramoa, C. E. A., Pires, P. S., & Añaña, E. S. (2021). Motorcycle tourism and nature: An analysis of motorcyclists' motivations to travel. Leisure Studies, Advance online publication. https://doi.org/10.1080/02614367.2020.1858327

[5] Cater, C. I. (2017). Tourism on two wheels: Patterns of motorcycle leisure in Wales. Tourism Management, 61, 180–189. https://doi.org/10.1016/j.tourman.2017.01.006

[6] Goossens, C. (2000). Price sensitivity in tourism markets. *Tourism Management*, 21(1), 89–96.

[7] Carey, M. J., & Aitken, M. E. (1996). Motorbike injuries in Bermuda: a risk for tourists. Annals of Emergency Medicine, 28(4), 424–429. https://doi.org/10.1016/S0196-0644(96)70011-0

[8] Ngan, T. (2021, January 25). Thị trường xe máy Việt Nam năm 2020 thiệt hại nặng nề nhất trong nhiều năm, không chỉ vì Covid-19. CafeF. Retrieved October 20, 2024, from https://cafef.vn/

[9] Nicolau, J. L., & Mas, F. (2006). The effect of price on tourist behavior. *Journal of Travel & Tourism Marketing*, 21(1), 5–20.

[10] Nikjoo, A. H., & Ketabi, M. (2015). The role of push and pull factors in the way tourists choose their destination. *Anatolia*, 26(4), 588–597.

[11] Pinch, P., & Reimer, S. (2012). Moto-mobilities: geographies of the motorcycle and motorcyclists. *Mobilities*, 7(3), 439–457.
[12] Prideaux, B., & Carson, D. (Eds.), (2010). Drive Tourism: Trends and Emerging Markets. Routledge.
[13] Scuttari, A. (2019). Cycling and Motorcycling Tourism. An analysis of physical, sensory, social, and emotional features of journey experiences. Eurac Research Bolzano.
[14] Reynolds, D. (1994). Food as a cultural experience: the role of culinary tourism. *Journal of Culinary Arts*, 5(2), 10–20.
[15] Scuttari, M. (2019). Interaction with nature: the role of motorcycle tourism. *Journal of Environmental Psychology*, 63, 1–9.
[16] Truitt, A. (2008). On the back of a motorbike: Middle-class mobility in Ho Chi Minh City, Vietnam. American Ethnologist, 35(1), 3–19. https://doi.org/10.1111/j.1548-1425.2008.00002.x
[17] Shih, H. Y. (2006). Network characteristics of drive tourism destinations: an application of network analysis in tourism. *Tourism Management*, 27(5), 1029–1039.
[18] Sykes, D. M., &. Kelly, K. G. (2014) Motorcycle tourism demand generators and dynamic interaction leisure. *International Journal of Culture, Tourism and Hospitality Research*, 8(1), 92–102.
[19] Vietnam National Administration of Tourism (VNAOT). (2016). Ho Chi Minh City Vespa tour. Retrieved October 8, 2024, from https://vietnam.travel
[20] Vietnam National Authority of Tourism. (2016, February 16). Tour du lịch khám phá thành phố Hồ Chí Minh bằng xe vespa. Vietnamtourism.gov.vn. Retrieved September 8, 2025, from https://vietnamtourism.gov.vn/post/19936
[21] Walker, L. (2011) Tourism and leisure motorcycle riding. In Prideaux, B., & Carson, D. (Eds), Drive Tourism: Trends and Emerging Markets, (pp. 146–158). New York, NY: Routledge.
[22] Misachi, J. (2019, August 14). Countries with the highest motorbike usage. World Atlas.
[23] Scherhag, K., Gross, S., & Sand, M. (2022). Adventures on two wheels–Comparative study of motorcycle adventure tourists in Germany, Austria and Switzerland. Zeitschrift für Tourismuswissenschaft, 14(3), 303-332. https://doi.org/10.1515/tw-2022-0017

9 Predictive analysis of stock prices based on social media data

Alaeddine Boubaker[a]

DBA Student, European School of Data Science and Technology, Switzerland

Abstract

Users of social media, such as those on Twitter, share their tweets to convey various reactions (opinions, emotions, ideas) about a subject. Our goal is to create a system that uses tweets to respond to inquiries such as: What are users' opinions about a company's stock? What is their view on the stock value of this company? Our study intends to conduct a sentiment analysis of tweets alongside real-time data related to that company, reflecting the status of its stock value and pricing. The objective of our research is to provide the XGBoost Algorithm with a training dataset, resulting in predictive analysis of a company's stock, enabling traders or individuals looking to buy or sell stocks to make informed decisions.

Keywords: Sentiment analysis, stocks, Twitter, XGBoost

Introduction

Forecasting the stock market is a task that can prove difficult for numerous researchers. This process is intended to assess the prospective value of a company's stock, assisting investors in making investment choices based on the analysis of the company's gains or losses, leading to decisions to buy or sell that stock. Sustainable investing represents a progression in investment practices, where investors prioritize environmental, social, social, and governance (ESG) aspects prior to making investment choices. Building on the technical and fundamental analysis of a company's stock, investors enhance their evaluation by assessing the company's sustainability. Social media platforms like Twitter, where millions of Tweets are shared each day, may play a role in the stock market prediction process. Twitter makes it easy for users to post their thoughts or emotions about a specific topic. Currently, Twitter users are allowed to compose tweets with a length of 280 characters. Consequently, the inquiry is: in what ways social media can assist investors in acquiring information and tackling the key issues concerning fundamental and technical analysis.

Literature Review

Most research focusing on the sentiment analysis of tweets aims to categorize them into three categories: positive, negative, and neutral. According to Ganthade et al. [2], the decision to "buy or sell" shares depend on the volume of positive and negative tweets. A study by Padmanayana and Bhavya [6] has shown that neutral tweets serve as a source of information that helps researchers gather more relevant data for fundamental and technical analysis. The classic approach before planning to buy or sell a company's stock involves conducting fundamental and technical analyses of that company. Research by Chakkera et al. [9] suggests that combining a sustainability analysis based on the evaluation of ESG metrics, with fundamental and technical analyses is relevant for predicting stock prices.

Research on preparing the data needed for fundamental and technical analysis and extracting relevant insights from sentiment analysis is still lacking, despite notable progress in stock market prediction based on Twitter sentiment analysis.

Research objectives

The primary objective of this study is to examine the impact of AI technology on assisting researchers in developing technical and fundamental analyses and predicting stock prices. Specifically, the research aims to:

[a]ala.boubaker@gmail.com

DOI: 10.4324/9781003739982-9

- Design a system that predicts the future stock value of a company based on a sustainability analysis and prepares data for analysis during the sentiment analysis.
- Assess how ESG metrics affect the development of stock prices.

Sentiment analysis
The tweet data is accessible through tweepy API, which includes username, text and timestamp. Company's stock market data are provided using Yahoo Finance API including close, open, low, adjusted and high values for a specific day Ganthade et al. [2]. Based on the historical data presented in Figure 9.1 for Nvidia's share values and Figure 9.2 for Tesla's share values, both companies have experienced an increase in stock prices over the past five years, making them more attractive to investors. Analyzing the Twitter data is one of the most challenging parts of our research because the combination of Twitter sentiment analysis and the company's stock data enables stakeholders to make informed choices about their future investments. For example, if most of the tweets are positive, the stock value of the company is likely to increase, and this is a good time to buy stocks and sell them later to make a profit. Conversely, if most of the tweets are negative, it indicates that the stock value of the company will decrease, and this is a bad time to buy stocks; it would be better for the trader to sell them to avoid future losses. Sentiment analysis involves handling tweet data. The processing of the data is divided into the following steps:

Optimization of the tweet data
Some characters must be removed from the tweet data, such as characters other than English characters. The designed system will manage tweets written in English; in this case, tweets written in foreign languages other than English are skipped from our design [2].

Tokenization of the Tweet data
The two characters @ and # play an important role in this process. The @ symbol enables us to know to whom the tweet may concern or refer. Furthermore, the # known as a hashtag determines the topics or thoughts. However, it might be unimportant. Every tweet is divided word by word, referred to as tokens. Furthermore, stop words such as {"he", "she", "a", "an", etc.} or symbols like {"&", "$", "/", "{", "}", etc.} also must be removed to execute the sentiment analysis [2].

Classification of the Tweet data
The tweet data are classified into three categories: positive, negative, and neutral. We will apply sentiment analysis to the Twitter data and group it into positive, negative, and neutral actions people display. Whenever a comment is optimistic or hints at positive feelings, it is seen as positive in this analysis. If the comment has a negative, unhappy attitude or if something is indicated with negative connections, it is considered a negative statement [6].

Collection of the company's data using the Yahoo finance API
Company data are fetched using the Yahoo Finance API. The adjacent closing values are so important that they are used by the model for the forecasting plan. Every stock is delivered with a unique ticker, which is used to identify the company in the database. Based on the ticker, start date, and current date, the company ' s data are available to the model [7].

Which business domain is affected by the technology?
Stock exchange prices and sentiment values are utilized by the portfolio management system that operates the model to predict long-term value and employs the expected values to make appropriate buy/sell decisions. Furthermore, banks and financial institutions could use this model to detect illegal activities such as money laundering and financial fraud based on the negative classification of tweets [8].

Forecasting the stock market is closely linked to the financial sector. Predictive models benefit investors and organizations in the finance industry by pushing them toward better investment choices and fewer risks. Tools from machine learning benefit people who must make financial decisions [5].

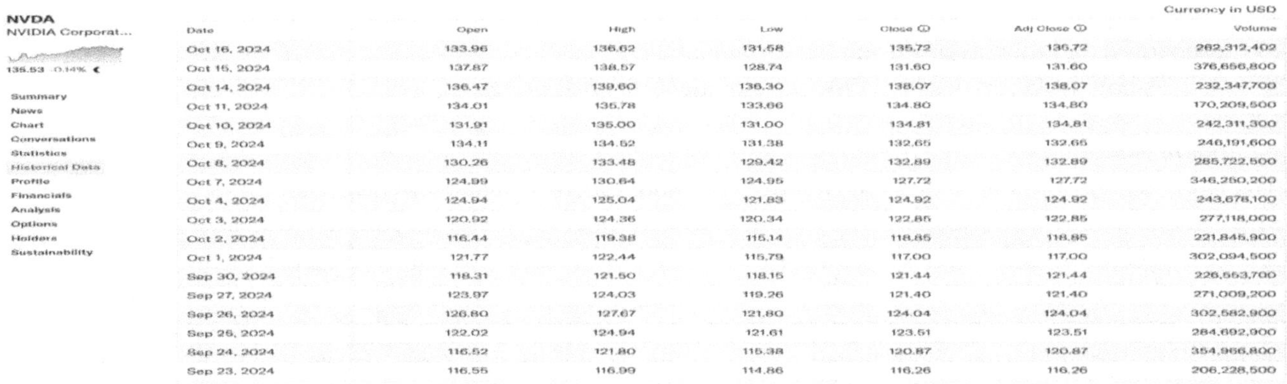

NVDA
NVIDIA Corporat...
135.53 -0.14%

Summary
News
Chart
Conversations
Statistics
Historical Data
Profile
Financials
Analysis
Options
Holders
Sustainability

Currency in USD

Date	Open	High	Low	Close	Adj Close	Volume
Oct 16, 2024	133.96	136.62	131.58	135.72	135.72	262,312,402
Oct 15, 2024	137.87	138.57	128.74	131.60	131.60	376,656,800
Oct 14, 2024	136.47	139.60	136.30	138.07	138.07	232,347,700
Oct 11, 2024	134.01	135.78	133.66	134.80	134.80	170,209,500
Oct 10, 2024	131.91	135.00	131.00	134.81	134.81	242,311,300
Oct 9, 2024	134.11	134.52	131.38	132.65	132.66	246,191,600
Oct 8, 2024	130.26	133.48	129.42	132.89	132.89	285,722,500
Oct 7, 2024	124.99	130.64	124.95	127.72	127.72	346,250,200
Oct 4, 2024	124.94	125.04	121.83	124.92	124.92	243,678,100
Oct 3, 2024	120.92	124.36	120.34	122.85	122.85	277,118,000
Oct 2, 2024	116.44	119.38	115.14	118.85	118.85	221,845,900
Oct 1, 2024	121.77	122.44	115.79	117.00	117.00	302,094,500
Sep 30, 2024	118.31	121.50	118.15	121.44	121.44	226,553,700
Sep 27, 2024	123.97	124.03	119.26	121.40	121.40	271,009,200
Sep 26, 2024	126.80	127.67	121.80	124.04	124.04	302,582,900
Sep 25, 2024	122.02	124.94	121.61	123.51	123.51	284,692,900
Sep 24, 2024	116.52	121.80	115.38	120.87	120.87	354,966,800
Sep 23, 2024	116.55	116.99	114.86	116.26	116.26	206,228,500

Figure 9.1 Nvidia's share value historical data between 19 September 2024 and 16 October 2024
Source: Investing.com [3]

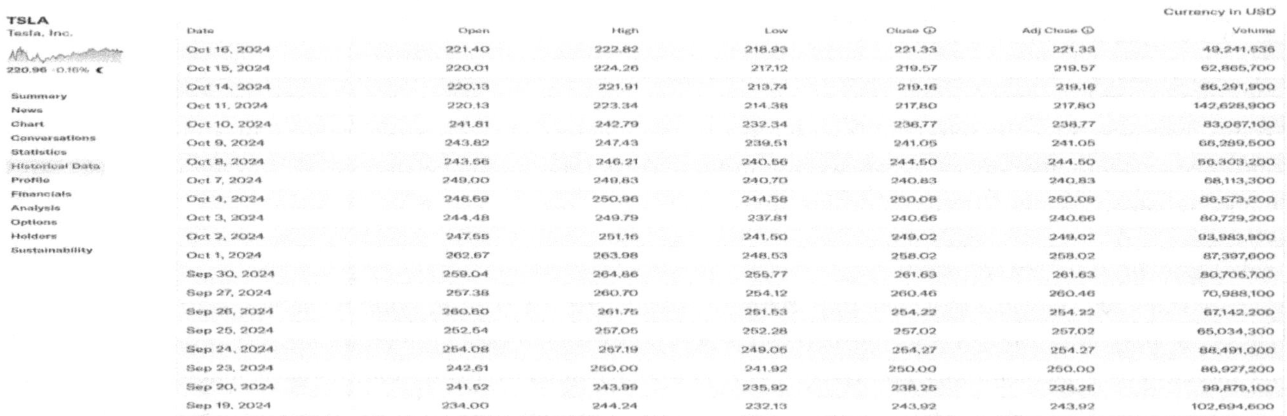

TSLA
Tesla, Inc.
220.96 -0.16%

Summary
News
Chart
Conversations
Statistics
Historical Data
Profile
Financials
Analysis
Options
Holders
Sustainability

Currency in USD

Date	Open	High	Low	Close	Adj Close	Volume
Oct 16, 2024	221.40	222.82	218.93	221.33	221.33	49,241,536
Oct 15, 2024	220.01	224.26	217.12	219.57	219.57	62,865,700
Oct 14, 2024	220.13	221.91	213.74	219.16	219.16	86,291,900
Oct 11, 2024	220.13	223.34	214.38	217.80	217.80	142,628,900
Oct 10, 2024	241.81	242.79	232.34	238.77	238.77	83,087,100
Oct 9, 2024	243.82	247.43	239.51	241.05	241.05	66,289,500
Oct 8, 2024	243.56	246.21	240.56	244.50	244.50	56,303,200
Oct 7, 2024	249.00	249.83	240.70	240.83	240.83	68,113,300
Oct 4, 2024	246.69	250.96	244.58	250.08	250.08	86,573,200
Oct 3, 2024	244.48	249.79	237.81	240.66	240.66	80,729,200
Oct 2, 2024	247.55	251.16	241.50	249.02	249.02	93,983,900
Oct 1, 2024	262.67	263.98	248.53	258.02	258.02	87,397,600
Sep 30, 2024	259.04	264.86	255.77	261.63	261.63	80,705,700
Sep 27, 2024	257.38	260.70	254.12	260.46	260.46	70,988,100
Sep 26, 2024	260.60	261.75	251.53	254.22	254.22	67,142,200
Sep 25, 2024	252.54	257.05	252.28	257.02	257.02	65,034,300
Sep 24, 2024	254.08	257.19	249.05	254.27	254.27	88,491,000
Sep 23, 2024	242.61	250.00	241.92	250.00	250.00	86,927,200
Sep 20, 2024	241.52	243.99	235.92	238.25	238.25	99,879,100
Sep 19, 2024	234.00	244.24	232.13	243.92	243.92	102,694,600

Figure 9.2 Tesla's share value historical data between 19 September 2024 and 16 October 2024
Source: Investing.com [4]

Table 9.1 Nvidia's and Tesla's overview.

Name of the company	Nvidia	Tesla
What does the company offer as a product?	GPU and Cloud solutions for Gaming users GPU for Data Centre supporting AI and Machine learning Hardware and Software for Self-Driving Technology Robotics and AI solutions	Clean energy company producing electric cars, solar panels and battery energy storage systems
CEO	Jensen Huang	Elon Musk

Source: Author

Case study: Nvidia vs. Tesla

Fundamental analysis

Nvidia is best known for its graphics processing units (GPUs) and cloud options aimed at players, as well as GPUs for data centres that run artificial intelligence (AI) and machine learning. Tesla, meanwhile, is a clean energy company that manufactures electric cars, solar panels, and battery energy storage systems

Table 9.2 Revenue and gains from Nvidia's stock between 2018 and 2023.

	2018	2019	2020	2021	2022	2023
Revenue	9,71	11,72	10,92	16,68	26,91	54
Gains	3,05	4,14	2,8	4,33	9,75	15

Source: Investing.com [3]

Table 9.3 Revenue and gains from Tesla's stock between 2018 and 2023.

	2018	2019	2020	2021	2022	2023
Revenue	21,46	24,58	31,53	53,82	81,46	96
Gains	-0,98	-0,86	0,72	5,52	12,58	15

Source: Investing.com [4]

Table 9.4 Company's market capitalization category.

Small Cap	Companies with market capitalization of up to 5 billion US dollars
Mid Cap	Companies with market capitalization between 5 and 10 billion US dollars
Large Cap	Companies with market capitalization between 10 and 200 billion US dollars
Blue Chips	Companies with market capitalization of more than 200 billion US dollars

Source: Author

Table 9.5 Nvidia's and tesla's market capitalization and caps.

Company	Market capitalization	Category (Caps)
Nvidia	2,98 trillion US dollars	Blue Chips
Tesla	832 billion US dollars	Blue Chips

Source: Author

in alignment with the company's mission of fostering sustainable transportation and renewable energy technology.

The Figure 9.1 shows that the stock price of Nvidia has increased from $4.76 on October 18, 2019, to $135.72 on October 16, 2024, achieving an increase of approximately 2,749% over the last five years. Meanwhile, Figure 9.2 indicates that the stock price of Tesla has risen from $15.52 on October 18, 2019, to $202.15 on October 16, 2024, resulting in an increase of about 1,219% during the same period.

In the Table 9.1 of Nvidia's gains and revenues, we can see that gains represented around 28% of revenue in 2023, compared to approximately 32% in 2018. In the Table 9.2 of Tesla's gains and revenues, we can see that gains accounted for approximately 15% of revenue in 2023, compared to 0% in 2018.

Market capitalization

Market capitalization is the total value of a company's stock, providing insight into how large the company is within its industry. Based on market capitalization and according to Table 9.3, companies can be categorized into four groups. According to Table 9.4, both Nvidia and Tesla are blue chips, which indicates that they both have strong positions in the world market. Nvidia, despite being one of the world's biggest technology companies, has a market cap of 2.98 trillion USD, dwarfing Tesla's 832 billion USD market cap.

Figure 9.3 Nvidia's share volume until October 2024
Source: Trading View [12]

Figure 9.4 Tesla's shares volume until October 2024
Source: TradingView [13]

Volume

Share volume refers to the number of shares traded during a specific period, providing insight into the liquidity level of a particular stock. In the case of Nvidia, Figure 9.1 indicates that the volume is 262.312 million shares, whereas Figure 9.2 shows that Tesla has a volume of 49.241 million shares.

Price-to-earnings ratio

This metric is used to evaluate a company's value by comparing its actual share price to its earnings per share (EPS). Divide the company's profit by the number of shares still available to the public to figure out earnings

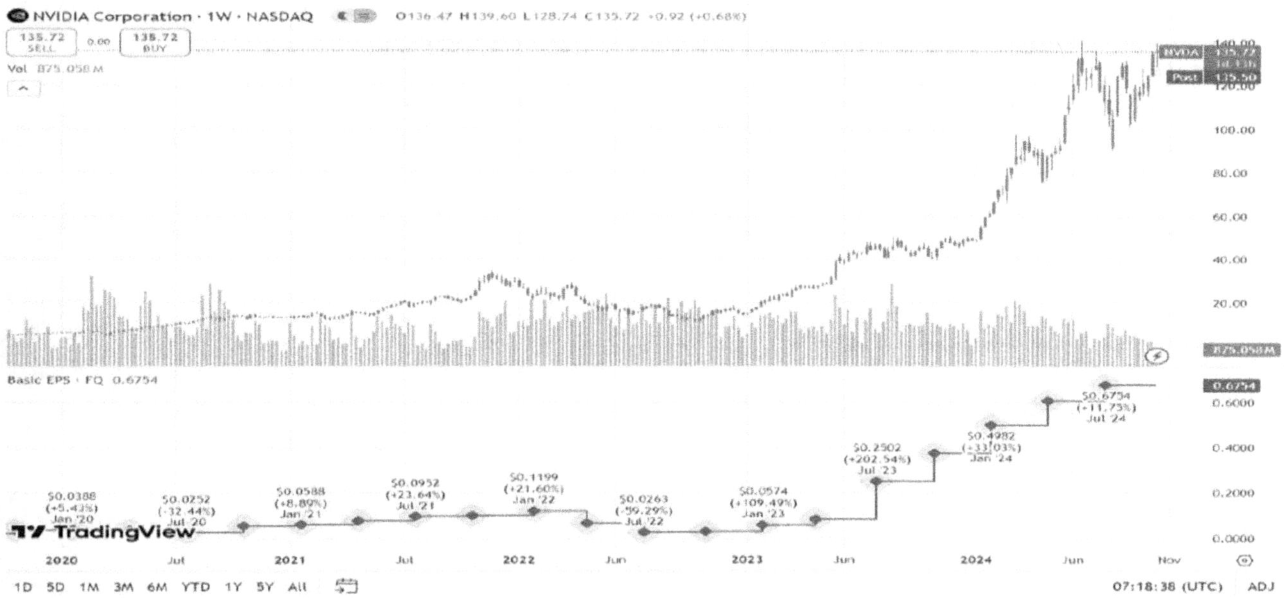

Figure 9.5 Nvidia's price-to-earnings ratio until October 2024
Source: Trading View [12]

Figure 9.6 Tesla's price-to-earnings ratio until October 2024
Source: Trading View [13]

per share. In the Figure 9.3, we can see that the EPS of Nvidia increased from $0.0388 in January 2020 to $0.6754 in July 2024. In contrast, In the Figure 9.4, we can see that the EPS of Tesla rose from $0.0389 in December 2019 to $2.4920 in December 2023 but then decreased to $0.4632 in June 2024.

The following list of questions helps researchers analyze the output of sentiment analysis and classify the data generated to assess the potential development of the company in the social media landscape.

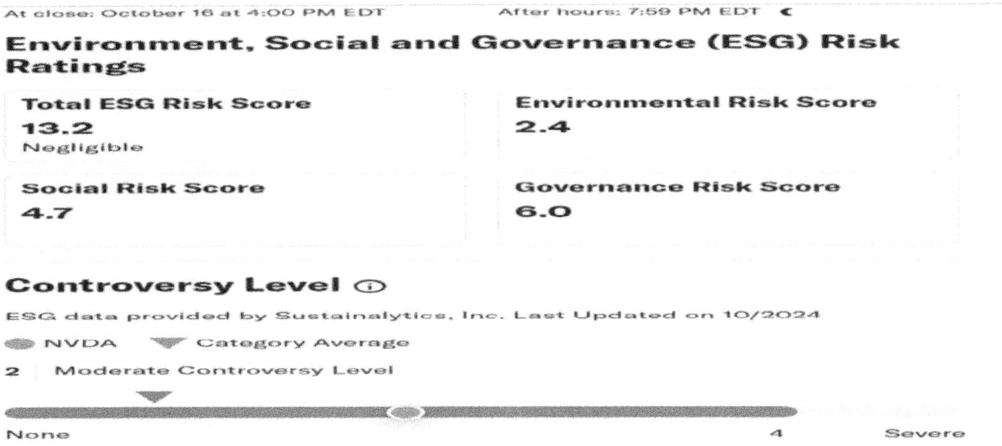

Figure 9.7 Nvidia's ESG risk ratings
Source: Yahoo Finance [14]

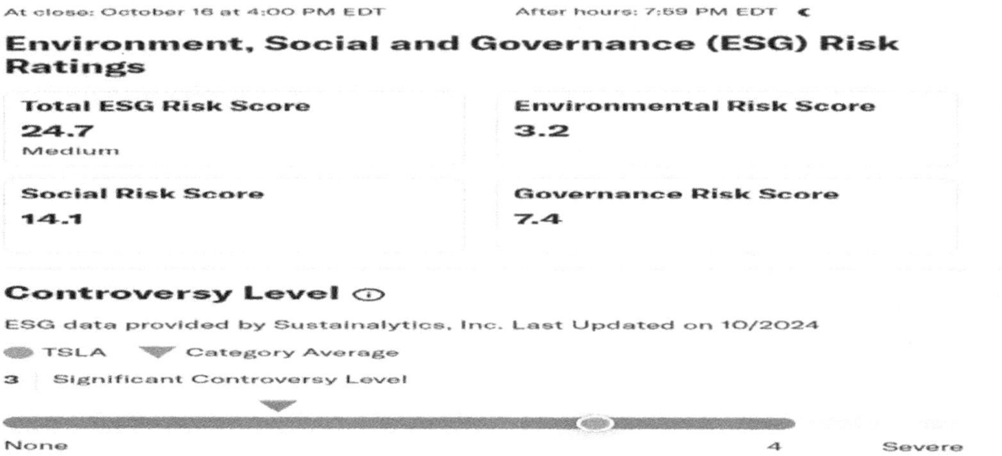

Figure 9.8 Tesla's ESG risk ratings
Source: Yahoo Finance [15]

Industry Growth
Does the company belong to a growing industry, such as artificial intelligence, renewable energy, or technology?

Product Innovation
Is the company offering innovative products or services? Could it increase its revenue and profits in the coming years?

Market Expansion
Does the company plan to enter new markets and create new customer segments?

Efficiency Enhancement
Is the company working on optimizing its business operations?

Company Mergers
Is the company planning to acquire other companies or access new markets?

Figure 9.9 Comparing Nvidia's share value with the moving average and the S&P 500 index in 2024
Source: Trading View [12]

Figure 9.10 Comparing tesla's share value with the moving average and the S&P 500 index in 2024
Source: Trading View [13]

Sustainability
ESG metrics assess a company's ESG activities. The outcomes of this assessment may help or hinder the company's financial results. The evaluation aims to categorize the companies into one of three risk levels: Low, Moderate, and High Risk. Low Risk companies effectively and efficiently manage ESG factors. Moderate Risk companies have some ESG issues but are also taking steps to minimize their risks. High

Risk companies face ESG-related challenges that could affect their image and performance. The total ESG Risk Score for Nvidia is 13.2, classifying it as a low-risk company. In contrast, Tesla has a score of 24.7, categorizing it as a moderate-risk company. Tesla is encountering issues related to social factors; as shown in the following ESG Rating chart, Tesla has a Social Risk Score of 14.1 compared to Nvidia's score of 4.7.

Technical analysis

The S&P 500 is a stock market index and economic indicator that reflects the performance of 500 companies from various sectors in the U.S. market. The Moving Average is used to analyse a stock 's performance over a period to identify its trend over time. We can observe in the Figure 9.5 that Nvidia's share value is above both the Moving Average and the S&P 500 index, indicating a positive trend and performance compared to the other 500 companies in the S&P 500. However, Figure 9.6 indicates that Tesla's share value is above the Moving Average but below the S&P 500 index, suggesting a negative trend and performance relative to the other companies in the index.

How Could the Business Domain Start with Technology

Naïve Bayes is most applied to sentiment analysis. This algorithm aims to give tweets one of three classifications: positive, negative, or neutral. Using Bayes' theorem, Naïve Bayes classifier forms Bayesian networks for a particular dataset. The dataset includes a feature for a class that can be separated from all other features. Let us suppose that an X has features that influence each other. Still, each sub-feature increases the likelihood that the object is X [10]. Naïve Bayes classifier predicts future results with the probability of different outcomes for an object. In sentiment analysis, we determine if a text contains a positive or negative thought. Written comments include a score that can serve as a dataset for sentiment analysis. The output generated from the sentiment analysis of tweets is in a Python dictionary format. The Naïve Bayes classifier, based on sentiment analysis, plays a significant role in supporting investors during their fundamental analysis. After categorizing the posts into three categories-positives, negatives, and neutrals-these posts can be analyzed more deeply to provide specific information related to price, CEO actions, branding, company secrets, and customers' willingness to change based on the sentiments expressed in the tweets. It can also analyze posts and news to address various questions regarding industry growth, product innovation, market expansion, efficiency enhancement, and company mergers, while gathering more specific information in terms of ESG metrics.

XGBoost is another classifier used to implement the prediction of stock prices. The output of the tweet sentiment analysis conducted by the Naïve Bayes classifier, along with the company data fetched from the Yahoo Finance API, market capitalization, volume, price -to-earnings ratio, moving average, and S&P 500 index, will serve as input for the XGBoost classifier [6]. A classifier is created by combining a series of tree models in the XGBoost decision tree boosting model. Each new tree is trained on the previous model, so the last results are adjusted each time a new tree is built. Finally, the scores corresponding to several trees obtained through training are summed up to provide the final predicted value of the stock [16].

Advantages of Using Technology

The Naïve Bayes classifier is one of the simplest classification algorithms, helping to create effective machine learning models that can lead the model to production. Padmanayana and Bhavya [6], XGBoost is a one of the most powerful machine learning algorithms. Padmanayana and Bhavya [6] opined that their research has greatly benefitted from using these two powerful merged algorithms, which helped in creating an asset for the stakeholder before planning to buy or sell a stock.

Conclusion

Twitter, as a social media platform, is a powerful source of millions of data points used in our research to perform a sentiment analysis based on the Naïve Bayes classifier. The data generated, accompanied by the company's data fetched from the Yahoo Finance API, contributes to the training of the algorithm, generating the prediction of the stock's value. The challenge in this research lies in how to effectively classify and categorize the output generated by sentiment analysis. This aims to assess how the company is developing in various areas: industry growth, product innovation, market expansion, efficiency enhancement, company mergers, and sustainability. This research could be further developed by investigating additional social media platforms, such as Facebook. The Facebook Prophet Tool, developed by the Meta Science Team as open-source software for forecasting research and predicting the stock market, would be helpful for advancing this study.

References

[1] A. Ganthade, E. Kulkarni, A. Agrawal, S. Garodia, Lahane and P, (2022). Stock market prediction based on Twitter, *International Journal of Advances in Engineering and Management (IJAEM)*, 4(5), 1087–1092.

[2] V. Padmanayana and K. Bhavya, (2021). Stock Market Prediction Using Twitter Sentiment Analysis, *International Journal of Scientific Research in Computer Science, Engineering and Information Technology (IJSRCSEIT)*, 7(4), 265–270.

[3] S. Chakkera, A. Anderson, B. White and J. Almasan, (2023). Analyzing the sentiment of tweets regarding sustainability practices to predict stock performance, *Journal of Student Research*, 12(4), 2023.

[4] N. Patil, R. Mutha, V. Pandey, R. Patil and V. Mane, (2022). SMAP-A Stock Market Analysis and Prediction Web Application, *ITM Web of Conferences (a peer-reviewed proceedings journal by EDP Sciences),* 44, 03038.

[5] Investing.com, NVIDIA Corp historical data. Investing.com, 16 October 2024. [Online]. Available: https://www.investing.com/equities/nvidia-corp-historical-data. [Accessed 16 October 2024].

[6] Investing.com, Tesla Motors historical data. Investing.com, 16 October 2024. [Online]. Available: https://www.investing.com/equities/tesla-motors-historical-data. [Accessed 16 October 2024].

[7] Z. Peng, (2019). Stocks analysis and prediction using big data analytics, *In 2019 international conference on intelligent transportation, big data & smart City (ICITBS)*, 309–312.

[8] A. Josey and N. Amrutha, (2024). Stock market prediction, *Indian Journal of Data Mining (IJDM)*, 4(1), 34–37.

[9] J. Chen, (2022). Market capitalization defined: Mega cap, large cap, mid cap, small cap, 31 March 2022. [Online]. Available: https://www.investopedia.com/investing/market-capitalization-defined/. [Accessed 16 October 2024].

[10] StatMuse, Nvidia market cap in October 2024, 16 October 2024. [Online]. Available: https://www.statmuse.com/money/ask/nvidia-market-cap-in-october-2024. [Accessed 16 October 2024].

[11] StatMuse, What is the market cap of Tesla October 2024, 16 October 2024. [Online]. Available: https://www.statmuse.com/money/ask/what-is-the-market-cap-of-tesla-october-2024. [Accessed 16 October 2024].

[12] TradingView, NVIDIA Corp, 16 October 2024. [Online]. Available: https://www.tradingview.com/chart/cDykJAL3/?symbol=NASDAQ%3ANVDA. [Accessed 16 October 2024].

[13] TradingView, Tesla Inc, 16 October 2024. [Online]. Available: https://www.tradingview.com/chart/cDykJAL3/?symbol=NASDAQ%3ATSLA. [Accessed 16 October 2024].

[14] Y. Finance, NVIDIA Corporation (NVDA) sustainability, 16 October 2024. [Online]. Available: https://finance.yahoo.com/quote/NVDA/sustainability/. [Accessed 16 October 2024].

[15] Y. Finance, Tesla, Inc. (TSLA) sustainability, 16 October 2024. [Online]. Available: https://finance.yahoo.com/quote/TSLA/sustainability/. [Accessed 16 October 2024].

[16] D. Mahajan Shubhrata, V. Deshmukh Kaveri, R. Thite Pranit, Y. Samel Bhavana and P. J. Chate, (2016). Stock market prediction and analysis using Naïve Bayes, *International Journal on Recent and Innovation Trends in Computing and Communication*, 4(11), 121–124.

[17] Y. Yang, Y. Wu, P. Wang and X. Jiali, (2021). Stock price prediction based on xgboost and lightgbm, *In E3s web of conferences*, 275, 01040.

10 Emerging trends in sustainable business models and practices: a bibliometric analysis

Udhaya Rekha, R.[1,a], *T. Shirmila*[2,b] *and G. David Abishek*[3,c]

[1]Pursuing (PDF) in Commerce, Lincoln University College, Selangor, Malaysia

[2]Associate Professor, Research Supervisor and Guide, Department of Commerce, Madras Christian College, Tambaram, Chennai (Affiliated to University of Madras, Chennai), India

[3]Ph.D. Research Scholar, Department of Commerce, Madras Christian College, Tambaram, Chennai (Affiliated to University of Madras, Chennai), India

Abstract

With the rising focus on sustainability, this trend has led businesses to develop new models that make them profitable by implementing ecological and social objectives. This bibliometric analysis explores changing research trends in sustainable business models and practices while revealing significant publication trends, productive authors, and novel thematic areas. This paper conducts a bibliometric analysis to identify the leading authors and journals, as well as map collaboration networks in the field using data collected between 2015 and 2024. We can also visualize the collaboration pattern and thematic evolution by approaching co-authorship network analysis, citation analysis, and keyword co-occurrence analysis over a decade. These discoveries provide a deep summary of the area with known gaps, facing research angles, and highlighting an increasing position of technology in sending. These findings deliver key implications for researchers, policymakers, and practitioners striving to foster a sustainable business operating model throughout diverse industries.

Keywords: Bibliometric analysis, business strategy, co-occurrence analysis, sustainability practices, sustainable business models

Introduction

Global regulatory frameworks, increasing consumer awareness, and global environmental concerns have made sustainability a crucial element of business strategy. Sustainable practices that cause businesses to think in innovative ways of economic viability that are socially and environmentally responsible. The therefore-yielding sustainability policy development domain in green finance, circular economy, responsible supply chains, and sustainability reporting has become a focal point for scholars and practitioners. For example, Bocken et al. [1] and Geissdoerfer et al. [2] highlight how new business model innovations and circular economy principles have become a strategic need for corporations. Using bibliometric analysis (employing tools such as Matplotlib and NetworkX for Python), this study analyses sustainable business model research from 2015–2024. We perform a systematic analysis of publication trends, thematic clusters, and collaboration networks to reveal salient research trends and identify prominent contributors in this field of study. The changeover of SDG, the effect of evolving technologies (e.g., artificial intelligence), and interdisciplinary connections in sustainability research are also assessed. This analysis aids in providing a structured bibliometric pathway to understand this nascent research area and identify the critical gaps that need expanding upon in future work.

Research objectives

- 2015 – 2024: A longitudinal analysis of sustainable business model research.
- Goal: To find out the top authors, journals, and institutions in the research on sustainable business models.
- To analyse the main themes and links in sustainability literature.
- Hence, to establish a robust bibliometric framework for further studies on in sustainability.

[a]rekha161987@yahoo.com, [b]shirmilastanley@mcc.edu.in, [c]davidabishek0822@gmail.com

DOI: 10.4324/9781003739982-10

Literature Review

Sustainable business model research: A review of the literature One such area has been green finance, which has been the subject of several studies on sustainable investing strategies, environmental, social and governance (ESG) indicators and carbon credits. Yet, researchers have delved into the means by which policy plays a role in pushing sustainability standards further, whilst maintaining profitability and compliance in a globalized world [4]. There has also been a considerable amount of research on the circular economy, especially in terms of waste reduction, eco efficiency, and closed loop supply chains. Sustainable companies are also found to experience increased brand value, improved regulatory compliance, and greater long-term resilience [3].

The increase in digital transformation in sustainability has also led to research on blockchain-based carbon trading, AI-driven ESG analytics, and smart sustainable supply chains. The growing dependence on automated sustainability reporting has, however, initiated critical conversations around data transparency, the use of AI for the ethical reporting of these corporate deposits and the standardization of ESG disclosures [5]. These studies point to the emergence of technology-sustainability intersections, where advances in pursuing data analytics and information systems are placed at the core of advancing corporate sustainability practices.

Methodology

Data collection

We used bibliometric analysis to review 635 research articles on sustainable business models published between 2015 and 2024. On February 6, 2024, the dataset was retrieved from academic databases (Scopus and Web of Science) according to a predetermined set of search criteria applied to titles, abstracts, and keywords of articles. This rich dataset provides the basis to explore sustainability research trends in the past 10 years.

A dual analytical approach was adopted. (1) the publication and citation structure of the literature was evaluated to reveal temporal trends in research output and to determine key impact publications. Figures showing the annual number of publications related to sustainability served to visualize these findings.

Secondly, we classified the literature into essential thematic domains of sustainability – circular economy, green finance, ESG strategies, digital transformation in sustainability, among others – to map diverse disciplinary contributions redefining sustainable business model research.

Data overview

The search criteria included keywords such as "Sustainable Business Models," "Green Finance," "ESG Strategies," "Circular Economy," "Sustainability Reporting," "Carbon Trading," "Corporate Sustainability," and "Digital Transformation in Sustainability," appearing in the title, abstract, or keywords of articles. This query returned 635 relevant articles (2015–2024). Table 10.1 summarizes the breakdown of articles by major topic/domain:

Coded each article against the domains based on its focus. This classification assisted in uncovering the range of research domains contributing to sustainable business model literature. Importantly, literature on all three domains – sustainable business models and circular economy as a combination – comes to a significant share, indicating a higher research interest in the core of business model innovation (resource efficiency).

Table 10.1 Categorization of the bibliometric dataset by key sustainability domains.

Title, Abstract, or Keyword	Number of Articles
Sustainable Business Models	250
Circular Economy	140
Green Finance & ESG	105
Digital Transformation in Sustainability	80
Policy & Regulations	60
Total	635

Source: Author

Emerging domains (e.g., digital transformation in sustainability) represent a less represented, but notable, portion of the research coverage.

Experiments and Results

Publication trend analysis (2015-2024)

The publication trend analysis (Figure 10.1) highlights a steady increase in research on sustainable business models over the past decade. In the early years from 2015 to 2017, the number of publications remained relatively low, indicating limited academic focus on structured sustainability frameworks. Between 2018 and 2020, there was a gradual increase, with publications rising to 28 in 2020, suggesting an emerging interest in corporate sustainability strategies.

A significant surge occurred in 2021 and 2022, where the number of publications increased to 45 in 2021 and 85 in 2022. This growth aligns with the increasing adoption of ESG regulations, circular economy principles, and digital sustainability solutions. The sharpest rise in 2023, with publications reaching 110, reflecting a paradigm shift toward AI-driven sustainability reporting, corporate accountability measures, and policy-driven green finance models (Figure 10.1).

Top 10 Authors in Sustainable Business Models

The analysis identified the top contributors to sustainable business model research, (Figure 10.2) highlighting ten authors with the highest number of publications and citations in the dataset. Svensson emerged as the most prolific author, followed by Di Vaio, Mangla, Padin, Lozano, and others. Collectively, their research has significantly influenced topics like corporate sustainability strategy, circular economy models, and ESG reporting.

- Svensson has the highest publication count, with influential work on business ethics and transformative sustainability models.
- Di Vaio specializes in the intersection of sustainability and digital transformation, contributing to our understanding of how technology drives sustainable business strategies.
- Mangla has extensively researched sustainable supply chain management and its role in business model innovation.
- Padin and Lozano are recognized for their contributions to corporate sustainability adoption and policy-driven green business practices.

Co-authorship network analysis (discussed below) suggests that these top authors frequently collaborate across institutions, particularly within Europe and North America. Their high citation counts underscore their global influence in shaping sustainability discussions.

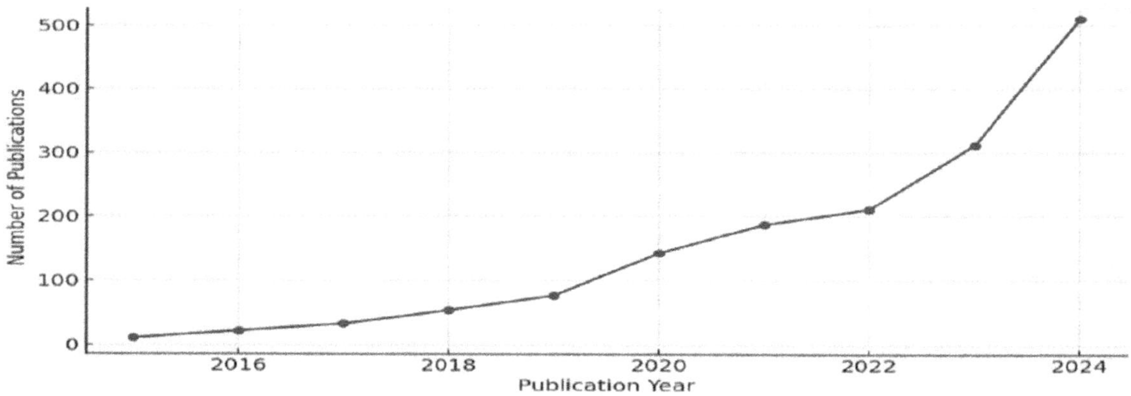

Figure 10.1 Publication trend analysis (2015-2024)
Source: Author

Keyword co-occurrence analysis

A keyword co-occurrence analysis was performed to identify dominant themes in sustainable business model research. The term frequency and co-occurrence were visualized (e.g., via a word cloud in Figure 10.3), revealing key areas of academic focus. The most frequently occurring keywords in the literature include "sustainability," "business model," "innovation," "supply chain," "firms," "companies," "practice," and "impact."

These frequent terms indicate that sustainability research is strongly linked to business model innovation, corporate practices, and strategic impact. The prominence of "innovation" suggests significant interest in new approaches to sustainability, such as technological advancements, digital sustainability initiatives, and novel business frameworks. The prominence of "supply chain" reflects a major research focus on sustainable supply chain management, including resource efficiency and ethical sourcing practices.

The frequent occurrence of terms like "firms," "companies," and "industry" emphasizes the practical, organizational perspective of much sustainability research, indicating that scholars are examining how businesses across various industries adopt sustainable models. Additionally, terms such as "relationship," "impact," and

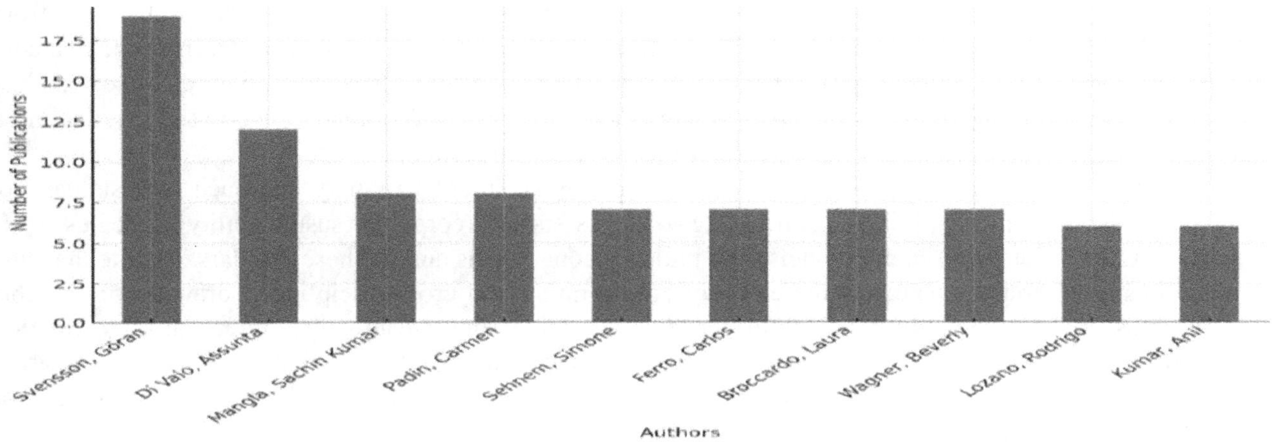

Figure 10.2 Top 10 Authors in sustainable business models
Source: Author

Figure 10.3 Keyword co-occurrence word cloud for sustainable business models research
Source: Author

"stakeholder" imply that researchers are investigating the broader effects of sustainability strategies on stakeholders (e.g., investors, customers, policymakers). The presence of words like "framework" and "methodology" suggests ongoing efforts to develop structured approaches for assessing and implementing sustainable business models. Finally, keywords like "challenge" and "strategy" hint at research addressing the barriers and complexities of integrating sustainability, such as financial constraints, policy enforcement issues, and organizational resistance to change.

Co-authorship network analysis

The co-authorship network analysis (Figure 10.4) sheds light on the collaborative structure of research in sustainable business models during 2015–2024. In this network, each node represents an author, and each connecting line (edge) represents a co-authorship relationship. Densely connected clusters of nodes indicate strong collaboration groups, whereas isolated nodes represent authors who have worked mostly independently.

The network analysis shows that while Svensson and Mangla are among the most prolific authors in this field, their positions in the network are relatively isolated, suggesting fewer direct co-authorships with other top scholars in this dataset. This may indicate that their contributions, though influential, often stem from independent or institution-specific research efforts rather than large collaborative projects. In contrast, a core group of researchers – including Di Vaio, Padin, Lozano, and Broccardo – forms a highly interconnected cluster. These scholars frequently co-author papers and engage in cross-institutional collaborations, reflecting a tight-knit research community in some areas of sustainability scholarship.

The strong connectivity within this core cluster suggests an interdisciplinary approach to sustainability research, with these authors jointly contributing to topics such as corporate sustainability strategies, ESG frameworks, and circular economy models. The multiple connections among these scholars indicate that sustainable business model research is increasingly collaborative and cross-disciplinary, drawing on insights from business management, environmental science, and public policy. Meanwhile, the partial fragmentation observed (e.g., Svensson and Mangla operating more independently) highlights that some leading researchers may be pursuing distinct agendas or working within specific collaborations, pointing to opportunities for broader engagement across currently separate clusters.

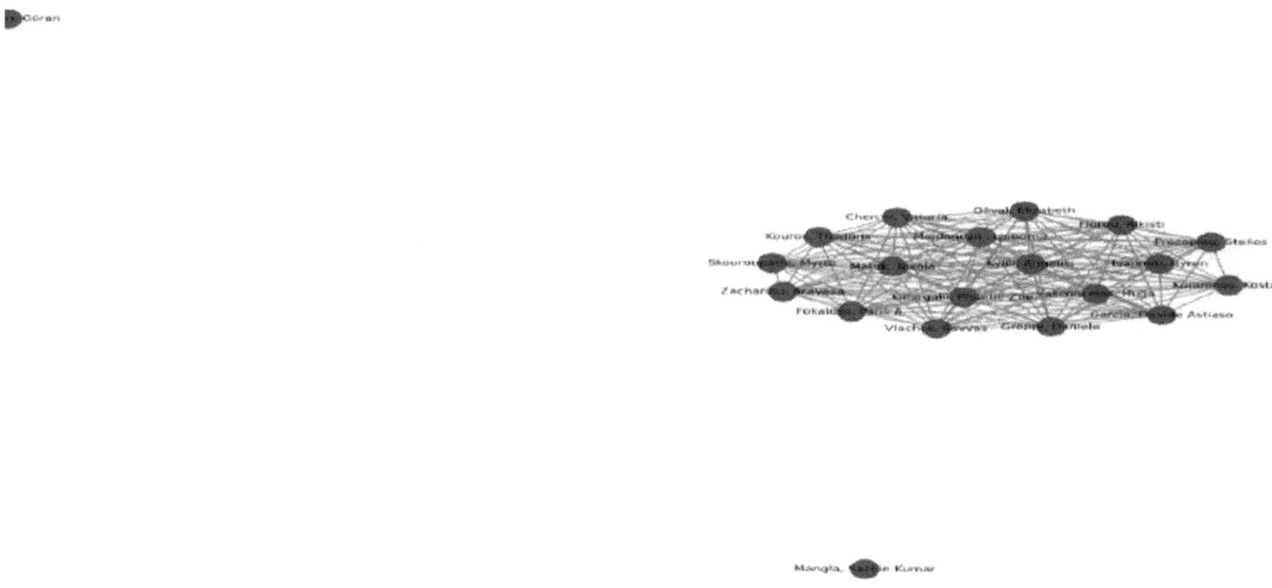

Figure 10.4 Co-authorship network analysis
Source: Author

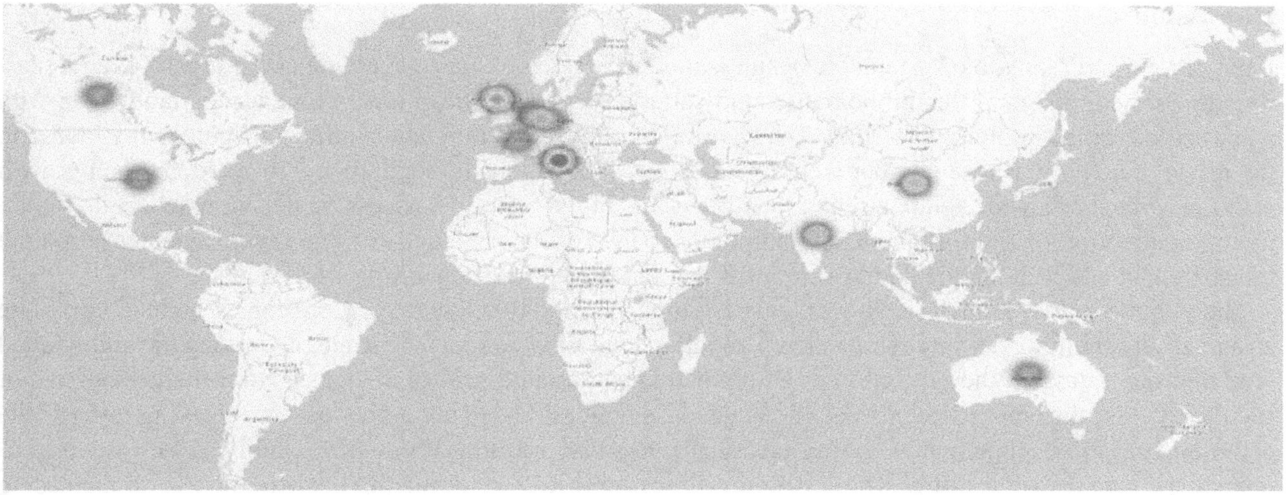

Figure 10.5 Global research distribution analysis
Source: Author

Global research distribution heatmap

A global distribution analysis was conducted to identify the geographic spread of research output in sustainable business models (2015–2024). The results were visualized as a world heatmap (Figure 10.5), where the intensity indicates the volume of publications originating from each country. Brighter areas on the map correspond to higher research output.

The analysis reveals that Germany, the United States, the United Kingdom, and China are among the most active contributors to this field, together accounting for approximately 60% of the total publications in our dataset. Germany leads with over 120 publications, aligning with the country's strong commitment to circular economy policies, robust ESG regulations, and corporate sustainability strategies. Germany's federal sustainability plans and industry initiatives have likely fostered significant academic output. The United States follows with around 110 publications, focusing largely on corporate sustainability strategies, responsible investment, and AI-driven ESG assessments. Numerous research collaborations between leading U.S. universities (such as Harvard, MIT, and Stanford) and industry partners have influenced sustainable business model frameworks and driven scholarly interest.

The United Kingdom contributed approximately 95 publications, bolstered by policy initiatives (like net-zero carbon goals and enhanced corporate governance regulations) and the presence of renowned academic institutions (Oxford, Cambridge, London School of Economics) that emphasize sustainability reporting and green finance. China produced roughly 85 publications, reflecting its growing emphasis on green finance, carbon neutrality commitments, and sustainable industrial practices. The Chinese government's policy goals (e.g., peaking carbon emissions by 2030 and achieving carbon neutrality by 2060) have spurred academic research in areas such as renewable energy policy and sustainable supply chain management.

Beyond these leading nations, other countries show moderate but notable research activity. For instance, India (around 65 publications), Canada (58), France (52), and Australia (49) have emerging contributions, often integrating ESG frameworks and corporate sustainability policies within their business contexts. However, the analysis highlights an uneven global distribution: developing regions, particularly parts of South America and Africa, account for less than 10% of the total publications. This disparity suggests that sustainability research output is concentrated in high-income countries with established regulatory and academic infrastructures, while many emerging economies remain underrepresented in the scholarly discourse.

This imbalance in global research output indicates a need for future efforts to broaden participation in sustainability research. Encouraging international collaborations and capacity-building initiatives in underrepresented regions could help bridge the knowledge gap and support global sustainability goals.

Discussion

It may prove surprising, but sustainable business model research has been evolving at a fast pace over the last decade, as the findings of this bibliometric study attest. We see a gradual increase in academic interest, with a marked increase in output post-2020. The analysis of publication timeline confirms a significant increase in the research activity, whose number went from just 28 publications up to 2020 to 110 in 2023. Such growth is in the context of a wider global trend towards sustainability-focused business models in practice, driven by the mass adoption of ESG principles by corporates; new regulatory mandates that require greater corporate transparency; and technological innovation that facilitates better sustainability assessments.

The citation network analysis shows what is going into today's literature. Core topics include corporate sustainability frameworks, circular economy adoption, and ESG compliance strategies among the highly cited works in our dataset. When the citation graph of frequently cited studies is viewed from the perspective of such a network, the emergence of a common agenda is noticeable – many individuals are working towards the common goal and in alignment with these seminal works that prioritize economic viability as well as environmental and social responsibility. These commonalities speak of a maturing field, where there is an increasing consensus on relevant theoretical constructs that matter (here, the triple bottom line and sustainability-oriented innovation).

Our analysis of co-authorship shows that sustainability research is getting more and more collaborative. The principal authors (Svensson, Di Vaio, Mangla, and Lozano) create recognizable co-authorship groups as a significant body of evidence of cooperative behavior that spans across disciplines, encompassing relations of management entrepreneurship, technological innovation, and environmental science. By bringing together diverse expertise and being built on trust, these collaborative networks have likely catalyzed knowledge development aimed at solving complex sustainability issues. One important detail is that some of the leading researchers operate in relative isolation (as represented by a few isolated nodes in the co-authorship network). That said, there is still a chance to enhance engagement among leading influencers in the professional field. Larger partnerships between today's separate research groups might catalyze new insights and unify approaches to sustainable business model innovation

The keyword co-occurrence analysis highlights the main themes and emerging interests in the literature. And the most frequent descriptors here, such as "sustainability," "business model," "innovation," "supply chain," and "ESG," affirm that integrating sustainability into core business strategy and operations remains the central preoccupation. The prevalence of tech-related keywords (such as "AI", "blockchain") found in the more recent publications shows an increasing interest in digital solutions for sustainability, indeed, emerging technologies are being explored as tools to enhance data analysis, reporting, and implementation of sustainability initiatives. This implies that future business models built on sustainability would be influenced by digital technology (i.e., adjust with the data ethics and interoperability of the system), ensuring, for example, a clear and unbiased AI in sustainability reporting (as the recent authors have indicated).

Research shows global distribution with both leadership and gaps. Advanced economies in Europe, North America, and East Asia produce the vast majority of academic output and lead the way with many sustainability frameworks due to robust institutional support and policy environments. The low output of developing regions, on the other hand, clearly points to the need for more inclusive research efforts. This presents a risk that sustainability solutions and business model innovations are being developed in silos without enough input from or applicability for emerging markets. The disparity highlights the need for more international collaboration and support for researchers from underrepresented areas of the world to develop practices and share knowledge on sustainability at the global scale, rather than being concentrated in a few areas.

Future Research Directions

While a growing body of literature is emerging on the relationship between sustainable business models and sustainability, there remain many critical areas that need to be investigated to move research in sustainable business models forward:

- AI and Sustainability Assessments: Future research should explore the ethical implications of AI-driven sustainability assessments and how reliable those assessments are. With more companies using artificial intelligence and machine learning to automate ESG assessments, there are questions over data accuracy, transparency, and the potential for bias in automated decision-making. Research may investigate frameworks for ensuring that AI tools improve (not hinder) the quality and trustworthiness of sustainability data
- Regulatory Issues Surrounding ESG Compliance: Although developed countries have set the ESG reporting standards as well as a regulatory framework, emerging economies have several loopholes in implementation and enforcement. Further studies are required on how different international agreements or policy interventions may uniquely target regional contexts to empower sustainability governance. This involves investigating the extent to which ESG benchmarks travel across geographies, as well as how local contexts impact adherence and performance.
- Sector-Specific Sustainable Practices: There were gaps for more sector-specific analyses of sustainability. Each industry (manufacturing, logistics, finance, etc.) has its own problems in implementing sustainable practices. In short, targeted research will help to identify barriers and success factors for corporations in their respective industries, allowing for the formulation of sector approaches for driving corporate ESG performance. Certainly, businesses can benchmark against peers and embrace best practices that are relevant to their industry.
- Overcoming research deficits in developing economies: There is a need for more global sustainability research efforts in underrepresented regions, especially regions in parts of Africa and South America. These could involve cross-border collaborations on research, funding and training opportunities for scholars in developing countries, and case studies on sustainability transitions in developing country contexts. Exploring more diverse economic and cultural environments in future research will improve the global relevance of sustainable business models and address knowledge inequities.

Conclusion

Through the extensive coverage of the data from 2015 to 2024, this study presents a comprehensive bibliometric analysis of sustainable business models and sustainable business practices, identifying key trends, prominent researchers, and emerging thematic areas in the literature. The sharp increase in academic output post-2020 is indicative of a heightened focus, both in academia and industry, on the integration of sustainability into corporate decision making. Sustainability research has matured through 'standing on the shoulders of giants' as documented by citation networks, and increasing collaboration and interdisciplinarity of the field as depicted in co-authorship and keyword analysis.

At the same time, the results highlight the unequal global distribution of sustainability research. Leading countries, such as Germany, the US, the UK, and China, all of which currently dominate these knowledge production metrics and research agenda-setting, while the contributions from developing economies remain low. This suggests that sustainability scholarship must become more inclusive if we expect knowledge and innovation to diffuse globally. Overcoming regulatory hurdles, understanding the growing pains of AI-driven sustainability tools, and adapting ESG frameworks to emerging markets are all important areas for future exploration.

To sum up, the field of sustainable business model research is evolving rapidly. As supportive policies, technology innovations, and interdisciplinary research endeavors integrate, the sustainable business practices landscape will evolve. Through these developments, corporate strategies and global sustainability governance will increasingly converge, with businesses and researchers collaborating to meld profit with pressing environmental and social imperatives.

References

[1] Bocken, N. M. P., Short, S. W., Rana, P., & Evans, S. (2014). A literature and practice review to develop sustainable business model archetypes. *Journal of Cleaner Production*, 65, 42–56.

[2] Geissdoerfer, M., Savaget, P., Bocken, N. M. P., & Hultink, E. J. (2017). The circular economy – a new sustainability paradigm? *Journal of Cleaner Production*, 143, 757–768.
[3] Lozano, R. (2020). Analysing the use of tools, initiatives, and approaches to promote sustainability in corporations. *Corporate Social Responsibility and Environmental Management*, 27(2), 982–998.
[4] Lüdeke-Freund, F., Gold, S., & Bocken, N. M. P. (2019). A review and typology of circular economy business model patterns. *Journal of Industrial Ecology*, 23(1), 36–61.
[5] Svensson, G., & Wagner, B. (2015). Implementing and managing economic, social and environmental efforts of business sustainability: propositions for measurement and structural models. *Management of Environmental Quality: An International Journal*, 26(2), 195–213.

11 AI driven digital marketing transforming digital landscape

Sonal Kapoor[a] *and Shruti Agrawal*[b]
Assistant Professor, DAV PG College, Varanasi, India

Abstract

Artificial intelligence (AI) and machine learning (ML) have rapidly progressed and are now influencing several industries, including digital marketing. Today, AI advancements give us an amazing chance to update how marketing and customer communication are done. AI can now change many parts of society, such as marketing. Because of artificial intelligence, companies can now analyze a huge amount of online customer data, understand emerging trends, and make good decisions. This study investigates how AI affects marketing by allowing businesses to enhance their ad strategies, give better consumer experiences, and boost their marketing outcomes.

With AI, businesses can deliver personalized messages, support customers with chatbots, sort audiences for targeting, and suggest online products. AI is very important for digital marketing because it helps change how we study consumer behavior and approach marketing. With AI, companies can choose customers they wish to reach, handle marketing according to data, and revise their messaging. Today, artificial intelligence supports marketing efforts through email, social media, content marketing, and communication. People working in digital marketing need to know how AI affects the field to have a strong impact.

Keywords: Artificial intelligence, chatbots, customer segmentation, digital marketing

Introduction

AI has swiftly altered the trends of the modern digital world and contributes significantly to consumer planning and competition [1]. Predictive marketing has helped us better understand the choices consumers make when shopping. Businesses are also using AI to gather consumer information to deliver goods and services suited to their clients. Operational marketing practices now use AI to target customers, examine customer information, and develop and select ads. However, businesses will likely make better decisions by applying computer science, knowledge representation, and intelligent algorithms to decision-making.

To help marketers understand their target audience better, this article looks closely at the impact of AI in digital marketing. Furthermore, outlining several methods of existing customer statistics, it acknowledges the importance of AI and predictive marketing for understanding modern and changing consumer behavior. The influence of artificial intelligence on digital marketing has been significant. To promote a range of products and services, digital marketers use electronic platforms [17, 26]. Fast technological progress leads many software developers to depend more on AI to improve marketing and succeed in the digital sphere. This paper seeks to explain how AI transforms how businesses work with their consumers, market their products, and grow in the digital era, drawing from recent research and industry practices.

Digital marketing

"Computerised promoting" is the term used to describe advertising that primarily uses the internet to reach the target audience through various innovative media channels [23]. It covers multiple platforms, including displaying content, SEO, email campaigns, web-based ads, adaptable marketing, and others, designed to help connect with consumers. A typical customer gathers information from the radio, TV, PC, tablet, mobile phone, and other traditional media. Along with advertising on TV, in newspapers, and on billboards, they depend on digital channels to help attract new buyers and to maintain contact with current clients.

[a]sonal.03dec@gmail.com, [b]ss.agrawal2011@gmail.com
DOI: 10.4324/9781003739982-11

Why is AI booming now?
Big data sets becoming more accessible has largely contributed to this. The amount of information created per second has increased exponentially as a result of the spread of technology and its increased accessibility. It is now more feasible to store these data sets on the cloud due to the decreased cost of storage.

The development of more potent computer systems is another element driving AI's expansion. Additionally, the COVID-19 pandemic has sped up firms' use of AI. Many businesses were forced to switch to remote work due to the pandemic, and in order to increase productivity and simplify processes; they looked to automation and artificial intelligence. Applications for AI include authoring tales or articles, producing realistic speech, making music, and creating art. A generative AI model, for instance, may be trained on a sizable picture dataset and then used to produce brand-new, previously unseen images that are stylistically and content-similar to the original dataset.

Research objectives
- To look at the most relevant and current research regarding the use of AI in online marketing.
- To study how artificial intelligence is applied in digital marketing.
- To learn about artificial intelligence's benefits and potential disadvantages in digital marketing plans.

Literature Review

In her research Rathore's [19] explores the potential applications of AI and the metaverse in marketing. They also examined how the metaverse and AI may change marketing tactics and enhance customer experience. The report points out that doing this can lead to stronger marketing, better communication with customers, and more loyal customers. Hadalgekar and Desai [9] looked at AI and how it supports digital marketing by improving strategies and methods of communication with clients. Figure 11.1 lists the different industries using AI in digital marketing, including e-commerce, start-ups, media and entertainment, real estate, travel agencies, education, and healthcare.

The contributors reviewed pertinent research on artificial intelligence and digital marketing to learn about the most recent data. They examined AI applications, including chatbots, recommendation engines, and pre-dictive analytics [10]. They found positives and negatives to using AI in digital marketing and suggested companies need to change to stay in step with today's requirements. In their report, Bawack et al. [2] explain

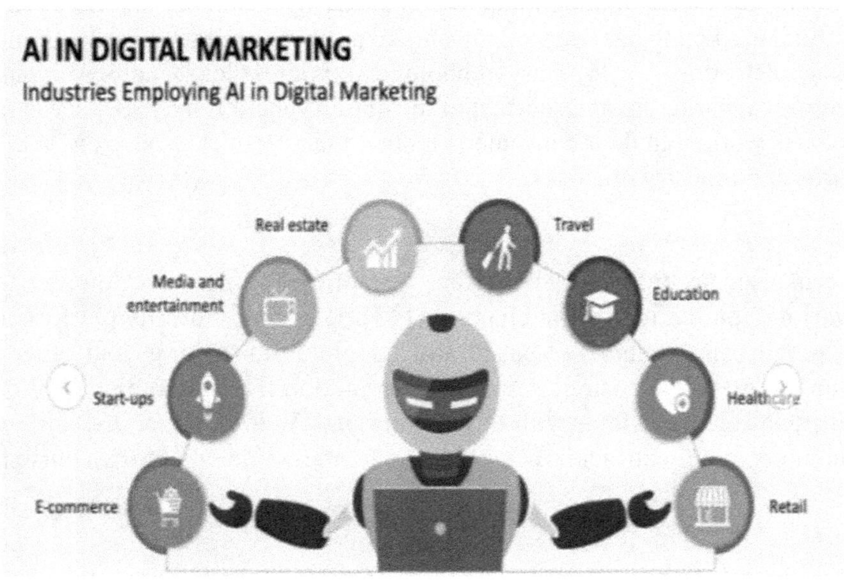

Figure 11.1 Various industries employing AI in digital marketing
Source: Orcun Sarioguz, Evin Miser, Falade Rhoda Adeola

that they used bibliometric analysis and literature reviews to study artificial intelligence and its role in e-commerce. Looking at numerous research papers from multiple databases allowed the authors to notice important themes in using AI in e-commerce.

The study pointed out that chatbots in customer service, individualized product suggestions, spotting fraud, overseeing the supply chain, and adjusting pricing are major ways AI is used in e-commerce. In addition, the poll revealed that more people are adopting natural language processing and machine learning as part of e-commerce [25]. In their study, Puttanna and Bashang identified that deep fakes can distribute false information, shape opinions among the public, and damage a person's reputation.

Types of digital marketing channels

The potential of AI in digital marketing is depicted in Figure 11.2. The top nine categories of digital marketing channels should be briefly reviewed before we go on to other facets of the field:

Website

In actuality, creating a website is the first step in the digital marketing process. The purpose of all other strategies is to direct visitors to the website. People use the website to imagine your business. The first thing you need is a visually appealing and mobile-friendly website. The goal of digital marketing is to increase website visitors.

Content marketing

AI may be used by content marketers to identify the kinds of material that their existing and prospective customers are interested in. AI-powered apps may be used for content creation and editing. For example, ChatGPT, Co-schedule, Grammarly, Hemingway Editor, and Jarvis are AI-powered tools that help content writers swiftly create attention-grabbing headlines for blogs and ad copy.

Search engine optimization

Using AI, online marketers can work on better link-building, assess their websites and find useful keywords. AI studies different data to discover what keywords your business needs for its services which helps boost your website's position in search engine rankings.

Figure 11.2 Prospects of AI in digital marketing
Source: Christos Ziakis and Maro Vlachopoulou

Email marketing

Businesses may build and maintain relationships with both current and future clients through newsletters, special offers, and other relevant information via email to foster client connections and foster consumer loyalty. Businesses may speed up the conversion process for potential clients by advertising goods and services through email promos, discounts, or exclusive deals.

Social media marketing

Social media gives businesses the ability to communicate directly with potential customers, build and enhance their brand image, distribute content, and engage with consumers. The target audience is informed, participation is encouraged, and the brand's values are reflected in this material. Businesses may interact directly with potential clients through social media platforms by answering queries, resolving customer grievances, and reacting to user comments, businesses may improve their connections with customers.

Mobile marketing

Mobile marketing includes strategies to reach the target audience via mobile devices, increasing brand recognition, encouraging consumer involvement, and increasing conversions, is a crucial part of online advertising. Businesses can interact with their target audience more directly thanks to mobile applications. Mobile applications can offer notifications, personalized information, special offers, and other features that enhance the user experience.

Online PR

Online public relations, commonly called E-PR or digital public relations, is where companies interact with existing and potential clients on the Internet. It tries to build positive relationships among users and decrease the comments or news that critics may post online about a company, its products, and its announcements. Content marketing and search engine optimization now play the most important roles for public relations and online marketing professionals.

Conversational AI

Conversational AI refers to chatbots and virtual agents that consumers use to communicate through messaging. They depend on data, machine learning, and natural language processing to attempt to recreate how humans communicate. They understand what is said and written and change it into the proper meaning in several languages. NLP and machine learning are included in the field of conversational AI.

Web analytics

Analyzing website data using web analytics enhances the user experience on the site. It can manage and improve websites, web applications, or other web products. By using data science, companies can improve their website's performance. Web analytics allows product managers, data scientists, UX designers, and others to enhance the product or website experience and satisfy customers.

Applications of AI in digital marketing

Figure 11.3 explains the vital role of digital marketing by making strategies more targeted and customer centric. Some of the most important applications are described below:

Customer segmentation

Kotler and Keller [15] point out that knowing customer segments helps businesses discover the most valuable customers, focus on specific advertising, and use their resources more wisely. With the help of AI, marketers now get clearer information about their target audiences, including their demographics, what they do online, and how they use social media [24]. Marketers want to group their clients by shared interests so that they can offer messages tailored to each group.

Personalized advertising

Advertising with personalized messages is a powerful approach to optimizing user relevance to advertising and marketers' return on investment. It does this because it can use online user data to target the ads to more of the right people with more meaningful advertising content, enhancing the user's and marketer's experiences with the service. These systems learn about a user's preferences by evaluating user activity data and can serve more relevant ads that drive the purchase. Organizations can increase conversion rates while improving a customer's experience through personalized advertising.

Content creation

Chatbots make it easy for customers to have fast exchanges about commonly asked questions and receive replies in real time. In addition, marketing teams can generate blog posts, social media updates, and email newsletters much more quickly with AI help. Gagnon [6] advises creating content that displays a company's expertise by saying 'show what you know. As part of any business strategy, it's important to have material that shares what the organization knows. According to Gagnon [6], learning in business leads to better organizational knowledge, allowing education to be beneficial and competing more effectively. As a result, customers can remember the products and buy from the company again when fulfilling their needs (Ibid). AI processes such as natural language processing (NLP) have made it much easier to create quality content without manual help [8].

Chatbots

Chatbots help digital marketers suggest ways to increase client participation while also handling normal conversational inquiries with AI technology [4]. People in regulated jobs, such as doctors and lawyers, sometimes use chatbots to communicate. Taxonomy, civic responsibility, consumer protection, cyber security, privacy, data protection, and IPR are all treated as human rights concerns [16]. With NLP and AI, chatbots can be programs that use everyday language to help customers buy from a website. Adding chatbots to a website or social media is a simple task. They can attend to multiple calls simultaneously, increase client engagement, and assist customers daily. Additionally, through voice-based or chat-based engagements, chatbots may instantly respond to consumer inquiries. Chatbots are already being used by several internet companies to provide better customer service. Surprisingly, in 2021, 85% of customer transactions were managed without human involvement, according to Gartner [7]. The amazing thing is that because chatbot conversations are so smooth and advanced users frequently may not even be aware that they are speaking with a machine.

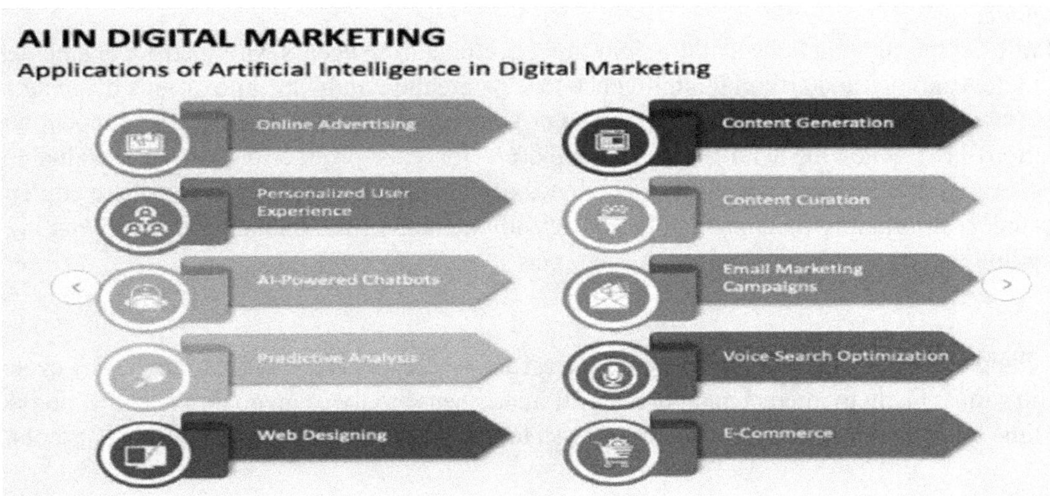

Figure 11.3 Application of AI in digital marketing
Source: https://www.sketchbubble.com/en/presentation-ai-in-digital-marketing.html

Semantic search

Semantic search is a helpful method that enables users to find answers to their search queries more rapidly and effectively. Semantic search is an advanced data searching technique that goes beyond traditional keyword-based search by attempting to understand what the user means behind the search query. Because of that, search results get better and better all the time, and we can deliver increasingly better answers to more users. Among its numerous factors are the user's search history, stored data, location, spelling changes, seasonality trends, local, synonyms, notional match, and search time.

Ad targeting

AI can create and promote internet ads, which are crucial for company marketing. It can create or enhance ad content according to the user's likes, dislikes, preferences, and interests. Machine learning and artificial intelligence are already used by Google Ad platforms to target users. AI can provide appropriate advertising to the right audience at the right time by using a variety of data, including search history, past purchases, demographics, interests, and more. Ads will have a higher return on investment (ROI) as a result.

Predictive marketing

Predictive marketing is the art of predicting marketing success, and artificial intelligence is often considered useful in helping marketers make exact business predictions. It uses data mining, machine learning, and artificial intelligence to predict future outcomes using past data. Each time you surf the internet, artificial intelligence gathers and examines data on what you do online. This data contains the user's brand preference and purchase frequency [12]. Artificial intelligence can understand the wants and demands of the customer with the data it has previously examined. Segmentation of the audience, which is done with the help of AI, lets companies understand what their consumers need. Your target customer's purchase habits help you predict it. Predictive analytics is built on supply and demand insights to help a business keep track of its production schedule.

Voice search

Fifty percent of all searches in 2020 were voice-based. According to a recent survey, 71% of customers would choose voice inquiries over typing by 2022. In addition, Google's algorithms are now so sophisticated that they have a 95% accuracy rate in understanding human language. Information may be found more quickly and easily with voice search. Is it not? Future SEO tactics will be altered by voice search; therefore, marketers must use voice-friendly long-tail keywords to improve their content. It is crucial to optimize your website for local search since people use phrases like "near me" in voice searches. Because Voice search is always searching for questions, provide web pages that offer straightforward solutions to the queries.

Target the right audience

Presenting the right offer to the right audience, at the right time, is crucial for success with internet businesses [21]. Experts use Google Analytics and artificial intelligence to separate their audience into groups by geography, psychographics (interests, preferences, attitudes, and so on), and demographics (age, gender, education, income, and occupation) [18]. Knowing who the right people are for your product or service is valuable. Digital marketers use artificial intelligence to analyze gigabytes of data about one client to distribute content correctly by client category. Marketing by email can be easier with the help of AI. Including a bit of your signature can bring attention to your emails, encouraging customers to respond to you.

Lead scoring

Lead scoring is the technique for grading leads to consumer interest and where they stand in their purchasing cycle. It's good to know who's most likely to interact and purchase. It makes sense to focus on quality leads, as no one wants to spend their time on unqualified leads. If businesses wish to lead, they might say 'hot', 'warm', or 'cold.'

- Hot – A lead who is five stages away from buying.
- Warm- A lead is interested in what your business offers.

- Cold- Someone who does not seem interested in what you offer.

Real hot leads may be automatically prioritized by artificial intelligence, which also proactively increases sales efficiency.

Data analysis

The AI systems allow marketers to quickly understand what customers prefer and how they act by processing a huge amount of information in real time [3]. Marketers who use AI to analyze data can easily tell what interests their customers and focus on their marketing correctly.

Advantages of bringing artificial intelligence to digital marketing

Improved client connections

Digital marketers can gather a great deal of consumer data using AI, which they can then utilize to create more engaging experiences. As a result, companies can discover that their clientele becomes better, and their brand becomes more recognizable.

Enhanced efficiency

AI can help digital marketers with a lot of difficult and time-consuming jobs. Your income will rise as a result, and you'll also save time and have some more money.

Effective marketing strategy

AI changes the way advertising typically works. AI data analysis platforms and tools can be used by digital marketers to optimize their work.

More return on investment

With AI, digital marketers will be able to decide better and publish more successful content. When they know their audience well, their digital marketing will be more effective.

Better experience for users

AI allows digital marketers to offer content to visitors most interested in it. People feel less nervous when they know what items to check. Based on research, AI brands are more successful at capturing customers. AI creates a new approach in advertising. Digital marketers have opportunities to improve how productively they work.

Challenges in the use of AI in digital marketing

The future of AI in digital marketing is depicted in Figure 11.4, which focuses on six significant developments that influence an industry.

Loss of jobs

Because AI has become more intelligent, many areas of internet marketing have experienced a lot of turmoil and commotion. The biggest reason is the growth of AI, which could put employees with industry knowledge at risk. In most cases, civilization depends on AI to adapt more easily. Employee personal improvement is important for organizations to keep their workforce up to date.

Lack of high-quality data

When data constantly grows, companies should use higher sales as a key tool for improving their marketing. A major disadvantage of AI is the lack of useful data. There are currently not many data sets that AI can work with.

Lack of transparency

Since AI is now used in marketing decisions, it can be hard to determine how choices are made. Spotting anything wrong in a system or ensuring this technology follows ethical standards can be hard.

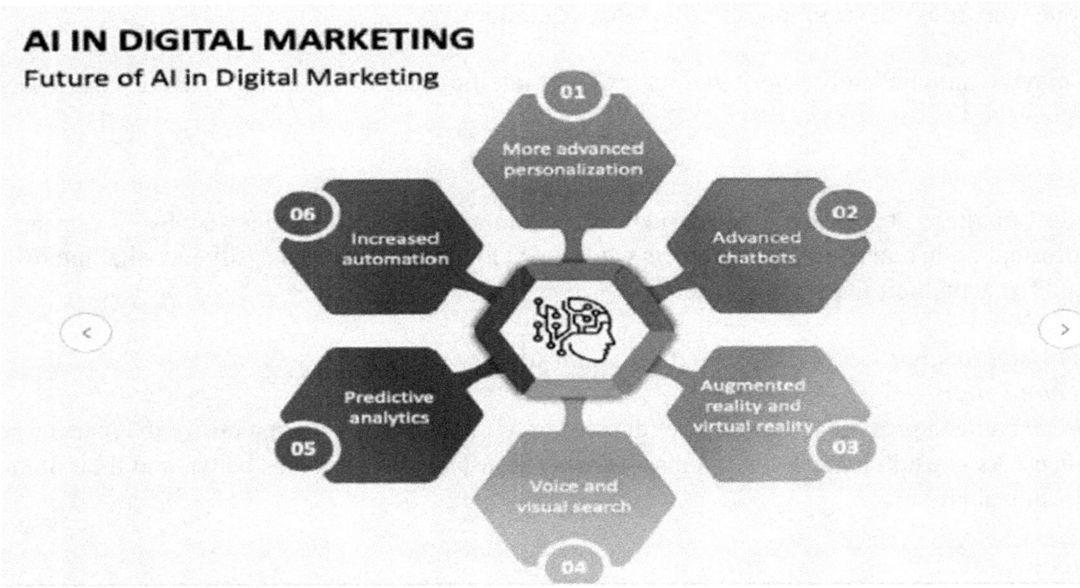

Figure 11.4 Future of AI in digital marketing
Source: https://www.sketchbubble.com/en/presentation-ai-in-digital-marketing.html

Lack of privacy
Most digital marketers are worried that the more AI progresses, the less secure our privacy will be. More and more people are starting to pay attention to their privacy and security worries.

Lack of creativity
AI can do many marketing chores, but it does not match people's originality and intuition. Consequently, marketing advertising that lacks real emotion or authenticity might appear.

The future of artificial intelligence in digital marketing
Artificial Intelligence's impact on marketing will undoubtedly boost businesses' and organizations' sales and profitability growth levels [22]. In the realm of marketing, artificial intelligence presents new possibilities. As soon as feasible, we can forecast the behavior of clients and customers with the aid of artificial intelligence.

By determining the degree of performance of digital marketing initiatives, AI may help the business increase sales volume, which in turn increases ROI [20]. By examining consumer insights, artificial intelligence will impact on the business's marketing plans [5]. AI is a useful technology that may help increase the productivity and efficiency of marketing managers [14].

Businesses may boost consumer and organizational value with the help of this revolutionary technology. AI's capacity to deliver a customized consumer experience stems from its power to leverage data to yield even greater advantages. Additionally, this will help customers make wise choices that will pay off in the long run by decreasing the frequency of purchases and discouraging overconsumption.

Conclusion

Artificial intelligence (AI) is making a large difference in digital marketing. The paper discusses AI in marketing by mentioning chatbots, automatically creating content, showing ads according to a user's interests, grouping customers, and balancing information presented in digital ads with users' privacy. This research also included AI's advantages and potential drawbacks in marketing plans. AI implementation may be challenging for small organizations with little financing and few resources. Lack of quick AI adaptability might lead to missed chances or inefficient tactics, underscoring the necessity of ongoing education and professional growth at the level of digital marketing. AI is capable of doing a number of digital marketing duties on its own. Human ingenuity and intuition in developing effective marketing efforts must still be acknowledged, though. AI has great promises for improving digital marketing. However, if used excessively, it may replace human contact and authenticity, which could lower customer engagement and brand loyalty.

References

[1] Bashang, S., & Puttanna, K. (2023). The role of artificial intelligence in digital marketing: a review. *International Research Journal of Economics and Management Studies*, 2(3), 125–133. https://doi.org/10.56472/25835238/IRJEMS-V2I3P118.

[2] Bawack, R. E., Wamba, S. F., Carillo, K. D. A., & Akter, S. (2022). AI in e-commerce: a Bibliometric study and literature review. Electronic Markets, 32, 1–27.

[3] Bughin, J., Hazan, E., Ramaswamy, S., Chui, M., Allas, T., Dahlstrom, P., et al. (2017). AI: The Next Digital Frontier? McKinseyGlobal Institute. https://apo.org.au/node/210501 (Accessed on 14 May 2024).

[4] Chopra, S. S. (2020). Helping entrepreneurs and small businesses make the digital transformation. In The Evolution of Business in the Cyber Age, (pp. 39–51). Apple Academic Press.

[5] Davenport, T., Guha, A., Grewal, D., & Bressgott, T. (2019). How AI will change the future of marketing. *Journal of the Academy of Marketing Science*, 47(3), 579–604. https://doi.org/10.1007/s11747-019-00696-0.

[6] Gagnon, E. (2014). Goodbye, B2B brand marketing: developing content-based marketing programs for the post-marketing Era. *International Management Review*, 10(2), 68.

[7] Gartner (2021). Report. https://www.gartner.com/en/marketing/research/consumer-trends. Accessed on 15 May 2024.

[8] Gupta, A., & Agrawal, R. K. (2019). AI in content creation: a systematic literature review. *Journal of Intelligent Information Systems*, 53(2), 209–238.

[9] Hadalgekar, A., & Desai, S. (2023). The role of AI in digital marketing. *Journal of Marketing Research*, 45(2), 123–137.

[10] Mohammed, I. A. (2020). Artificial Intelligence for cybersecurity: a systematic mapping of literature. *International Journal of Innovations in Engineering Research and Technology*, 7(09), 172–176. https://repo.ijiert.org/index.php/ijiert/article/view/2797.

[11] Jain, K. (2020). Artificial intelligence applications in handling infectious diseases. *Primary Health Care: Open Access*, 10(5), 1–3.

[12] Jain, P., & Aggarwal, K. (2020). Transforming marketing with artificial intelligence. *International Research Journal of Engineering and Technology*, 7(7), 3964–3976.

[13] Jarrahi, M. H. (2018). Artificial intelligence and the future of work: human-AI symbiosis in organizational decision making. *Business Horizons*, 61(4), 577–586. https://doi.org/10.1016/j.bushor.2018.03.007.

[14] Kardon, B. (2019). Five AI solutions transforming B2B marketing. *MIT Sloan Management Review*, 22(7), 15–24.

[15] Kotler, P., & Keller, K. L. (2016). Marketing Management, (15th edn.). Pearson Education Limited.

[16] Leaua, C., & Didu, I.-A. (2021). Chat bots. Legal challenges and the Eu legal policy approach. *Perspectives of Law and Public Administration*, 10(3), 210-216.

[17] Mkwizu, K. H. (2020). Digital marketing and tourism: opportunities for Africa. *International Hospitality Review*, 34(1), 5–12. https://doi.org/10.1108/IHR-09-2019-0015.

[18] Prabha, & Sheetlani, J. (2017). Fingerprint-based automatic human gender identification. *International Journal of Computer Applications*, 170(7), 124.

[19] Rathore, B. (2023). Furture of AI and generation alpha: ChatGPT beyond boundaries. *International Peer Reviewed/Refereed Multidisciplinary Journal (EIPRMJ)*, 12(1), 63–68.

[20] Schrage, M., & Kiron, D. (2018). Leading with next-generation key performance indicators. *MIT Sloan Management Review*, 16(June), 1–2.

[21] Shaikh, S. (2022). Internet of things: designing digital eco-systems for competitive tourism related micro and small enterprises in Pakistan. In Technology Application in Tourism in Asia, (pp. 349–365). Singapore: Springer. DOI: https://doi.org/10.1007/978-981-16-5461-9_21.

[22] Singh, A., & Kushwaha, T. (2017). Role of customer relationship management (CRM) strategy in the development of business organization. *International Journal in Management and Social Science*, 5(1), 275–285.

[23] Smith, K. (2007). What is digital marketing? *Digital Marketing*, 101. 20–22.

[24] Smith, J., Johnson, A., Brown, M., & D avis, R. (2019). AI algorithms enable marketers to segment their target audience more effectively by analyzing demographic data, online behavior patterns, and social media interactions. *Journal of Marketing Research*, 45(2), 123–135.
[25] Syam, N., & Sharma, A. (2018). Waiting for a sales renaissance in the fourth industrial revolution: machine learning and artificial intelligence in sales research and practice. *Industrial Marketing Management*, 69, 135–146.
[26] Yasmin, A., Tasneem, S., & Fatema, K. (2015). Effectiveness of digital marketing in the challenging age: an empirical study. *International Journal of Management Science and Business Administration*, 1(5), 69–80.

12 Navigating regulatory challenges in e-government: a bibliometric study

Marina Crasta[1,a], *T. Shirmila*[2,b] *and Dulsin Crasta*[3,c]

[1]Research Scholar, Madras Christian College, Tambaram, Affiliated to University of Madras, Chennai, India

[2]Associate Professor, Madras Christian College, Tambaram, Affiliated to University of Madras, Chennai, India

[3]Research Scholar, Rani Channamma University, Belagavi, Karnataka, India

Abstract

In recent years many governments have digitized public administration and services to bring transparency and easy accessibility. This paper has used bibliometric analysis to investigate the broad overview of regulatory challenges in e-government. The study was conducted on 97 documents extracted from Dimensions database from 2001-2025. The results reveal that the Government Information Quarterly journal is the leading publisher with 26.57% of total citations and the United States as the most contributing country with highest documents (14) and (655) citations. Co-citation and country collaboration analysis linkages are low, and it suggests that each author has dwelled upon the regulatory aspects of one's own country. In addition, the research indicates that technological innovation, infrastructural development, and multidisciplinary research have contributed towards the growth of research literature in recent years. This paper contributes to future research by providing a solid framework with meaningful insights for those seeking to explore and enhance their knowledge.

Keywords: Bibliometric analysis, e-government, regulatory challenges, technological innovation

Introduction

E-Government comprises hyper-connected and socially inclusive digital infrastructure developed with adaptive architecture to improve public service delivery with accountability and transparency [10]. The prudent implementation of e-government facilitates governance towards sustainable development. Song et al. [16], Tonetto [18], mentioned that the widespread adoption of e-government can improve efficiency and effectiveness of public administration, fostering significant interest in this research domain.

The literature reveals that there are many challenges for implementing e-government of which Arief [2], through a systematic literature review has highlighted 34 main barriers. Therefore, this bibliometric analysis is done to make a study on one of the barriers in e-government, such as regulatory challenges.

Chen [3], observes that bibliometrics serves as a powerful tool for analyzing literature by applying statistical and mathematical methods, and assess the existing knowledge as well as identify development trends". The distinct objectives of this analysis include the following:

To study collaboration of authors, keyword co-occurrence and the impacting countries

To observe the descriptive key factors of research literature and

To examine the details of significant documents and prominent authors

Literature Review

Bibliometric analysis, as mentioned by Donthu [6], is a well-established and scientific method of examining and interpreting extensive data that helps in understanding the gradual development of a particular discipline as well as showcasing latest advancements. Many researchers have applied bibliometric analyses to study the research literature pertaining to the e-government landscape. Developments in e-government are identified and analyzed by examining document metrics, author-based information and progression of research themes by employing a certain time frame [16].

[a]marinacrasta@gmail.com, [b]shirmilastanley@mcc.edu.in, [c]dulcinecrasta@yahoo.co.in

DOI: 10.4324/9781003739982-12

Arias [1] by using the bibliometrics, analyzed 161 documents from 37 publisher sources indexed in the WOS database. In this paper research literature on e-government in public administration was categorized into subfields based on mainstream research, and intellectual influence.

Another study was conducted in the same year by Dias [5], on 1129 documents extracted from the Scopus® database on e-government, published during the period of 2003 - 2017. The presented analyses consisted of specific research themes, prominent researchers, significant study areas and international cooperation patterns namely within the Ibero-American Community.

VOSviewer, Biblioshiny and Bibexcel were used by Ramzy [13], to visualize and analyze 21320 documents on e-government, retrieved from the Digital Government Reference Library and Scopus database, published during 2000–2019. The findings show the average citation as 12.34 and yearly increase as 21.50% in the research literature.

To trace the evolution in e-government Song [16], examined 4536 research documents from the Web of Science database that were published from 2000 to 2023. The results highlight that the focus in research is shifting from electronic transformation to innovation.

Recently a few bibliometric studies combining other variables with e-government have emerged. Research was conducted by Nindito [12], using 87 documents published between 2000 and 2020, on tourism and e-government indexed in Scopus database. An in-depth analysis conducted by Elmatsani [7], of 358 scholarly articles, spanning from 2004 to 2023, using the Scopus database, outlines the progression of leadership from the era of e-government to the current digital epoch.

Scopus and Web of Science databases were used by Mushtaq [11] that identified 3790 documents from January 2015 to January 2025. The aim of this research was to study cyber security issues in e-government. The key insights from the research suggest that user trust, security and privacy issues are attended to but aspects like cybercrime mitigation strategies remain unexplored. Hence, this study makes an attempt to study the regulatory challenges by employing bibliometric analysis.

Method and Materials

Bibliometric data was extracted from Dimensions database on 27 February 2025. The following search string with a broad array of keywords pertaining to regulatory challenges in e-government, was used to capture the full data.

"Digital era government" OR "digital government" OR "e-government" OR "smart government" OR "open government" OR "digital era governance" OR "digital governance" OR "e-governance" OR "electronic governance" OR "smart governance" OR "digital public services" AND "regulatory challenges" OR "regulatory barriers" OR "policy challenges" OR "regulatory constraints" OR "regulatory issues" OR "governance issues".

The documents published between 2001 and 2025 that include the search query in the title and abstract were identified. The English language documents were only considered by manually checking the data. All the needed data were extracted in CSV format containing details of author and publication, author affiliation with organization and country, title, abstract and cited references as presented in multi-phase process (Figure 12.1) as being relevant for the study.

The descriptive statistics and visualization of leading authors' collaboration, networking countries, citation and maps of keywords based on co-occurrence data is done by using VOSviewer software tool [19].

Findings

Outline of key features

An outline of key features of research literature on regulatory challenges in e-government used in this bibliometric analysis is presented in Table 12.1. This study relies on a total of 97 documents written by 182 authors in the period 2001–2025. In this research data, about 47.42% were written by a single author and the number of authors per document is 2.09. The relative majority (55.67%) of the documents have at least one citation

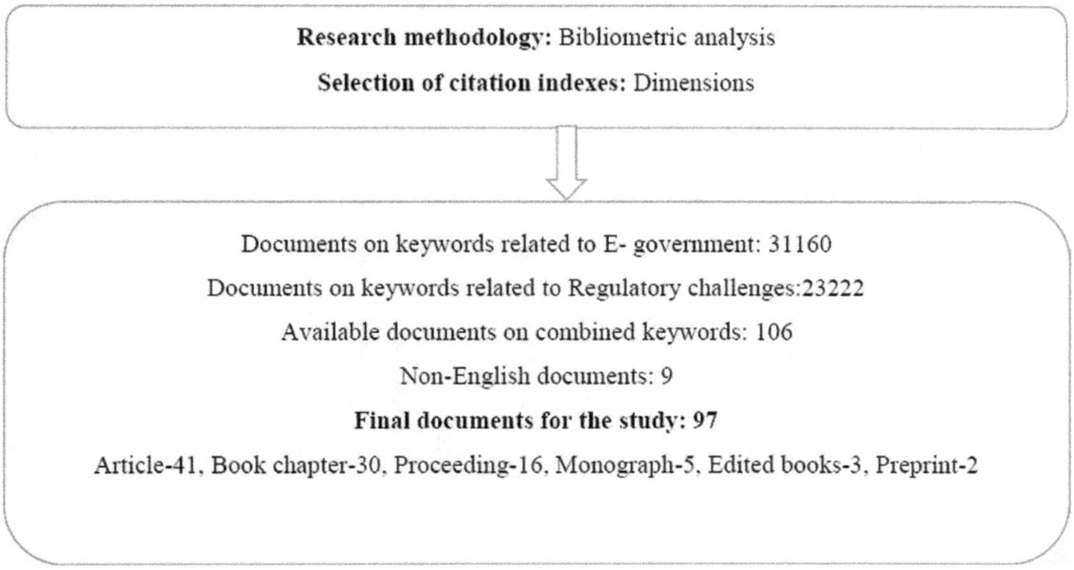

Figure 12.1 Flowchart determining the data
Source: Author

Table 12.1 Outline of key features of research literature on regulatory challenges in e-government.

Bibliometric items	Findings
Timespan	2001-2025
Documents	97
Sources (Journals, books, etc)	76
Publications with minimum of one citation	54
Distinct authors	182
Single-authored publications	46
Authors per publication	2.09
Average reference per publication	95.30
Mean citation count per document	12.45

Source: Author

while the average citation is 12.45 per document. Finally, bibliometric indicators show that each document contains an average of 95.30 references.

Figure 12.2. presents a numerical analysis of documents, citations and cumulative citations between 2001 and 2025. During this period, there are 97 documents that received 1208 cumulative citations. Research data was not found for the years 2002, 2003, 2005 and 2007. In the year 2010, 2023 and 2024 the highest number of documents (12, 11 and 13 respectively) were written. There is a steady growth in the research literature from the year 2022-2024, with 5 in 2022, 11 in 2023 and 13 in 2024. This surge in research relating to e-government is due to the development of infrastructure and innovation in technology Song [16], such as Artificial Intelligence, blockchain, robotic process automation, Virtual Reality and Augmented Reality, and associated software applications [9]. It also suggests the possibility of having substantial and sustained growth in the research on regulatory challenges in e-government [14].

Table 12.2. gives an account of most relevant authors in which OECD has the highest number of documents, and all other authors have two each document. However, the research by Dawes Sharon S. with 286 citations, and Bertot John Carlo as well as Choi Heeyoon on big data with 273 citations has significant influence in the given research field.

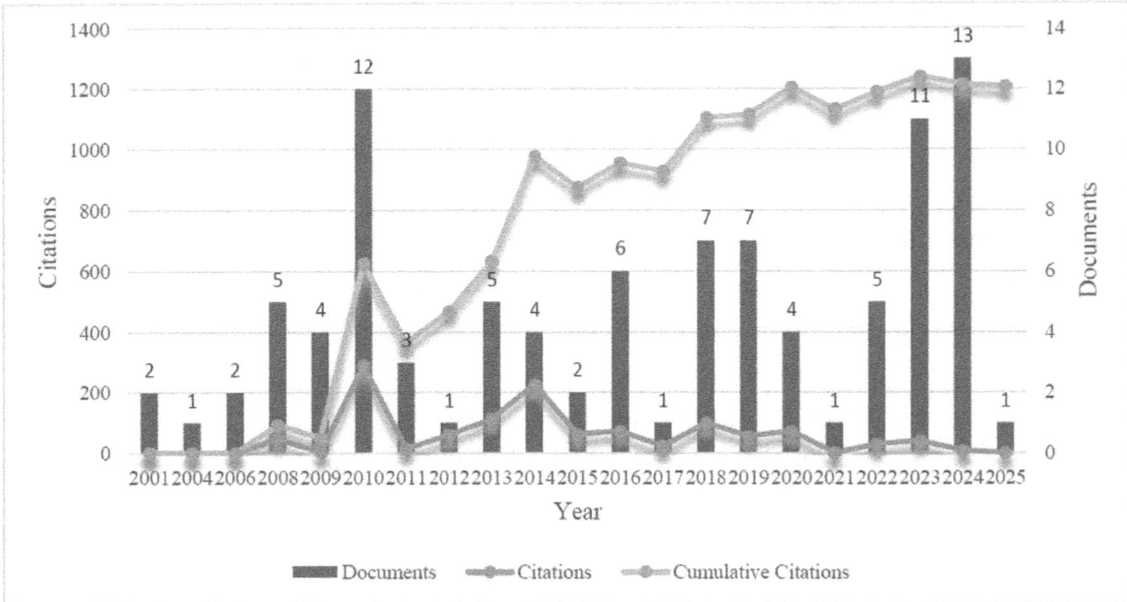

Figure 12.2 Distribution of documents, citations and cumulative citations (2001–2025)
Source: Author

Table 12.2 Highly published authors.

Authors	Documents	Citations
OECD	14	12
Bertot John Carlo	2	273
Choi Heeyoon	2	273
Conklin Arthur	2	0
Dawes Sharon S.	2	286
Hepburn Paul Anthony	2	10
Jobodwana Z.	2	0
Vaughn Rayford B.	2	0
White Gregory B.	2	0

Source: Author

Table 12.3 highlights the ten most relevant and frequently cited documents during 2001-2025. The article by Dawes [4], "Stewardship and usefulness: Policy principles for information-based transparency" is the most cited document of all. The most recent relevant document is, "From Digital Government to Digital Governance: Are We There Yet?" by Erkut [8], that has 63 citations. There are only two documents with published source as Government Information Quarterly in the entire documents under the study and both are in the top ten document list with a total of 321 (26.57%) citations.

Visualization and analysis of networks

Co-author analysis

Figure 12.3 shows the co-authorship network, and in this network, there is only one cluster consisting of three authors namely Conklin Arthur, Vaughn Rayford B and White Gregory B who have two documents published in Hawaii International Conference in 2014 and 2016 with 4 total link strength. They belong to the same country (United States) but different organizations. However, these documents seem to be of less significance as they do not have any citations.

Table 12.3 Most relevant documents and their author with number of citations.

Author (s)	Year	Document Title	Source Title	Cita tions
Dawes Sharon S.	2010	"Stewardship and usefulness: Policy principles for information-based transparency"	*Government Information Quarterly*	269
Bertot John Carlo, Gorham Ursula, Jaeger Paul T., Sarin Lindsay C., Choi Heeyoon	2014	"Big data, open government and e-government: Issues, policies and recommendations"	*Information Polity*	167
Bertot John Carlo, Choi Heeyoon	2013	"Big data and e-government"	*Proceedings of the 14th Annual International Conference on Digital Government Research*	106
Brous Paul, Janssen Marijn, Vilminko-Heikkinen Riikka	2016	"Coordinating Decision-Making in Data Management Activities: A Systematic Review of Data Governance Principles"	*Lecture Notes in Computer Science*	64
Erkut Burak	2020	"From Digital Government to Digital Governance: Are We There Yet?"	*Sustainability*	63
Chun Soon Ae, Luna-Reyes Luis F., Sandoval-Almazán Rodrigo	2012	"Collaborative e-government"	*Transforming Government People Process and Policy*	59
Lægreid P., Sarapuu K., Rykkja L. and Randma-Liiv, T.	2014	"Organizing for Coordination in the Public Sector, Practices and Lessons from 12 European Countries"	*Public Sector Organizations*	58
Ojo Adegboyega, Mellouli Sehl	2018	"Deploying governance networks for societal challenges"	*Government Information Quarterly*	52
Jung Kwangho, Lee Sabinne	2015	"A systematic review of RFID applications and	*Journal of Open Innovation:*	48

Source: Author

Co-citation analysis

The co-citation analysis explores the underlying relationship network between the key papers and identifies the major research trends [17]. The Figure 12.4 displays a co-citation network that was conducted to know the highly referenced researchers. There is a cluster consisting of six authors who have co-cited each other's research. These authors have one each citation with a total strength link of five each.

Global collaboration network

Figure 12.5 depicts the collaboration at the global level in the research literature on regulatory challenges in e-government. The most relevant countries are highlighted based on the publication contribution and document reference, between the time period of 2001 and 2025.

There are 28 countries where the research is published but we limit the presentation to countries where a minimum of 2 documents is published. Only seven countries meet this threshold. These countries have 36 documents and 1189 citations. The United States has the highest documents (14) with 655 citations.

The country collaboration clusters represent a group of countries that share significant linkages in scholarly literature, with the normative citation values indicating the strength of influence within the network [15]. In this study there are 4 countries collaborating with each other forming three clusters.

Figure 12.3 Co- author links
Source: Author

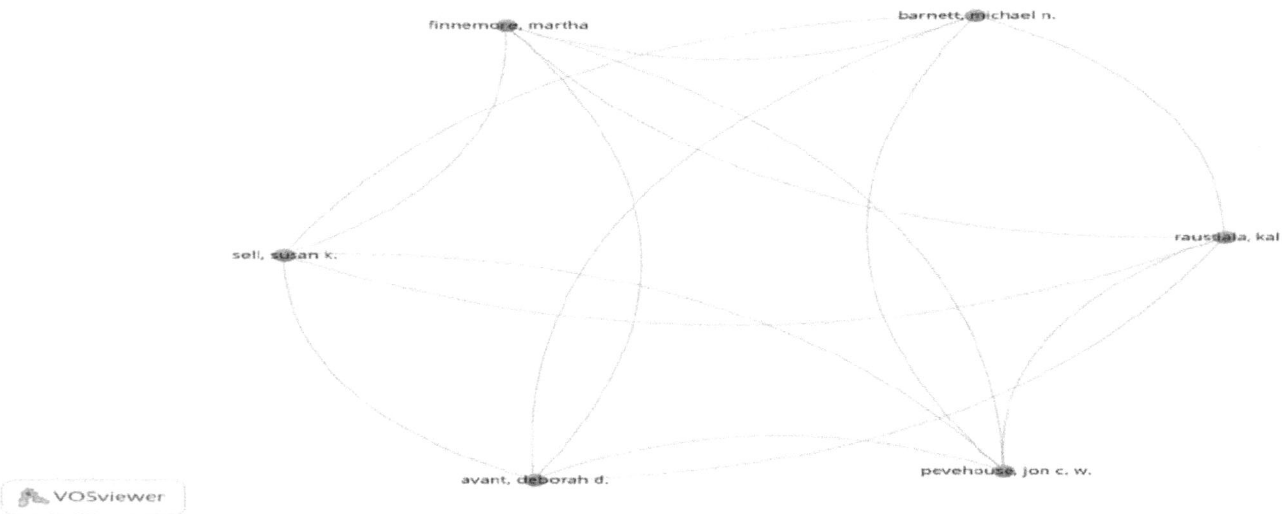

Figure 12.4 Co- citation network analysis on authors
Source: Author

Cluster 1 consists of Canada and the United States, with one and six total link strength respectively with 16 total documents and 707 total citations. Cluster 2 consists of the Netherlands with three documents, 95 citations and a network link with the United States. Cluster 3 consists of South Korea that has 3 documents with 321 citations and four total link strength.

Although India stands second in terms of highest documents (8) with 30 citations, China as well as United Kingdom with 3 each document with 25 and 11 citations respectively, they do not share any network with other countries.

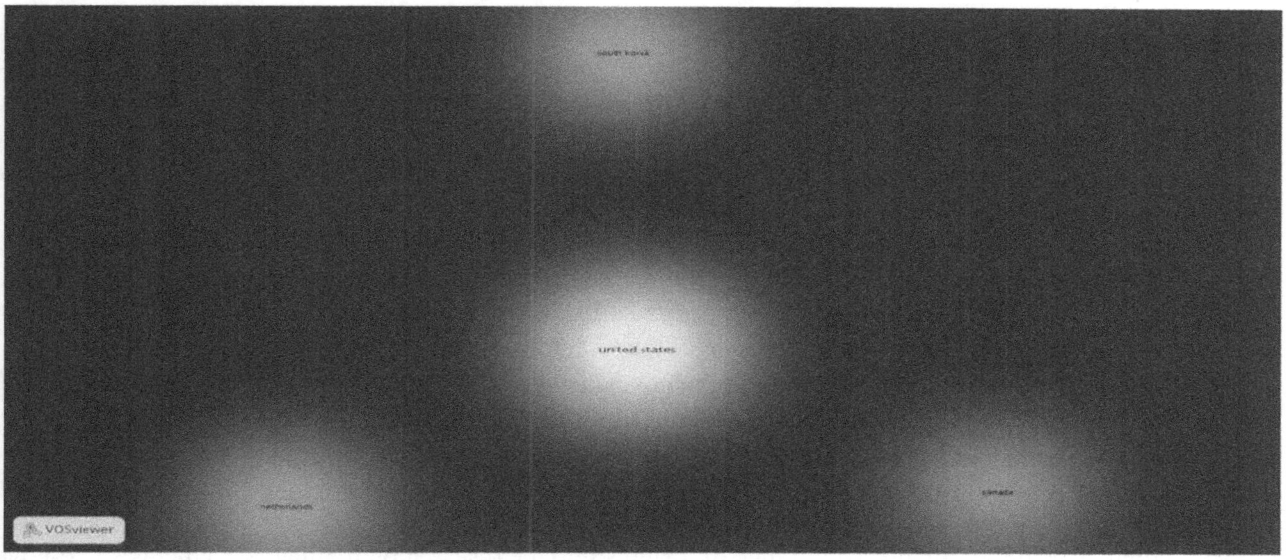

Figure 12.5 Major research hubs
Source: Author

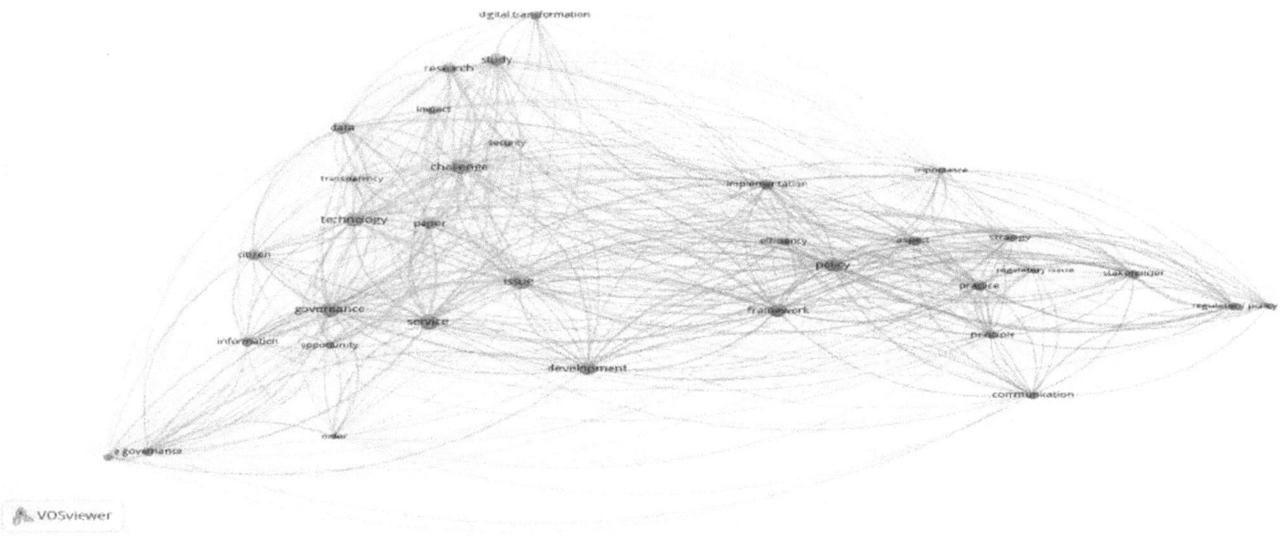

Figure 12.6 Co-occurrence of keywords
Source: Author

Co-occurrence analysis

The keywords analysis is used to represent the domain space and to identify the primary content within a particular theme [20]. The Figure 12.6 shows the co-occurrence of key term analysis undertaken by extracting the abstract, title and keywords, by setting it to "full counting" with the threshold of 15 words as the minimum number of occurrences. Totally 41 keywords met the criteria, of which 85% of items formed 3 clusters.

Cluster 1 (Red) consists of 14 keywords, with 'policy' and 'framework' occurring 90 and 66 times respectively highlighting the regulatory aspect. Cluster 2 (Green) consists of 13 words, of which 'challenge', 'issue' and 'technology' have maximum occurrence. Finally, cluster 3 (Blue) has eight terms which mainly speak of 'governance', 'development' and 'service'.

Conclusion

This paper presented a bibliometric analysis of 97 manuscripts published on the subject of regulatory challenges in e-government, between 2001 and 2025. Dimensions were used as the database and VOSviewer as the visualization software.

The findings highlight an upsurge in the research publications in the recent years in the given field mainly due to the infrastructural development and innovation in technology.

It is noticed that each country has its own regulatory challenges and regulatory frameworks in implementing e-governance. Therefore, the authors collaborate within the limits of their own country which leads to a lesser international network. Further, the developing countries like India and China too have contributed actively towards the research and it denotes the relevance of the research area.

The articles have scattered themes of e-government when the aspect of regulatory challenges was combined with it. However, in the article titles alone, under the study, the words- policy, strategy and better regulation occur 14, 11 and 9 times respectively which denotes that the regulation theme is highlighted.

The documents under Government Information Quarterly have higher citation count which indicates that this publisher source seems to publish qualitative research.

Even though this study provides wide-range of insights into the research on regulatory challenges in e-government, it has some limitations. The Dimension database may not include all the documents on the research topic and also there might be variations in the citation count due to low index rate. The search term combination reduced the research literature as the authors have used specific regulatory challenges or regulatory frameworks as research topics pertaining to their own country. This might have narrowed down the scope of this research.

The future research should integrate broader data foundations, refine research points and diversify the data gathering techniques that cover comprehensive literature. Advanced bibliometric tools or combinations of other tools like systematic literature review could be applied. This paper contributes to future research by providing a solid framework with meaningful insights for those, seeking to explore and enhance their knowledge.

References

[1] Arias, M. I., Serra, F., Guerrazzi, L., & Ferreira, M. P. (2019). Intellectual foundations and mainstream research of e-government in public administration. *Management Research*, 17(1), 89–115. https://doi.org/10.1108/MRJIAM-07-2018-0844.

[2] Arief, A., Wahab, I. H. A., & Muhammad, M. (2021). Barriers and challenges of e-government services: a systematic literature review and meta-analyses. In IOP Conference Series: Materials Science and Engineering, (Vol. 1125, p. 012027). https://doi.org/10.1088/1757-899X/1125/1/012027.

[3] Chen, H., Jiang, W., Yang, Y., Yang, Y., & Man, X. (2016). State of the art on food waste research: a bibliometrics study from 1997 to 2014. *Journal of Cleaner Production*, 140. 840–846. https://doi.org/10.1016/j.jclepro.2015.11.085.

[4] Dawes, S. (2010). Stewardship and usefulness: policy principles for information-based transparency. *Government Information Quarterly*, 27(4), 377–383.

[5] Dias, G. (2019). Fifteen years of e-government research in Ibero-America: a bibliometric analysis. *Government Information Quarterly*, 36(3), 400–411.

[6] Donthu, N., Kumar, S., Mukherjee, D., Pandey, N., & Lim, W. M. (2021). How to conduct a bibliometric analysis: an overview and guidelines. *Journal of Business Research*, 133(C), 285–296.

[7] Elmatsani, H., Widianingsih, I., Nurasa, H., Munajat, M., & Suwanda, S. (2024). Exploring the evolution of leadership in government: a bibliometric study from the e-government era into the digital age. *Cogent Social Sciences*, 10(1), 32.

[8] Erkut, B., (2020). From digital government to digital governance: are we there yet? *Sustainability*, 12(3), 860.

[9] Malhotra, C., & Anand, R. (2020). Cyber security as a key enabler for Industry 4.0 adoption. edge computing, process automation through robotics, industry 4.0 and cognitive technology (EPIC). In National Conference by Computer Society of India, Visakhapatnam, India.

[10] Malodia, S., Dhir, A., Mishra, M., & Bhatti, Z. A. (2021). Future of e-government: an integrated conceptual framework. *Technological Forecasting and Social Change*, 173(1), 16.

[11] Mushtaq, S., & Shah, M. (2025). Mitigating cybercrimes in e-government services: a systematic review and bibliometric analysis. *Digital*, 5(1), 3. 10.3390/digital5010003.

[12] Nindito, H., Prabowo, H., Hendric, S. W. H. L., & Sfenrianto, S. (2021). A bibliometric analysis on e-government and tourism. (pp. 599–603). https://doi.org/10.1109/ICIMTech53080.2021.9534960.

[13] Ramzy, M., & Ibrahim, B. (2024). The evolution of e-government research over two decades: applying bibliometrics and science mapping analysis. *Library Hi Tech*, 42(1), 227–260.

[14] Ravšelj, D., Umek, L., Todorovski, L., & Aristovnik, A. (2022). A review of digital era governance research in the first two decades: a bibliometric study. *Future Internet*, 14(5), 126. https://doi.org/10.3390/fi14050126.

[15] Shirmila, T., & Abishek, D. G. (2024). Navigating sustainability: a bibliometric exploration of sustainable business models, green finance, and environmental conservation. *International Management Review*, 20(1), 15–24.

[16] Song, Y., Natori, T., & Yu, X. (2024). Tracing the evolution of e-government: a visual bibliometric analysis from 2000 to 2023. *Administrative Sciences*, 14(7), 133. https://doi.org/10.3390/admsci14070133.

[17] Tang, K.-Y., Chang, C.-Y., & Hwang, G.-J. (2021). Trends in artificial intelligence-supported e- learning: a systematic review and co-citation network analysis (1998-2019). *Interactive Learning Environments*, 31(4), 2134–2152. https://doi.org/10.1080/10494820.2021.1875001.

[18] Tonetto, J. L., Fochezatto, A., & Pique, J. M. (2023). The impact of the COVID-19 pandemic on the use of the menor preço brasil application. *Administrative Sciences*, 13(11), 229. https://doi.org/10.3390/admsci13110229.

[19] Van Eck, N., & Waltman, L. (2010). Software survey: VOSviewer, a computer program for bibliometric mapping. *Scientometrics*, 84(2), 523–538.

[20] Wang, C., & Si, L. (2023). A bibliometric analysis of digital literacy research from 1990 to 2022 and research on emerging themes during the COVID-19 pandemic. *Sustainability*, 15(7), 5769. https://doi.org/10.3390/su15075769.

13 Attention based AI-powered environment sentiment prediction: enhancing safety and personalization in public spaces

Sarin Kumar Thayyilsubramanian[1,a], *Lakshmi Ethirajan*[2,b] *and Manoj Nath*[3,c]

[1]Doctoral Researcher, Rushford Business School, Switzerland

[2]Software Architect, Boeing India Pvt Ltd, Bangalore, Karnataka, India

[3]Associate Technical Fellow, Boeing India Pvt Ltd, Bangalore, Karnataka, India

Abstract

In this paper, we introduce a deep learning-based AI system that analyses emotions in surveilled public space by using image captioning and natural language processing so that risk can be proactively managed in tandem with security activity and economic robustness in spite of an emergent reaction or a disturbance. This system can be used to analyze images containing several individuals, detect people using a region of interest (ROI) detection technique, and generate descriptive captions. These summarized captions are then categorized by the system to allow the overall mood and sentiment of the environment to be assessed for proactive risk management. Our methodology produces superior outcomes when detecting people along with generating emotional captions contrary to conventional image processing methods. The results confirm that the approach is effective compared to the traditional approaches. Public safety performance strengthens substantially when organizations adopt data-based intelligent interventions. Such approaches enable organizations to gain a better understanding of the changed environmental context which, in turn, benefits from security coverage, strategic planning, and real-time situational awareness. The applications of this technology are not confined to the domain of security; they can also be used to improve customer experience in retail environments as well as to quantify the level of audience involvement and enthusiasm during event management, etc. Effective crowd management helps businesses empathize with their customers, enhancing spatial experience, supporting human-centric design thinking.

Keywords: Customer experience, emotion detection, generative AI, image captioning, public safety, risk management, sentiment detection

Introduction

Widespread adoption of Artificial Intelligence (AI) technologies in in industries has led to new opportunities of improving security measures and economic activities by means of sophisticated monitoring systems. AI cameras for surveillance in public spaces have a big potential for adding safety, and creating economic efficiency, since they provide instant insights and allow them to proactively mitigate risks. AI technologies integrated with surveillance systems have changed the entirety of the monitoring and securing of the public space dramatically. With their capabilities to analyze huge visual data in real-time, these systems are able to recognize with precision possible security threats, suspicious behavior, or emergency cases. By making this capability available, local governments can react quickly and increase the effectiveness in the allocation of overall security, hence creating safer environments for their citizens and visitors. Additionally, AI powered cameras can enable traffic management, crowd management, even help in tracing the missing persons, thus adding public safety and operational efficiency [11].

From the business and urban planners' point of view, AI driven surveillance systems bring substantial economic profits. These technologies can provide a very meaningful insight on the foot traffic patterns, consumer behavior and space utilization, and hence help businesses make better decisions on how to optimize their operations and marketing strategies.

Though current image analysis techniques have increased our utility in scene understanding as well as the detection of emotions, they aren't able to generate informed analysis of emotional context in complex

[a]talk2sarin@gmail.com, [b]lakshmi1212@gmail.com, [c]manojnath4u@gmail.com

DOI: 10.4324/9781003739982-13

environments, which consequently deteriorates sentiment analysis [4]. Although these methods can recognize broad emotional themes, or even identify single emotional facial features, they do not combine these in a single cohesive understanding of the emotional atmosphere. This is most apparent in crowded or dynamic situations where the circumstances in which they interact increase the emotional context. In addition, there does not exist comprehensive systems which can identify people and evaluate their emotional states by means of image captioning and natural optical language methods.

Currently, there are no comprehensive systems that enable a computer vision and natural language processing system to identify a large number of unorganized individuals and unstructured emotions all at once in a crowded environment. For such a system, the image captioning system would have to include advanced image captioning techniques that would describe the visual elements that are in the scene and a natural language processing system that would need to infer emotional states from these descriptions. In addition, the algorithms used should be robust to perform person detection and tracking to isolate individual subjects from a crowd and finally advanced facial expression recognition to gauge the emotional states of the subjects. Taking one step further, developing such a holistic approach will not only improve sentiment analysis at a complex level, but will also enable usage on many occasions, such as in the arena of public safety, event management or human-computer interactions.

The proposed AI system comprises computer vision and natural language processing with the ability of running computer vision processes on surveillance footage in real time. Through deep learning algorithms, the system could detect and categorize an extensive variety of human emotions from facial expressions, body language and signs related to context. We would combine object detection, scene understanding, and an emotional assessment to generate detailed and descriptive captioning that summarizes the overall situation in these public spaces.

Such a system could easily be use for more than just basic security monitoring. It can aid urban planners in making more user-friendly spaces, event organizers in quick crowd dynamics management, emergency responders in quick situation assessment and prioritization. Furthermore, the human readable descriptions that are generated by the system can help operators and decision makers communicate more efficiently, which may allow for quicker and proper responses to arising situations. Though such a system is possible, the implementation of this process would also require thought regarding privacy issues and ethical concerns to guarantee the moral utilization of the innovation.

The key objectives of this research

- To develop a surveillance system that detects emotions through natural language processing and predicts the sentiment of the environment in real time.
- To advance the methods for image captioning and natural language processing, multi-person detection, along with their emotions within crowded spaces.
- To develop a robust algorithm that detects emotions by splitting into multiple regions of interest and aggregating the results to predict the sentiment of the environment.
- To execute complex-level sentiment analysis and implement a holistic approach in applications that fall in the categories of public safety, event management, and human–computer interactions.
- To create detailed and descriptive captioning of objects detected to summarize the overall situation of public spaces based on different fields, such as scene understanding and emotional assessment.

Literature Review

Region of interest (ROI)

The YOLO (You Only Look Once) family of models Cheng and Li [2], are a great improvement in object detection. They are known to be the fastest and most accurate models for real-time object detection. The latest model by Ultralytics, YOLOv8, continues this legacy though, providing very strong performance [15, 12, 3]. It is known that YOLO models are effective in various applications, such as human detection. One of the most common benchmarks used for training robust object detection models is COCO dataset, which is a dataset used to train models that detect humans in most varied environments. We use the pre-trained YOLOv8 model on the COCO dataset Sorboni et al. [13], to compute the human region of interest. This builds on the existing literature of object detection.

In a variety of image analysis tasks, extraction of human Regions of Interest (ROIs) Zhang et al. [16] is an important preprocessing step. Most research about detecting and segmenting humans has been previous research using traditional image processing techniques or previous iterations of object detection models. Nevertheless, YOLOv8 shows high computational efficiency as well as accuracy, making it a clear win for real time or big scale applications. Human ROI extraction facilitates downstream analysis, such as pose estimation, action recognition, and biometric analysis. To take advantage of the functionality that YOLOv8 offers, this work sets out to provide a robust and efficient approach for human ROI extraction which in turn can impact the greater field of human centric image analysis [9]

Image captioning

In recent times, there have been many improvements in image captioning which have led to an increase in the accuracy and relevance of the generated captions, and researchers have explored a multitude of approaches to improve the contextual understanding and semantic coherence of the generated captions. However, although there has been a lot of progress in captioning each object and scene in an image, the problem of describing a multi person or group image is still an active area of research.

Concept based modelling is one such approach to image captioning which was successfully implemented in different linguistic contexts. As an example, a new Vision based Multi Encoder Transformer Architecture (ViMETA) was presented to cope with multi output concept modelling while captioning [10]. With both quantitative and qualitative results, this technique proved promising with its enhanced caption relevance in compound visual scenes. Secondly, we have another significant development, namely Word Guided Attention (WGA) mechanism, that improves attention-based models by integrating word information into attention results. By improving visualization of regions of attention in object coverage and caption detail, this method is competitive with state-of-the-art on the MSCOCO dataset [14]. This motivates the use of such attention-based strategies for multi person image captioning where understanding a person's contribution to a scene is essential for coherent description.

In recent times, the research on vision language task has shifted towards Transformer based architecture Kumari and Kaul [6], Alayrac et al. [1], Li et al. [7], Liu et al. [8], such as Flamingo and BLIP, which has shown superior performance on the same. Cross modal reasoning helps Flamingo to be able to provide more contextually relevant captions, and the bootstrapped image language pretraining approach in BLIP brings image captioning accuracy to the latter. Because these models are shown to be effective at processing complex visual inputs and generating more human-like descriptions, these models are well suited for multi-person and group image captioning. Although most previous research on image captioning has concentrated on captioning individual objects or separate scenes, multi person and group image captioning require more advanced approaches. However, existing methods fail at differentiating multiple people, modelling their interactions, and representing relationships, all of which are crucial for describing realistic natural interactions. To tackle these problems, novel advanced attention mechanisms, a state-of-the-art multimodal feature fusion technique, and context aware modelling are employed to make captions appropriately describe the dynamics of group interactions.

Finally, as image captioning research progresses, such novel architectures and learning strategies are applied to improve the quality and context relevance of the generated descriptions. As multi-person and group image captioning receives more attention, future advancements will likely be made to models that can interpret complex social interactions and relationships in the image. More human-like captioning systems will live out from continued exploration in the domain and increase the accuracy and contextual consensus of multi-entity visual descriptions.

Research Methodology

Data

The EMOTIC dataset served as a part of our research methodology, and we used it to train our model [5]. It has a large number of images with labels on emotion as well as contextual information and can thus be used for studying multi-person and group interactions. This study utilized 1200 unique images from the EMOTIC dataset, focusing on four core emotions: happiness, sadness, anger, and fear. The dataset was divided into training and testing sets with an 80:20 ratio to train the model.

Architecture

As shown in Figure. 13.1, the proposed architecture has three key components.

1. Image caption generator: identifies the individuals in the image and describes them along with their attributes.
2. Caption summarizer: Merges separate descriptions of an individual scene/caption to generate a complete scene/caption, so that the generated captions are coherent.
3. Sentiment analyzer: Takes the class of summarized captions and obtains the general emotional context of the environment.

To improve the accuracy of our analysis, we applied ROI technique to segment within the image so that each individual is properly segmented and captioned. This enables the model to discern people in a scene and provide more refined and precise sentiment analysis with captions for people in the scene.

To qualitatively verify the results of our approach, we processed an image from the EMOTIC dataset using two distinct pipelines: one representing the traditional method and the other implementing our proposed approach.

Pipeline 1: Image captioning models to generate captions as the first stage, LLMs classify captions to get emotions as the second stage. However, these captions only give a high-level description, without any of the emotional details (Figure 13.2).

Pipeline 2: In the second pipeline, our approach can be described more accurately as follows: Region of Interest (ROI) segmentation is used to identify individuals (Figure. 13.3).

The ROI was cropped and processed individually. For example, each participant receives his or her captions about facial expressions, body postures, and gestures. All emotional elements are included in the summarized captions to improve the classification accuracy.

However, such prior work has been largely centered on captioning individual objects or isolated scenes, leaving a need for more advanced solutions to the problem of multiple person and group image captioning.

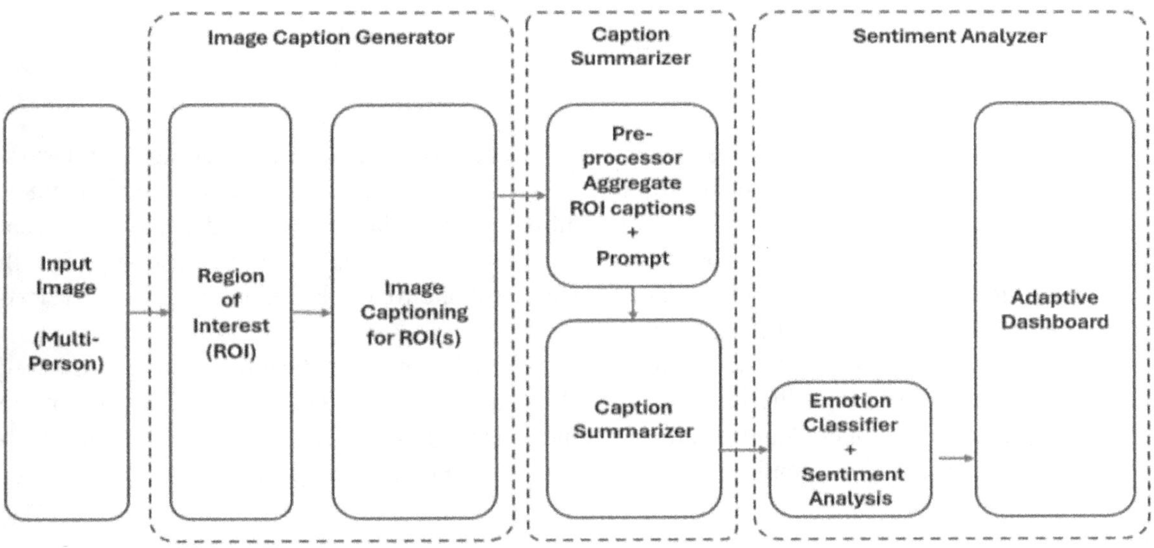

Figure 13.1 Architecture overview diagram
Source: Author

Figure 13.2 Pipeline 1 - Existing approach
Source: Created by author using data from [5] Emotic Dataset

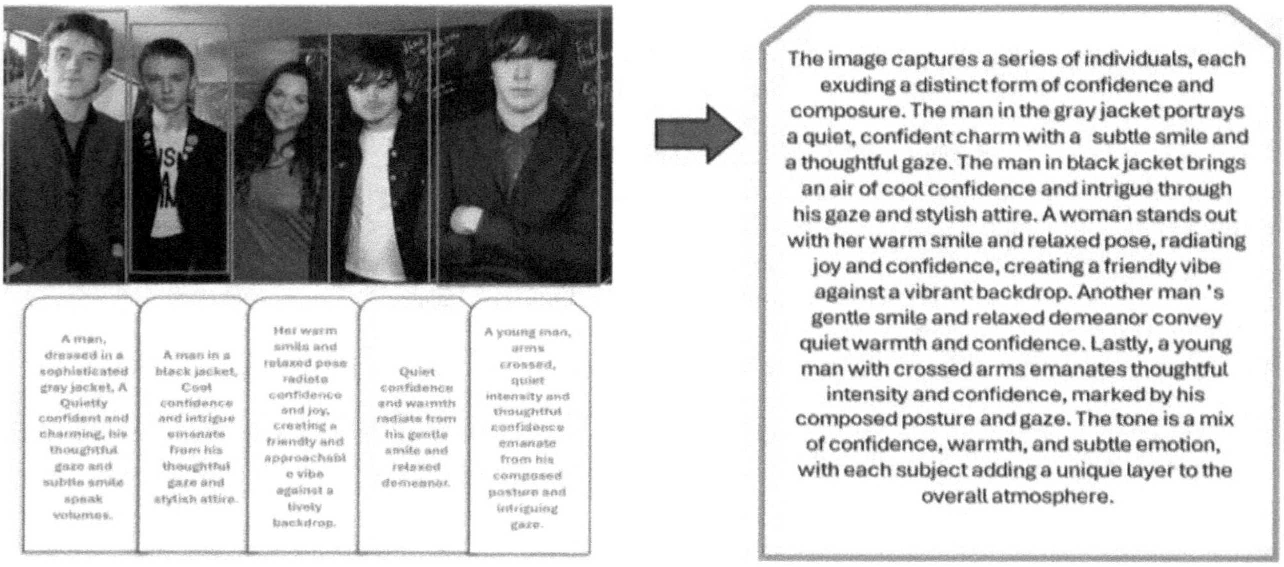

Figure 13.3 Pipeline 2 - Proposed approach
Source: Created by author using data from [5] Emotic Dataset

Nevertheless, all these methods impose challenges on person differentiation, interaction modelling and relationship representation, which are important for providing informative descriptions. To address these challenges, one should create advanced attention mechanisms that combine multimodal features and context-apparent modelling to enable the caption to follow group interaction dynamics. Research on image captioning is still evolving, and better algorithms are still being introduced, such as the one we explained in the paper and strategies to improve the quality and context of the generated descriptions.

Finally, the overall emotion was determined by processing the final summarized caption with a text-based classifier. Pipeline 1 yields more atmospheric or less detailed captions than Pipeline 2, which gives more detailed captions, and hence better understands characters' emotions in the scene. This shows that our methodology was able to classify emotions as Confidence and Positive sentiment in our evaluation.

Evaluation metrics

To evaluate our idea of image captioning and emotion detection, we used captions generated by the first and second pipelines. The standard method by the industry is Pipeline 1 and our proposed approach is Pipeline 2.

Precision, recall, F1-score, and accuracy were used as emotion classification metrics to evaluate the effectiveness of the NLP-based mood classifier model.

The Bilingual Evaluation Understudy (BLEU) score was used to tune the linguistic quality and relevance of the generated captions. In this sense, this comparative evaluation is used to evaluate the effectiveness of our proposed model in capturing emotions and generating contextually rich captions in multi-person and group images.

With our approach, we demonstrate that we can outperform standard methods not only in emotional nuance - although this is informative yet unsurprising - but also quantitatively, in the sense that, just as a caption generator, we provide an effective description of the given image that is significantly more detailed. This allowed us to correctly classify emotions, hinting that our methodology can help gain further insight into the context of images regarding emotion. The evaluation process used a suite of motivated metrics to evaluate the emotional accuracy and linguistic quality of the generated captions. Furthermore, we compared our proposed model with the state of industry in a complex setting describing multiple people or objects (pipeline 2) with pipeline 1 in terms of emotion classification metrics and BLEU scores to understand how well it can generate contextually rich captions with an emotionally accurate representation.

Hardware and software recommendation

For training: High-performance GPUs/TPUs, cloud computing, PyTorch, and Hugging Face models.

For inference & deployment: Optimized CPU/GPU servers, API-based processing with FastAPI/Flask, and cloud storage.

For real-time applications: Edge AI devices (NVIDIA Jetson) or cloud-based serverless inference (AWS Lambda, Google Cloud Functions).

For evaluation: scikit-learn, BLEU, METEOR, ROUGE for accuracy measurement

Results and Discussion

In this section, we compare our new solution pipeline 2 with existing industry solution pipeline 1. The calculated values of accuracy, precision, recall and F1-score were measured as the weighted mean over the classes to account for possible class imbalances. Table 13.1 shows the results obtained with pipeline 1 (traditional approach) and Table 13.2 depicts the results from pipeline 2 (our proposed approach). As can be seen from the results, there is a significant improvement in all the metrics with pipeline 2.

Table 13.1 Pipeline 1.

	Accuracy	Precision	Recall	F1-score
Random Forest	0.486111	0.503433	0.486111	0.477002
XGBoost	0.402778	0.385455	0.402778	0.388360
Gradient Boosting	0.416667	0.421820	0.416667	0.408313

Source: Evaluated on test images from the Emotic Dataset [5] and results computed by author

Table 13.2 Pipeline 2.

	Accuracy	Precision	Recall	F1-score
Random Forest	0.722222	0.746914	0.722222	0.727358
XGBoost	0.722222	0.730085	0.722222	0.722224
Gradient Boosting	0.638889	0.651455	0.638889	0.643301

Source: Evaluated on test images from the Emotic Dataset [5] and results computed by author

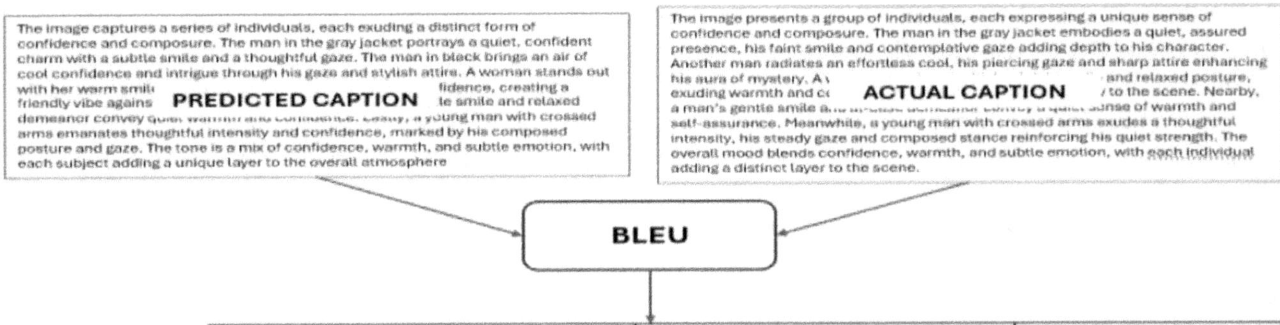

Type	Weights	BLEU_Score
1-gram BLEU Score	(1, 0, 0, 0)	0.6
2-gram BLEU Score	(0, 1, 0, 0)	0.34
3-gram BLEU Score	(0, 0, 1, 0)	0.2
4-gram BLEU Score	(0, 0, 0, 1)	0.14
1,2-gram BLEU Score	(0.5, 0.5, 0, 0)	0.45
1,2,3-gram BLEU Score	(0.33, 0.34, 0.33, 0)	0.34
1,2,3,4-gram BLEU Score	(0.25, 0.25, 0.25, 0.25)	0.27

Figure 13.4 BLEU score results

Source: Evaluated on test images from the Emotic Dataset [5] and results computed by author

Regarding the BLEU score, the captions generated by pipeline 2 are rich, detailed, and accurate in context. Although the individual words were similar, there was almost no similarity between the consecutive word patterns obtained using the two captioning methods. Figure 13.4 shows the results of the BLEU score between the predicted caption and the actual caption.

The fact that BLEU scores decrease as n increases indicates that phrases are quite dissimilar between the two methods, including the use of correct words but with very different phrasing. Furthermore, the combined BLEU scores (0.27–0.45) demonstrated that there was a combination of correct words, but dissimilar structures. A key limitation of BLEU is that it depends on the exact word and phrase match, disregarding synonyms and paraphrases.

Other, more complete evaluation metrics for caption quality may include METEOR, ROUGE, and human review to see how similar the captions are to human-generated captions and whether the captions are fluent enough to read. In future studies, these additional evaluation methods will be explored to further understand the performance of the proposed approach

Conclusion

The proposed AI system will be able to enhance security measures and situational awareness as well as provide useful information related to urban planning and event management in the case of emotion-based image captioning and emotion analysis in public spaces. By proposing a system that relies on techniques of advanced computer vision and natural language processing, with deep learning algorithms, a system that is more certain, context-wise, and incorporates more nuances for the analysis of complex social environments, can be proposed when compared to traditional image processing methods. Results show that pipeline 2, which is the proposed methodology, produced more emotionally rich and detailed captions as well as a high classification accuracy as compared to the standard industrial approach (pipeline 1). We further explain the reasons for the improved performance in the segmentation of the Region of Interest (ROI), individual captioning, and emotion-based summarization. Although the system has potential, there is a need to address existing ethical concerns and privacy issues when widely adopted. Further investigation should be conducted to enhance the model's capability to decipher intricate social interactions, fare better in caption coherence in multi-person scenes, and harmless use of the technology within public areas. Much alike, this AI orientated approach is also an achievement in the domain of intelligent surveillance and emotion recognition, where its numerous applications can be seen in public safety, urban development, human–computer interaction, etc. The continued development and ethical implementation of such systems could provide more effective, safer, more efficient, and responsive public environments.

The proposed AI system processed images to detect emotions and generate a descriptive caption of environmental mood. This aids in advancing public safety by providing the ability to identify potential threats and provide them to identified threat actors in real time so that they can be proactive in engaging in risk management. The user experience is improved, and users can manage public spaces better, and so, for authorities, they can take data-driven decisions with respect to crowds and security control.

Recommendations and Future Work

Beyond security applications, this technology can be extended to any domains such as:

Retail: To analyze shopper's emotions and behaviors and enhance customer experience.

Event Management: Assessing audience engagement and sentiment in large gatherings.

In future, we plan to develop predictive models where the analysis will integrate the live insights with the historical data to enable better forecasting of possible security risks and mood swings, boosting the performance in public spaces.

Acknowledgement

The authors would like to thank Mr. Vineet Garg, Senior Manager (Boeing EAI&D-IT&DA), and Prof. Anuj Kumar Ph.D. (Head of Research - Rushford Business School) for their invaluable support throughout this research and technical guidance of the paper

References

[1] Alayrac, J.-B., Menick, J., Cabi, S., Barreira, R., Miech, A., Reynolds M., et al. (2022). Flamingo: a visual language model for few-shot learning. Cornell University, 29 April. Available from: https://doi.org/10.48550/arxiv.2204.14198.

[2] Cheng, K., & Li, Q. (2023). Application of acquiring region of interest based on the YOLOv5 model in terahertz digital holography. *Applied Optics*, 62(14), 3589.

[3] Chuai, Q., He, X., & Li, Y. (2023). Improved traffic small object detection via cross-layer feature fusion and channel attention. *Electronics*, 12(16), 3421.

[4] Kopalidis, T., Solachidis, V., Daras, P., & Vretos, N. (2024). Advances in facial expression recognition: a survey of methods, benchmarks, models, and datasets. *Information*, 15(3), 135.

[5] Kosti, R., Alvarez, J. M., Recasens, A., & Lapedriza, A. (2019). Context-based emotion recognition using Emotic dataset. *IEEE Transactions on Pattern Analysis and Machine Intelligence*, 42(11), 2755–2766.

[6] Kumari, M., & Kaul, A. (2023). Recent advances in the application of vision transformers to remote sensing image scene classification. *Remote Sensing Letters*, 14(7), 722–732.

[7] Li, J., Xiong, C., Li, D., & Hoi, S. (2022). BLIP: bootstrapping language-image pre-training for unified vision-language understanding and generation. Cornell University, 28 January. Available from: https://doi.org/10.48550/arxiv.2201.12086.

[8] Liu, W., Hu, K., Wu, H., Cheng, X., & Luo, Q. (2021). A scientometric visualization analysis of image captioning research from 2010 to 2020. *IEEE Access*, 9, 156799–156817.

[9] Lu, K., Zhang, Y., Xu, X., & Zhao, F. (2023). An object detection algorithm combining self-attention and YOLOv4 in traffic scene. *Plos One*, 18(5), e0285654.

[10] Osman, A., Soliman, M., Elsayed, K., & Shalaby, M. (2024). Ar-CM-ViMETA: Arabic image captioning based on concept model and vision-based multi-encoder transformer architecture. *The International Arab Journal of Information Technology*, 21(3), 458–465. Available from: https://doi.org/10.34028/iajit/21/3/9.

[11] Park, J., & Kang, D. (2024). Artificial intelligence and smart technologies in safety management: a comprehensive analysis across multiple industries. *Applied Sciences*, 14(24), 11934.

[12] Abid, M. S. Z., Jahan, B., Mamun, A. A., Hossen, M. J., & Mazumder, S. H. (2024). Bangladeshi crops leaf disease detection using YOLOv8. *Heliyon*, 10(18), e36694.

[13] Sorboni, N. G., Wang, J., & Najafi, M. R. (2024). Automated first floor height estimation for flood vulnerability analysis using deep learning and google street view. *Journal of Flood Risk Management*, 17(2), e12975. Available from: https://doi.org/10.1111/jfr3.12975.

[14] Tang, Z., Yi, Y., & Sheng, H. (2021). Attention-guided image captioning through word information. *Sensors*, 21(23), 7982.

[15] Xue, Y., Wang, H., Hu, Y., Cheng, L., Wang, Q., & Qian, Y. (2024). FL-YOLOv8: lightweight object detector based on feature fusion. *Electronics*, 13(23), 4653.

[16] Zhang, Q., Kim, C.-H., & Byun, H. W. (2022). Multi-Finger-Based Arbitrary Region-of-Interest Selection in Virtual Reality, *International Journal of Human–Computer Interaction*, vol. ahead-of-print, no. ahead-of-print, pp. 3969–3983, Aug. 2022, doi: 10.1080/10447318.2022.2108666.

14 Analyzing spillover effects of international monetary policies on the green bond market

Nguyen Thi Vu Ha[a] *and Dang Hong Duong*

Faculty of International Business and Economics, VNU University of Economics and Business, Hanoi, Vietnam

Abstract

The impact of international monetary policy (IMP) plays a crucial role in stabilizing inflation and fostering economic growth, in addition to contributing to the development of global financial markets such as the green bond market (GBM). Hence, it is meaningful and interesting to investigate the global monetary policy impact on GBMs via spillover effects The objective of this paper is to analyze the spillover effects of international monetary policies—from the United States (US), the European Union (EU), the United Kingdom (UK), and Japan—on the Solactive Green Bond (SGB) Index and the S&P Green Bond (SPGB) Index during the period 2014–2021. To account for the dynamic effects of these factors over time, we use a TVP-VAR model. The results suggest that US monetary policy has significant effects on the performance of green bonds, the majority stemming from interest rate and exchange rate channels, and the effects are more significant in the period of monetary easing. However, such spillover effects are attenuated during periods of global instability, i.e., COVID-19, possibly because of higher levels of systemic risk. The findings imply some policy implications for central banks and developing countries, especially including green finance tools in monetary regulatory frameworks and international regulation for sustainable development.

Keywords: Global financial stability, green bonds, IMP, spillover effects, TVP-VAR model

Introduction

Since IMP continues to be regarded as a powerful tool not only to ensure price stability and foster economic stabilization, but also to shape the dynamics of global financial markets, including the nascent GBM. After the international financial crisis of 2007–2009, the world's big central banks—the FED, ECB, BoE, and BoJ—adopted a series of non-conventional policy instruments such as QE and the accounting of negative interest rates. Although those interventions have been conducted with the stricter purpose of enhancing domestic liquidity and containing the costs of borrowing, they have also had noticeable cross-border spillover effects – consistent with earlier evidence on financial contagion [13] – and thus indirect implications for the performance and growth of financial instruments with sustainability features, such as green bonds.

There has been increasing demand from the other side of the institutional spectrum for green bonds post-pandemic—debt securities issued for the purpose of financing environmentally friendly projects. There is growing interest in these instruments as they offer a double-edged promise of providing financial returns as well as helping to meet climate-related objectives. The value of new green bond issuance was USD 5.174 billion in 2021 with an 85% year-on-year growth rate, indicating the increasing presence of sustainable financing in the international capital markets [11].

Though GBM has developed rapidly in recent years, its linkage with the IMP has received less attention. In SSF, there is a large body of research concerning the effects of monetary policy on conventional markets, but the studies on green bonds are still scarce [21, 4]. Hence, the aim of this paper is to contribute to the academic literature by analyzing the spillover effects of monetary policy changes in some developed economies -such as the USA, EU, Japan, and United Kingdom- on the GBM. In this regard, this study uses two representative indices to assess the impact of IMP on the GBM: the SGB Index illustrates market volatility, while the SPGB Index indicates the global market capitalization of green bonds [18]. These indexes give an indication to appraise the reaction of green bonds to monetary policy at the time. Moreover, SSR, which are often utilized for unconventional monetary policy purposes, are used as the policy proxies, particularly

[a]hantv@vnu.edu.vn

DOI: 10.4324/9781003739982-14

when conventional policy rates are either bounded from below by the zero level or slip into the negative [7, 14].

Drawing on the intertemporal asset-pricing model, the study investigates the pass-through of monetary policy renovations from advanced economies to other countries' financial markets. Green bonds, for instance, are the outcome of the global transmission of liquidity, interest rates, and capital flows from developed markets to the international preference for environment-related securities [5, 23]. We, however, defensively argue that the reactions of green bonds to monetary policy changes might not be in line with those of conventional bonds, given their specific features, particularly in relation to environmental and sustainability objectives (i.e., Lin and Su [21]). The empirical analysis period runs from 31 July 2014 through 31 December 2021, encompassing extreme policy experiment times, such as during the pandemic caused by COVID-19. In particular, attention is given to the ways that monetary policy might be reoriented in order to further broader sustainability goals, thus entrenching the transmission mechanism from macroeconomic stability to long-run environmental goals.

Literature Review

Besides its domestic objectives, monetary policy exerts an important influence on international financial markets through several transmission channels, such as interest rates, capital flows, and exchange rate changes [2, 5, 10, 23]. Central banks introduced their own policies that have been crucial in determining these cross-border impacts, particularly the use of non-standard monetary policies such as quantitative easing (QE) and negative interest rates following the 2007–2009 global financial crisis [15, 6, 8]. Although academic literature has focused on the impact of these policies on standard financial markets, other market segments - such as green bonds - have recently gained attention in policy spillover discussions.

The pass-through of IMP varies significantly across asset classes and is critically dependent on the state of the global economy and the instruments used [16]. Antonakakis et al. [3] introduced the time-varying parameter vector autoregressive (TVP-VAR) specification. They documented an increase in the spillover transmission of US policy during the crisis of 2009. Likewise, Sugimoto and Matsuki [23] found that US monetary tightening had significant impacts on Asian stock markets, whereas Bhattarai et al. [5] emphasized how QE was among the factors that led to greater volatility in exchange rates and sovereign bonds in emerging economies. Similarly, Evon et al. [20] demonstrated that U.S. balance sheet policy affected foreign holdings of Malaysian government securities. However, these papers mostly focus on traditional assets, and there is scarce empirical evidence on how a relatively recent and differentiated product such as green bonds reacts to these policy events.

Most research on the bond market focuses on the government and corporate bond markets, two instruments that are directly affected by changes in interest rates and macro-financial conditions. For example, Gagnon et al. (2018) demonstrated the long-term interest rate and capital flow impact worldwide of the Federal Reserve's QE. This is supported by Fratzscher et al. [15] found pronounced spillovers from US monetary policy to global equity and bond markets, a view further supported by Ahmed et al. [1], who emphasized that both the nature of U.S. monetary shocks and the vulnerabilities of emerging markets play key roles in transmission. However, green bonds are distinct from these ordinary instruments not only in terms of purpose and investor composition but also in the nature of financing for long-horizon environmental investments that characterize their sustainability-linked missions [21].

Unlike traditional bonds, green bonds are sensitive not only to financial factors but also to the variation in sustainability-related demand and the evolution of policy in the long run. Lin and Su [21] discovered that the issuance of green bonds contracts under monetary tightening, mainly because of the higher cost of capital. Further, Azhgaliyeva and Kapsalyamova [4] highlight the significance of global cooperation and the use of cost-reduction measures to strengthen and develop green finance markets.

GBM has experienced an increase in popularity over the past few years, especially in light of the outbreak of the COVID-19, yet research on the GBM and its association with market-wide monetary policy is limited. Wang et al. [25], for instance, used the quantile connectedness approach to measure interconnections between China and US GBMs and found high volatility during economic uncertainty. Turn, Gyamerah, and Asare [17] also examined the effect of global policy uncertainty on green bond returns, while Mzoughi et al. [22] studied the influence of blockchain assets on green finance instruments in volatile financial environments.

The development of GBM can be divided into three stages. Issuance soared between 2014 and 2017, reflecting in part the 2016 Paris Accord and global climate targets (International Energy Agency, 2017). This progress, however, slowed between 2017 and 2019 due to monetary tightening in a variety of advanced economies, most notably the US (Federal Reserve, 2018). The third phase (2020–2021) was marked by a revival in issuance, attributed to expansionary monetary and fiscal stimulus measures implemented in response to the pandemic [11].

However, a clear lack of understanding remains regarding the exact mechanisms through which IMP is transmitted to the global GBM. Although traditional bonds have been widely studied in terms of interest rate and liquidity dynamics, the particular nature of green bonds and their policy relevance make it necessary to conduct more empirical work. This paper attempts to fill this void by examining the transmission of short-term interest rate (STIR) shocks from leading economies to the global GBM. To this end, it aims to contribute to the literature on sustainable finance, as well as provide analytical support for aligning monetary policy with long-term climate and development goals.

Research Methodology

Research model

In this study, the Time-Varying Parameter Vector Autoregression (TVP-VAR) model is employed to examine the spillover effects of IMP on the global GBM. Originally developed by Koop and Korobilis [19], the TVP-VAR framework is particularly well-suited for analyzing relationships that evolve over time, especially under conditions of macro-financial instability and shifting policy regimes. The model facilitates the identification of changing linkages between monetary policy variables and green bond performance by accounting for temporal dynamics in parameter estimates.

The preference for the TVP-VAR approach lies in its methodological advantages over traditional sliding-window or fixed-parameter techniques. Specifically, the model estimates time-varying coefficients through the use of the Kalman filter, thereby enhancing estimation accuracy while avoiding the data loss commonly associated with moving-window estimators. In the context of this analysis, monetary policy stance is proxied by SSR, which are capable of capturing the effects of unconventional policy tools in low or negative interest rate environments. The model enables the tracking of how the association between SSR, and key green bond indices changes over time, thus providing a dynamic perspective on policy transmission.

The formal specification of the model is presented as follows:

$$\Delta x_t = \beta_t \Delta x_{t-1} + \epsilon_t \, \epsilon_t \sim N(0, \Sigma_t) \quad (1)$$

$$vec(\beta_t) = vec(\beta_{t-1}) + \upsilon_t \, \upsilon_t \sim N(0, R_t) \quad (2)$$

Where:

- Δx_t represents the vector of variables at time t, comprising changes in green bond indices and monetary policy variables.
- β_t denotes the time-varying parameter matrix.
- ϵ_t is the error term, which is assumed to follow a normal distribution with a time-varying covariance matrix Σ_t.
- v_t reflects innovations to the parameters, following a normal distribution with covariance R_t.

To enhance the understanding of spillover dynamics beyond the baseline TVP-VAR model, this study further incorporates the Generalized Forecast Error Variance Decomposition (GFEVD) technique. As proposed by Diebold and Yilmaz [12], the GFEVD allows for the quantification of directional spillovers by measuring the extent to which forecast error variances of one variable—such as green bond indices—can be attributed to innovations in another variable, specifically SSR as a proxy for IMP shocks. This approach provides an additional layer of granularity in identifying the relative influence of external monetary disturbances on GBM.

In parallel, wavelet coherence analysis, introduced by Torrence and Compo [24], is applied to examine the co-movement between green bond indices and monetary policy indicators across multiple frequency bands. By decomposing the time series into localized time-frequency space, wavelet analysis facilitates the identification of varying degrees of association over short-, medium-, and long-term horizons. This method is particularly useful in highlighting temporal episodes where strong covariance emerges between monetary policy changes and green bond dynamics.

The integration of TVP-VAR, GFEVD, and wavelet-based analysis forms a comprehensive methodological framework. This enables a multi-dimensional assessment of spillover effects that are both dynamic and time-varying in nature, thereby improving the explanatory power of the empirical investigation and aligning with the complexity of global financial interdependencies.

Research data and variables

For our empirical analysis, we examine daily data over the period from July 31, 2014, to December 31, 2021, which comprises a broad range of both conventional and unconventional monetary policy, including the introduction of QE and the introduction of negative interest rate policy. This period was chosen to ensure that monetary policy transmission effect in different macroeconomic environments, particularly their effects on the global GBM can be identified. Two indices are employed to represent this market: the SGB Index and the SPGB Index (SPGB), as presented in Table 14.1

The SGB Index serves as the primary proxy for GBM volatility. It covers a wide range of green bonds denominated in different currencies and from different regions, which allows us to consider cross-border effects. In order not to outweigh individual issuers, the index places a cap on the contribution of any one bond (5%), and this cap limits concentratiandand also makes the index more representative. The index structure allows us to represent the market behavior in less volatile and more diversified fashion, thus suitable for volatility analysis [18].

In comparison, the SPGB Index (SPGB) is constructed using a market-value weighting scheme and is used primarily to validate the robustness of the results obtained from the Solactive Index. It places greater emphasis on the scale of bond issuance, thereby reflecting aggregate market value trends. Bonds included in the SPGB must conform to the eligibility standards set by the Climate Bonds Initiative, ensuring alignment with established environmental criteria. The use of this secondary index allows for cross-verification of findings under alternative market representations [11].

Monetary policy conditions are proxied through SSR, which can reflect both conventional policy rate changes and non-traditional policy measures, particularly in low or negative rate environments. SSR data is obtained from LJK Limited and includes series for four major economies—namely the US (US.SSR), the EU (EU.SSR), Japan (JP.SSR), and UK (UK.SSR)—chosen for their systemic importance and established influence on international capital markets [5, 14].

In terms of data processing, missing observations are imputed using linear interpolation to maintain time-series continuity. Outlier detection is performed using a robust z-score approach, with economically meaningful extreme values retained to preserve informational content. Where necessary, a moving average smoothing technique is applied to mitigate the influence of anomalous data points that could distort the estimation outcomes. These processes ensure that the dataset remains reliable for rigorous analysis.

Table 14.1 Summary of variables.

No.	Symbol	Meaning	Unit	Source
1	Solactive Index	SGB Index		Solactive
2	SPGB	SPGB Index		S&P Global
3	US.SSR	Shadow STIR of the US	%	LJK Limited
4	EU.SSR	Shadow STIR of the EU	%	LJK Limited
5	UK.SSR	Shadow STIR of UK	%	LJK Limited
6	JP.SSR	Shadow STIR of Japan	%	LJK Limited

Source: Authors for expressing both authors' work

Table 14.2 Preliminary statistics of variables.

	SPGB	Solactive index	US.SSR	EU.SSR	JP.SSR	UK.SSR
Mean	0.000	0.000	0.001	0.000	0.001	0.000
Variance	0.000***	0.000***	0.000***	0.000***	0.000***	0.000***
Skewness	–0.526***	–0.202***	–1.199***	0.780***	0.393***	0.942***
	0.000	0.000	0.000	0.000	0.000	0.000
Kurtosis	5.630***	27.279***	9.635***	2.146***	1.289***	7.085***
	0.000	0.000	0.000	0.000	0.000	0.000
JB	2526.842***	57341.467***	7595.291***	542.565***	175.616***	4141.261***
	0.000	0.000	0.000	0.000	0.000	0.000
ERS	–17.259***	–15.443***	–5.094***	–9.230***	–7.003***	–10.659***
	0.000	0.000	0.000	0.000	0.000	0.000
Q(20)	37.580***	23.008***	3243.256***	5118.220***	7461.216***	3978.667***
	0.000	0.005	0.000	0.000	0.000	0.000
Q2(20)	498.871***	386.366***	1844.094***	2572.772***	3633.569***	3106.172***
	0.000	0.000	0.000	0.000	0.000	0.000

Source: Authors for expressing both authors' work

Note: ***, **, and * represent significance levels of 1%, 5%, and 10%, respectively; Skewness: D'Agostino test (1970); Kurtosis: Anscombe and Glynn test (1983); J.B.: Jarque-Bera normality test (1980); ERS: Stock (1996) unit root test; Q (20) and Q2(20): Fisher and Gallagher (2012) weighted portmanteau tests

Research Results

Descriptive statistics

The descriptive statistics reveal a consistent increase in the shadow STIRs of the US and Japan from 2016 to 2021, while the Solactive index, SPGB, and the interest rates of the EU and United Kingdom remained stable. The minimal variance in these variables supports the stationary nature of the time series, a key requirement for time series analysis (see Table 14.2).

Figure 14.1 presents the time series plots of the model's variables. The shadow STIRs of the US and UK remained relatively stable, reflecting a consistent monetary policy stance during the study period. The shadow STIR of the EU exhibited more significant variation, suggesting continuous adjustments in its monetary policy. A monetary policy shock around 2019 saw STIRs in the US, EU, and Japan decline sharply, followed by a recovery after six months. This suggests aggressive monetary easing during this period. Although UK also experienced a decline, it remained within a relatively stable range. This policy shock impacted GBM, reflected in the sharp decline of the Solactive and SPGB Indices, consistent with the findings of Lin and Su [21], who noted a drop-in green bond activity during periods of eased monetary policy.

Skewness and kurtosis measures indicate that the SPGB, Solactive index, and US SSR exhibit right-skewed distributions, while the SSR for the EU, Japan, and UK are left-skewed. These characteristics reflect differences in market responses to each region's monetary policies.

The correlation analysis reveals that the shadow STIRs in the studied countries negatively correlate with the SPGB and Solactive index, while the SSRs across these countries correlate positively with each other. The high correlation between SPGB and Solactive suggests that both indices effectively represent the global GBM. The Augmented Dickey-Fuller test confirms stationarity for all series, and the SBIC criterion suggests a lag length of 2 for the VAR model.

TVP-VAR results with Solactive index

The results from the TVP-VAR model indicate that US monetary policy exerts a dominant influence on the global GBM. The total connectivity index (TCI) is 43.47%, showing that nearly half of the forecast error variance in the model is driven by the spillover effects between international monetary policies and the GBM.

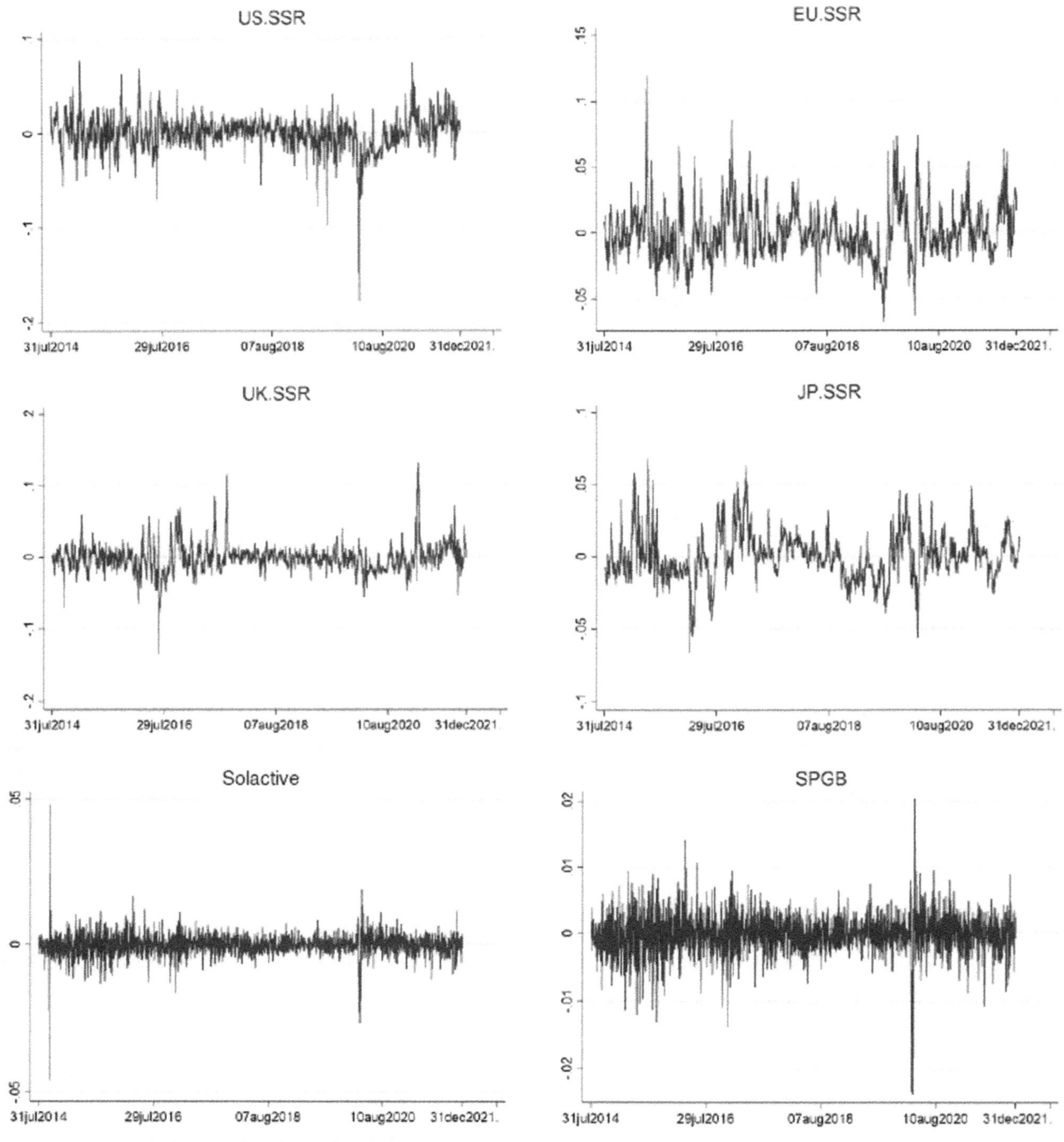

Figure 14.1 Time Series plots of variables in the model
Source: Authors for expressing both authors' work

The US SSR emerges as the most significant transmitter of monetary shocks, with a connectivity index of 5.98, highlighting its substantial role in influencing green bond dynamics. This confirms the significant global impact of US monetary policy, particularly during periods of quantitative easing. In contrast, the UK SSR has the lowest spillover effect, indicating that UK monetary policy has a relatively minor role in influencing global GBM.

Table 14.3 presents the average connectivity indices for the model's variables. EU.SSR has the highest overall spillover index (64.86), underscoring its importance as a major shock transmitter in the international

Table 14.3 Average connectivity indices.

	Solactive index	US.SSR	EU.SSR	JP.SSR	UK.SSR	FROM
Solactive index	75.74	9.67	5.76	3.64	5.19	**24.26**
US.SSR	**5.98**	55.23	16.31	2.65	19.83	44.77
EU.SSR	5.58	17.47	53.56	4.79	18.61	46.44
JP.SSR	5.72	15.39	21.63	45.50	11.76	**54.50**
UK.SSR	3.30	20.46	21.16	2.48	52.60	47.40
TO	20.57	62.99	**64.86**	13.55	55.38	217.36
Inc Own	96.31	**118.22**	**118.42**	59.06	107.99	**cTCI/TCI**
Net Spillover	**-3.69**	18.22	18.42	**–40.94**	7.99	**54.34/43.47**
NPT	1	4	3	0	2	

Source: Authors for expressing both authors' work

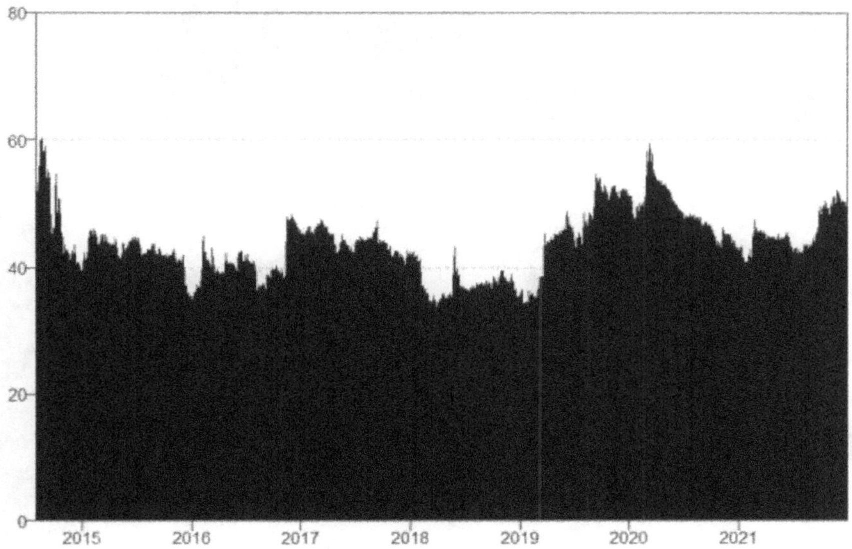

Figure 14.2 Dynamic spillover index
Source: Authors for expressing both authors' work

financial system. Conversely, Japan's SSR (JP.SSR) has the highest "FROM" value (54.5), meaning that Japan's monetary policy is more susceptible to external shocks than other countries, particularly from the US and EU

Dynamic spillover effects

The dynamic spillover index (Figure 14.2) shows how the connectivity between monetary policies and GBM evolves over time. The index peaked at 60% around July 2014, indicating a period of heightened global financial interconnectedness. During 2015-2016, the spillover effect remained relatively stable at about 50%, but the effect started to decrease due to the widespread adoption of quantitative easing and negative interest rates.

After 2018, the spillover effects increased again, peaking in 2020 at the onset of the pandemic caused by COVID-19, when global financial markets became more volatile. The index declined to around 40% in 2021 as the focus of many central banks shifted to stabilizing domestic economies and managing the economic consequences of the pandemic.

The dynamic spillover "TO" effect (Figure 14.3) shows that the Solactive Index initially strongly influenced other variables, with a spillover index of nearly 200% at the start of the study. This influence dropped sharply between 2016 and 2019 but rebounded slightly in late 2020, reflecting the resurgence of green bond

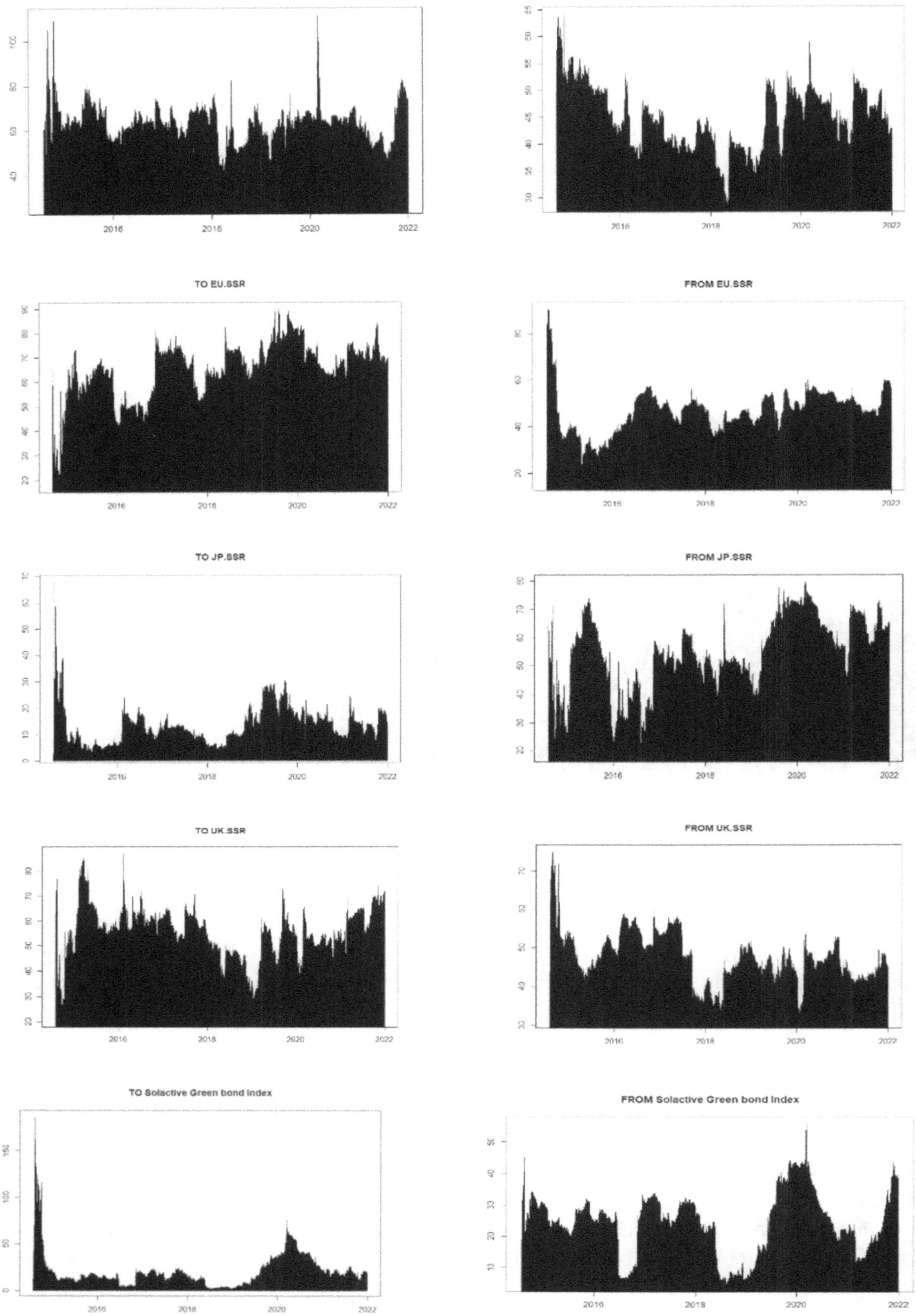

Figure 14.3 Spillover "TO" and "FROM" effects among variables
Source: Authors for expressing both authors' work

investments. US.SSR and EU.SSR displayed consistent spillover levels throughout the study, emphasizing their central role in transmitting monetary policy shocks to the GBM.

In contrast, Japan's SSR and the Solactive index exhibited lower "FROM" values, indicating that they are more influenced by external monetary shocks rather than acting as transmitters. The pandemic caused by COVID-19 appears to have amplified the role of the GBM as a recipient of these shocks, particularly as governments shifted their focus to domestic policy measures.

The impact of monetary policy on the GBM

The spillover index and wavelet analysis reveal the impact of IMP on the GBM. The results reveal three primary transmission channels: US.SSR, EU.SSR, and UK.SSR. These STIRs are key indicators of how monetary policies in these regions affect the GBM.

The continuous wavelet method Torrence and Webster [24], examined the co-movement between the SPGB Index and these shadow STIRs across short, medium, and long-term periods (Figure 14.4). The findings show that US monetary policy significantly influences the GBM in the medium term, particularly from 2019 to 2020, with an inverse relationship observed. This indicates that GBM activity tends to decline when US monetary policy is eased.

In contrast, the EU's monetary policy has a more profound effect over the long term, with its influence on green bond performance becoming more pronounced from 2018 onward. The UK monetary policy demonstrated a notable impact during the medium term (late 2015 to 2017), but this influence diminished in the long term, reflecting the limited role of the UK in the broader global GBM.

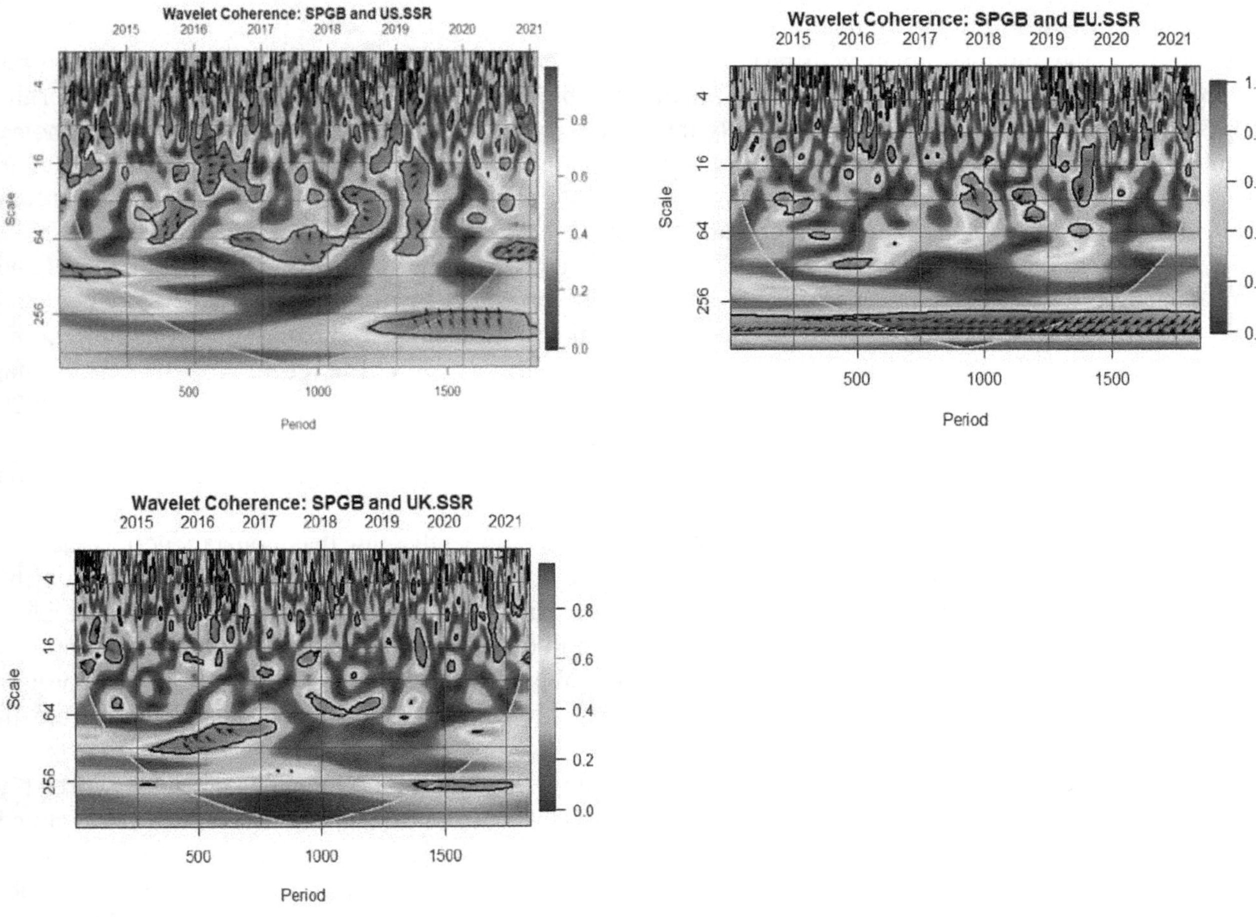

Figure 14.4 Combined wavelet spectrum of the SPGB Index and SSR of various countries

Source: Authors for expressing both authors' work

Robustness check

To ensure the reliability of the results, a robustness check was performed by substituting the Solactive index with the SPGB Index in the TVP-VAR model. The results remained largely consistent, with the total connectivity index increasing slightly by 0.5%. The US.SSR and EU.SSR continued to play dominant roles in transmitting shocks, while Japan remained the most affected by monetary policy changes.

The difference in spillover intensity between the SGB Index and the SPGB Index can be attributed to some extent to the underlying weighting methodology employed for each index. Although the SPGB Index leverages market value in its index construction (favoring larger issuances), the Solactive mandates a cap of 5% on an individual bond's weight to avoid issuer concentration. This structural distinction could explain the sensitivity differences to outsider monetary shocks, considering that the SPGB Index puts more emphasis on the aggregate of market valuation and thus perhaps has captured a broader number of reactions from those largest, more active issuers.

Discussion

The empirical analysis based on the TVP-VAR model and the related dynamic spillover network implies that international monetary policies—especially those of the US—are clearly shaping the global GBM. Of the countries covered, the US has the greatest net spillover index at 5.98, meaning that it plays a crucial role in transferring monetary shocks to this asset class. This finding is in line with the previous investigations of Fratzscher et al. [15] and Bhattarai et al. [5], who also reported the international transmission of US monetary spillover, particularly when the US launched or withdrew policies of QE and MT. The ability of US policy to serve as a source of global liquidity and as a definer of interest rate expectations will likely prove to be a critical channel of transmission, affecting the allocation of capital (and of long-duration instruments like green bonds) around the world.

By contrast, the spillover effect with respect to the UK seems to be much weaker, as shown by the net spillover index of 1.15. This relatively limited impact may be due to the fact that, compared to the US or the EU, the UK's GBM is smaller and less globally integrated into sustainable finance flows. The UK economy traditionally draws more on conventional instruments, while the architecture of green finance is still evolving. Increased policy uncertainty related to Brexit developments over the sample period could also have constrained the role of the UK in influencing global GBM trends.

The dynamic spillover results also support the temporal nature of these spillovers, peaking in 2014H2 and decreasing dramatically during the COVID-19 outbreak. The apex in 2014 coincides with a recovery in global financial markets following the 2007–2009 global financial crisis, when central banks—most notably in the US and EU—adopted a dovish stance with respect to their monetary policy. The recent drop may also signal a change in the focus of central banks globally toward the stability of domestic economies during the 2020 pandemic, which in turn reduced interest in international trends like green bonds. That being said, the spillover effects by the end of 2020 suggest a quick recovery of global financial markets, propelled by the reintroduction of easing measures in large economies.

These findings are in line with the general macroeconomic literature indicating that monetary policies abroad also affect green or other financial securities. However, the green bond reaction seems more reliant on the wider macro context. In periods of crisis, such as during the pandemic caused by COVID-19, the globalizing tendency of financial markets is usually reversed, which could moderate the immediate effect of international monetary policies. In the context of a post-crisis recovery, the GBM also appears to benefit from improved liquidity and lower interest rates, which reinforces its character as a rather sustainable financing instrument within the emergence of the postulated sustainable finance taxonomy.

Empirically, the results of this paper are mostly consistent with previous literature and have underscored the international spillovers of US monetary policy. Notably, Fratzscher et al. [15] and Bhattarai et al. [5] illustrated the global reach of US monetary actions on bond rates and capital flows in both developed and emerging markets. The findings of this study confirm such patterns in GBM, where changes in US monetary policy, particularly those related to quantitative easing, have contributed to the transmission of changes in global liquidity, interest rate expectations, and green bond dynamics.

Meanwhile, this paper also provides several new contributions that not only complement but also go beyond existing literature. Whereas much of the existing research has concentrated on traditional fixed-income instruments, the current study demonstrates how green bonds—a fast-growing market sector intuitively connected to long-term sustainability goals—behave differently. Green bonds are less negatively impacted than standard bonds during rebound periods, such as in late 2020 after the initial outbreak of COVID-19. This resilience can be explained by investor confidence in the environmental authenticity and policy backing of green instruments—an angle not directly investigated in previous studies examining monetary policy transmission [9].

Further, the study deviates from the literature by highlighting cross-regional differences in the transmission of monetary policy responses. While previous studies often singled out the UK as a financial center with significant overseas influence, the results here show that the UK-GBM relationships are actually weaker globally compared to those of the US and the EU This might be in part due to institutional reasons, such as the still-in-flux regulatory framework for green finance in the UK and persisting uncertainty about the post-Brexit policy environment.

Lastly, the present research adds value by infusing a dynamic front to the examination of spillover effects, rather than the static lens used in prior studies. Results using time-varying models suggest that the impact of IMP is not constant over time but varies in line with international business cycles. The spillover effect becomes stronger when expansionary policies are active or when global systemic risk—such as during the COVID-19 crisis—is low.

Conclusion and Recommendations

Our study examines the transmission mechanisms of IMP spillovers to the global GBM, paying special attention to the part that can be played by monetary authorities in the US, the EU, UK, and Japan. The analysis points to shadow STIR fluctuations as the main channel for the transmission of policies. In periods of accommodative monetary policy actions, including quantitative easing or policy rate cuts, the appeal of green bonds is more apparent given more liquidity and lower borrowing costs. Rather, the transmission channels are weakened during periods of crisis, such as during COVID-19 (worldwide), possibly reflecting increased systemic risk and changes in investor sentiment.

This study adds to the literature by specifically looking at green bonds as a unique type of asset class. First, existing literature focusing on traditional bonds is expanded by providing evidence on the differentiated response of green bonds to exogenous monetary shocks. Results indicate that green bonds are more resilient following crisis-recoveries, which may be related to their alignment with long-term environmental aims. Second, the paper detects regional dispersions in policy effectiveness, where US monetary policy indicators have a substantially stronger global impact than those from other parts of the world. These divergences indicate that the major markets of green finance are not evenly integrated or influential.

The results of the present study have several implications at the policy level. For emerging market economies, the findings highlight the possible payoffs from harmonizing domestic regulatory architecture with global norms of green finance, especially when global monetary conditions are loose. Enhanced disclosure aligned sustainability standards, and more standardized issuance can help create interest among foreign investors and provide more confidence that the market is transparent. Engagement with international institutions in emerging markets such as Vietnam could help provide coherent legal and institutional structures (Climate Bonds Initiative). These actions can help domestic markets slowly connect to international financial networks and facilitate access to climate-aligned investment.

Central banks, on the other hand, could also consider using green bonds as part of their monetary operations, particularly when policy is loose. Green monetary tools in asset purchase programs can also serve to stabilize financial markets and incentivize environmental goals, to render monetary frameworks consistent with sustainability, more broadly.

Furthermore, the results indicate that the green bond has strategic impact in economy recovery of recession. Green bonds could finance climate-resilient infrastructure, renewable energy and other environmentally friendly activities, both as a short-term stimulus and as a long-term way support transitions to a greener future.

Despite its valuable insights, the study has some inevitable limitations. The analysis uses two global benchmarks — the SGB Index and the SPGB Index — that predominantly reflect activity in developed markets. Consequently, generalization to smaller or less developed markets should be approached with caution. Future research would benefit from using country-level or regional indices that better capture market-specific attributes.

Also, although shadow STIRs are a useful approximation for monetary policy, they do not consider other key drivers such as fiscal dynamics, geopolitical risk, or changes in investor sentiment. Integration of these dimensions within future empirical frameworks can provide a more holistic picture of the forces driving the performance of green bonds.

Last, this research is constrained by time due to the exceptional policy actions in response to the worldwide spread of the novel coronavirus, up to 2021. To make these findings more general, it would be open for investigating -in a pre-pandemic analysis- on how the nature of the relationship between monetary policy and sustainable finance changes over time. As the field of market-related research continues to grow, much will be required to untangle how innovation, regulation and global macroeconomic trends coalesce to shape green finance over time.

References

[1] Ahmed, S., Correa, R., & Coulibaly, B. (2021). *U.S. monetary policy spillovers to emerging markets: Both shocks and vulnerabilities matter* (International Finance Discussion Papers No. 1321). Board of Governors of the Federal Reserve System. https://doi.org/10.17016/IFDP.2021.1321

[2] Ahmed, S., Coulibaly, B., & Zlate, A. (2017). International financial spillovers to emerging market economies: How important are economic fundamentals? *Journal of International Money and Finance*, 76, 133–152. https://doi.org/10.1016/j.jimonfin.2017.05.001

[3] Antonakakis, N., Gabauer, D., & Gupta, R. (2019). International monetary policy spillovers evidence from a time-varying parameter vector autoregression. *International Review of Financial Analysis*, Article 101382. https://doi.org/10.1016/j.irfa.2019.101382

[4] Azhgaliyeva, D., & Kapsalyamova, Z. (2021). *Policy support in promoting green bonds in Asia* (No. 1275). ADBI Working Paper. https://hdl.handle.net/10419/249454

[5] Bhattarai, S., Chatterjee, A., & Park, W. Y. (2021). Effects of US quantitative easing on emerging market economies. *Journal of Economic Dynamics and Control*, 122, 104031. https://doi.org/10.1016/j.jedc.2020.104031

[6] Borio, C., & Zabai, A. (2018). Unconventional monetary policies: a re-appraisal. In *Research handbook on central banking* (pp. 398–444). Edward Elgar Publishing. https://doi.org/10.4337/9781784719227.00026

[7] Çekin, S. E., Hkiri, B., Tiwari, A. K., & Gupta, R. (2020). The relationship between monetary policy and uncertainty in advanced economies: evidence from time-and frequency-domains. *The Quarterly Review of Economics and Finance*, 78, 70-87. https://doi.org/10.1016/j.qref.2020.05.010

[8] Chadha, J. S., & Waters, A. (2014). Applying a macro-finance yield curve to UK quantitative easing. *Journal of Banking & Finance*, 39, 68–86. https://doi.org/10.1016/j.jbankfin.2013.11.008

[9] Chen, Q., Filardo, A., He, D., & Zhu, F. (2016). Financial crisis, US unconventional monetary policy and international spillovers. *Journal of International Money and Finance*, 67, 62–81. https://doi.org/10.1016/j.jimonfin.2015.06.011

[10] Ciminelli, G., Rogers, J., & Wu, W. (2022). The effects of U.S. monetary policy on international mutual fund investment. *Journal of International Money and Finance*, 127, 102676. https://doi.org/10.1016/j.jimonfin.2022.102676

[11] Climate Bonds Initiative (2022). GBM Summary. Climate Bonds Initiative.

[12] Diebold, F. X., & Yılmaz, K. (2014). On the network topology of variance decompositions: Measuring the connectedness of financial firms. *Journal of econometrics*, 182(1), 119–134. https://doi.org/10.1016/j.jeconom.2014.04.012

[13] Eichengreen, B., Rose, A. K., & Wyplosz, C. (1996). Contagious currency crises. *Scandinavian Journal of Economics*, 98(4), 463–484. https://www.nber.org/system/files/working_papers/w5681/w5681.pdf

[14] Elsayed, A. H., & Sousa, R. M. (2022). International monetary policy and cryptocurrency markets: dynamic and spillover effects. *The European Journal of Finance*, 30(16), 1855–1875. https://doi.org/10.1080/1351847X.2022.2068375

[15] Fratzscher, M., Lo Duca, M., & Straub, R. (2018). On the international spillovers of US quantitative easing. *The Economic Journal*, 128(608), 330–377. https://doi.org/10.1111/ecoj.12435

[16] Gabauer, D., & Gupta, R. (2018). On the transmission mechanism of country-specific and international economic uncertainty spillovers: evidence from a TVP-FAVAR model. *Economics Letters*, 171, 59–63. https://doi.org/10.1016/j.econlet.2018.07.007

[17] Gyamerah, S. A., & Asare, C. (2024). The impacts of global economic policy uncertainty on green bond returns: a systematic literature review. *Heliyon*, 10, e25076. https://doi.org/10.1016/j.heliyon.2024.e25076

[18] Kanamura, T. (2020). Are green bonds environmentally friendly and good performing assets?. *Energy Economics*, 88, 104767. https://doi.org/10.1016/j.eneco.2020.104767

[19] Koop, G., & Korobilis, D. (2013). Large time-varying parameter VARs. *Journal of Econometrics*, 177(2), 185–198. https://doi.org/10.1016/j.jeconom.2013.04.007

[20] Evon, Z., Lee, H., & Joe, H. Y. (2020). FTSE WGBI, US Balance Sheet Policy And Foreign Holdings Of Malaysia Government Securities. In Z. Ahmad (Ed.), Progressing Beyond and Better: Leading Businesses for a Sustainable Future, vol 88. European Proceedings of Social and Behavioural Sciences (pp. 88–97). European Publisher. https://doi.org/10.15405/epsbs.2020.10.8

[21] Lin, B., & Su, T. (2022). Green bond vs conventional bond: Outline the rationale behind issuance choices in China. *International Review of Financial Analysis*, 81, 102063. https://doi.org/10.1016/j.irfa.2022.102063

[22] Mzoughi, H., Amar, A. B., Guesmi, K., & Benkraiem, R. (2024). Blockchain markets, green finance investments, and environmental impacts. *Research in International Business and Finance*, 69, 102249. https://doi.org/10.1016/j.ribaf.2024.102249

[23] Sugimoto, K., & Matsuki, T. (2019). International spillovers into Asian stock markets under the unconventional monetary policies of advanced countries. *Journal of the Japanese and International Economies*, 52, 171–188. https://doi.org/10.1016/j.jjie.2018.10.001

[24] Torrence, C., & Compo, G. P. (1998). A practical guide to wavelet analysis. *Bulletin of the American Meteorological Society*, 79(1), 61–78. https://doi.org/10.1175/1520-0477(1998)079<0061:APGTWA>2.0.CO;2

[25] Wang, M. C., Jiang, P., & Chang, T. (2025). Re-examining China and the U.S.'s respective green bond markets in extreme conditions: Evidence from quantile connectedness. *The North American Journal of Economics and Finance*, 75, 102286. https://doi.org/10.1016/j.najef.2024.102286

15 AI and ML enabled smart city initiatives for sustainable development – a mixed method approach

Rajani H. pillai[1,a] *Deeksha, S.*[2,b], *Vernachris Rhoda Bonjour*[3,c] *and Roopa Adarsh*[4,d]

[1]Associate Professor, School of Commerce, Mount Carmel College, Autonomous, Bengaluru, Karnataka, India

[2]Full Time Research Scholar, Bengaluru City University, Commerce Block, Bengaluru City University, Bengaluru, Karnataka, India

[3]English Teacher, Clarence High School ICSE .Bangalore, Karnataka, India

[4]Associate Professor, School of Humanities and Social Sciences, Mount Carmel College, Autonomous, Bengaluru, Karnataka, India

Abstract

Smart City practices have benefited from innovation in artificial intelligence (AI) and machine learning (ML) to enhance urban decision-making and management. All these technologies have helped the cities to embrace data and analytics to predict and manage urban systems, efficiently deliver services and enhance the welfare of the citizens. AI and ML are now ground breaking elements within smart city that enable decision and preventive or mitigating actions in complex urban structures. The research objectives are to understand the present state of Internet of Things (IoT) and machine learning applications in selected smart cities , to evaluate the smart city management AI and ML paradigms and to learn how policymakers view the artificial intelligence and machine learning models employed in smart city management. The research methodology of the present paper is based on concurrent triangulation convergence model. Data was gathered from: smart city residents, specialists of internet of things, machine learning developers, policymakers, and AI specialist engaged with smart city projects. Due to the case-based character of qualitative research, in-depth analyses require relatively small samples. Additionally, qualitative samples are hand-picked because of the wealth of precise information they can provide on the phenomena under study. Therefore, 10 policy makers were considered for the study. Focusing on ten smart cities in the Indian state of Karnataka, this study examines their smart service, economics, mobility, environment, people, and governance initiatives. Research into the association between SDGs and smart city is the aim of this paper. Consideration is given to SDGs 3, 7, 8, 9, and 11 in order to measure sustainable development. The research seeks to develop a better smart city management method through confluence of artificial intelligence, IoT, and machine learning technologies. This research used IBM SPSS Version 28, AMOS version 22 for statistical inferences, and NVivo for analysing qualitative data. AI and ML-based smart city management gets its main factors from Smart mobility, Education, Health, Living, Environment, Economy and Governance. The information collected by smart cities can be handled using AI and ML technologies in multiple ways that include predictive data analysis and live tracking and individual customization. The implementation of these technologies enables official city representatives to make well-informed decisions and boost performance outcomes and living quality throughout their communities. The functionalities of cities receive improvement through AI and ML technologies. These technologies enable both easier and better operational results in smart cities management. These technologies can have a significant impact on Sustainable Development Goals (SDGs). The emphasis is placed here on the SDGs 3, 7, 8, 9 and 11, which aim to improve health, energy, jobs, infrastructure and sustainable cities. In conclusion, AI and ML technologies play a crucial role in improving the management of smart cities.

Keywords: Artificial intelligence, machine learning, smart cities, sustainable development

Introduction

Human activity has gathered in urban centers across the world due to accelerated widespread urbanization during the 21st century. Statistical data shows that urban population exceeds 55% worldwide but experts predict this number will rise to 68% by the middle of 2050. Cities face substantial challenges to

[a]rajani.h.pillai@mccblr.edu.in, [b]raju.deeksha1994@gmail.com, [c]vernaj09@gmail.com, [d]roopa.adarsh@mccblr.edu.in

DOI: 10.4324/9781003739982-15

serve their growing population because United Nations released a report in [29] about resource requirements and infrastructure needs and services delivery. The current management approaches for existing cities lack effectiveness for proper handling of modern urban life issues. Smart city technology advances because it enables better metropolitan living standards through sustainability and efficiency and effective living situations. The urban transformation takes place through smart cities which adopt Internet of Things (IoT), artificial intelligence (AI) and machine learning (ML) technologies according to Alahi et al. [2]. By combining various information resources that encompass sensors with social media systems urban areas can enhance their swift decision-making ability to build superior services and develop economic power and advance neighborhood living quality [28]. Modern urban areas address their fundamental traffic and energy and waste management and security concerns using effective technological strategies in smart cities [23].

Smart cities strongly depend on the IoT because this technology links various automated systems which continuously gather and transfer data [15]. The collection of data via sensors cameras and smart meters in addition to numerous other parameters including air quality and traffic density is a function of IoT devices. These devices gather data that enables city planners along with managers to discover how they should effectively use their resources to enhance urban services [24]. The real-time identification of traffic congestion through a traffic management system based on IoT technology permits the system to modify traffic controls for better flow optimization [18]. The combination of AI technology with ML capabilities helps identify maximum energy usage periods across areas to reduce supply wastage while using historical patterns for traffic predictions that guide urban development plans [26].

The Indian Smart Cities Mission established in 2015 serves among multiple initiatives dedicated to improving urban areas. The mission will create new cities throughout the following century which will concentrate on developing transportation systems and power distribution infrastructure while managing water resources and waste disposal and establishing administrative systems [21]. The state of Karnataka under its leadership oversees this project which earned recognition for its technological achievements. The three cities of Bengaluru, Mysuru and Mangaluru work on smart city programs digital technologies like AI, IoT, and machine learning for attaining the sustainable goals [8]. The cities implement strategic development methods through contemporary technology usage which confirms their ability to implement efficient smart solutions for modern urban operations [25].

Urban decision-making along with management practices in Smart City systems have improved because of AI) and ML innovations. The emergence of AI and ML represents two fundamental features of modern smart city systems which produce operational decisions and enabling preventive or mitigating responses to complex urban structures [4]. The processing of extensive data through AI and ML systems enables the identification of signals and characteristics which subsequently produces predictive outcomes from existing and previous information only [15]. These propositions enable cities to develop advanced abilities in forecasting and addressing urban problems that result from traffic congestion and energy distribution and security risks. The combination of AI and ML technologies improves city management systems so cities achieve better governance outcomes [10].

Decisions makers throughout cities benefit from AI and ML to enhance resource productivity together with strategy development for better urban solution creation. These technologies enable discovery of how social groups implement choices through systems that combine live operational data with prediction mathematical models and advanced beyond classic urban decision systems. Predictive analytics represents a fundamental element of smart cities because AI and ML enable the use of gathered data to create probable outcomes for similar cities. The city's future issues including traffic congestion and fluctuating energy needs may be predicted which allows preventive actions to minimize those problems. Predictive modeling delivers benefits to cities through three application fields including resource distribution systems and service provision networks and resource consumption patterns [10].

AI together with ML technologies help define urban environment qualities while performing analytical tasks on all urban-related data. These technologies facilitate the evaluation of different planning choices through assessments of policy effectiveness in addition to managing urban land use and transport and infrastructure systems across cities. AI and ML applications enable cities to establish sustainable friendly urban spaces for people [3].

With this background, this study examines the utilization of IoT, AI, and ML in the sustainable development of smart cities, specifically in Karnataka, India. This analysis of theoretical frameworks, technological components, and practical applications demonstrates that these technologies have the potential to transform urban living and promote sustainable development.

The flow of the paper is structured as, Section 2- covers the review literature. Section 3-discuss the research methodology. Section 4-highlights the findings of empirical results, and the end the section-5 summarizes the scope of further research.

Literature Review

A systematic literature review was conducted and studies concerning AI and ML use in smart cities and its impact on sustainable development were studied extensively.

The concept of smart cities uses next-level technical solutions for achieving better citizen quality of life and reduced environmental impact and productivity growth as described by Jyothi et al. [17]. The unlimited number of possibilities for transformation exists between data-driven governance and IoT-powered infrastructure. Numerous privacy and security standards must be implemented to manage smart city data. The AI-DMS system for Smart Cities exists to overcome the identified difficulties during development. The AI-DMS system aims to accomplish maximum operating efficiency by optimizing the entire data pipeline between extraction and publication steps. Additional to its main functionality the Multi-Level Sensitive Model functions as an extra feature to classify data into three categories: sensitive, quasi-sensitive or public. The model allows complex data exchange procedures. Through PCA monitoring features while manipulating and normalizing selection and mapping processes the system presents an all-inclusive protection method for privacy.

Smart cities require effective load control as an essential part of sustainable energy usage because they accelerate the process of urban development through IoT networks [32]. This research presents an MSLL technique strengthened by AI that focuses on achieving secure IoT network load control. MMStransformer functions as one of the transformer-based models utilized by the proposed approach because it processes multiple correlated variables and understands long dependencies in forecasting load data. MMStransformer employs multi-mask learning-to-learning procedures that increase CPU efficiency without affecting accuracy levels. The study uses numerous operational and environmental variables to analyze the intricate smart city data processing nature and its dynamic features. We dedicate our highest priority to the secure handling of data and its secure transmission methods. This study investigates the privacy and security matters which affect IoT networks exclusively. The experimental data indicates that the proposed method achieves better performance than conventional as well as baseline models. AI technology solutions have proved the potential to improve both smart city infrastructure protection and load prediction accuracy according to experimental findings. The research findings help progress the deployment of AI systems for power management in addition to sustainable urban development.

The paper authored by Kalusivalingam et al. [18] demonstrates how uniting IoT data analytics with AI and its machine learning algorithms shows promise to disrupt smart city building procedures. The concept of "Smart Cities" arises as a sustainable answer to rising resource requirements and urban growth because these urban networks enhance management systems and deliver better life quality. The study examines approaches where artificial intelligence methods can advance urban planning as well as traffic management systems and power distribution and public security measures. Global city case studies show that machine learning algorithms possess significant potential to cope and interpret the volumious data generated by devices. The algorithms reach optimal process performance through their capability to execute real-time decisions and obtain predictive data. The study presents data security together with infrastructure costs and robust regulatory frameworks among the implementation challenges that become obstacles for the plan. The article presents possible solutions that combine collaborative governance with adaptive learning systems to address the described issues. The essay depicts future smart cities through internet of things technologies along with AI by showing their development into environmentally conscious and socially accepting technological urban centers. Data scientists together with city planners and legislators require formation into multidisciplinary teams to achieve operational smart city ecosystems.

Ullah e al. [28] explained that the development of "smart cities" seeks to optimize metropolitan management of expanding populations along with energy usage and natural habitat protection as well as resident income and life quality improvement while integrating new information technology systems. The development of smart city is supported by Information and communication technology (ICT). The central focus of this research is to evaluate the impact of AI, ML and DRL on smart city project expansion. Using these techniques enables the effective management of numerous difficult problems associated with smart cities. This survey explores smart transportation systems (ITSs), cyber-security, energy-efficient smart grid (SG) utilization, smart healthcare in a smart city, and the efficient use of UAVs to provide the best 5G and B5G communications services.

Smart city management system development aims to enhance city resident quality of life through economic and energy efficiency growth while ensuring environmental sustainability as explained by Varshney et al. [30]. Information and communication technology (ICT) serves as the main foundation for deciding policies and applying existing methods in constructing smart cities. The main objective of this project focuses on analyzing smart city development methods that use AI and ML technologies. This survey examines existing publication trends related to ICT data flow through identification of leading technologies facilitating this communication. This study offers complete AI and ML introduction by focusing on smart transport systems and concrete mix design prediction along with mechanical property forecasting.

The fastest growing human population drives rapid urbanization which makes it essential for Ahmad et al. [1] to study the maintenance of standards of living in cities. Data-driven AI services in smart cities need people to understand two essential points: technology effectively enhances city conditions and social equity through proper institutional development and governance frameworks; these smart cities exist to help individuals and society prosper. Researchers have established connections between particular technological elements and business methods and several social complications including extremism and social division as well as disinformation and Internet addiction. The eventual development of future city technology depends on these research results so the attention to philosophical and ethical standards for creating simple and secure AI systems has become critical. Scientists across the world strive to create technology that shows increased person-centeredness and compassion in its design.

Heidari et al. [14] presents the final purpose of smart city and society management as achieving maximum resource utilization alongside enhanced population quality of life. Three modern technologies which make urban sustainability possible for smart cities include the IoT, the Internet of Drones (IoD) and the Internet of Vehicles (IoV). Analyzing the data generated by smart city and society technology through analytics processes enables operators to obtain new findings that boost operational efficiency. Municipal surveillance and smart buildings and smart healthcare monitoring and smart traffic management and smart power and energy management make up the most widespread uses of smart cities. Automated smart city processes assign promising outcomes through the utilization of AI and ML with DL. This paper examines research areas and possible future investigation pathways to actualize the smart city concept using the described methodologies.

Sarker [26] demonstrates how the Fourth Industrial Revolution (4IR) uses technological and operational improvements in cities which "data science" drives through its development. An automated intelligent city system development begins with constructing a data-model which matches findings extracted from municipal data. Scientists who analyze real occurrences with historical data employ different scientific methods together with machine learning techniques and processes to develop systems. This term describes the process of extracting knowledge from various data sources which includes sensors and Internet-connected devices through data mining operations. The goal is to both improve decision-making capabilities and present advanced public services to the citizens through the system. Municipal data analysis could be enhanced by using artificial intelligence while machine learning analytical modeling remains a specific core principle in achieving these results.

Urban areas currently face challenges in sustaining sustainable living conditions for their citizens because of insufficient investments in intelligent technology innovation and growing urban development [2]. The future administration and development of smart cities become possible because the vast data made available by IoT allows new opportunities for exploration. AI operates as an integral component throughout this procedure.

This paper explores smart cities by examining their defining features and develops an exploration of their underlying structure that utilizes IoT technology. The article features knowledge expert opinions about future smart city development which outlines 5G network and AI capabilities to boost modern urban environments. The analysis shows by the authors how IoT collaboration with AI opens new remarkable opportunities for existing scholarly works. Smart cities based on these opportunities work to enhance sustainability alongside productivity and urban lifestyle quality for residents.

A research analyzes the predominant position held by artificial intelligence combined with machine learning for smart cities [11]. This study identifies the different urban aspects like public safety and sustainability from AI and ML transformative powers, with the support of government operations and infrastructure. This study explains what constitutes a smart city by describing its characteristics along with main components and technological advancements that drive smart city projects. The researchers analyzed extensive materials about smart city AI and ML to establish their study findings. Relevant understanding about how AI and ML help smart cities optimize infrastructure and enhance public safety along with citizen service delivery was extracted from online research. Research findings confirm that AI and ML enable all three aspects of optimized smart city development including data-informed choices and predictive analytics capabilities. The five essential functions of transportation network improvements, energy distribution optimization and public safety enhancement and governmental efficiency improvements and healthcare service transformations depend on these technologies. To achieve moral deployment of AI and ML in urban smart cities certain technical problems need resolution along with protecting individual privacy. The study concludes by identifying the obstacles and foreseeable directions for AI and ML to affect cityscapes while underlining essential responsible teamwork and utilization. These research findings prove that AI and ML technology can transform the entire process of smart city development together with service provisioning and sustainability measurements. Research aims to establish future policy frameworks for dealing with AI and machine learning technological challenges alongside developing transparency protocols and fairness standards for their smart city implementation.

The smart city implements ICT through Chen et al. [9] to fight against urbanisation-caused complications while supporting sustainable development methods. The data management interface of smart city infrastructure forms an essential element for meeting requirements from smart city applications regarding privacy and security together with secrecy and authenticity. This paper presents HBDIAIM as an interface security and privacy approach that combines artificial intelligence with big data technology to address current security and privacy issues. The system provides useful applications for multiple smart city functions. The implementation of HBDIAIM includes a differential evolutionary algorithm which protects smart city applications' secret data management interfaces sufficiently. The differential evolutionary algorithm employs the Big Data analytics assisted decision privacy method to enable data accessibility and scalability in data management interfaces through storage placements. An adaptable interface design method exists to manage private data while also dealing with smart-city-application scalability through improved versions that aim to improve user interface capabilities. Multiple tests based on security, accuracy, performance and scalability demonstrate the reliability of the proposed framework.

Finch [12] applies modern advanced technology for urban space longevity while enhancing efficiency which signifies "Smart City" as a significant milestone in urban planning evolution. This article explains how AI together with Machine Learning serves as a fundamental component during smart city initiative orchestration efforts. The worldwide examination of different applications demonstrates how ML and AI systems enable improvement of safety-related city services and energy management systems and transportation networks while simultaneously making cities adapt to population behaviors and demands. The research strengthens ongoing city planning conversations through a rigorous analysis of AI-based solutions that transform cities into greener and efficient and comfortable locations. The analysis develops both specific areas for additional study including data governance construction and deployment strategies across different types of urban environments.

Cities require niche technologies according to Allam and Dhunny [5] to solve their complex socioeconomic and ecological and morphological issues. The IoT delivers great support to the new "Smart Cities" concept by enabling sensor integration and Big Data sharing. The potential use of municipal planning techniques and administrative systems related to big data resembles the business potentials this data surge creates. Big Data processing under AI management stands to deliver superior city life quality though sustainability must remain the foremost priority. This paper evaluates AI's potential role in urban environments before presenting a framework to link AI technology with urban centers for successful smart city implementation and Sustainable Development Goal 11 accomplishment along with the New Urban Agenda fulfillment. The research integrates three fundamental elements which include Culture, Metabolism and Governance. Engineers together with data scientists and policymakers who wish to advance AI and Big Data collaboration in Smart Cities form the main audience for this research paper that seeks to strengthen urban infrastructure through boosted economic expansion and potential development.

The technology enabled by machine learning helps to automate numerous operations according to Mazhar et al. [22]. Intelligent buildings equipped with computers and mobile devices would simplify the management of internal temperature controls while keeping watch over security and doing regular maintenance operations. Intelligent buildings achieve connectivity through the Internet of Things among all their components. Smart grids continue to integrate with larger networks because the IoT attracts increased attention. Smart grids heavily depend on the IoT because it delivers essential services which benefit residents and provides security through established life support systems. The goal of this research focuses exclusively on discovering the underlying reasons behind installing intelligent building IoT devices. The infrastructure that provides support to IoT devices and components becomes essential in this situation.

Soomro et al. [27] clarifies As ICT supports more and more functions in smart cities the demand for big data analytics solutions continues to escalate. Relevant fields have achieved success by implementing solutions based on artificial intelligence and data science and machine learning principles in various domains such as climate research and energy control and transit management as well as clean air regulation and weather condition interpretation. This paper conducts an extensive review dedicated to the analysis of big data in smart cities. The evaluation includes materials from multiple repositories which were selected through a systematic data mining process. Our evaluation presents both the topical and technical results of a literature review about different approaches in data mining and machine learning methods. We developed a classification model after conducting this analysis which includes four primary aspects of research within this field. The research area includes data models together with computer models and privacy and security aspects and crucial commercial factors observed in smart cities.

Gharaibeh et al. [13] explains that achieving a smart city framework requires IoT technology to link every embedded system and electronic device present in our environments. Urban residents obtain better entertainment and operational efficiency through the massive data output of the IoT. Efficient data processing of this extensive dataset remains crucial for implementing smart cities throughout their existence. Research makes an data-focused contribution which diverges from earlier smart city surveys by defining fundamental data management strategies required to produce flexible and reusable data from the Internet of Things systems that run smart cities. Integral data management alongside privacy and security layers of protection with supporting infrastructure plays an essential role in managing smart city data from the start to the end. Researchers explain which network and computer systems enable smart cities then detail the security protocols for preserving data privacy. Smart city features have proved their successful implementation as one of the numerous achievements.

It is becoming more challenging to store and process such massive data sets with conventional software as the traffic volume continues to rise. In order to store and analyze such massive amounts of data, a parallel computing paradigm and a collection of storage devices are required. One such framework is Hadoop, which offers a dependable cluster storage capacity, facilitates fast parallel processing via its MapReduce framework, and stores massive amounts of data in a distributed fashion utilizing a unique file system. To give end users traffic analysis and helpful forecasts, MapReduce makes it easy to recover filtered data flow [20].

Research gap

Finding a model to make Indian cities sustainable through AI and ML theories represents an ongoing challenge because research on this subject of intelligent city maintenance through IoT is scarce. Indian city administrators face a dual challenge of absent solid plans and implementation frameworks and operational paradigms to achieve their IoT and AI management objectives for smart cities. Unified efforts between government agencies tech businesses and academic institutions are required to conduct more research for developing innovative solutions based on their close collaboration. The analysis of big data through technological means will enhance both sustainable development achievements and urban living conditions for India's city populations.

Research objectives

1. To understand the present state of IoT and machine learning applications in selected smart cities.
2. To evaluate the smart city management AI and ML paradigms.
3. To learn how policymakers view the artificial intelligence and machine learning models employed in smart city management.

Research Methods

Research strategy

The study incorporated concurrent triangulation convergence model , which is based on both qualitative and quantitative methods. According to Ivankova and Creswell [16] it offers multiple viewpoints on research, which can lead to a full understanding of the topic. By combining three or more approaches, the validity and trustworthiness of the results can be enhanced. Furthermore, utilising multiple methods together allows the researcher to highlight specific interrelatonships among variable.Data gathered mostly from: smart city residents who are engaged with (i) IoT specialists, (ii) AI specialists, (iii) .ML developers, and policymakers involved with smart city projects.

Research sample size

Based on the Cochran formula, when the population is unknown then at 10% margin of error, 100 citizen respondents can be considered for the study. Due to the case-based character of qualitative research, in-depth analyses require relatively small samples. Additionally, qualitative samples are hand-picked because of the wealth of precise information they can provide on the phenomena under study. Therefore, 10 policy makers were considered for the study.

Focusing on ten smart cities in the Indian state of Karnataka, this study examines their smart service, economics, mobility, environment, people, and governance initiatives. Research into the relationship between Smart City management and sustainable development is the focus of this project. Consideration is given to SDGs 3, 7, 8, 9, and 11 in order to measure sustainable development. Ultimately, the study hopes to suggest an improved Smart City management strategy utilising IoT, AI, and ML.

Research tests and tools

The tools used for the study are –

Qualitative analysis-NVivo Wong [33]

Inferential statistics -IBM SPSS Version 28 Verma [31] and Bala [6]

Multivariate statistics-IBM SPSS AMOS Version 22 Barnidge and De Zúñiga [7] and Kline [19]

Empirical results

Demographic profile of the citizens

According to the above data representation, the gender disparity of respondents seems to contribute to noticeable variability. Males within this population stand at 60% while females stand at 40%. The highest percentage of persons are found in the age range of 20-29yrs [26.8%] and 40–49 years [32.4%]. This means that the majority of the group is young adults and mid-career persons. The 30-39 years age group constitutes 24.6%; there is a significant representation of the young adults. Though, there is a slight digression as per the 50-59 years age group where only 14.6 the percentage reflects that fewer people are in their working years of retirement age. Also, the group represented the least for the last age bracket below, "Above 60 years" which accounted for 1.6%. According to results of the presented data, the majority of families can be characterised as nuclear, with 74.8% of families being identified as such. The majority of the respondents possess college education most of which are graduations (40.6%) and post graduations (20.8%). This therefore infers that the group is one the is well educated and a considerable number of those that belong to the group have been to University. Nevertheless, one can find a smaller number of low-educated people such as 8.8 % were having basic schooling and 9.4 % done professional course.This means that there is still growth in education as a sphere; more attempts have to be made to give a chance to people who did not receive as many educational opportunities as they can be provided with. While only two percent of the respondents have Masters degree while another two percent have a post graduate diploma, a very low proportion, that is, one point six percent, have a PhD. This is a good indication as there are some people within the group that have attained at least up to the advanced education level. The analysis shows that an approximate of 47.6% of the respondents are currently employed within the private sector. This figure shows that the private sector is the biggest employer and how the private sector can affect the economy. Also, the freelancing or business ownership is quite widespread among the general population: 25% of the sample is self-employed. On the other hand, the probability of not working is 22.2%, making the question about unemployment, availability of employment, choices not to seek employment.

Identifying determinants of smart city

H1: Smart mobility, education, health, living, environment, economy and governance are determinants of smart city is accepted

Model fit statistics - When analysing statistical data, model fit statistics are useful for summarizing how well a model fits the data. The Chi sqr/degree of freedom should be below < 0.500 and it is 3.287 in the current model. The goodness of fit index should be greater than 0.900 and in the current model the GFI value is 0.917. One way to evaluate a model's ability to capture the data accurately is by looking at its root mean square residual, or RMR. A better match is indicated by a decreased RMR number, and a perfect fit is represented by an RMR of zero. A worse fit is indicated by a higher RMR value. RMR is 0.045 and statistically significant at $p< 0.05$ which indicates model fit.

The given information in Table 15.1 and Figure 15.1 presents standardized estimates for various aspects of a smart city, which are further categorized into five main sub-domains: Smart Mobility; Smart Living; Smart Economy; Smart Health; Smart Governance. Such estimations indicate the level of consultation of each sub-domain to the notion of a smart city.

Initially, evaluation of the smart mobility domain reveals an estimate of 0.953 signifying that smart mobility is strongly aligned to the concept of smart city. This might mean that efficient transport systems; connected automobiles, electrical transportation, and wise traffic systems, are at the core of smart city making. Better transportation reduces traffic congestion and duration, and the emissions of greenhouse gases making city residents' quality of life better.

Table 15.1 Standardized estimates - determinants of smart city.

Standardized estimates			**Estimate**
Smart_Mobility	←	SMART_CITY	0.953
Smart_Living	←	SMART_CITY	0.917
Smart_economy	←	SMART_CITY	0.842
Smart_Health	←	SMART_CITY	0.984
Smart_Governance	←	SMART_CITY	0.97
Smart_Env	←	SMART_CITY	0.975
Smart_Education	←	SMART_CITY	0.942

Source: Author

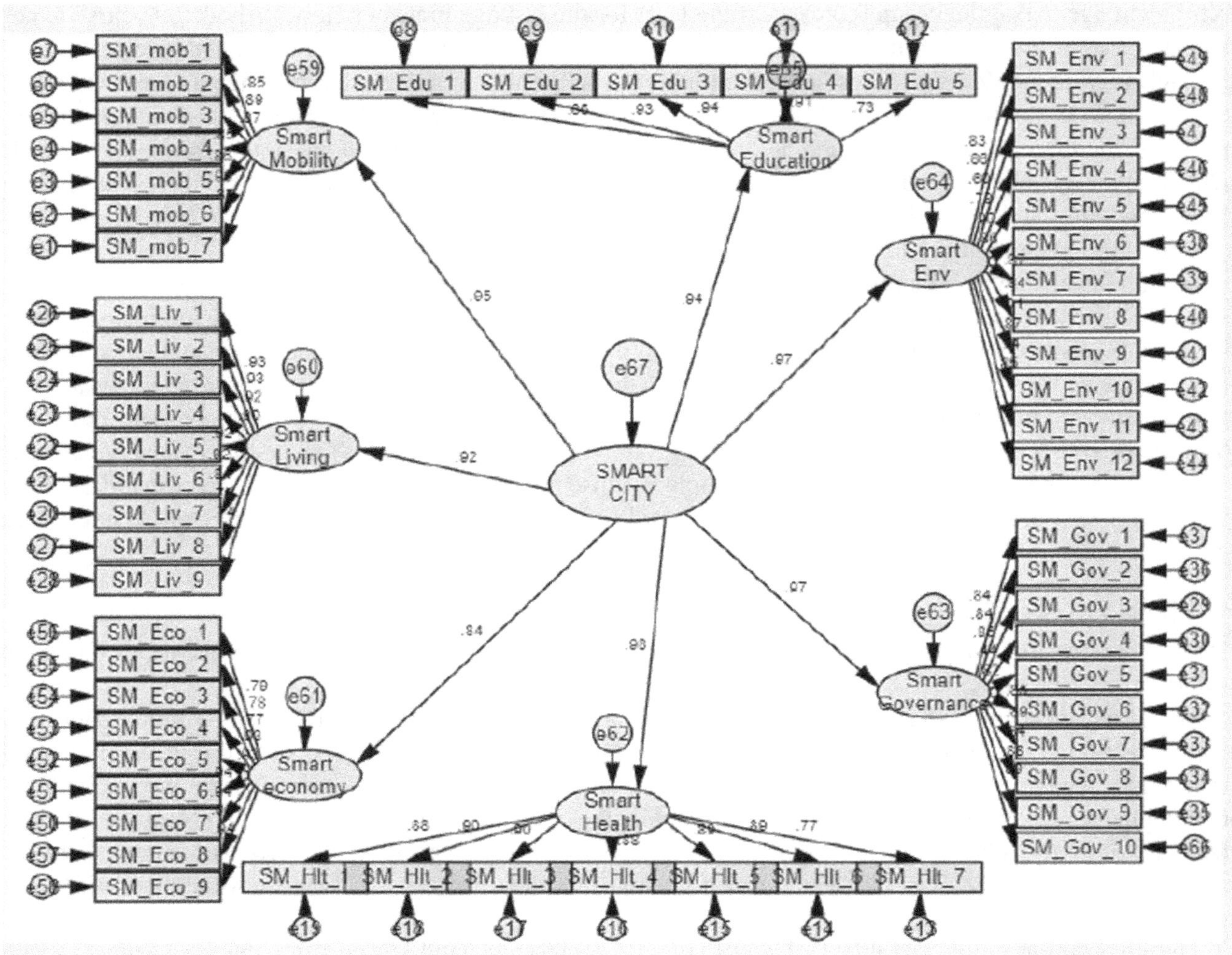

Figure 15.1 Structural equation model results - determinants of Smart City
Source: Author

Secondly, Smart Living, with an estimate of 0.917, is equally important in a smart city. This aspect covers smart living elements of the city, such as smart homes, smart wearables, and connected home appliances. These technologies increase the comfort, convenience, and well-being of people, improve sustainability, and save energy.

Thirdly, Smart Economy has an estimate of 0.842 to help in the formation of a smart city. One of the dependent domains within smart specializations is the domain of the economic development of smart technologies and innovation. Smart Economy consists of measures like start-ups, business to consumer or business to business sales and big data analysis to allow companies to be as effective as possible within the global market.

Fourthly, Smart Health is estimated to be 0.984 and is an essential characteristic of a smart city. The use of telemedicine, remote care, and electronic health records improves the health results, make healthcare services more available, and efficient. This is valid especially given that healthcare needs of a large and densely packed population may be hard to contain.

Last but not the least, Smart Governance is expected to be equal to 0.97 and is a constituent of a smart city since this framework stresses the value of the usage of the processed information and predictive analysis for making better decisions and enhancing public service delivery. The elements of big data, artificial intelligence and other technologies will enable the city authorities to get a 'sense' of the citizen's needs and put resources where they are most needed.

In addition, the estimate of the Smart Environment is 0.975, which demonstrates that it is an element that supports sustainable development of smart cities. Increased emphasis on clean energy technologies, green infrastructure, and other environmentally friendly transport systems can help to minimize an urban area's carbon emissions and enhance the quality of life for residents of the city.

Last but not least, Smart Education has an estimated value of 0.942. The use of technology may bring about more fulfilling and effective teaching-learning activities in learner this is by coming up with-filled and more conducive learning environment. They may also encourage innovation, creativeness, and critical thinking skills that are vital part of a city's economy.

On this note, the standardized estimates also show that each of the five sub domains is highly significant in developing a holistic smart city. Every sub-domain dwells differently in fostering the overall concept and it is evident that Smart Mobility and Smart Living sub-domains play an essential role in fostering overall concept. By concentrating on these domains and fostering the corresponding growth, the city can become the smart city that will use technologies to enhance people's experience.

Alternate hypothesis - Smart mobility, Education, Health, Living, Environment, Economy and Governance are determinants of smart city is accepted

Profile of the policy makers

The data illustrates the distribution of responders among five unique organisations: AMRUT, JnNURM, Municipal Corporation, SCM, and SPV – Belagavi Smart City Ltd. Significantly, AMRUT and JnNURM, which pertain to the physical planning and infrastructure development of urban regions, collectively account for half of the total respondents, each representing 28%. This demonstrates the dominance and activity of these programs throughout the sector. The Municipal Corporation and SCM are two significant entities linked to municipal governance, tasked with the sustainable management of resources; nonetheless, they represent just 16% of responses, with SCM accounting for 8%. Finally, 28% of the total respondents belong to the category identified as SPV - Belagavi Smart City Ltd, likely a special purpose vehicle established in alignment with the smart city aim.

Role of AI and ML in smart cities

Concepts of smart cities as urban construction and management systems introducing superior technologies and innovative measures for enhanced living standards and sustainability have gained importance in current earlier years. AI and ML are currently among the most influential driving forces that define the smart city project. As it was found out analyzing 20 files cum 268 references, the implication of AI and of ML can be seen to be significant in enhancing different facets of smart cities as seen in Figure 15.2.

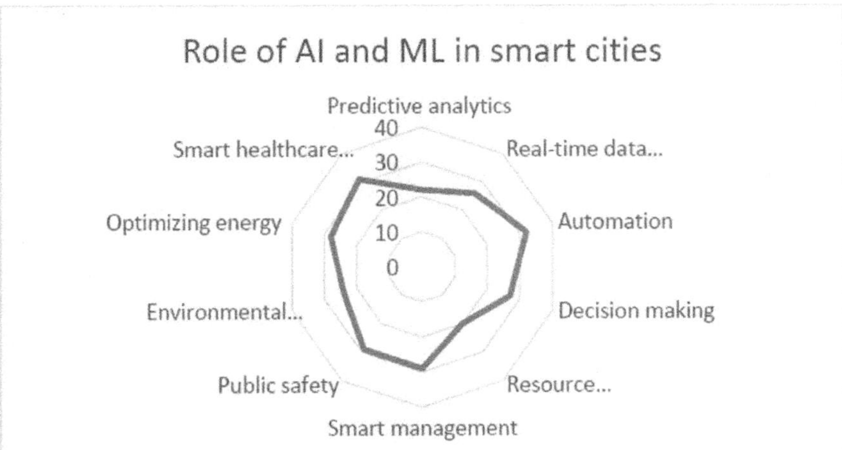

Figure 15.2 Role of AI and ML in smart cities
Source: Author

A subset of big data analytics, which entails the identification of trends or patterns within a large data set, coupled with the creation of accurate forecasts is referred to as Smart Cities Predictive analytics. Predictive analytics' application in urban planning is possible to solve challenges of population growth predicting, traffic jams, and infrastructure, as evidenced in 17 files and 22 references. The use of real-time analysis also means that city authorities are able to act on the basis of the changes of traffic flow or an incident, thereby increasing overall safety and productivity of city traffic (17 files, 26 references).

The fourth promising application where AI and ML are utilized in smart cities is automation. AI and ML algorithms have potential consequences in the daily functions with the routine aspects, for instance, energy partition, mass transit services, and waste handling, with the intention of raising resource effectiveness (18 files, 32 references). As pointed out in 17 files and 27 references, new ways of making decisions help urban planners to allocate resources and manage the public services efficiently.

Intelligent traffic systems and other increaser management systems that come in use in cities, aim at decreasing traffic and enhancing transportation generally. Application of AI and ML algorithms can improve such systems leading to better public safety measures and faster response to the emergencies (17 files, 29 references). Also, the opportunity to take into account the pollution and natural disasters becomes critical for effective urbanization. By using AI and ML, these factors can easily be observed and controlled, as supported by 19 files and 24 references.

Energy efficiency control also appears to be a critical issue in smart cities. City energy can be made sustainable if energy consumption data is analyzed by using AI and ML algorithms (17 files 28 references). In addition, AI and ML can be employed to design new smart healthcare solutions and enhance medical treatment as well as patient care and decrease the cost of healthcare (16 files, 31 references).

In conclusion, the presence of AI and ML technologies in smart cities is pivotal to enhancing a number of facets that make up the city community including resource utilization, transport, safety, energy consumption, and healthcare. The evaluation of the files and references provided here also confirms that AI and ML can be valuable in designing cities with sustainable, efficient, and high quality.

Data entities for smart city management

This paper has presented a number of code which have been derived from the given problem and these are data entities for smart city management, traffic patterns, energy consumption, environmental data, public safety incidents, healthcare metrics, waste management data and citizen feedback. The files and references related to these themes as shown in Figure 15.3 will be discussed below:

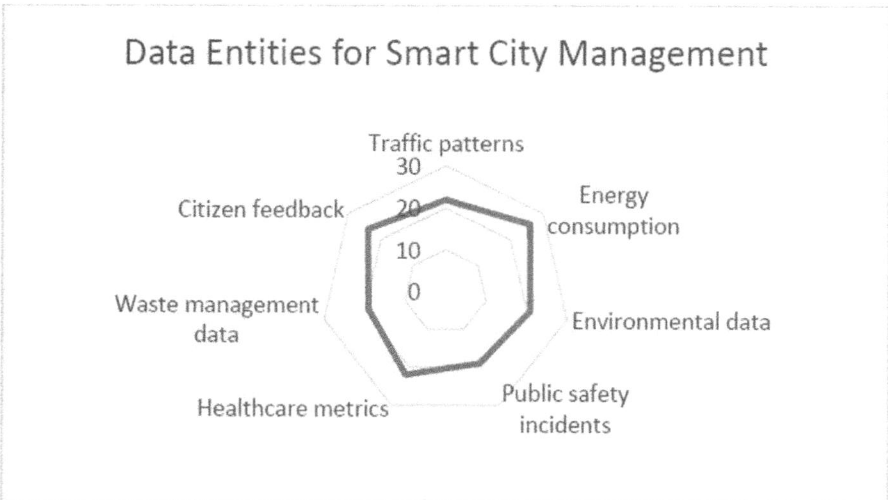

Figure 15.3 Data entities for smart city management
Source: Author

1. Data entities for Smart City management: In the same case, the theme with the highest amounts of files (20) and references (153) shedding light on smart city management shows the subject is of immense interest in this field. Data entities are important in that they provide a mechanism for a city to integrate and coordinate various aspects of a city. The number of files and references proves the significance of efficient utilizing and managing data as the foundation for smart city strategies and decisions.
2. Traffic patterns: The second most discussed theme has 15 files and contains 22 references. Traffic flow is an important aspect in analysis and planning of transport in urban centers to guarantee smooth traffic flow and to avoid congestion. The large number of files and references mean that traffic patterns are of especial importance in smart city management, and their identification and regulation are among the most important tasks of smart city systems.
3. Energy consumption: The third theme includes 14 files and 26 references. Energy is another strategic aspect of a smart city because it entails the efficient use of energy in a city as well as promotion of conservation. The large amount of files and references indicates that energy consumption is one of the most popular and widely used fields in smart cities, focused on their effective use and utilization to reduce costs and a negative impact on the environment.
4. Environmental data: This theme has 12 files and contains 21 references. Environmental information is significant in tracking and evaluating impacts of trends such as urbanisation on environmental habitat, pollution rates and the environment at large. The large number of files and references present show that environmental data is highly crucial in the decision making and management of smart cities especially as relates to sustainable development and environmentally friendly practices.
5. Public safety incidents: This theme has 13 files and 19 references and showcases how public safety is of essence in managing smart cities. Security of people is paramount and given that there are so many files and references available it is evident that there are different technologies and solutions being used to improve security through smart cities project.
6. Healthcare metrics: This theme comprise of 17 files and 22 references. Healthcare parameters are important for health assessment of a city's population and to carry out effective health administration. Such a large number of files and references confirms that healthcare metrics are an important part of managing a smart city, the objective of which is to improve the health of citizens.
7. Waste management data: This theme has 13 files and it contains references of 19. Smart city waste data is important if only because waste collection, sorting and recycling in smart cities needs to be efficient. The large amount of files and references found also points out that waste management should also become one of the priorities of smart city management, which aims at the quality of the environment and the reduction of waste production.
8. Citizen feedback: The last theme has 12 files and 24 references. Public views are crucial to meet citizens' expectations, address their concerns or understand their preferences for applying suitable interventions in smart city operation. The large number of files and references proves that people's feedback is an essential element of smart city projects, the main goal of which is to involve citizens and enhance their quality of life.

Therefore, the evaluation of the themes in the smart city management shows that data entities, traffic characteristics, energy, and environment, safety occurrences, health indicators, waste data, and citizens' feedback are the most important. Thus, the many files and references related to these topics indicate their relevance and the burgeoning interest in building and realizing smart city strategies for the improvement of urban life.

Challenges in sustainability development programs

The issues of the themes found in the study are discussed in the framework of sustainability development programs. Of files there are 20 and of references 166 that contain information on various aspects of these programs as depicted in Figure 15.4.

The first source of data relates to three major themes namely; The first theme is uso, this involves an assessment of the current programs in use. There is proof that the current Sustainability Development Programs

Figure 15.4 Challenges in sustainability development programs
Source: Author

work, as indicated 11 files and 26 references. This success is an indication that the programs' interventions are exerting the intended efforts and the beneficiaries are reaping the benefits.

However, there are several problems associated with the employment of the programs. The first general challenge mentioned in 11 files and 27 references is managing with delay and setbacks. However, there is still improvement still being made present as evidence by the involved parties who remain determined.

Second, the notion of targeting rural populations is highlighted, which has received 11 files and 20 references. The realization in the developed nations have reached a considerable level in the urban areas, thus creating pressure to focus on the rural sectors. This shows the need to care for all the regions in equal measures from the sustainability development programs not limiting to only the urban centers.

Regarding the upcoming activities, the goals for the future are quite innovative and correlate with the objectives of the nation, as 15 files and 32 references testify. This optimism on future development indicates that the programs under the Act are geared towards achieving long term objectives of addressing social needs with positive impact on the society.

However, funding hurdle is highlighted as described in 14 files and 20 references. One of the main challenges that can be inherent to these programs is the struggle with the issues concerning the acquisition of the necessary funds, which, in its turn, can have an impact on the results of the programs implemented. These are important factors that need to be managed to see that the Sustainability Development Programs sustains itself.

The benefits of the programs to the affected communities form the cornerstone of our present analysis as derived from the evaluation of 13 files and 20 references. This paper provides evidence of the positive impact on the communities in the area and therefore supports the need for such programs in society.

Finally, integrating technological element is becoming prominent, 14 files and 21 references have noted that for the future plan the tendency for integrating technology is high. This suggests the need to accept Innovative Practices in an effort to make the Sustainability Development Programs better and more effective.

Thus, the themes that have been evidenced in the course of the current study are quite informative about the state and the future directions of Sustainability Development Programs. Such factors include the fact that the programs are successful, that they target rural areas and that they have a beneficial effect on society. However, amongst such opportunities, there are also threats, for example, delays in programs' implementation and funding problems must to be solved for further successful development of such programs. In the last one, the adoption of technology in future planning will help in advancing and refining future plans.

Conclusion

This AI and ML can be used to manage data in various ways, such as:

Predictive analytics - that is, artificial intelligence (AI) and machine learning (ML) algorithms—can examine past data and project future trends, occurrences, and patterns. This will enable local officials to make wise decisions and implement preventative action to handle possible problems.

Real-time monitoring transforms possible because AI and ML track multiple city aspects such as traffic patterns and energy consumption and air quality tracking happens in real-time. This approach enables administrators to detect developing problems so they can execute repairs instantly which enhances operative effectiveness while boosting residential quality standards.

AI working with ML technologies merges information that originates from various monitoring systems including sensors and cameras and social media to build complete operational reports about municipal features. The data provides city authorities with resources for developing policies that are based on facts and make better decisions.

AI together with ML technology provides city authorities the opportunity to dedicate their attention to critical priorities because it performs multiple routine jobs such as data entry and analysis and reporting tasks. Efficiency improvements together with reduced costs for smart city data management become feasible through these measures.

AI and ML enable public servants to deliver customized traffic alerts together with energy-minimization tips to residents. The implementation of smarter cities through these methods supports user-friendly interfaces that result in higher life quality for residents.

AI and ML methods enable organizations in smart cities to handle acquired data through predictive analysis as well as real-time tracking and adaptive applications. The application of these technology enables better official decisions and increased operational efficiency and superior residential standards for cities.

Two key technological developments that enable better city operation consist of AI and automated learning (ML). Modern administrative practices within smart cities become more efficient because of these technologies. These technologies have strong positive effects on the Sustainable Development Goals (SDGs). SDGs 3, 7, 8, 9 and 11 represent the focus of this segment because they focus on promoting health along with advancing energy systems and creating employment opportunities and constructing infrastructure and building sustainable cities. AI and ML technology improves the management of smart cities to a powerful degree.

References

[1] Ahmad, K., Maabreh, M., Ghaly, M., Khan, K., Qadir, J., & Al-Fuqaha, A. (2022). Developing future human-centered smart cities: critical analysis of smart city security, data management, and ethical challenges. *Computer Science Review*, 43, 100452.

[2] Alahi, M. E. E., Sukkuea, A., Tina, F. W., Nag, A., Kurdthongmee, W., Suwannarat, K., et al. (2023). Integration of IoT-enabled technologies and artificial intelligence (AI) for smart city scenario: recent advancements and future trends. *Sensors*, 23(11), 5206.

[3] Alam, M., & Khan, I. R. (2022). Application of AI in Smart Cities. In Industrial Transformation, (pp. 61–86). CRC Press.

[4] Allam, Z. (2020). Big data, artificial intelligence and the rise of autonomous smart cities. In *The rise of autonomous smart cities: technology, economic performance and climate resilience.* (pp. 7–30). Cham: Springer International Publishing.

[5] Allam, Z., & Dhunny, Z. A. (2019). On big data, artificial intelligence and smart cities. *Cities*, 89, 80–91.

[6] Bala, J. (2016). Contribution of SPSS in Social Sciences Research. *International Journal of Advanced Research in Computer Science*, 7(6), 250.

[7] Barnidge, M., & De Zúñiga, H. G. (2017). Amos (software). *The international encyclopedia of communication research methods*, 1, 1–3.

[8] Chatterjee, S., Kar, A. K., & Gupta, M. P. (2018). Success of IoT in smart cities of India: An empirical analysis. *Government Information Quarterly*, 35(3), 349–361.

[9] Chen, J., Ramanathan, L., & Alazab, M. (2021). Holistic big data integrated artificial intelligent modeling to improve privacy and security in data management of smart cities. *Microprocessors and Microsystems*, 81, 103722.

[10] Cugurullo, F., Caprotti, F., Cook, M., Karvonen, A., M A., M, P., & Marvin, S. (2024). The rise of AI urbanism in post-smart cities: a critical commentary on urban artificial intelligence. *Urban Studies*, 61(6), 1168–1182.

[11] Deep, G., & Verma, J. (2023). Embracing the future: AI and ML transforming urban environments in smart cities. *Journal of Artificial Intelligence*, 5, 57–73.

[12] Finch, E. G. (2019). The integration of ML and AI in developing smart cities. *Integration*, 10(1), 22.

[13] Gharaibeh, A., Salahuddin, M. A., Hussini, S. J., Khreishah, A., Khalil, I., Guizani, M., et al. (2017). Smart cities: a survey on data management, security, and enabling technologies. *IEEE Communications Surveys and Tutorials*, 19(4), 2456–2501.

[14] Heidari, A., Navimipour, N. J., & Unal, M. (2022). Applications of ML/DL in the management of smart cities and societies based on new trends in information technologies: A systematic literature review. *Sustainable Cities and Society*, 85, 104089.

[15] Herath, H. M. K. K. M. B., & Mittal, M. (2022). Adoption of artificial intelligence in smart cities: a comprehensive review. *International Journal of Information Management Data Insights*, 2(1), 100076.

[16] Ivankova, N. V., & Creswell, J. W. (2009). Mixed methods. *Qualitative Research in Applied Linguistics: A Practical Introduction*, 23, 135–161.

[17] Jyothi, V., Sreelatha, T., Thiyagu, T. M., Sowndharya, R., & Arvinth, N. (2024). A data management system for smart cities leveraging artificial intelligence modeling techniques to enhance privacy and security. *Journal of Internet Services and Information Security*, 14(1), 37–51.

[18] Kalusivalingam, A. K., Sharma, A., Patel, N., & Singh, V. (2021). Enhancing smart city development with AI: leveraging machine learning algorithms and IoT-driven data analytics. *International Journal of AI and ML*, 2(3), 17–19.

[19] Kline, R. B. (1998). Software review: Software programs for structural equation modeling: amos, EQS, and LISREL. *Journal of Psychoeducational Assessment*, 16(4), 343–364.

[20] Bijjaragi, K., & Tijare, P. (2016). Big data approach for secure traffic data analytics using hadoop. *International Journal on Recent and Innovation Trends in Computing and Communication*, 4(5), 539–542.

[21] Kumar, N. M., Goel, S., & Mallick, P. K. (2018). Smart cities in India: features, policies, current status, and challenges. In 2018 Technologies for Smart-City Energy Security and Power (ICSESP), (pp. 1–4).

[22] Mazhar, S. A., Anjum, R., Anwar, A. I., & Khan, A. A. (2022). Methods of data collection: a fundamental tool of research. *Journal of Integrated Community Health*, 10(1), 6–10. (ISSN 2319-9113).

[23] Oladipo, I. D., AbdulRaheem, M., Awotunde, J. B., Bhoi, A. K., Adeniyi, E. A., & Abiodun, M. K. (2021). Machine learning and deep learning algorithms for smart cities: a start-of-the-art review. *IoT and IoE Driven Smart Cities*, 143–162. ISSN 2522-8609.

[24] Prawiyogi, A. G., Purnama, S., & Meria, L. (2022). Smart cities using machine learning and intelligent applications. *International Transactions on Artificial Intelligence*, 1(1), 102–116.

[25] Ramaswamy, R., & Madakam, S. (2013). The state of art: smart cities in India: A literature review report. *International Journal of Innovative Research and Development, II*, 12, 115–119.

[26] Sarker, I. H. (2022). Smart city data science: towards data-driven smart cities with open research issues. *Internet of Things*, 19, 100528.

[27] Soomro, K., Bhutta, M. N. M., Khan, Z., & Tahir, M. A. (2019). Smart city big data analytics: an advanced review. *Wiley Interdisciplinary Reviews: Data Mining and Knowledge Discovery*, 9(5), e1319.

[28] Ullah, Z., Al-Turjman, F., Mostarda, L., & Gagliardi, R. (2020). Applications of artificial intelligence and machine learning in smart cities. *Computer Communications*, 154, 313–323.

[29] United Nations, Department of Economic and Social Affairs, Population Division. (2019). World Urbanization Prospects: The 2018 Revision (ST/ESA/SER.A/420). New York, NY: https://www.un.org/development/desa/en/news/population/2018-revision-of-world urbanization-prospects.html.

[30] Varshney, H., Khan, R. A., Khan, U., & Verma, R. (2021). Approaches of artificial intelligence and machine learning in smart cities: critical review. In IOP Conference Series: Materials Science and Engineering (Vol. 1022, No. 1, p. 012019). IOP Publishing.

[31] Verma, J. P. (2012). Data Analysis in Management with SPSS Software. Springer Science and Business Media.

[32] Wang, B., Dabbaghjamanesh, M., Kavousi-Fard, A., & Yue, Y. (2024). AI-enhanced multi-stage learning-to-learning approach for secure smart cities load management in IoT networks. *Ad Hoc Networks*, 164, 103628.

[33] Wong, L. P. (2008). Data analysis in qualitative research: a brief guide to using NVivo. *Malaysian family physician: the Official Journal of the Academy of Family Physicians of Malaysia*, 3(1), 14.

16 Analyzing the role of Netflix in digital transformation: a comprehensive research study

Shreshtha Sharma[a]

Assistant Professor, Faculty of Commerce and Management, Apex University, Jaipur, Rajasthan, India

Abstract

The digital transformation of the entertainment industry has reshaped content creation, distribution, and consumption. Netflix has played a key role in this shift by adopting cloud computing, AI, data analytics, and personalized recommendations. Its innovations have set industry benchmarks, changing how users engage with digital content. This study explores Netflix's impact on digital transformation and its influence on technological adoption, content strategies, and user experience. This study examines how Netflix has influenced digital transformation in entertainment. It evaluates the impact of its technology adoption, content delivery, data-driven content creation, user experience design, and recommendation system. The goal is to understand how Netflix's innovations have reshaped industry practices and consumer behavior. A mixed-methods approach was used with data from 132 participants, including consumers, industry professionals, and digital experts. Surveys measured behavioral trends, and interviews provided qualitative insights. Statistical analysis was done using SPSS 27.0, while NVivo 14 was used for qualitative data. Reliability testing showed strong internal consistency ($\alpha = 0.89$). Netflix has significantly influenced digital transformation. Its cloud infrastructure adoption reached 78.5%, AI integration 65.7%, and data analytics 82.4%. Its content delivery model increased weekly viewing hours by 35% and reduced content discovery time by 67%. Data-driven content creation improved success rates by 130.9% over traditional models. Its user experience innovations had a 92.3% industry adoption rate. AI-driven recommendations increased engagement by 43.8% and retention from 56.4% to 88.3%. Netflix has pioneered digital innovation in entertainment. Its technology adoption, content approach, and user experience innovations have revolutionized industry best practices. AI, cloud computing, and data analytics have increased content delivery and audience interaction. Its impact has established streaming as the digital entertainment mode of choice, setting the pace for future industry directions.

Keywords: AI, cloud computing, content delivery, data analytics, digital transformation, Netflix, recommendation system, streaming, user experience

Introduction

The entertainment sector has been transformed beyond precedent in the digital era, fundamentally reshaping classical paradigms of content creation, distribution, and consumption. The transformation of Netflix from a DVD rental service to a worldwide streaming giant is a testament to its role as a change agent in digital transformation. Established in 1997 by Marc Randolph and Reed Hastings, the business originally used a subscription-based DVD rental service where customers could rent movies over the internet and have them mailed to them. This method revolutionized traditional video stores by providing increased convenience and variety. Despite that, high costs of operation and a small initial catalog were problematic, and so Netflix built a logistics network of more than 50 warehouses and added 'Cinematch' in 2000, a recommendation engine that improved user activity by examining rental history to recommend films [9]. Taking advantage of technology, Netflix moved to streaming services in 2007 with the growth of high-speed internet. This shift not only reduced distribution costs but also aligned with changing consumer preferences for on-demand content. The company's strategic use of data analytics has been central to its success; by analyzing user behavior and preferences, Netflix offers personalized content recommendations, significantly enhancing user satisfaction and retention. This data-driven approach extends to content creation, exemplified by the production of "House of Cards," which was greenlit based on insights indicating a high probability of success among subscribers [33]. Netflix's marketing strategy is characterized by innovation and agility. The platform continuously adapts to market needs and user demands, evolving its tactics to maintain engagement. Through regular analysis and

[a]sharmashreshtha96@gmail.com

DOI: 10.4324/9781003739982-16

optimization, Netflix ensures its advertising strategy remains user-centric and personalized, strengthening customer connections and serving as a model for other brands aiming to enhance exposure and market value [1].

In its pursuit of global expansion, Netflix has invested heavily in producing original content that caters to diverse audiences worldwide. This move not only differentiates Netflix from competitors but also allows greater control over content distribution. By 2016, Netflix had expanded its services globally, amassing over 100 million subscribers by the end of 2017 [9]. The company's culture emphasizes the integration of algorithms and data at its core, with significant investments in original content and technological innovation. This approach has attracted top tech talent and enabled Netflix to stay ahead of competitors [27]. Despite facing powerful competitors, Netflix remains a dominant force in the streaming and entertainment world. As of the first quarter of 2024, the subscription-based streaming service has over 270 million paid subscribers and reported revenue of over $9.4 billion. Its use of artificial intelligence algorithms enables Netflix to personalize the user experience, with over 80% of the shows people watch on the platform based on its recommendations. To boost revenue and attract more subscribers, Netflix offers a range of subscription plans, including 'Standard with adverts', 'Standard', and 'Premium'. The launch of the lower-cost subscription in November 2022 was intended to attract more cost-conscious users after a sharp decline in the first half of the year [18].

Netflix in Digital Transformation

Netflix's journey from a DVD rental service to a dominant global streaming platform is a prime example of digital transformation and disruption in the entertainment industry. Digitalization, the process of converting analog information into digital formats, has revolutionized various sectors, including entertainment, introducing new business dynamics and forcing traditional companies to adapt swiftly [15]. Netflix successfully disrupted the physical video rental industry, particularly Blockbuster, by leveraging data analytics, innovative subscription models, and original content production [30].

The era of digital disruption in entertainment: The entertainment industry has undergone significant disruption, with online streaming services redefining content consumption patterns. Netflix pioneered this shift by using advanced algorithms and personalized recommendations, transforming how audiences engage with digital media [5]. Unlike traditional broadcasting, Netflix's on-demand subscription-based model eliminated late fees and encouraged binge-watching, a phenomenon that increased global user engagement [14, 3]. The company's strategic response to the COVID-19 pandemic, where it gained millions of new subscribers due to lockdown restrictions, further cemented its place as a market leader [23].

Evolution of Netflix's business model: Founded in 1997 by Reed Hastings and Marc Randolph, Netflix initially operated as an online DVD rental service. In 1999, the company introduced a subscription model, offering unlimited rentals for a fixed monthly fee, which gained popularity [13]. The company's initial public offering (IPO) in 2002 further fueled its expansion, and by 2006, it had amassed 6.3 million subscribers [16]. The transition to online streaming in 2007 marked a major turning point, enabling Netflix to move away from physical rentals and embrace a digital-first strategy.

Netflix as a market disruptor: Netflix's competitive edge lies in strategic innovation. By using user analytics to personalize recommendations, Netflix disrupted Blockbuster's rental model, leading to Blockbuster's decline [30, 28]. The company further distanced itself from traditional television by launching Netflix Originals in 2012, allowing it to control content production and distribution [20]. This move proved crucial in distinguishing Netflix from competitors and establishing a self-sustaining content ecosystem.

Digital transformation strategies: Netflix's digital transformation relied on data-driven decision-making and predictive analytics. The company used sophisticated AI algorithms to recommend content, increasing user engagement and retention [33]. The 2013 Netflix Long-Term View report outlined its vision of internet TV replacing traditional cable TV, a prediction that has largely materialized [17, 32]. Additionally, Netflix's investment in global content expansion and regional productions helped it capture diverse international markets.

Netflix's growth and adaptability: Netflix's ability to adapt and innovate has been central to its success. Despite market challenges and rising competition, the company set revenue records and expanded its global user base, particularly during the pandemic [11]. By 2020, Netflix had 182 million subscribers worldwide, growing to 221 million by the end of the year [24]. Its direct-to-consumer streaming model disrupted traditional TV networks by eliminating intermediaries and establishing a direct revenue stream from subscribers [26].

Literature Review

The digital transformation of the entertainment industry has led to significant changes in business models, consumer behavior, and technological advancements. Several studies have analyzed the case of Netflix, a company that has successfully navigated the digital landscape to establish itself as a leader in online streaming. The evolution of Netflix is deeply tied to the broader theme of digital transformation. Margiono [12] identifies two primary paths that companies follow when undergoing digital transformation: an offensive path characterized by aggressive investments in digital assets and a defensive path that involves the gradual development of digital capabilities. Netflix has been the classic example of the offensive strategy through strategic buys, original content investment, and expansion.

In the same vein, Vu ković and Gavrilović [29] compare and contrast Netflix's and Blockbuster's digital transformation paths and point out how Netflix's foresight digital actions saw it succeed, whereas Blockbuster's inability to embrace digital ultimately changed and destroyed the company. This speaks volumes for the role that timely and strategically directed digital transformation can play in keeping businesses sustainable.

Some studies have attempted to analyze Netflix's evolving business model and how it affects customer behavior. Au-Yong-Oliveira et al. [2] analyzed the trend towards shifting away from traditional television towards streaming media by carrying out a survey. They report that online streaming media is being adopted increasingly instead of traditional television channels, and among them, Netflix dominates the market. The transition in consumer behavior reflects the wider digitalization wave in which ease of use and convenience become determinants. Pratama et al. [21] also examines the effects of digital transformation on business models within the entertainment sector. Their studies based on Netflix and Spotify reflect the need for ongoing evolution in response to dynamic business environments, with a focus on innovation in driving growth. Hora [6] also elaborates on how servitization—shifting from product-centered to service-centered business models has been key to the success of such firms as Netflix. The research identifies how the transition from ownership to usership increases customer experience by way of customization, convenience, and co-creation.

Technology has been instrumental in the success of Netflix. Ruiz-Navas et al. [22] carried out a longitudinal examination of the technological capabilities of Netflix and picked out major changes that helped the company shift from being a DVD rental service to a world leader in streaming. Their research identifies three separate stages in Netflix's technological development and its initial emphasis on IT-based retailing, the shift to VOD service with digital processing capacity, and its move into overseas markets with emphasis on data processing and communication infrastructures. Hsiao [7] goes on to explore Netflix's technological innovations further, such as AI-powered recommendation systems, VR and AR adoption, and international expansion and localization strategies. The research focuses on how personalization enhances customer engagement and quality of service. Juteau [8] also investigates the journey of Netflix as a technologically empowered company, focusing on how it applied cloud computing, artificial intelligence, and blockchain technology to advance its operations and user experience.

The pandemic attributed to COVID-19 had a strong influence on the streaming industry, motivating research on the financial trends and market positioning of Netflix. Lozic et al. [10] examine Netflix's post-pandemic financial performance, illustrating the decline in revenue growth and saturation in the market. The research explains the trend due to higher production expenses for original content as well as stiffening competition in the streaming sector. Although the number of users is increasing, Netflix's expansion into new markets seems to be the main source of its growth and does not increase user activity within markets. The performance of digital marketing practices in streaming platforms has also been investigated by contemporary literature. Gadiya and Bhatt [4] emphasize the role of Netflix's landing pages on user behavior and conversion. Their research uses a mixed-methods design, investigating user behavior to maximize digital marketing efforts. The results highlight the significance of well-designed landing pages in maximizing digital marketing effectiveness. Paul et al. [19] offer a multidisciplinary overview of digital transformation, investigating new technologies like IoT, social media, AI, and metaverse. Their editorial perspective offers insights into the multifaceted impact of these technologies on business transformation and future research directions. Additionally, Walter [31] compares digital transformation efforts in corporate and national context highlighting Netflix's agility in responding to digital challenges in contrast to a national case study on El Salvador, where a lack of digital strategy hindered innovation.

Research Objectives

Drawing from prior research and identifying gaps in literature, this study aims to

1. Analyze Netflix's influence on industry-wide digital transformation strategies and technology adoption patterns;
2. Evaluate the impact of Netflix's content delivery model on consumer behavior and viewing preferences;
3. Assess the relationship between Netflix's data analytics implementation and content creation effectiveness;
4. Measure the influence of Netflix's user experience, design industry standards and platform development;
5. Examine the effectiveness of Netflix's recommendation systems in shaping content discovery and consumption;

Research Hypotheses

Based on existing literature and preliminary research, we propose the following hypotheses:

H1: Netflix's digital transformation strategies have a significant positive correlation with industry-wide technological adoption rates;
H2: Netflix's content delivery model has significantly influenced consumer viewing preferences and behaviors;
H3: Netflix's data analytics practices have transformed industry approaches to content creation and distribution;
H4: Netflix's user experience design has established new industry standards for platform development;
H5: Netflix's recommendation system has significantly impacted content discovery and consumption patterns;

Methodology

This research employed a comprehensive mixed-methods approach conducted over four months from October 2024 to January 2025. The study design incorporated both quantitative and qualitative methodologies to ensure robust data collection and analysis. A stratified random sampling technique was implemented to ensure representative data collection across diverse demographic and professional segments.

The sample population (N = 132) was carefully structured to represent key stakeholder groups within the digital entertainment ecosystem. The consumer group (n = 85) was stratified based on age, location, usage patterns, and subscription duration. The industry professional group (n = 30) included executives, content creators, and technology managers from various entertainment companies. The digital transformation expert group (n = 17) comprised technology consultants, digital strategy advisors, and academic researchers specializing in digital media transformation.

Data collection utilized multiple instruments to ensure comprehensive insights. Quantitative data was gathered through structured online surveys featuring 45 items measuring various aspects of digital transformation impact. These surveys employed 5-point Likert scales for attitude measurement and included behavioral tracking metrics. Qualitative data collection involved in-depth interviews lasting 60–90 minutes, focus group discussions, and detailed case study analyses.

Table 16.1 Digital transformation implementation metrics.

Technology component	Adoption rate	Implementation success	ROI Impact	Correlation coefficient	Standard error	t-value	p-value
Cloud Infrastructure	78.5%	72.3%	+85.4%	0.684	0.058	11.79	<0.001
Data Analytics Systems	82.4%	75.8%	+92.7%	0.725	0.052	13.94	<0.001
AI/ML Integration	65.7%	58.9%	+67.3%	0.592	0.064	9.25	<0.001
Microservices Architecture	71.2%	64.5%	+72.8%	0.635	0.061	10.41	<0.001
DevOps Automation	74.8%	68.7%	+78.5%	0.658	0.059	11.15	<0.001

Source: Author

Table 16.2 Statistical analysis of content delivery impact.

Delivery metric	Pre mean (SD)	Post mean (SD)	t-value	p-value
Weekly Viewing Hours	8.51 ± 1.83	14.23 ± 2.37	12.45	<0.001
Content Discovery Time	38.44 ± 6.26	12.64 ± 2.87	15.67	<0.001
User Satisfaction Score (out of 5)	3.42 ± 0.69	4.21 ± 0.40	9.82	<0.001
Platform Retention Rate	62.38 ± 8.42	84.59 ± 6.25	11.34	<0.001
Cross-Device Usage	1.89 ± 0.56	3.27 ± 0.77	10.56	<0.001

Source: Author

All research instruments underwent rigorous validation through a pilot study with 15 participants, leading to refinements in question structure and measurement scales. Reliability testing using Cronbach's alpha showed high internal consistency ($\alpha = 0.89$) across measurement items. Data analysis employed both statistical and thematic analysis approaches, utilizing SPSS 27.0 for quantitative data and NVivo 14 for qualitative content analysis.

Results

Digital transformation impact analysis (H1)

The results in this Table 16.1 highlight the significant role of Netflix in driving digital transformation across the entertainment industry. The high adoption rates of cloud infrastructure (78.5%), data analytics systems (82.4%), and DevOps automation (74.8%) reflect how Netflix has led the way in implementing advanced technologies. The return on investment (ROI) impact is particularly substantial with data analytics yielding a 92.7% return, demonstrating its effectiveness in optimizing content delivery and operational efficiency. The high correlation coefficients (0.592 to 0.725) indicate a positive relationship between Netflix's technological innovations and their effective adoption in the industry. Moreover, the statistical significance ($p<0.001$) in all the measures ensures the success of these digital transformation strategies. In light of these results, the hypothesis (H1) that Netflix's digital transformation strategies have a significant positive correlation with industry-wide technological adoption rates is accepted. The statistics offer strong proof that Netflix has played a central role in driving the uptake of new technology in the entertainment industry, providing a model for other players in the industry to emulate.

Content delivery model impact (H2)

Table 16.2 illustrates a thorough evaluation of how Netflix's model of content delivery has impacted consumer viewing habits. The statistics reflect a staggering growth in weekly viewing time, increasing from 8.51 hours to 14.23 hours, showing a change in user engagement based on Netflix's on-demand streaming model. Further, time spent discovering content was greatly minimized from 38.44 minutes to 12.64 minutes, reflecting the effectiveness of Netflix's AI-based recommendation engine. Satisfaction of users also increased

Table 16.3 Content creation performance metrics.

Content metric	Traditional model	Netflix model	Percentage change	F-value	p-value
Success rate (%)	32.45 ± 5.25	74.80 ± 6.18	+130.9%	45.67	<0.001
Development time (months)	18.24 ± 2.82	11.03 ± 1.92	-37.9%	38.92	<0.001
Audience match (%)	45.27 ± 7.18	82.34 ± 5.84	+82.1%	52.34	<0.001
Cost efficiency	100.0 ± 15.35	168.55 ± 12.46	+68.5%	41.76	<0.001
Content ROI	100.0 ± 18.63	223.40 ± 21.22	+123.4%	48.23	<0.001

Source: Author

Table 16.4 User experience performance metrics.

UX Element	Industry adoption	User satisfaction	Engagement impact	t-statistic	p-value
Interface Design	84.24 ± 7.15	4.53 ± 0.41	+76.3%	16.78	<0.001
Navigation System	87.62 ± 6.61	4.37 ± 0.53	+82.1%	18.92	<0.001
Personalization	92.38 ± 5.70	4.71 ± 0.33	+89.4%	22.45	<0.001
Content Layout	89.17 ± 6.27	4.47 ± 0.49	+79.8%	19.34	<0.001
Search Functionality	86.59 ± 7.30	4.24 ± 0.53	+74.2%	17.56	<0.001

Source: Author

significantly, with an increase from 3.42 to 4.21 on a 5-point scale, and retention rates of the platform went up from 62.38–84.59%, implying that the platform's easy and intuitive user interface is instrumental in subscriber retention. Furthermore, cross-device usage increased from 1.89 to 3.2,7 reinforcing the seamless accessibility of Netflix's streaming service across multiple devices. Given the statistically significant improvements ($p < 0.001$) in all measured parameters, the hypothesis (H2) that Netflix's content delivery model has significantly influenced consumer viewing preferences and behaviors is accepted. The findings clearly illustrate how Netflix's innovative streaming technology has redefined content consumption, making digital streaming the dominant mode of entertainment.

Data analytics impact on content creation (H3)

Table 16.3 compares the performance of traditional content creation methods with Netflix's data-driven approach. The success rate of Netflix-produced content is significantly higher at 74.80% compared to 32.45% for traditional content, indicating that Netflix's reliance on audience insights and predictive analytics leads to more successful content. Additionally, the content development time has decreased from 18.24 months to 11.03 months, showcasing improved efficiency in production timelines. Audience alignment has also been optimized, with audience match percentages rising from 45.27% in the traditional model to 82.34% under Netflix's model. Furthermore, cost efficiency improved by 68.5%, and content ROI increased by 123.4%, reinforcing that Netflix's data-driven content strategies not only enhance viewer engagement but also maximize financial gains. Statistical significance ($p < 0.001$) reaffirms that the improvements are significantly reliable. The hypothesis (H3) regarding Netflix's data analytics practices has revolutionized content creation and delivery approaches in the industry and is supported by such high evidence. The results highlight the fact that the capability of Netflix to use viewer data and predictive modeling has redefined content creation to ensure that new releases capture viewer tastes and optimize profitability.

User experience design impact (H4)

Table 16.4 analyzes Netflix's influence on UX design, measuring elements including interface design, navigation, personalization, content layout, and searchability. Netflix's UX elements have very high industry adoption rates: personalization at 92.38%, content layout at 89.17%, and navigation at 87.62%, illustrating

Table 16.5 Recommendation system performance metrics.

Metric	Traditional system	AI-Driven system	Percentage change	Z-score	p-value
Content discovery	45.63 ± 6.13	82.32 ± 4.26	+80.5%	25.67	<0.001
User engagement	3.25 ± 0.56	4.65 ± 0.33	+43.8%	22.34	<0.001
View time	92.79 ± 15.67	168.46 ± 12.32	+81.7%	19.89	<0.001
Retention rate	56.43 ± 5.22	88.27 ± 3.81	+56.4%	28.45	<0.001
Recommendation aaccuracy	42.31 ± 5.80	78.62 ± 4.16	+85.8%	24.78	<0.001

Source: Author

the pervasive impact of Netflix's design benchmarks. In addition, user satisfaction ratings are always over 4.2 on a 5-point scale, reflecting the success of Netflix's easy-to-use and intuitive interface. The engagement impact scores between 74.2% and 89.4% also attest to the fact that Netflix's UX innovations play a major role in improving user interaction and retention. Based on these strong findings, the hypothesis (H4) that Netflix's user experience design has set new industry benchmarks for platform creation is accepted. Statistics emphasize Netflix's position in influencing how digital platforms are structured, guaranteeing easy navigation, high customization, and higher usability, which all contribute to a better viewing experience.

Recommendation system impact (H5)

Table 16.5 evaluates the effect of Netflix's AI-powered recommendation system over conventional content discovery techniques. The findings reveal an immense improvement in content availability with an 80.5% increase in the efficiency of content discovery, making it possible for users to access relevant content significantly quicker than in the past. Moreover, user interaction scores also increased from 3.25 to 4.65, and session view time increased from 92.79 minutes to 168.46 minutes, proving that personalized recommendations make users watch more content. The retention rate also increased drastically from 56.43% to 88.27%, proving that the recommendation system of Netflix is an important factor in retaining subscribers. In addition, the precision of recommendations was improved from 42.31% to 78.62%, illustrating how AI-powered personalization is improving content discovery. The statistical significance (p-value < 0.001) supports that these findings are extremely reliable. Based on these results, the hypothesis (H5) that Netflix's recommendation system has greatly influenced content discovery and consumption habits is accepted. The evidence supports that AI-driven recommendations not only enhance content availability but also increase user engagement and retention, making them an essential factor in Netflix's success.

Conclusion

This research validates that Netflix has played a pivotal role in driving digital change in the entertainment sector. Its visionary deployment of cloud computing, artificial intelligence, and data analysis has created new standards, which have shaped technology innovation and business models throughout the industry. The study emphasizes that Netflix's content delivery model has profoundly changed viewing habits among consumers, enhancing audience engagement and shaping content consumption habits. The transition from broadcast television to streaming on demand has been hastened by Netflix's intuitive user experience, data-backed content creation, and recommendations based on personal tastes. The study reveals that Netflix's investment in predictive analytics and AI-based recommendations has enhanced discovery of content and user retention and made personalized streaming experiences the new norm. The research also illustrates how Netflix's content strategy, supported by audience insights, has boosted content success rates and minimized production time and cost. In addition, the universal use of its user experience design principles by competitors reinforces Netflix's position in defining the wider digital entertainment space.

Overall, Netflix innovations have revolutionized entertainment, laying the groundwork for future digital transformation. As streaming becomes more advanced, the sector will witness even greater development in

AI-based content curation, more personalized experiences, and new interactive viewing experiences. This research confirms that businesses looking to achieve successful digital transformation can borrow a page from Netflix's book as a blueprint for harnessing technology, enhancing user experience, and maintaining growth in an ever-evolving digital world. Future research directions involve longitudinal studies of emerging market growth, examination of AI incorporation in content production, and study of changing consumer behavior trends in reaction to new technological abilities.

References

[1] Arun, A. (2024). A case study on netflix marketing strategy. Available from: https://www.simplilearn.com/tutorials/marketing-case-studies-tutorial/netflix-marketing-strategy (Accessed: 29 January 2025).

[2] Au-Yong-Oliveira, M., Marinheiro, M., & Costa Tavares, J. A. (2020). The power of digitalization: the Netflix story. In Trends and Innovations in Information Systems and Technologies, (Vol. 3, pp. 590–599). Springer International Publishing. http://dx.doi.org/10.1007/978-3-030-45697-9_57.

[3] Broe, D. (2019). Birth of the Binge: Serial TV and the End of Leisure. Wayne State University Press.

[4] Gadiya, K., & Bhatt, A. S. (2024). Analyzing the influence of Netflix landing pages on digital marketing success. *International Journal of Research Publication and Reviews*, 5(4), 5100–5103.

[5] Green, J. (2023). Netflix's complicated role as an innovative disruptor in the film industry. *ESIC Digital Economy and Innovation Journal*, 2, e057. http://dx.doi.org/10.55234/edeij-2-057.

[6] Hora, M. (2022). Role of servitization in transitioning from scarcity to abundance paradigm. *Frontiers in Research Metrics and Analytics*, 7, 1016432. https://doi.org/10.3389/frma.2022.1016432.

[7] Hsiao, Y. H. (2024). The business strategy analysis of Netflix. Transactions on Social Science, Education and Humanities Research, 11. https://doi.org/10.62051/tjhh1617.

[8] Juteau, S. (2025). Netflix: Disrupting the entertainment market with digital technologies, time and again. *Journal of Information Technology Teaching Cases*, 15(1), 163–166. http://dx.doi.org/10.1177/20438869231226394.

[9] Saldanha, T. (2019). Why digital transformations fail: The surprising disciplines of how to take off and stay ahead. Berrett-Koehler Publishers, 2(4), 13.

[10] Lozić, J., Vojković, G., & Čiković, K. F. (2024). Business analysis of the Netflix platform in the post-COVID-19 time. In 2024 47th MIPRO ICT and Electronics Convention (MIPRO), (pp. 945–950). http://dx.doi.org/10.1109/MIPRO60963.2024.10569212.

[11] Mandal, G. K., Diroma, F., & Jain, R. (2017). Netflix: an in-depth study of their proactive and adaptive strategies to drive growth and deal with issues of net-neutrality and digital equity. *IRA-International Journal of Management and Social Sciences*, 8(2), 152–161.https://dx.doi.org/10.21013/jmss.v8.n2.p3.

[12] Margiono, A. (2021). Digital transformation: setting the pace. *Journal of Business Strategy*, 42(5), 315–322. https://doi.org/10.1108/JBS-11-2019-0215.

[13] Allen, G., Feils, D., & Disbrow, H. (2014). The rise and fall of Netflix: what happened and where will it go from here?. *Journal of the International Academy for Case Studies*, 20(1), 135.

[14] Matrix, S. (2014). The Netflix effect: teens, binge watching, and on-demand digital media trends. *Jeunesse: Young People, Texts, Cultures*, 6(1), 119–138. http://dx.doi.org/10.1353/jeu.2014.0002.

[15] McAfee, A., & Brynjolfsson, E. (2017). Machine, Platform, Crowd: Harnessing Our Digital Future. W. W. Norton and Company. ISBN: 978-0-393-35606-9.

[16] de Zilwa, D. K. (2024). Netflix: rise, fall and recovery. Journal of Business Strategy, 45(6), 405–413.

[17] United States Securities and Exchange Commission (2013). Annual report pursuant to section 13 or 15(d) of the Securities Exchange Act of 1934.

[18] O'Brien, C. (2025). The unstoppable success of Netflix. Available from: https://digitalmarketinginstitute.com/blog/the-unstoppable-success-of-netflix (Accessed: 6 August 2025).

[19] Paul, J., Ueno, A., Dennis, C., Alamanos, E., Curtis, L., Foroudi, P., et al. (2024). Digital transformation: a multidisciplinary perspective and future research agenda. *International Journal of Consumer Studies*, 48(2), e13015. https://doi.org/10.1111/ijcs.13015.

[20] Pilipets, E. (2019). From Netflix streaming to Netflix and chill: The (dis) connected body of serial binge-viewer. Social Media+ Society, 5(4), 20–26. http://dx.doi.org/10.1177/2056305119883426.

[21] Pratama, O., & Narimawati, U. (2023). The influence of digital changes on media and entertainment business models: a case study of Netflix and Spotify. *Journal of Principles Management and Business*, 2(02), 108–121. https://doi.org/10.55657/jpmb.v2i02.116.

[22] Ruiz-Navas, S., & Miyazaki, K. (2017). Adapting technological capabilities for world digital business: the case of Netflix. In 2017 Portland International Conference on Management of Engineering and Technology (PICMET), (pp. 1–10). IEEE. http://dx.doi.org/10.23919/PICMET.2017.8125430.

[23] Soldo, L., & Schagerl, C. (2023). Impact of the COVID-19 pandemic on Netflix. *MAP Education and Humanities*, 3(1), 75–82. https://doi.org/10.53880/2744-2373.2023.3.1.75.

[24] Stoll, J. (2022). Netflix: number of subscribers worldwide 2011–2022. Statista. Available from: https://www.statista.com/statistics/250934/quarterly-number-of-netflix-streaming-subscribers-worldwide/(Accessed: 27 January 2025).

[25] Talukdar, P. (2024). Digital transformation of Netflix. Available from: https://www.linkedin.com/pulse/digital-transformation-netflix-poulomi-talukdar-ff7vc (Accessed: 4 February 2025).

[26] Thompson, B. (2017). The great unbundling. Stratechery. Available from: https:// stratechery.com/2017/the-great-unbundling/. (Accessed: 25 January 2025)

[27] Venkatraman, N. V. (2017). Netflix: a case of transformation for the digital future. Available from: https://medium.com/@nvenkatraman/netflix-a-case-of-transformation-for-the-digital-future-4ef612c8d8b (Accessed: 3 February 2025).

[28] Voigt, K. I., Buliga, O., & Michl, K. (2017). Entertainment on demand: the case of Netflix. In Business Model Pioneers: How Innovators Successfully Implement New Business Models, (pp. 127–141). http://dx.doi.org/10.1007/978-3-319-38845-8_11.

[29] Vučeković, M., & Gavrilović, K. (2021). Digital transformation and evolution of business models. *IPSI BGD Transactions on Internet Research*, 17(1), 29–35.

[30] Walker, R., Jeffery, M., So, L., Sriram, S., Nathanson, J., Ferreira, J., et al. (2017). Netflix leading with data: the emergence of data-driven video. *Kellogg School of Management Cases*, 1–19. http://dx.doi.org/10.1108/case.kellogg.2016.000232.

[31] Walter, Y. (2023). The centrality of a digital strategy for societal and business innovations. *Digital Transformation and Society*, 2(1), 27–41. https://doi.org/10.1108/DTS-06-2022-0027.

[32] Wayne, M. L. (2018). Netflix, Amazon, and branded television content in subscription video on-demand portals. *Media, Culture and Society*, 40(5), 725–741. http://dx.doi.org/10.1177/0163443717736118.

[33] Wessel, M., Levie, A., & Siegel, R. (2016). The problem with legacy ecosystems. *Harvard Business Review*, 94(11), 68–74.

17 Understanding the impact of perceived liquidity crisis on customers' trust in banks and bank runs

Nishikant Jha[1,a] *and Irvin Kaur*[2,b]

[1]Vice Principal, Thakur College of Science and Commerce; Research Guide, University of Mumbai, Maharashtra, India

[2]Research Scholar, Department of Banking and Finance, K.P.B. Hinduja College of Commerce, University of Mumbai, Maharashtra, India

Abstract

Banks are pillars of any economy, and their foundation is laid upon customers' trust. Banks need to maintain sufficient funds at all times to maintain stability. Should they experience a liquidity crisis, customers' trust in them will evaporate, leading to heavy withdrawals, consequently inducing a bank run. This research aims to find out the impact of perceived liquidity crises on customers' trust in banks and bank runs. Primary data was collected from 202 respondents who had a bank account and were selected for the study. Data is analyzed using simple percentages, a heat map, a chi-square test, and a phi coefficient. The results revealed that the liquidity crisis significantly impacts the customers' trust in banks. Furthermore, this study articulated that a liquidity crisis will precipitate a bank run.

Keywords: Banking system, liquidity, liquidity crisis, trust

Introduction

Trust is a qualitative construct that forms the genesis of all relationships. Mosch and Prast [16] asserted trust as a prerequisite for confidence. Trust entails willingly opening oneself to risk by forging a relationship with another party [29]. Trust requires readiness to expose oneself to a certain amount of risk while transacting with another. The reliability of a person or a thing can be determined only where there is an existence of trust, making the concept of trust highly relevant for financial institutions, as their existence is possible only when people can rely on and trust them to keep their money safe and return it on a future date while readily accepting the risk involved in it. Ampudia and Palligkinis [2] pointed out that a lack of trust in banks can lead to detrimental effects on financial inclusion, which makes the role of trust significant for banks. Trust can be stratified into narrow trust in an institution or broad scope, i.e., trust in the banking system as a whole. This research focuses on narrow-scope trust, i.e., trust in one's bank.

Liquidity is a short-term concept that refers to the potential of converting an asset into cash without any reduction in its worth. The Basel Committee on Banking Supervision in 2008 described liquidity as the ability of a bank to fund an increase in assets and discharge its obligations as and when they become due, without sustaining any unwarranted loss. To ensure trust in a bank, they need adequate liquidity and to always fulfill the demand deposits of customers. Kumar and Yadav [15] accentuated liquidity risk with funding long-term bank assets against short-term liabilities. The banking structure suffers vulnerability due to these long-term loans being illiquid and balanced against highly liquid demand deposits, placing banks' liquidity position at a high-risk [7]. This research will address the impact of liquidity crises on the trust of bank customers, as during normal times, people have faith in their bank, but this same trust evaporates during crises.

A bank run is a result of panic withdrawals by customers on a massive scale. When a bank faces a severe liquidity crisis, it makes the public ponder the stability of the bank and motivates customers to make panic withdrawals, which happened in the case of YES Bank in 2020 and Lakshmi Vilas Bank in 2020. Banks that maintain a strong relationship with their customers are less likely to face a run during crises [10]. Bijlsma et al. [4] also stated that trust serves as an essential factor for financial inclusion and stability, which can help avoid bank runs. A high level of societal trust results in lower market risk for banks. Societal trust can perform the

[a]drnishikantjha@gmail.com, [b]irvinkaur18@gmail.com

DOI: 10.4324/9781003739982-17

function of informal governance to control market risk when formal governance is inefficient [1]. Found that during crises, people who lose trust in banks will withdraw money, creating panic among others and resulting in a run. This research is grounded on the premise that liquidity crises make customers lose trust in banks, which causes them to panic withdrawals, resulting in a run.

Concepts and Literature

Liquidity crises and trust

At times when economies are suffering from concerns of financial instability, liquidity serves as a key ingredient to absorb the shock. Emphasizing the importance of liquidity, Van der Cruijsen et al. [20] stated that individuals having lower trust in the bank prefer them to have higher liquidity. Bertrand et al. [3] illustrated the strong association between liquidity and trust in banks using Gallup's survey and deduced that liquidity and trust move in the same direction, indicating a positive relationship between them. They also stated that this association intensifies during economic crises. Fungáčová et al. [8] also uncovered that individuals implicated by crises have lower trust in banks. Knell and Stix [14] identified that people's assessment of their financial position is a subjective factor for running trusts with banks. They inferred that financial crises cause a sizeable reduction in trust, emphasizing the fragility of public confidence. Van der Cruijsen et al. [19] studied data from banks in the Netherlands and determined that the financial crisis has a detrimental impact on trust and hurts trust. Jiang and Lim [12] analyzed data from banks in the US and highlighted that trust is a strong determinant of choices made by households. Emphasized that trust creates positive economic outcomes. Ampudia and Palligkinis [2] also pointed out that a lack of trust in banks can lead to detrimental effects on financial inclusion. Mosch and Prast [16] stated that trust is a prerequisite for confidence. Low trust can result in financial usability, and prior negative experiences will create an image that their bank cannot be trusted [13].

H_0: There is no significant association between perceived liquidity crisis and trust in the bank

Liquidity crises and bank run

The banking system depends on the deposits received from the customers (a liability of the bank), which are employed to extend loans (which become an asset). It is rational for a bank to have a fragile structure harboring the possibility of a bank run due to the functions it provides. Banks grant illiquid loans and demand deposits, rendering banks susceptible to a run. The system is extremely frail, as the liquid liabilities are to be balanced against illiquid assets. Economies in severe crises face panic withdrawals from the banks, and the illiquid nature of banks' assets acts as a hindrance, as the full value of it cannot be recovered at that particular time, making repayment of deposits perplexing [6]. Diamond and Rajan [7] elaborated on various situations in which the liquidity of a bank is affected, triggering a bank run. Additionally, they suggested measures to be taken in those situations. If a bank is incapable of repaying its customers due to the illiquid nature of its assets, it may start losing trust in the bank, intensifying the situation to a bank run [3]. Ippolito et al. [9] analyzed banking data during the 2008 crisis and discovered that a liquidity crisis may result in double bank runs on the asset side as well as the liability side. They further emphasized the significance of ex-ante liquidity risk management to prevent a double bank run.

H_0: There is no significant association between perceived liquidity crisis and bank run.

Research gap

The banking crisis of 2008 had a profound impact on the banking system, prompting researchers to focus on trust in banks, financial crises, and bank runs. Currently, multiple studies are undertaken to explore drivers of trust in banks [18], financial crises and trust Roth [17], van der Cruijsen, et al. [20], bank runs Ippolito et al. [9], and also liquidity and trust [4]. Merely a handful of studies analyzed the effects of liquidity crises, and the ones that did, focused on the liquidity crises as a quantitative concept derived from numerical values of banking transactions, whereas the current study is based on perceived liquidity being a qualitative concept stemming from experiences and perceptions of the respondents.

Research Methodology

Instruments

The study follows a quantitative research design. Bank customers are likely to be unaware of the actual liquidity position of their banks, so perceived liquidity is considered for analysis. Our first hypothesis examines the impact of perceived liquidity crises on trust in banks with variables: liquidity crises (independent variable) and trust (dependent variable). Our second hypothesis focuses on the impact of perceived liquidity on bank runs, involving two variables: liquidity crises (independent variable) and bank runs (dependent variable).

Sampling design

Data is collected employing judgmental and purposive sampling. A survey was undertaken to collect data from respondents residing in the Mumbai district of India through a structured questionnaire that was circulated electronically. The questionnaire was filled out by 202 respondents holding a savings bank account.

Software used

The collected data was analyzed using Python software, which is a high-powered statistical software with extensive libraries, thereby providing deep insights into data and excellent tools for testing hypotheses.

Tools applied

Initially, a heat map was plotted to analyze the role of demographic variables: age, gender, and income. Since the data is categorical, a chi-square test of independence was applied to establish the association between liquidity crises and trust and liquidity crises and bank runs. The Phi coefficient is applied to test the strength of association established by the Chi-Square test.

Data analysis and interpretation

H_1: There is a significant association between liquidity crises and customers' trust in banks

To measure the impact of liquidity crises and customers' trust, respondents were asked a "yes" or "no" question: "If your bank faces a liquidity crisis, will it affect your trust in the bank?"

Demographic analysis

Figure 17.1 shows a gender-wise classification of the effects of liquidity crises on the trust of 89.3% (100) of women and 85.6% (77) of men. The difference between men and women is dwarfed, which aligns with the study by Carbó-Valverde et al. [5], which found that demographic characteristics like gender do not have a significant impact on trust and stated that women trust banks slightly more than men.

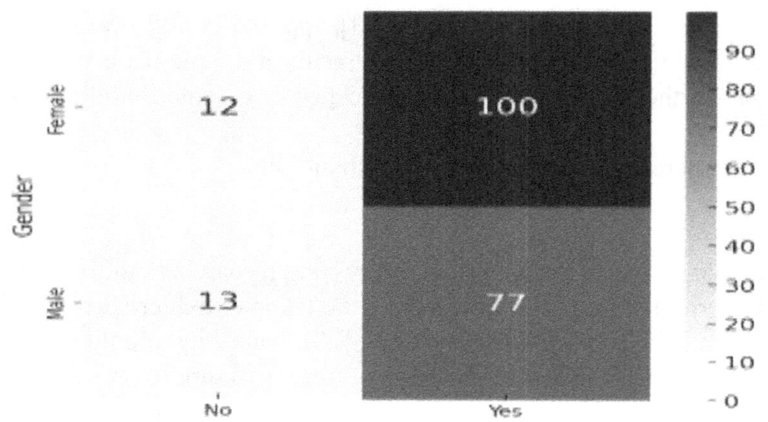

Figure 17.1 Effects of liquidity crises on trust: gender-wise classification
Source: Author

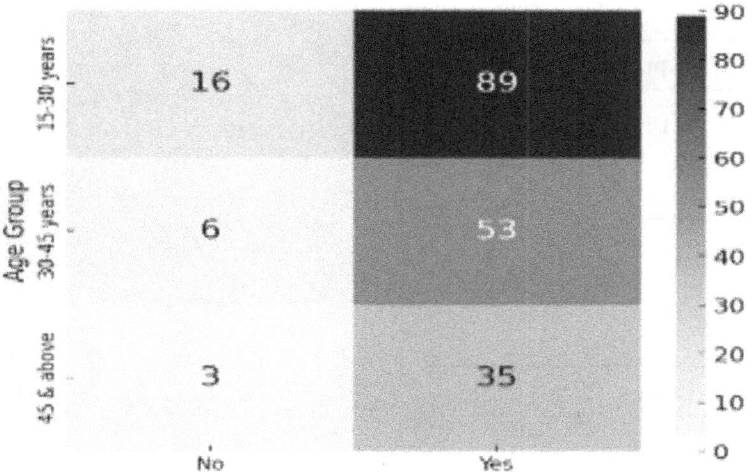

Figure 17.2 Effects of liquidity crises on trust: age-wise classification
Source: Author

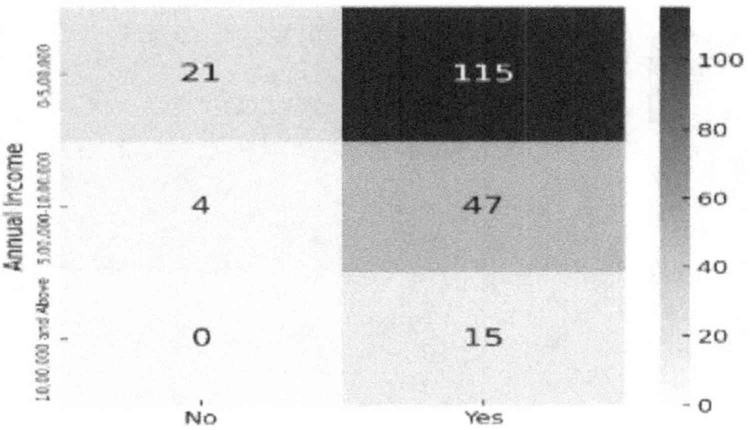

Figure 17.3 Effects of liquidity crises on trust: income-wise classification
Source: Author

Figure 17.2 shows the age-wise classification of the effects of liquidity crises on trust. Due to liquidity crises in the age group of 15-30 years, trust of 84.8% (89), 30-45 years trust of 89.8% (53), and trust of 92.1% (35) of individuals above 45 age group will be impacted. As age increases, trust decreases, which is similar to the results of Fungáčová et al. [8].

Figure 17.3 displays the income-wise classification of liquidity on trust. The trust of 84.6% (115) of respondents will be affected due to liquidity crises in income level 0-500,000, 92.2% (47) in the age group 500,000-1,000,000, and 100% (15) in the age group above 1,000,000, which makes it evident that trust decreases with an increase in age, matching with the conclusion of Fungáčová et al. [8].

Summary statistics

The p-value, obtained using the chi-square test on observed and expected frequencies listed in Table 17.1, is less than 0.01, rejecting the null hypothesis. This indicates a significant association between liquidity and customers' trust in the bank, as shown in Table 17.2.

The value of the Phi coefficient is 0.75, establishing a strong relationship between liquidity crises and trust based on Cohen's criteria. This signifies that if a bank suffers from a liquidity crisis, it will certainly impact trust in the bank.

Table 17.1 Contingency table.

Category	Observed frequency	Expected frequency
Yes	177	101
No	25	101
Total (N)	202	202

Source: Author

Table 17.2 Chi-Square and Phi coefficient test results.

Statistics	Value
Chi-square statistics (χ^2)	114.38
P-Value	<0.01
Phi Coefficient	0.75

Source: Author

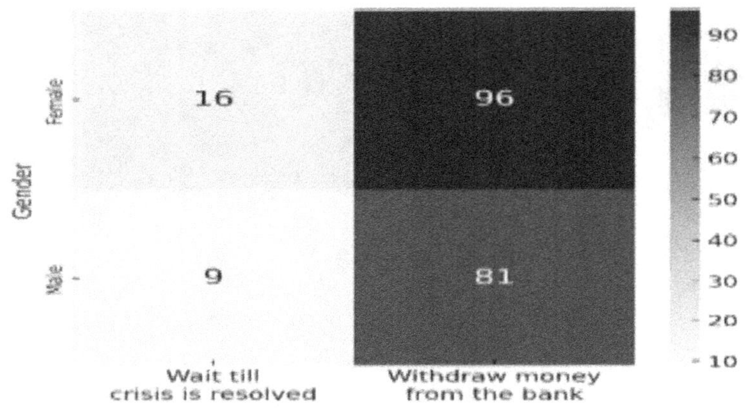

Figure 17.4 Effects of liquidity crises on bank run: gender wise classification
Source: Author

The results highlight that if banks maintain a high level of liquidity, trust in the bank will be high. On the other hand, if the bank is facing a liquidity crisis, customers are more likely to lose trust in their bank, which is in agreement with the conclusion of the Centre for European Policy Studies working paper (2009).

H_2: There is a significant association between liquidity crisis and bank run

To test the relation between a liquidity crisis and a bank run, respondents were asked the question, "If your bank faces a liquidity crisis, what will you do?" Wait till the crisis is resolved, or withdraw money from the bank.

Demographic analysis

Figure 17.4 illustrates that only 14.3% (16) of women and 10% (9) of men will wait for the resolution of liquidity crises; others will choose to withdraw from the bank. Such massive withdrawals by over 85% of the population will likely result in a run. Again, the results are familiar; there is no significant difference between the behavior of men and women during a run.

Figure 17.5 provides an age-wise classification of the effects of liquidity crises on bank runs. In case of a liquidity crisis, individuals in the age group of 30–45 years are most likely to run (91.5%), followed by

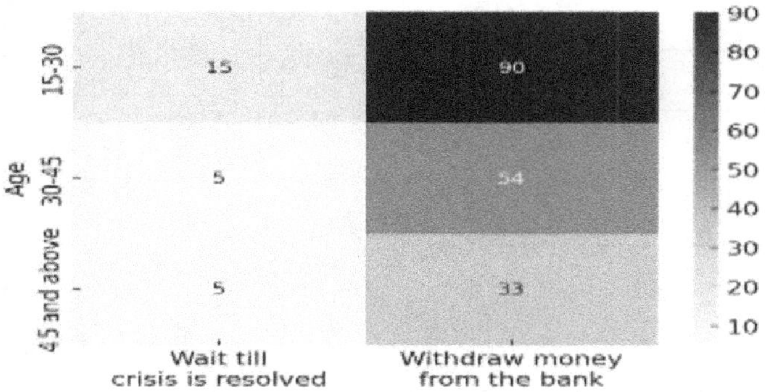

Figure 17.5 Effects of liquidity crises on bank run: age-wise classification
Source: Author

Table 17.3 Contingency table.

Category	Observed frequency	Expected frequency
Wait till the crisis is resolved	25	101
Withdraw money from the bank	177	101
Total (N)	202	202

Source: Author

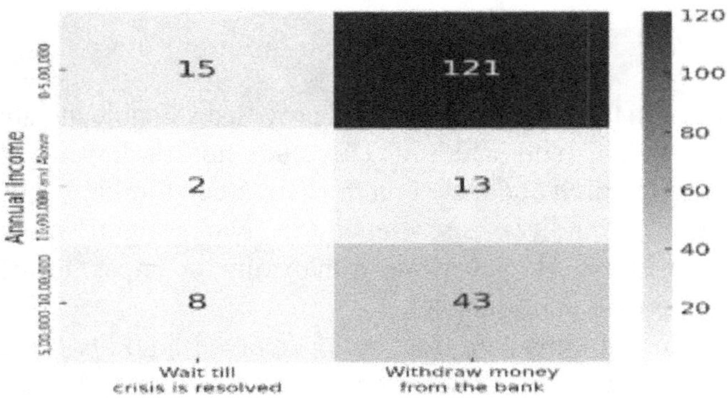

Figure 17.6 Effects of liquidity crises on bank run: income-wise classification
Source: Author

individuals above 45 years, who are 86.8% likely to run, and lastly, individuals in the age group of 15–30 years, who are 85.7% likely to run. Overall, there is no major difference between the age groups, as all are likely to run in case of liquidity crises.

Figure 17.6 represents the income-wise classification of the relationship between liquidity crises and bank runs. Respondents with income up to 500,000 have an 89% (121) possibility of a run, 86.8% (43) in income level 500,000–1,000,000, and 86.7% (13) in income above 10,000,000. This makes it evident that there is no significant difference in the possibility of a run with an increase in income level.

Summary statistics

A chi-square test is performed on frequencies in Table 17.3 to analyse the association between liquidity crises and bank runs. The results of the chi-square test in Table 17.4 highlighted a p-value less than 0.01, i.e., significant at 1%, establishing a strong association between a liquidity crisis and bank run, matching the outcome of [20].

Table 17.4 Chi-Square and Phi coefficient test results.

Statistics	Value
Chi-square statistics (χ^2)	114.38
P-Value	<0.01
Phi Coefficient	0.75

Source: Author

The Phi Coefficient value is 0.75, closer to 1, validating a significant relationship between liquidity crises and bank runs. This establishes that a bank's liquidity crisis compels customers to withdraw money, resulting in a bank run.

These findings highlight a significant connection between a bank's liquidity position and its susceptibility to causing a run. When a bank doesn't have sufficient liquid assets to meet its short-term obligations, customers are prone to lose trust in the bank and pull out their funds.

Limitations of the Study

This research is subject to limitations, such as a limited sample size and a geographical area limited to Mumbai. The study is based on perceived liquidity crises, analyzing how individuals will respond during a crisis scenario. However, their reaction during an actual crisis may differ from the perceived reaction. This research focuses on banks in general; a comparative study of trust levels comparing different types of banks will enable an in-depth understanding of the subject that is not covered in this research.

Conclusion

The present study analyzed the influence of liquidity crises on trust and bank runs and provided valuable insight into the impact of liquidity crises on customers' trust in the bank and bank run. This study holds relevance in today's time when banks are facing financial distress, and research conducted on this is scarce in India.

An analysis of the demographic profile exhibited that in a liquidity crisis, women trust banks slightly more than men, and trust in banks decreases with age and income level. However, while analyzing the impact of the liquidity crisis, the bank run demographic profile did not pose a major impact.

The findings highlight that liquidity crises have a significant impact on trust, as a perceived liquidity crisis can reduce trust in banks drastically. The influence can be seen in large-scale withdrawals by the customers of banks during a perceived liquidity crisis, transforming the scenario into a bank run. The research results are significant at the current time, as many cooperative banks in India are failing, and people are losing trust in them. Not only in India, but banks all over the globe are struggling, as in many countries, liquidity requirements under BASIL III norms are not yet followed. A liquidity crisis can result in a trust crisis, which would erode the trust of customers not only in failing banks but in the entire banking system.

Banks should focus on creating bank-depositor relationships to decrease fragility and avoid bank run. Strengthening banks' governance, stringent regulatory compliances, and increasing the deposit insurance cover should be considered for preventing a bank run.

References

[1] Abdelsalam, O., Chantziaras, A., Joseph, N. L., & Tsileponis, N. (2024). Trust matters: a global perspective on the influence of trust on bank market risk. *Journal of International Financial Markets, Institutions and Money*, 92, 101959. https://doi.org/10.1016/j.intfin.2024.101959.

[2] Ampudia, M., & Palligkinis, S. (2018). *Trust and the household-bank relationship* (ECB Working Paper No. 2184). European Central Bank. https://doi.org/10.2139/ssrn.3266282

[3] Bertrand, J., Klein, P. O., & Soula, J. L. (2022), Liquidity creation and trust environment. *Journal of Financial Services Research*, 62(3), 201–232. https://dx.doi.org/10.1007/s10693-021-00353-0.

[4] Bijlsma, M., van der Cruijsen, C., & Koldijk, J. (2022). Determinants of trust in banks' payment services during COVID: an exploration using daily data. *De Economist*, 170(2), 231–256. https://doi.org/10.1007/s10645-022-09405-9.

[5] Carbo-Valverde, S., López, E., & Rodríguez-Fernández, F. (2013). Evidence from the Spanish financial crisis (August 14, 2013). In 26th Australasian Finance and Banking Conference 2013, http://dx.doi.org/10.2139/ssrn.2310273.

[6] Diamond, D. W., & Dybvig, P. H. (1983). Bank runs, deposit insurance, and liquidity. *Journal of Political Economy*, 91(3), 401–419. https://doi.org/10.1086/261155.

[7] Diamond, D. W., & Rajan, R. G. (2001). Liquidity risk, liquidity creation, and financial fragility: a theory of banking. *Journal of Political Economy*, 109(2), 287–327. http://dx.doi.org/10.2139/ssrn.112473.

[8] Fungáčová, Z., Hasan, I., & Weill, L. (2019). Trust in banks. *Journal of Economic Behavior and Organization*, 157, 452–476. https://doi.org/10.1016/j.jebo.2017.08.014.

[9] Ippolito, F., Peydró, J. L., Polo, A., & Sette, E. (2016). Double bank runs and liquidity risk management. *Journal of Financial Economics*, 122(1), 135–154. https://doi.org/10.1016/j.jfineco.2015.11.004.

[10] Iyer, R., & Puri, M. (2012). Understanding bank runs (2012): The importance of depositor-bank relationships and networks. FDIC Center of Financial Research, Working Paper No. 2008-11. http://dx.doi.org/10.1257/aer.102.4.1414.

[11] Jansen, D. J., Mosch, R., & Van Der Cruijsen, C. (2013). When does general public lose trust in bank? DNB Working Paper No. 402. https://dx.doi.org/10.2139/ssrn.2373084.

[12] Jiang, D., & Lim, S. S. (2018). Trust and household debt. *Review of Finance*, 22(2), 783–812. http://dx.doi.org/10.2139/ssrn.1954790.

[13] Kidron, A., & Kreis, Y. (2020). Listening to bank customers: the meaning of trust. *International Journal of Quality and Service Sciences*, 12(3), 355–370. http://dx.doi.org/10.1108/IJQSS-10-2019-0120.

[14] Knell, M., & Stix, H. (2010). Trust in banks - evidence from normal times and from times of crises. Beiträge zur Jahrestagung des Vereins für Socialpolitik 2010: Ökonomie der Familie - Session: Trusting Banks in a Financial Crisis, No. A1-V1, Verein für Socialpolitik, Frankfurt a. M.

[15] Kumar, M., & Yadav, G. C. (2013). Liquidity risk management in bank: a conceptual framework. *AIMA Journal of Management and Research*, 7(2/4), 0974-497. http://dx.doi.org/10.33094/ijaefa.v14i2.689.

[16] Mosch, R. H. J., & Prast, H. (2008). Confidence and trust: empirical investigation for the Netherlands and the financial sector. *DNB Occasional Studies*, 6(2). 1–48.

[17] Roth, F. (2022). The effect of the financial crisis on systemic trust. In Public Support for the Euro. Contributions to Economics, (pp. 209–224). Cham: Springer. http://dx.doi.org/10.1007/978-3-030-86024-0_11.

[18] Sekhon, H., Ennew, C., Kharouf, H., & Devlin, J. (2014). Trustworthiness and trust: influences and implications. *Journal of Marketing Management*, 30(3-4), 409–430. https://doi.org/10.1080/0267257x.2013.842609.

[19] Van der Cruijsen, C., de Haan, J., & Roerink, R. (2023). Trust in financial institutions: a survey. *Journal of Economic Surveys*, 37(4), 1214–1254. https://doi.org/10.1111/joes.12468.

[20] Van der Cruijsen, C., de Haan, J., & Jansen, D.-J. (2016). Trust and financial crisis experiences. *Social Indicators Research*, 127(2), 577–600. https://doi.org/10.1007/s11205-015-0984-8.

[21] Mayer, R. C., Davis, J. H., & Schoorman, F. D. (1995). An Integrative Model of Organizational Trust. *The Academy of Management Review*, 20(3), 709–734. https://doi.org/10.2307/258792.

18 IPOS underpricing and long-term performance: evidence from the Bulgarian Stock Exchange

Vasia Manolova[a] *and Marcellin Yovogan*[b]

Department of Finance and Accounting, Sofia University St. Kliment Ohridski, Sofia, Bulgaria

Abstract

The current research examines the IPO underpricing and issuers' long-term performance from the first IPO launched in 2004 to July 2023. The study gives additional insight into the Standard Equities segment IPOs and contributes to a better understanding of the IPO process, trends, relationships, and market opportunities on the Bulgarian Stock Exchange. We used a descriptive and analytical approach to explore the Standard Equities and Beam market IPOs in terms of volume, number of issues, current market segmentation, and default rate. Then, we examined the IPO price change compared to the SOFIX index. The results showed that the prevailing IPOs launched before the financial crisis of 2008 tend to decrease in price on the first day of trade or to be overpriced. However, they outperformed the market index by 0.37% on an annual average in the long term. Since then, BSE IPOs, including Beam IPOs, have shown a tendency of IPO underpricing and benchmark underperformance in the long term. The industry analysis results showed market outperformance of businesses operating in the manufacturing, communication service, real estate, information technology, and financial sectors.

Keywords: IPO, performance, underpricing

Introduction

The Bulgarian Stock Exchange(BSE) is a relatively young and is still characterized by the features of a typical emerging and developing markets. The Initial Public Offering (IPO) on the BSE and post-IPO performance is highly influenced by the global financial trends, but it has its particularities considering the local regulatory factors, sectoral specifics, and investors' biases. Most IPO issues on BSE were launched during the market boom in 2005–2007, but after the global financial and real estate crisis in 2008, Standard Equities/SE/IPO activities dropped significantly both in volume and number.

The Bulgarian capital market is not researched enough regarding the IPO underpricing and long-term performance. The current paper examines the IPO values, the prices variations, the market performance, and the default rate from the first IPO launch in 2004 to July 2023. The study gives additional insight into the Standard Equities and Beam market IPOs and contributes to a better understanding of the BSE IPO process, trends, and market opportunities.

The objective of this research is to examine the IPO historical development and trends on BSE by focusing on the Standard Equities and Beam markets.

The used secondary data is collected from public online resources, among which are the Bulgarian Stock Exchange; and the Bulgarian Registry Agency [21]; as well specialized financial markets websites such as Infostock.bg, [11], and x3News.com [26].

The paper is structured in two main parts. In the first part, we present the theoretical background, literature review, and the methodology of the research. The second part includes the data analysis, the findings, and the limitations of the study. It's concluded with some discussions.

Theoretical Background and Literature Review

Theoretical background

IPO as a way to become a public company

Companies have generally two paths to raising money: debt or equity financing. The last could be performed through the issuance and sale of new shares to existing or new shareholders on a closed private deal or

[a]vimanolova@uni-sofia.bg, [b]myovogan@feb.uni-sofia.bg

DOI: 10.4324/9781003739982-18

through a public offering of shares on a regulated or non-regulated market. The initial offering of existing shares or issuance of new ones to the public on a stock exchange is referred to as an IPO. However, an IPO is not the only path to becoming public. As stated by Huang et al. [7], private companies that plan to go public can perform a traditional IPO, a direct listing, merging with a special purpose acquisition company (SPAC), or being acquired by a public company. The IPO implies the issuance of new shares and usually involves an investment intermediary, which underwrites the issue and determines the issue price. In a direct listing, a private company lists its common shares on the capital market without using underwriters. Direct listing does not involve a capital increase, only existing, outstanding shares are offered to the public. During 2020–21 SPACs became popular in the US. A SPAC raises capital via an IPO, deposits the proceeds in an escrow account, and searches for a private company to merge with. In case of no merger, the SPAC liquidates and distributes the funds to its shareholders. The last way for a company to become public is through an acquisition by a public company.

Listing process

Most commonly an IPO commences with the preparation of a prospectus for an initial public offering of securities, which together with other required by law documents are submitted to the regulatory authority/Financial Supervision Commission in Bulgaria for approval. Following the approval of the Prospectus by the regulatory authority and its publication on the website of the company, the securities could be admitted to trading on the regulated market/BSE in Bulgaria. The regulated stock exchange approves the application for issue admission given that: the Prospect is approved; the securities are registered at the depositary institution; the issuer is not in liquidation or bankruptcy proceedings; financial statements for a 3 to 5-year historic period or other required financial information are submitted; declaration confirming the issuer's consent to apply the principles of corporate governance as approved by the stock exchange. Upon successful subscription of the determined in the Prospectus minimum number of shares, the IPO is considered successful and its shares start trading on the secondary market of the stock exchange.

Intermediaries

The role of the investment banks is substantial for IPO effectiveness. Burton et al. [5] outline the important contribution of the investment banks in the IPO process, in several directions: 1) design of the new issue, including advice on the amount and type of securities (shares or bonds) and establishing an appropriate price; 2) consider a good timing: a recommended time to initiate IPO is during a period of high stock prices and bullish market; 3) assist corporations in filling out and prospectus documents to the regulatory institution according to local legislation and stock exchange regulations; 4) underwrite and market the securities: the underwriter purchases the entire issue at a fixed contracted price and in that way takes the whole risk for the success of the issue. To mitigate the risk, the investment bank usually defines a lower IPO price.

The IPO on BSE is usually undertaken by an ***investment intermediary***.

Reasons to go public

As stated by Khurshed [14] generalizes that the driving reason for IPO is the need for capital for companies' expansion. Among other reasons are: to repay loans due; to achieve better terms on future debt due to higher transparency; offering part of the shares to the employees as compensation helps the firm to attract, motivate, and retain employees. Ritter and Welch [22] suggest that companies initiate IPOs in favorable market conditions, but only when they reach a certain stage of development. The authors find a positive relationship between the issuing activity and the capital market development. Despite offering prices being lowered, many firms withdraw their offers rather than proceed with an IPO, which raises the interesting question of why IPO volumes depend on market boom (downturn), instead of observing price adjustment. Brau and Fawcett [1] argue that the driving reason for IPO is to favor Mand A, and the companies choose to stay private to keep management and ownership.

IPO advantages and disadvantages

Becoming a public company through IPO is accompanied by pros and cons. As defined by Khurshed [14], after an IPO completion, some competitive advantages occur: improved reputation and publicity; the public trade of shares allows the initial shareholders to deprive the profit from their investment and diversify their portfolio by selling part of their shares. In addition, Zhang [27] identifies the following IPO advantages: increased available capital, improved global recognition, enhanced user confidence, liquidity benefits to owners of capital, higher employee incentives, and larger market cap due to increased transparency. Apart from the benefits, Khurshed points out the disadvantages: public companies need to follow regulatory requirements about information disclosure, including disclosure of price-sensitive information, and managerial and financial data, which is both expensive and reveals sensitive information to peers. An additional negative outcome is that the management usually does not have an ownership stake in the company, often resulting in short-term-oriented executive decisions shifting away from good investment projects with long-term pay-offs. Another point is that increased transparency facilitates Mand A, and opens opportunities for unsolicited acquisitions. Zhang [27] also outlines the negative impact of disclosing sensitive information to the public on certain industries like biotech companies, whose exposure to the public might reduce their competitiveness. A final concern is that conducting an IPO is not a cheap process. According to Dahlquist and Knight [6], an IPO procedure can expect to incur costs of 5% to 8% or more, calculated based on the value of the IPO.

Literature Review

According to Roopa [23], capital markets observe sizable differences between the IPO offer price and the opening price on the first day of trade, allowing investors to make substantial single-day gains. This is referred to as ***underpricing***. The initial underpricing of the IPOs is a broadly discussed issue, which usually leads to underperformance in the long run. According to Roopa [23], underpricing arises from trading unpredictability thus compensating the investors for the risk they take. Another argument is that the issuer possesses inside information and the firm should offer a lower price to incentivize buyers to participate in the public offering. Ilbasmis [8] summarized four theories for IPO underpricing: asymmetric information, ownership and control considerations, institutional and behavioral explanations. Furthermore, Ritter and Welch [22] point out that asymmetric information theories cannot justify the underpricing of 65 percent on IPOs within the Internet bubble in the USA in 1999-2000. They consider that underpricing is mainly due to agency conflicts and share distribution problems combined with behavioral theories but cannot find a leading theory to explain the phenomena, which is a persistent feature of the US IPO market. Huang et al. [7], suggest that agency problems are less pronounced in countries with higher democracy and media independence and have better-established management practices.

Most IPO underpricing research are based on the US market. Ritter and Welch [22] examine the IPO first-day return and subsequent performance for the period 1980-2001. They calculate average first-day returns between 9.8% and 22.3% within the period from 1990 to 1998, the astonishing 71.7% in 1999 and 56.1% in 2000 during the Internet bubble, falling back to 14% in the next year /2001/. The authors observe that the higher IPO activity corresponds to a higher first-day return rate but cannot find a clear correlation between short-term and long-term performance. Recent studies on the US capital market outline the advantages of IPOs, which according to Zhang [27] outweigh the disadvantages, turning the IPO into a key process of a successful business.

Khurshed et al. [15], examine UK IPO performance and observe a significant decline in the post-issue price change of the Official List IPOs on the London Stock Exchange. On the contrary, the Alternative Investment Market (AIM) allows firms to raise fresh funds without sacrificing profitability. Authors conclude that the AIM represents the first segment where the financial results do not deteriorate following the IPO.

While underpricing is usually related to stock market bubbles, Ilbasmis [8] studied an interesting underpricing phenomenon during COVID-19 on the Istanbul stock exchange. Ilbasmis found out that the IPO prices during the pandemic were reduced to a greater extent relative to the pre-pandemic period. The author also observes that the short-term prices of companies that launched IPOs during the pandemic increased, and those companies' IPOs outperformed relative to the former periods IPOs.

Shukla and Shaw [24] analyzed the long-term returns of the IPO companies in India launched from Apr 2000 to Mar 2015, suggesting that in contrast to the US studies, Indian IPOs do not show evidence of underperformance in the long term. However, in single cases, the authors find negative returns. Furthermore, they observe that a median IPO company underperforms the benchmark, explained by the fact that most IPOs are launched during the market boom periods.

Another research by Komenkul and Kiranand [16] about Asian countries' market performance shows that biopharmaceutical and healthcare IPOs achieved a positive return in the long run after going public opposite to current US healthcare studies. Malaysian and Thai healthcare and biopharmaceutical IPOs outperform in the long run, whereas the Singaporean IPOs show comparable results to the US studies regarding an inverse correlation between short-term and medium-term (3-year) performance. The authors argue that emerging markets have different patterns regarding IPO returns and suggest longer-holding period investment strategies.

Sustainability and the greenness level impact on public companies' performance is another topic of discussion. Meles et al. [17], study the EU capital market from 2003 to 2019 including the BSE market among 35 EU countries. The research focuses on green innovation and its correlation to the default risk, using OLS regression and GMM analysis. The results show a negative relationship between green innovation and the default rate suggesting that green innovation increases the firms' value and revenues. Furthermore, a greenness index was proposed by Mumtaz and Yoshino [19] calculated according to emissions level. The authors find that the greenness level depends on the market sector, the highest ones belonging to the financial and services sectors. They also observe that high-green companies achieve lower returns in the short term but perform better in the long term than low-green companies.

Kaserer and Treßel [13] studied the regulatory complexity and its impact on the IPO activity in 12 European markets and the US, including 27 companies listed on the BSE. The research covers the period 2016–2022 using word count and difference analysis and finds that the listing requirements could be simplified without limiting investor protection.

The behavior of IPO hot markets in Bulgaria during the period 2006-2007, as stated by Ivantchev [12] has the same basic characteristics as those in other countries, within the setting of hot markets, but with a larger underperformance. The author argues that the results can be explained by the higher amplitude of optimism bias of investors during the hot market combined with the highly overvalued shares. In addition, Vasileva [25] reviews the stock market indicators on BSE such as market capitalization, turnover, transaction and issues number, BSE indices, and development during the period. The study covers a longer 20-year period but does not focus on IPO issues. Nenkov [20] studied the main indexes' performance pre and post-global crisis period, including price to earnings (PE) and price to book value (PBV) ratios on US and Bulgarian markets. Nenkov concentrates on the global financial crisis period (2008) and the largest stock market bubble at that time but does not discuss IPOs.

The prevailing papers related to the IPO dynamics, analyze the reasons, advantages, and disadvantages of going public, and discuss common IPO problems such as underpricing and long-term underperformance, concerning developing markets, and measures to reform the regulatory and legislative framework. As expected, most researches focus on the biggest capital markets like the US, China, India, Asia, and the UK. Local researchers from Turkey, Kazakhstan, Ukraine, and Bulgaria discuss the IPO market performance and regulatory and other internal factors on the corresponding domestic market.

This paper presents the global trends and challenges and gives an in-depth understanding of the Bulgarian IPO market, and in that way contributes to the capital market research studies.

Methodology

In this research, we use the following approach:

- Focusing on the literature review that helps to understand the IPO process, fundamentals, and specific requirements for Standard Equities IPOs and Beam IPOs; exploring some IPO-related papers on developed and developing capital markets;
- The historic-analytical method: observing the historic development of Standard Equities IPOs and Beam IPOs related to the number, volume, and market segmentation, including BSE reclassification; this method aims to examine the IPO activity, volume, and default rate using the retrieved data for the period 2004 – 2023;
- We applied the boxplot visualization in the Seaborn library of Jupyter notebook, provided by Anaconda PowerShell Prompt program, and using the Python programming language.
- Research-analytical: analyzing the outperformance of IPOs on BSE, including the first day of trade price change and long-term market performance; IPO calculations on equity segment and Beam market are performed, regarding underpricing and annual compound market performance, using the SOFIX index as a market benchmark.

We used the following definitions and formulas:

IPO underpricing

We used an IPO underpricing formula to assess the BSE IPOs' first day of trade performance. We define IPO underpricing as the difference between the percentage price change in stock price and the percentage change of the SOFIX index from the starting date for shares' subscription in IPO until the first day of trading.

IPO underpricing is calculated using the formula:

$$IPO\ underpricing = \frac{Pt - Po}{Po} - \frac{St - So}{So}$$

Where:

- Po represents the IPO price;
- Pt represents the closing price on the first day of trading of IPO stocks;
- So is the SOFIX index value at the starting date for shares' subscription;
- St is the SOFIX index value on the first day of trading.

IPO long-term performance

IPO long-term performance is used to assess the IPO success rate and is defined as the adjusted market benchmark price change between the IPO price and the July 2023 issue price, computed on an annual compound basis. We apply the SOFIX index as a benchmark to compute the market outperformance/underperformance for the given period. We first define the IPO price market outperformance/underperformance for the whole period, using the following formulas:

$$\Delta IPO = \frac{Pj - Po}{Po} - \frac{Sj - So}{So}$$

Where:

- **Po** represents the IPO price (IPO proceeds divided by the number of shares subscribed);
- **Pj** represents the closing price as of the end of July 2023;
- **So** is the SOFIX index value at the starting date for shares' subscription in the IPO;
- **Sj** is the SOFIX index value as of the end of July 2023.

Then we annualize the result to receive a comparable annual long-term outperformance/ underperformance, by using the compounded period formula:

$$IPO\ annual\ market\ outperformance\ = \sqrt[n]{\Delta\ IPO + 1} - 1$$

Where:

- Δ IPO represents the computed issue market outperformance/underperformance for the period;
- n is the number of periods in years.

The result shows the annualized return of the issue over the market benchmark. In case of positive value, the issue outperforms the market and given the result is negative the issue underperforms the market.

IPO default rate
The IPO default rate is indicative of the IPO issues sustainability and is calculated based on the number of delisted and in liquidation companies /excluding delisted by shareholders/ within the period 2004–2023, compared to the total number of initiated IPOs within the same period. We use the following formula:

Data Collection

The analyzed data is collected from public online resources, among which are the Bulgarian Stock Exchange (IPO statistical data); and the Bulgarian Registry Agency [21], (financial statements); specialized online media such as Infostock.bg, Investr.bg, and x3News.com [26] (price statistics, news, and announcements) and companies' websites (IPO Prospectus documentation). During the analysis, 46 public companies were reviewed, representing all standard equities IPOs (including BEAMs) listed on the BSE within the period 2004–2023. All of these are included in the survey statistics, figures and graphics. The delisted issues are excluded from the long-term performance calculations since they do not support the current market price.

$$IPO\ default\ rate = \frac{number\ of\ IPO\ issuers\ in\ bankruptcy\ or\ liquidation}{total\ number\ of\ IPOs}$$

Data Analysis

IPOs on BSE
After the fall of the communist regime in 1989, the capital market was re-established. Six years later in 1995, BSE was founded. During the following several years the first shares of companies participating in the Privatization Process were listed, alongside the implementation of many regulatory and structural changes. The first IPO was carried out in 2004, and from then until July 2023 45 new IPOs were successfully launched on BSE on the Standard Equities IPO segment and Beam market.
The activity of the BSE market is organized in several markets - a regulated market, consisting of BSE Main Market and BaSE Alternative Market, and a non-regulated market, comprising Beam market and MTF BSE International. These markets are determined according to issuers' qualitative and quantitative criteria, among which are market capitalization, free float, financial performance, trade activity, and others.

BSE delists companies from the capital market in case of bankruptcy (liquidation or upon acquisition by shareholders). Issues from the SME growth Beam market can be moved into the main market in case they meet the BSE main market criteria for the standard equities segment. For that reason, the Beam market is considered a steppingstone to the regulated market. However, since the Beam market introduction in 2021 until 2023, no Beam issues have been transferred into the main market, but no Beam issues have been delisted either.

As shown in Figure 18.1, Premium and Standard Equities represent 33% of the IPO issues on the main market segment, Beam equities account for 30%, 20% of all issues are moved to trade on the alternative market, and 17% are delisted from BSE.

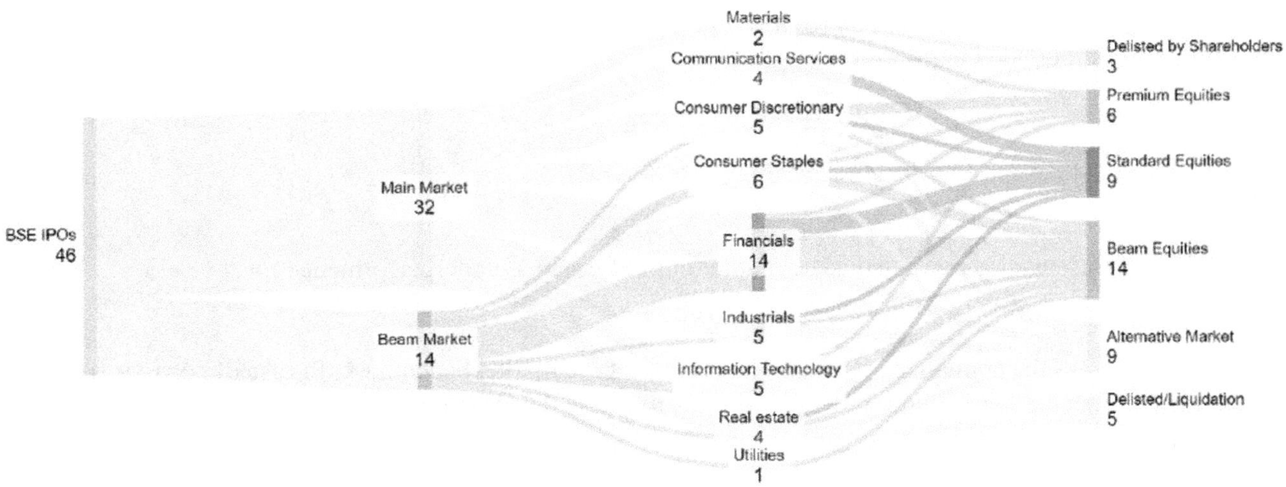

Figure 18.1 BSE IPOs sector and market segment overview (Unit: number of issues)
Source: BSE statistics, Infostock.bg data BSE [2, 3], Infostock.bg [9, 10]

The prevailing IPO issues belong to the financial sector (30%), and consumer goods and services (24%). Figure 18.1 also indicates the movement of issues from the main market to the alternative market (28%), and from the standard equities segment to premium equities (19%). In addition, the rate of the delisted companies is 17% and the IPO default rate which reflects the rate of the delisted companies due to bankruptcy or liquidation is 11%.

The IPO historic IPO development in respect to number and volume of Standard Equities IPOs and Beam IPOs is presented in Figure 18.2.

The major percentage of IPOs on BSE took place between 2004 and 2008, when 78% of all IPO funds were raised, corresponding to approximately 50% of the total number of IPO issues. Since 2009 the IPOs decreased both in volume and number, showing some activity from single issues like Gradus AD /chicken producer/, who managed to raise over EUR 20 million in 2018, making it the largest IPO since the global financial crisis in 2008. During 2021–2023, smaller Beam market issues were successfully launched on BSE, raising only 10% of overall IPO funds, but representing 30% of the total number of IPOs. A tendency can be observed toward dominance of Beam market issues since their launch in 2021, reaching 14 issues compared to only one new listing on the BSE main market within the same period (2022).

IPO underpricing

Unlike developed capital markets, BSE does not show evidence of IPO underpricing. As presented in Figure 18.3, the IPO's 1st day of trade market adjusted percentage price change varies from overpricing to underpricing and a clear tendency cannot be outlined: the first issues during the IPO boom period 2004-2007 tend to decrease in price in the first day of trade or to be overpriced, performing with an average of 42% under the benchmark within the first day of trade; issues launched within 2008 show an underpricing or an increase by 34% average in the 1-st day of trade; the period following the financial crisis from 2009 till 2023 is characterized with a volatile performance of the standard equities without prevailing trend for IPO overpricing or underpricing. Beam market issues show evidence of underpricing with an average 17% higher return than the benchmark within the first day of trade.

One of the main reasons for the lack of clear underpricing or overpricing is that the investment intermediaries facilitating IPOs on BSE typically do not underwrite the issues. Underwriters tend to set a lower offer price in an IPO to secure investment interest and the potential net gain on the sale of the shares. Since BSE IPO issues are not underwritten, we cannot observe a downward pressure on the IPO price. The evidence of underpricing Beam issues and standard equity issues in 2007–2008 can be explained by the increased investment interest during the market boom and in light of the new Beam market opportunities.

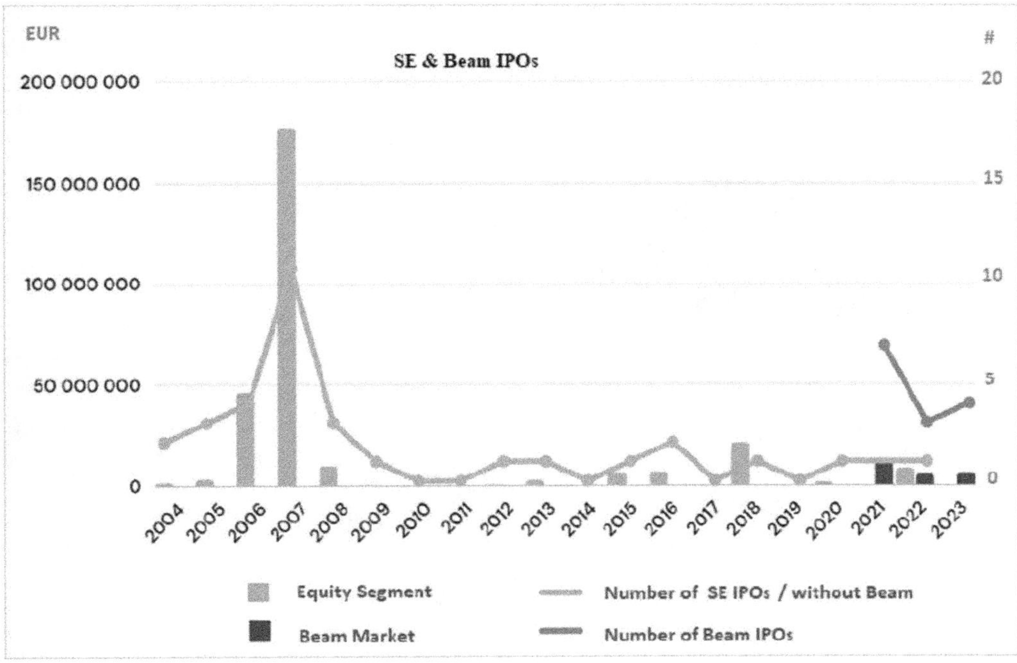

Figure 18.2 Funds raised through IPO and number of IPOs on Standard Equities segment and Beam market (Units: line - number of IPOs; box – funds raised in EUR)
Source: BSE statistical data BSE [2, 4, 3]

Figure 18.3 BSE IPO underpricing/ overpricing, adjusted by SOFIX index (Unit: percentage)
Source: Authors' calculation

IPO underpricing/overpricing breakdown by sectors is presented in Figure 18.3. The sectoral classification is performed according to the Global Industry Classification Standard /GICS/ [18].

IPO underpricing can be observed to the greatest extent in the industrial and consumer staples sectors (Figure 18.4). The predominant issues within the other sectors tend to be overpriced, particularly the information technology and real estate sectors.

IPO long-term performance

The results show that most IPOs initiated until the end of 2007 or with the first day of trade until mid-2008 outperform the SOFIX index with a 0.37% annual average (Figure 18.5). At the same time, the majority of

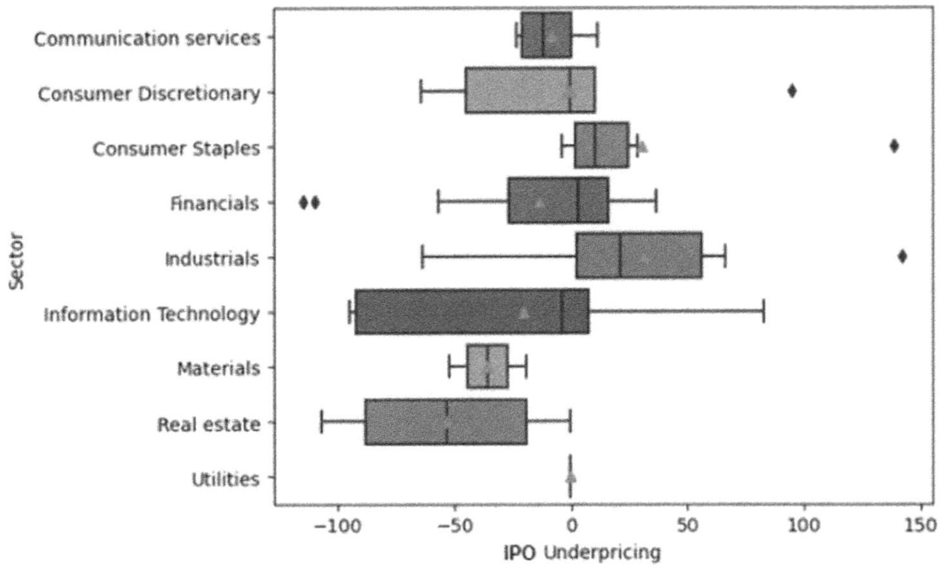

Figure 18.4 IPO underpricing/overpricing breakdown by sectors[1] (unit: percentage)
Source: Author

delisted IPOs /75%/, which are excluded from long-term performance, fall into the same period. Within the next period – from mid-2008 until July 2023, SE IPOs listed on the main market underperform the benchmark and show 6.59% lower returns. In the latter period, however, only 25% of the issues delisted by the BSE fell. On average, the SE achieved a 2.53% lower return than the SOFIX index without considering the default rate which contributes to further underperformance.

The analysis of the Beam market IPOs that effectively commenced in 2021 is consistent with the SE IPOs but with a greater magnitude: Beams underperform the SOFIX index by 13.79% on average.

The compound annual market long-term performance indicates that only 12 issues or 26% of all IPOs managed to outperform the market benchmark since launch till July 2023. The best-performing companies operate in the following sectors: industrials, communication services, real estate, and information technology (Figure 18.5). The average obtained outperformance, computed on compound annual average base, of these 12 issuers is 16%.

On the other side, there are the IPO companies with a drop in price compared to the SOFIX index, representing 67% of all IPOs with an average underperformance of 14.5%, excluding delisted and liquidation companies. A major part of the second group of IPOs was launched during the IPO boom in 2004–2008 when issues were generally overvalued.

A breakdown of the outperformance and underperformance by sectors is presented in Figure 18.6.

A relationship between IPO underpricing and IPO long-term performance cannot be observed except for the industrials sector, which shows the highest average value of both underpricing and long-term outperformance.

It can be concluded that the majority of IPO companies, that are launched before the financial crisis in 2008 support more stable prices, but at the same time show a higher default rate. Post-crisis issues from 2008–2015 underperform the benchmark by -15% and are still struggling with the consequences of the financial collapse not being able to return to IPO price values. Newer IPO issues (after 2016) are more volatile, with stocks showing higher amplitude in market performance. The newly introduced Beam market IPOs underperform the SOFIX index by -13.79%.

1 The middle line in the box represents the median; the triangle within the box represents the arithmetic average value; the box indicates the interquartile range from the 25th to 75th percentile; the whiskers represent the range; diamonds are outliers.

Figure 18.5 IPO long-term performance: annualized benchmark outperformance (unit: percentage)
Source: BSE statistics, Infostock.bg data BSE [2, 3], Infostock.bg [9, 10]

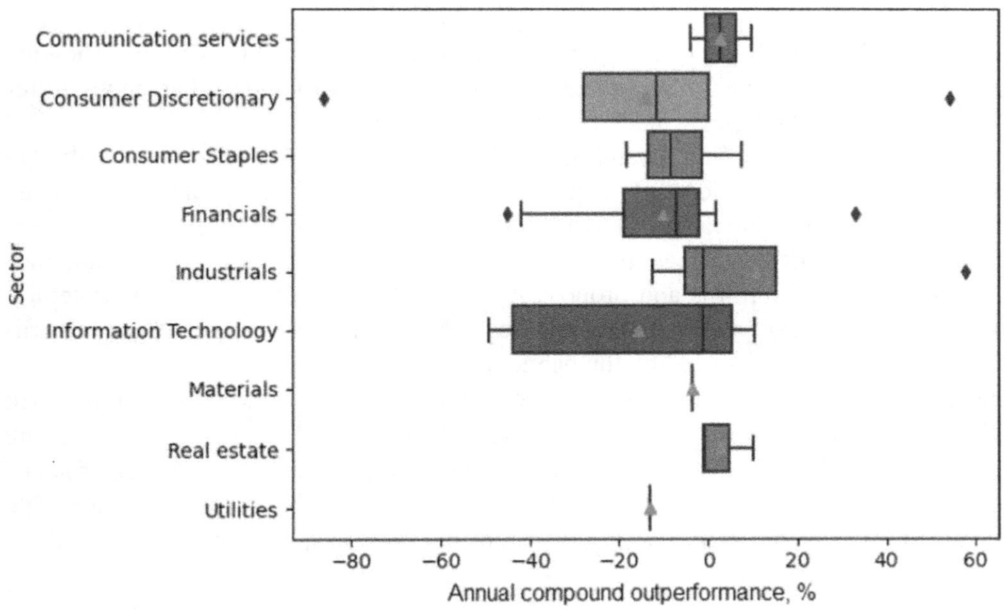

Figure 18.6 IPO Annual compound outperformance/underperformance breakdown by sectors (unit: percentage)
Source: BSE statistics, Infostock.bg data BSE [2, 3] Infostock.bg [9, 10]

Findings and Results

This research examines the IPO activity, IPO underpricing, and long-term performance in the Bulgarian capital market.

IPO activity

As a whole, BSE experienced a prompt acceleration in market capitalization during the market boom in terms of its development opportunities as a frontier capital market in Southeast Europe. This result is consistent with Ritter and Welch's [22] research which found a positive relationship between the issuing activity and capital market development. The subsequent 2008 global financial crisis caused a considerable decline in both IPO volume and the number of IPOs. A tendency can be observed toward dominance of smaller Beam market issues since their launch in 2021 as we evidence 14 Beam issues raised 10% of the overall IPO funds. Since Beams IPOs are less regulated than standard equities IPOs we can conclude that the lower regulatory requirements do not affect investment interest which agrees with the findings Kaserer and Treßel [13] that the listing requirements could be simplified without limiting investor protection.

IPO underpricing

BSE does not show clear evidence of IPO underpricing. IPO's 1st day of trade market adjusted percentage price change varies from overpricing to underpricing depending on the reviewed period: the first issues during the IPO boom period 2004–2007 tend to be overpriced;

The period following the financial crisis from 2009 to 2023 is characterized with volatile performance without prevailing trend for IPO pricing.

The Beam market shows evidence of underpricing with an average of 17% benchmark adjusted increase in the price within the first day of trade.

Long-term performance

Most IPOs initiated until the end of 2007 or with the first day of trade until mid-2008 outperformed the SOFIX index with a 0.37% annual average. The results differ from a study performed by Ivantchev [12] who finds a larger underperformance during the hot market period 2006-2007. The difference in findings is due to the shorter period observed by the author.

Within the period –mid-2008 to July 2023, Standard equities IPOs underperform the benchmark, showing 6.59% lower returns. On average, it achieved a 2.53% lower return than the SOFIX index. The newly introduced Beam market IPOs underperform the SOFIX index by 13.79% on average.

The results are similar to those observed by Shukla and Shaw [24] who suggest that in contrast to the US studies, Indian IPOs do not show evidence of underperformance in the long term, but the median IPO company underperforms the benchmark, explained by the fact that most IPOs are launched during the market boom periods. Our study does not support the results by Komenkul and Kiranand [16] who suggest that emerging markets have different patterns regarding IPO returns and propose longer-holding period investment strategies. They observe Malaysian and Thai healthcare and biopharmaceutical IPOs, which may achieve better returns since those sectors have not been negatively affected by the pandemic.

Though the study has insightful findings, it has its own limitations. Firstly, the results cannot be generalised since the data and analysis are fetched and done specifically for the Bulgarian market, which is a developing economy. Secondly, there is a possibility of survivorship bias while determining the long term performance since the study has excluded delisted firms. Finally, the study has relied totally on secondary data available from public sources. However, this study can act as a background for future research that incorporates a mixed approach with both primary and secondary data.

Conclusions

We applied historical reviews, and research analytical methods to explore the BSE IPOs from 2004 to 2023. It can be concluded that the prevailing IPOs, that are launched before the financial crisis in 2008 tend to decrease in price on the first day of trade or to be overpriced, but at the same time, they outperform the benchmark by 0.37% annual average in the long-term. BSE IPOs, including Beam IPOs, have shown a tendency of IPO underpricing and benchmark underperformance in the long term.

The sectoral analysis indicates a predominant market outperformance of the issuers operating in the industrial sector, communication service, real estate, information technology, and financial sectors. We can also observe a few outliers driving the average outperformance in a positive or a negative direction. Considering the segmentation, the relationship between IPO underpricing and IPO long-term performance cannot be observed except for the industrial sector, which shows the highest average value of both underpricing and long-term outperformance.

Beams are usually technological and innovative start-ups and are not traded on the regulated market, which assumes a higher return on investment. BSE investors' biases are towards riskier Beams, indicating that the investors on BSE did not become more cautious after the real estate crisis in 2008 and the financial crises in 2022–2023, causing the collapse of many technological and financial companies.

References

[1] Brau, J., & Fawcett, S. (2006). Initial public offerings: an analysis of theory and practice. *The Journal of Finance*, LXI(1), 399–436.

[2] BSE-listed instruments. July10. Accessed 07 10, 2023. https://bse-sofia.bg/en/listed-instruments.

[3] BSE (2023). BSE Statistics. July10. Accessed 07 10, 2023. https://bse-sofia.bg/en/statistics.

[4] Bulgarian Stock Exchange (2023). Interim Report on the Activity of the Bulgarian Stock Exchange for the First Year-half of 2023. Sofia: BSE. https://www.bse-sofia.bg/en/bse-reports/2023.

[5] Burton, M., Nesiba, R., & Brown, B. (2010). An Introduction to Financial Markets and Institutions, (p. 46). Taylor and Francis.

[6] Dahlquist, J., & Knight, R. (2022). Principles of Finance. OpenStax, Rice University.

[7] Huang, R., Ritter, J., & Zhang, D. (2023). IPOs and SPACs: recent developments. *Annual Review of Financial Economics*, 15, 595–615.

[8] Ilbasmis, M. (2023). Underpricing and aftermarket performance of IPOs during the Covid-19 period: evidence from Istanbul Stock Exchange. *Borsa Istanbul Review*, 23(3), 662–673.

[9] Infostock.bg. (2023). Infostock Issues. July 05. Accessed 07 05, 2023. https://www.infostock.bg/infostock/ control/ issues.

[10] Infostock.bg. (2023). Infostock quotation data and graphics. July 05. Accessed 07 05, 2023. https://www.infostock.bg/infostock/.

[11] Investor. BG (2023). Investor.bg trades. July 09. Accessed 07 09, 2023. https://www.investor.bg/trades.

[12] Ivantchev, B. (2015). IPO hot markets: In Bulgaria: Performance, Investor Biases. *Journal of Advancements in Economics, Finance and Accounting*, V(1), 26–32.

[13] Kaserer, C., & Treßel, V. (2024). The EU prospectus regulation and its impact on SME listings. *Journal of International Financial Markets, Institutions and Money*, 93, 101983.

[14] Khurshed, A. (2011). Initial Public Offerings: The Mechanics and Performance of IPOs. Harriman House Ltd.

[15] Khurshed, A., Paleari, S., & Vismara, S. (2005). The operating performance of initial public offerings: the UK experience. *Universita di Bergamo Working Paper*. Available at SSRN: https://ssrn.com/abstract=439240.

[16] Komenkul, K., & Kiranand, S. (2017). Aftermarket performance of health care and biopharmaceutical IPOs: evidence from ASEAN countries. *Inquiry*, 54.

[17] Meles, A., Salerno, D., Sampagnaro, G., Verdoliva, V., & Zhang, J. (2023). The influence of green innovation on default risk: evidence from Europe. *International Review of Economics and Finance*, 84, 692–710.

[18] MSCI (2024). GICS classification. July 28. Accessed 07 28, 2024. https://www.msci.com/our-solutions/indexes/gics.

[19] Mumtaz, M., & Yoshino, N. (2021). Greenness index: IPO performance and portfolio allocation. *Research in International Business and Finance*, 57, 101398.

[20] Nenkov, D. (2017). Relative valuation and stock-market bubbles. *Economic Alternatives*, 3, 363–378.

[21] Registry Agency (2008-2023). Published reports. July 20. Accessed 07 20, 2024. https://portal.registryagency.bg/CR/en/Reports/VerificationPer- sonOrg.

[22] Ritter, J., & Welch, I. (2002). A review of IPO activity, pricing, and allocations. *The Journal of Finance*, 57(4), 1795–1828.

[23] Roopa, P. (2016). A study on initial performance of IPO's in India during 2015-16 - comparison of book building and fixed price mechanism. *International Journal of Science Technology and Management*, 5(05), 81–88.

[24] Shukla, A., & Shaw, S. (2023). Long-run stock return of IPO firms in India: examining investment and profitability hypothesis. *Vikalpa*, 48(1), 21–38.

[25] Vasileva, V. (2023). Bulgarian capital market dynamics (2001-2021). *Economic and Social Alternatives*, 29(1), 24–37.

[26] X3News (2023). X3News Reports. July 20. Accessed 07 20, 2023 https://www.x3news.com/?page=Reports.

[27] Zhang, R. (2023). IPO as a key process for a successful company. *BCP Business and Management*, 46, 178–183.

19 Transforming the shopper's journey: the impact of augmented reality on consumer decisions and brand loyalty - a bibliometric analysis

Swetha, P.[1,a] *and T. Shirmila*[2,b]

[1]Research Scholar, Department of Commerce, Madras Christian College, Chennai, India

[2]Associate Professor, Department of Commerce, Madras Christian College, Chennai, India

Abstract

By bridging the gap between physical and digital commerce, augmented reality (AR) is transforming the customer buying experience into a retail environment that is becoming more and more competitive. This study adds to the expanding body of research on innovative digital marketing and offers useful advice to companies attempting to negotiate the quickly changing terrain of augmented reality-enhanced retail. This study employs a bibliometric analysis of literature on augmented reality (AR)'s influence on brand connection and purchasing behavior across various retail contexts. By enabling real-time product visualization, AR can help to close the gap between online and offline purchasing and speed up decision-making.

Keywords: Augmented reality, brand trust, consumer decision-making, digital marketing innovation, shopper's journey

Introduction

The arrival of augmented reality (AR) is truly a transformative moment for online shopping, opening up a world of possibilities that break down the barriers we've always faced. Imagine being able to visualize products in our own home, feeling a sense of connection and excitement as we shop. It's not just about convenience; it's about creating a more personal and engaging experience that brings us closer to the things we love. Regular online shopping only offers limited interaction; however, AR as the cutting-edge technology allows users to break all of that and have a seamless crossover of our digital and real lives. AR technology enhances online shopping by bridging the gap between digital and real life, allowing for immersive interactions. This improves customer engagement and encourages thoughtful purchasing decisions. In the retail sector, the adoption of AR technology was diverse and widespread with ongoing development in Internet technology and smart devices. Thanks to the virtual fitting room and real-time product demonstration with the help of AR technology, we are able to know more about the structure of the product. The more consumers use AR to experience the product, the more confidence they will have in purchasing, and this leads to a better customer shopping experience. By integrating online and offline operations with the use of AR Technology the retailers offer a wider range of shopping choices to their consumers. This study investigates the influence of AR technology on consumers' assurance in making their purchases and to improve their shopping experiences which brings about a transformation in the retail industry. The introduction of AR technology has drastically changed the shopping behavior and decision-making of consumers in a more interactive way. In addition, this AR technology enables new brands and gives the user an active and interactive relationship with the products. In the case of the AR advertising system, a more considered perception of the product features, traits, and use may be gained by the user. This integration of AR technology on social media media is a new way to share and experience its content.

Objectives

To review the main research trends in AR and consumer behavior.

To highlight the most influential authors, journals, and publications in AR.

[a]swethapetchi21@gmail.com, [b]shirmilastanley@mcc.edu.in

DOI: 10.4324/9781003739982-19

Literature Review

In their research, Chakkambath et al. [1] concluded that AR makes it possible for the users to have a virtual experience with the product before making a purchase, which increases the customer trust in the product. In retail, AR enhances the in-store experience by enabling consumers to easily view product information, test different colors or customizations, and expedite the purchasing choice. This paper addressed the effect of AR on consumers' purchase intention. Descriptive research design was employed with a structured questionnaire and convenience technique for the 146 respondents to elicit the information. These analyses included correlational analyses and exploratory factor analysis (EFA) with varimax rotation, which produced two factors as part of conducting the EFA. With the launch of AI platforms, augmented reality is aimed to get more acceptance among the consumers in the future. The insights from this research paper would pinpoint some of the major factors that have an impact on consumers' decision-making.

On their study, the team investigated how AR technology reshapes retail by delivering an engaging and immersive shopping experience [2]. AR blends digital elements with the real world, fostering stronger connections between customers and retailers. Features like virtual fitting rooms and live product displays elevate the shopping process, making it more interactive. The study shows AR increases shoppers' confidence and purchase intent. However, it also points out hurdles like technical issues and gaining wider market approval that need to be overcome for AR's full impact to be realized.

The researchers explored how information technology (IT) has reshaped retail, moving from traditional stores to dynamic omnichannel platforms. These platforms use omnichannel strategies to offer a smooth and connected shopping experience across online, mobile, and in-store channels. Despite their growing importance, the study points out a gap in academic research on this topic. By expanding the Unified Theory of Acceptance and Use of Technology (UTAUT2), the study strengthens its application to omnichannel retailing [3].

Research Methodology

In this study, bibliometric analysis was conducted to understand how literature on a new topic has evolved. They used two main approaches: performance analysis and scientific mapping. Performance analysis examined publication trends by country, author, and institution, while also tracking changes over time. Scientific mapping included techniques like analyzing citations, co-citations, bibliographic connections, shared keywords, and collaborations between authors. By combining these methods with network analysis, the study provided a clear picture of the research field's structure and growth. In this study, dimensions (an extensive research database) were used to collect the data source. Papers that were published between 2016 and 2024 were gathered and processed in the VOS viewer tool for network analysis. To carry out the bibliometric analysis, there are several procedures that need to be followed:

1. Complete the data search procedure
2. Filtering by bibliography
3. Verify the bibliometric features and perform bibliometric analysis
4. **Initial search procedure:** The first step is to explore the database, searching for "augmented reality" in titles, abstracts, and keywords. This brought up a whopping 143,004 documents, from articles and books to conference papers, giving them a broad pool of AR-related research.
5. **Focusing on research:** To get more specific, the results are further filtered to include studies that also mentioned "Brand Trust" and "Consumer Decision-Making." This helped the research hone in on how AR shapes customer trust and buying decisions in retail environments.

This research study has collected the data that were published from the years 2015–2024, ie.178 articles. The data were extracted in csv format. Furthermore, csv data is processed and filtered for this research study.

1. **Collecting core insights:** Post-filtering, I gathered data on AR research trends, top authors, key topics, highly cited papers, and top journals/publishers, outlining AR's retail impact.

Table 19.1 Publication trends 2016-2025.

Year	2016	2017	2018	2019	2020	2021	2022	2023	2024	2025
Publication (Total)	1	3	3	22	9	15	18	48	59	0

Source: Author

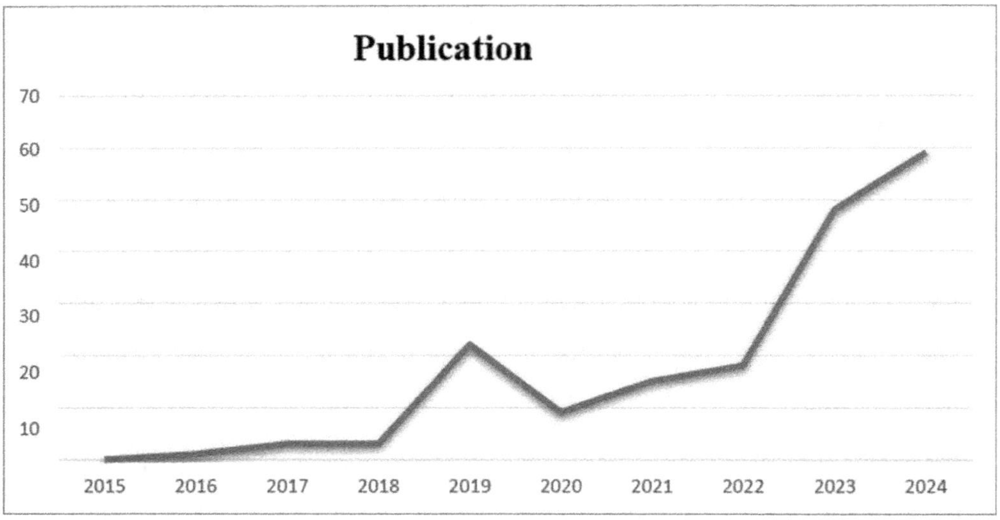

Figure 19.1 Distribution of augmented reality throughout the year of publication
Source: Author

2. **Visualizing with VOSviewer**: I used VOSviewer to map study, author, and journal connections via citations and keyword networks, highlighting brand trust and consumer decision-making in AR research [4].

Results and Discussion

Growth of augmented reality research over time

Using the Dimensions database, searching for keywords: "AUGMENTED REALITY," "BRAND TRUST," and "CONSUMER DECISION-MAKING," finding 178 relevant articles. Table 19.1 below shows publication trends from 2016–2025.

In the year 2016, the papers published were comparatively less or constant however, from 2019–2024 it gradually increased and used by many authors. Starting with one article in 2016, AR research grew significantly from 2019, peaking at 59 articles in 2024, reflecting its rising relevance in retail.

Research across disciplines

The above chart shows that the leading field of research area with 106 articles were published in commerce, management, tourism and services followed by information and computing sciences (40 articles) and least area (1) was for economics, history, heritage and archaeology as shown in Table 19.2.

Mapping authors and co-authors

The visualization shows a network of five key authors: Glavas Charmaine, Mulcahy Rory, Russell-Bennett Rebekah, McAndrew Ryan, and Letheren Kate, connected through their collaborative work. The nodes (representing each author) are labelled with their names, and the lines between them illustrate co-authorship relationships, with thicker lines indicating stronger collaboration (i.e., more co-authored papers). Only five authors met the requirement (2 documents, 10 citations), highlighting the field's concentrated influence. These

Table 19.2 Research disciplines.

Category	Fields of research (ANZSRC 2020)
Commerce, management, tourism and services	106
Information and computing sciences	40
Language, communication and culture	11
Human society	8
Psychology	7
Biomedical and clinical sciences	5
Creative arts and writing	4
Built environment and design	3
Engineering	3
Law and legal studies	3
Philosophy and religious studies	3
Agricultural, veterinary and food sciences	2
Biological sciences	2
Education	2
Economics	1
History, heritage and archaeology	1

Source: https://app.dimensions.ai/discover/publication

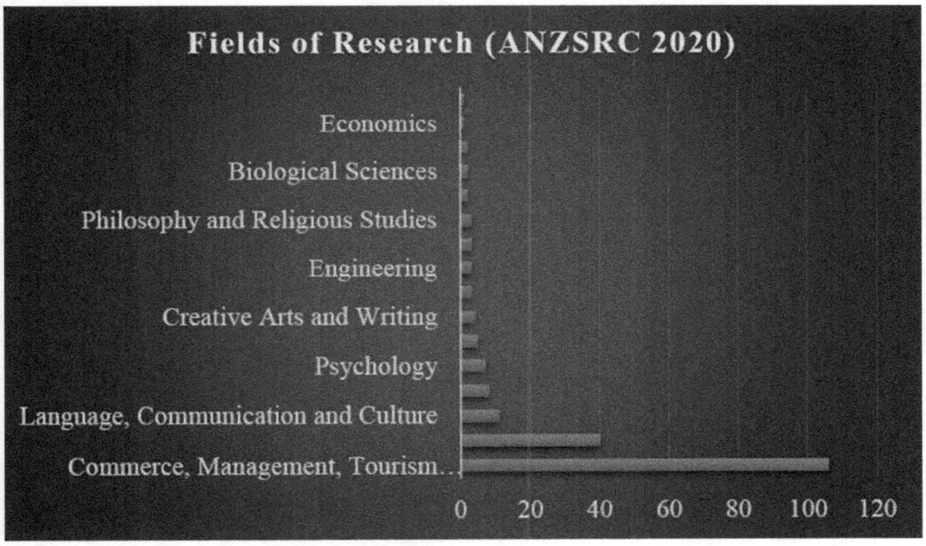

Figure 19.2 Articles based on the field
Source: Author

researchers are expected to be influential in determining how augmented reality is perceived in retail settings, particularly in terms of brand trust and purchasing decisions.

Leading countries

In this study, the maximum number of papers published in a country was limited to 25. The minimum number of documents and citations of a country was limited to 5, out of 46 countries, only 10 meets the thresholds. It was identified that in AR research, setting a minimum of five documents and citations (max 25 papers). Ten of 46 countries emerged in two clusters. The first cluster includes: United Kingdom, United States, Australia, France and India. The second cluster includes: South Korea, Spain, China, Indonesia and Pakistan.

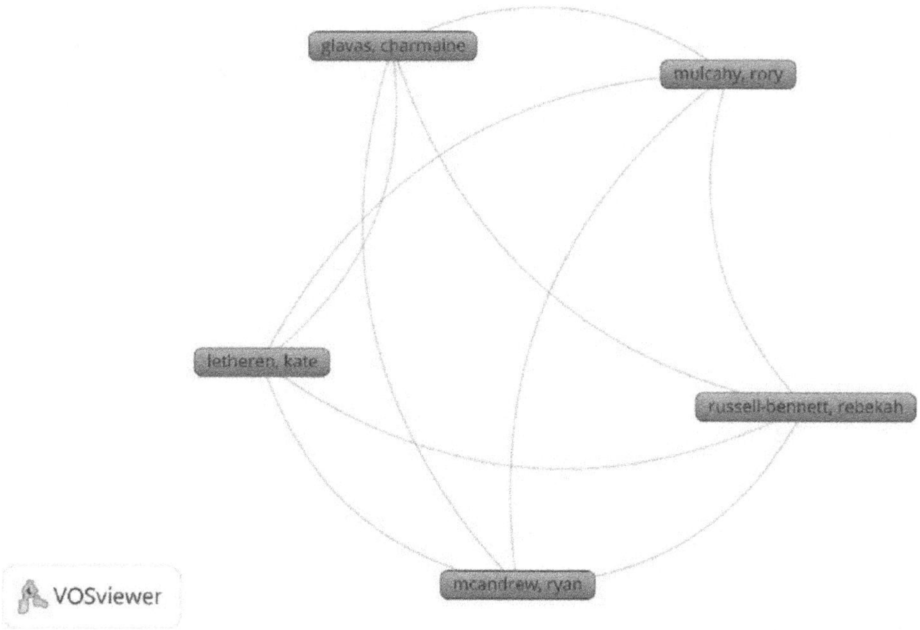

Figure 19.3 Authors and co-authors network
Source: https://www.vosviewer.com/

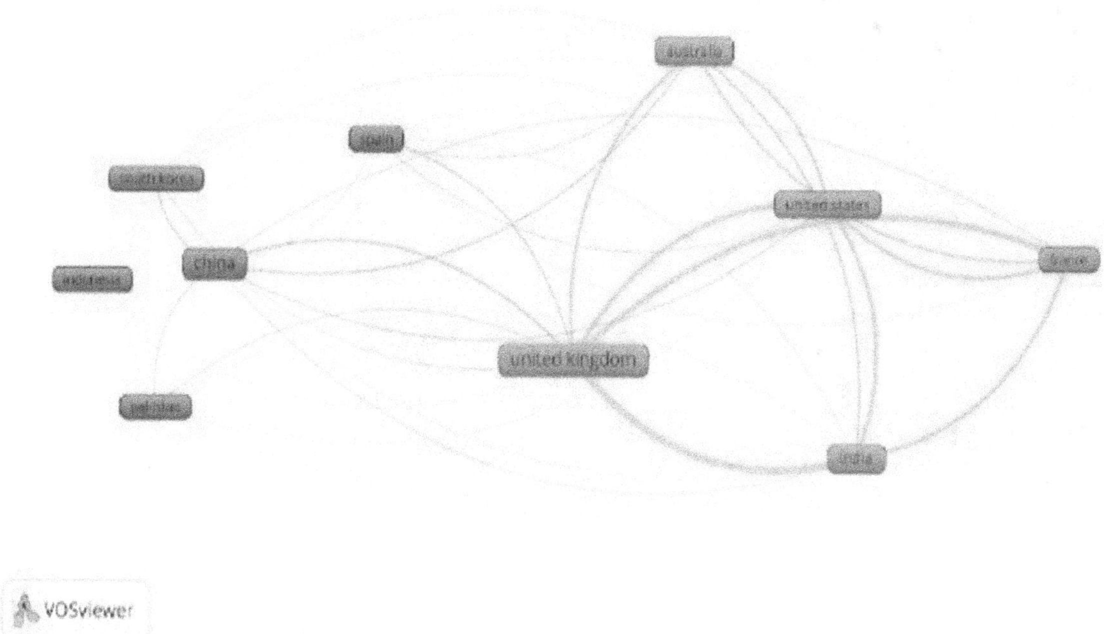

Figure 19.4 Top 10 leading countries in this area of research
Source: https://www.vosviewer.com/

The distribution of keywords based on their co-occurrence

Through network analysis, the co-occurrence of keywords is divided into five clusters.

1. Cluster 1 in red color shows significant impact on the keywords such as Purchase Intention, customer engagement and Augmented reality.

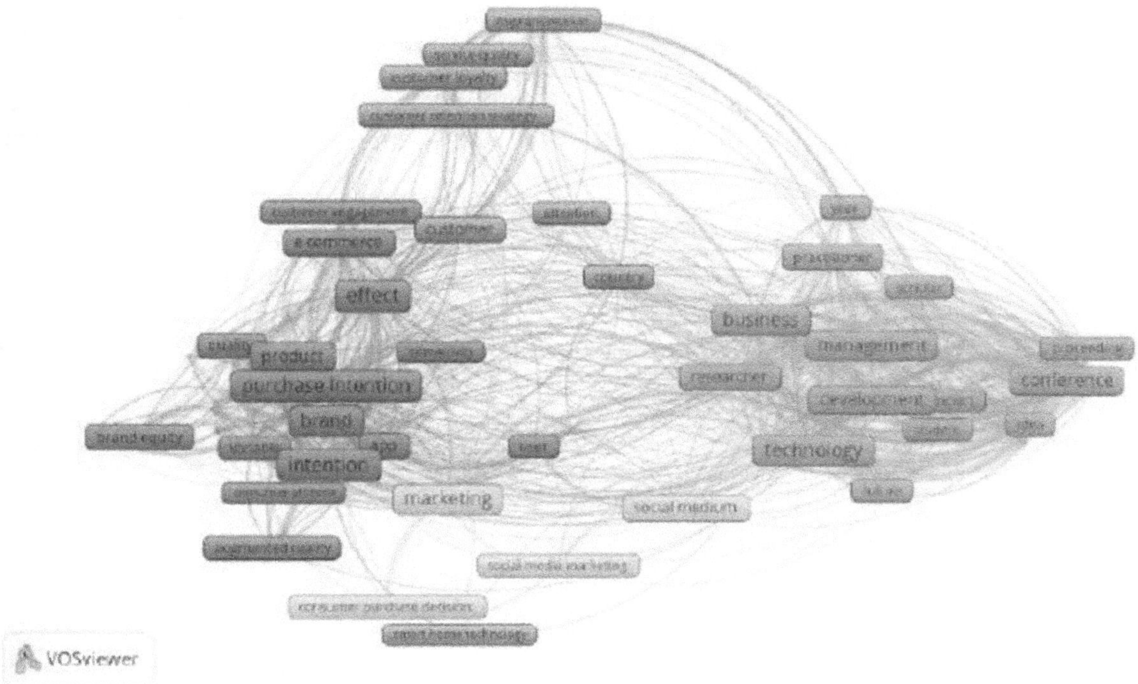

Figure 19.5 Keyword connections
Source: https://www.vosviewer.com/

2. Cluster 2 in blue color shows connection with AR in terms of customer loyalty, customer retention strategy and service quality.
3. Cluster 3, which is in green color has significant concerns on the key words such as development, management and technology
4. Cluster 4 in yellow color has significant contributions on the keywords such as consumer purchase decisions and social media marketing.
5. Cluster 5 of purple color shows emerging smart home technology.

This study explores AR through a bibliometric lens, using Dimensions to map research trends, identify emerging areas, and track AR applications. It offers insights for researchers and practitioners to understand AR's societal impact and future potential.

Conclusion

This bibliometric study, covering 178 papers by 435 authors, demonstrates that augmented reality (AR) in retail drives growth in purchase intention and customer loyalty. It highlights AR's capacity to reshape consumer behavior and improve e-commerce performance. These insights provide actionable directions for businesses and future research. Integrating AR into e-commerce requires continuous innovation to maximize its potential in the evolving digital landscape.

References

[1] Chakkambath, R. S., Sukumaran, S., & Kizhakilode, S. (2024). A study on the influence of augmented reality (AR) in enhancing consumer behaviour and decision-making. *International Journal of Progressive Research in Engineering Management and Science (IJPREMS)*, 4(7), 43–47. ISSN 2583-1062.

[2] Liu, R., Balakrishnan, B., & Saari, E. (2024). The impact of augmented reality (AR) technology on consumers' purchasing decision processes. *Frontiers in Business, Economics and Management*, 13, 181–185. 10.54097/1r7f1x56.

[3] Wahib, N., Jailani, N., & Ismail, M. (2023). Factors influencing generation Z's purchase intention in omnichannel retail settings. *Advanced International Journal of Business, Entrepreneurship and SMEs*, 5, 167–172. 10.35631/Aijbes.518016.

[4] Wang, C., & Si, L. (2023). A bibliometric analysis of digital literacy research from 1990 to 2022 and research on emerging themes during the COVID-19 pandemic. *Sustainability*, 15(7), 5769. https://doi.org/10.3390/su1507576.

20 Sustainable digital transformation in higher education: redefining the role of Edtech platforms

Gandhali Sewak[a]

Doctor of Business Administration Scholar, Rushford Business School, Switzerland

Abstract

This paper is entitled “sustainable digital transformation in higher education: redefining the role of Edtech platforms. This paper explores how digital technologies are changing the face of higher education. It explains how the digital shift improves access, equity, and sustainability, while there are risks of the digital divide, environmental footprint, and financial barriers. The paper uses India as a case study and explains how online platforms solve the problem of infrastructure and overcrowded classrooms. The ongoing digital transformation must be sustainable from an environmental, social, and economic perspective. To promote sustainable, long-term growth that includes all communities, the energy consumption of data centers, e-waste, costly digital devices, and the lack of connectivity in marginalized communities need to be addressed. The paper calls for action on multiple fronts. Governments should create better policies and funding. Universities should promote hybrid learning models, leading to a sustainable future. Rural areas need affordable and sustainable digital platform options from edtech companies. However, the paper does not cover extensive empirical data or long-term impact assessments of the suggested solutions for sustainable digital transformation. The study focuses on policy and technological interventions but does not have adequate bandwidth to discuss the practical implementation challenges that institutions and learners face in various contexts. In the end, the paper has a hopeful vision. The digital revolution can expand the frontiers of higher education to more people. It may create equal opportunities, promote innovation, and offer environment-friendly options for the planet.

Keywords: Ed-tech-platforms, education-technology, higher education, sustainable education

Introduction

Higher education plays a critical role in developing a nation. It provides people in different communities with higher-level skills, fosters innovation, and supports economic development. In the context of higher education, digital transformation comprises the integration of technology into the teaching, learning, and administration process of institutions. It makes education more available, versatile, and personalized by using technology. Technology acts as an enabler for remote learning, automates processes, and fosters globalization. This change is worldwide as it is being adopted to meet new challenges for students, educators, and industry. Let’s look at some facts before we dive into the analysis of online education:

1. Worldwide, about 49% of students have opted for some online learning.
2. Online learning is one of the fastest-growing markets in the world. – It has grown 900% since its creation in 2000.
3. 70% of students have expressed an opinion that the quality of online learning is comparable to traditional classroom learning.
4. The number of online learning users is expected to increase to 57 million by 2027.
5. 80% of businesses now offer online learning or training solutions.
6. Online learning can reduce the time needed to learn a subject by 40–60%.
7. The online learning industry is projected to be worth more than $370 billion by 2026 (*Source*: Peck [4]).

Online platforms and virtual classrooms are reaching all corners of the world and are set to break the barriers to quality education, even in remote areas. This shift was accelerated by the COVID-19 pandemic, which exposed the shortcomings in the digital infrastructure. However, it also led to the fact that the change

[a]sgandhali@gmail.com

DOI: 10.4324/9781003739982-20

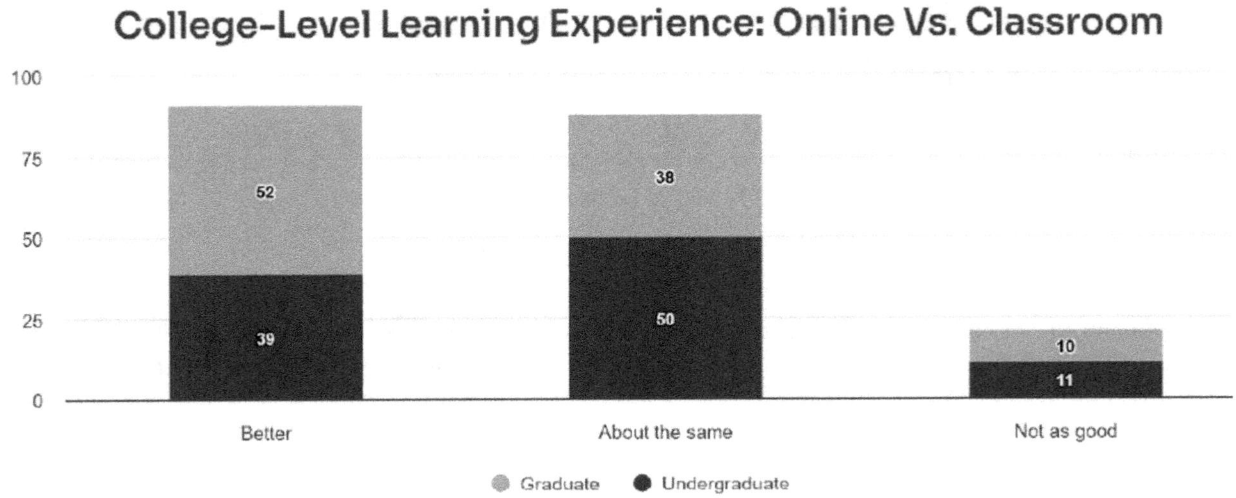

Figure 20.1 Quality of online learning
Source: Statista [6]

can be long-lasting. Schools and Universities use technology to increase the impact of programs, lower costs, and offer different approaches to learning. However, it is not just about better tools but also about rethinking education's strategies and values. With a large young population and growing internet access, online learning platforms are attracting more and more people all over the world. In developing nations like India, technology offers a solution to problems like overcrowded classrooms, inadequate infrastructure, and the increasing need for skill-based education. Universities now offer flexible learning, industry-relevant courses, and global connections to make education more accessible to everyone. According to a survey by Research.Com [5], learners find the experience of online and classroom learning comparable (Figure 20.1).

By addressing environmental, social, and economic factors, this study seeks to ensure that digital change in higher education may be sustained. Energy use, carbon emissions, and technological trash are some environmental harms caused by the growing use of digital instruments. Institutions should, therefore, use green technologies to reduce their impact. Socially, digital transformation should be for the inclusion of all and everyone. It enhances access to education, but poor execution can lead to a digital divide. Affordable devices and reliable internet access must be available for all equally to achieve equity. Economically, institutions must manage resources, decrease costs, and maintain quality. While doing this, they should also engage in the development of sustainable, affordable solutions. They should train teachers to use digital tools, improve cybersecurity, and foster innovation through technology partnerships.

Problem Statement

1. **Maintaining accessibility, affordability, and the quality of education are the major hurdles in the digital transformation of higher education.**
   Many students in remote and underserved areas cannot access reliable internet and digital devices, which widens the digital divide. The cost of tuition and other expenses like laptops, software, and high-speed internet are out of the reach of low-income students, and therefore, education is unaffordable to them. Despite the fact that digital education is easier to access, quality remains an issue. These problems hinder the full scope of digital revolution in the provision of inclusive and meaningful education for all.
2. **Equity in education faces significant challenges due to systemic disparities in access to technology and resources and the shortcomings of current edtech platforms.**
   The digital divide poses additional hurdles for underrepresented groups like women, rural people, and learners from low-income backgrounds. Most edtech solutions are not designed for diverse learners, for

example, learners with disabilities or cultural differences, and thus only contribute to the existing oppression. If we do not include everyone in the design of digital transformation, then it may become the digital division that keeps the existing barriers for learners.

3. **Current edtech platforms struggle to tackle these challenges sustainably while balancing technological progress with environmental and economic factors.**
   Many platforms focus on scalability and profitability, which leads to environmental harm through energy-heavy data centers, electronic waste, and the carbon emissions associated with digital infrastructure. Economically, the high costs and subscription models make these tools hard to access for smaller or underfunded institutions. These practices should minimize environmental impact and efficiently promote economic resource use.

Objectives

1. To examine how Edtech platforms can contribute to sustainable digital transformation.
2. To study the Indian context while comparing it with global trends.
3. To suggest a framework for integrating edtech solutions sustainably into higher education.

Methodology

This study uses a multi-method research approach, comprising case studies and a literature review, to examine the part that edtech platforms play in enabling sustainable digital transformation. Based on a review of the literature on sustainability, digital transformation, and educational technology to develop a theoretical framework, the Research highlights significant trends, challenges, and opportunities within the field. To support the theoretical insights, it examines case studies of edtech platforms from India and other countries. These case studies are real-world examples of successes, impacts, and limitations of digital transformation in higher education. The study covers a comprehensive perspective as the case-study examples cover platforms that are popular in the world, as well as specifically in India.

Sustainability in higher education

The main goal of sustainability in higher education is to create a long-term system that does a proper job of meeting economic, social, and environmental goals. It isn't about being more productive. This encourages diversity and focuses on building the foundation for access equity. This means motivating innovation while attempting to limit the use of resources for the sake of future generations. This point of view emphasizes the importance of education for economic development, eliminating social inequalities, and environmental protection.

The United Nations' Sustainable Development Goals (SDGs) emphasize the importance of education in promoting global progress. Among these, SDG 4—Quality Education—is particularly significant. While encouraging lifelong learning opportunities for all, it focuses on providing an inclusive, equitable, and high-quality education.

This goal aligns with the core mission of higher education. It aims to

- Empower individuals
- Address inequalities
- Support sustainable economic and social progress.

Strengthening key pillars is a must for achieving true sustainability across higher education.

Digital and physical infrastructure: A combination of digital and physical infrastructure is necessary for a long-lasting, sustainable solution. We must close the access divide, where the availability of internet access, classroom facilities, and technology in urban and rural areas varies widely. Embracing a green campus helps minimize an institution's environmental impact and reinforces sustainability.

Pedagogy: Teachers must learn to teach students of a diverse digital population. Flexible blended learning models that combine online and in-person tutoring are sustainable and effective.

Curriculum design: Review and regular curriculum updates to cover the latest and cutting-edge knowledge in a format that is suitable for digital delivery should be adopted as a standard practice.

Learner engagement: Sustainability is only ensured when students are actively involved. Thus, inclusive approaches to meet the needs of all learners and their learning styles and backgrounds should be developed using AI-driven platforms, gamification, and immersive technologies.

Faculty development: Educators are the main drivers of sustainability in education. This is done through ensuring that there is a constant development of professionals in the new technologies, teaching methods, and interdisciplinary strategies.

Sustainability in higher education is not a dream; it is a necessity. The sustainability principles can be incorporated into every aspect of the learning process and thus change individuals' and societies' lives for the better, leading to a better future for coming generations.

Role of edtech platforms

E-learning platforms are no longer just places where people can only find videos with lectures and e-books; now, they are smart and adaptive environments. The current generation of platforms supports collaborative learning, real-time feedback, and adaptive assessments to facilitate the easy transition between online and offline learning. This change has made education more creative, convenient, and student-oriented. E-learning platforms no longer play a role only in teaching and learning. It covers some crucial aspects of administration, testing, grading, and many more.

The paper concentrates on how Edtech platforms can play a larger role in bringing in sustainability in all social, environmental, and economic aspects as shown in Table 20.1.

Inclusive edtech solutions

Around the world, Edtech platforms have displayed how to make their products inclusive. With an eye on inclusivity and accessibility, edtech can make sure that leaving or income does not stop a learner from joining. Edtech platforms should pay more attention to these points to become more inclusive:

1. Serving various groups speaking different languages by providing tools in different regional languages.
2. By teaming up with device makers, the government hopes to provide students with cost-effective hardware.

Table 20.1 Role of e-learning platforms.

Key Area	Description
Digital learning (LMS and CMS)	DL enables flexible and personalized learning experiences through online courses, virtual classrooms, and digital tools, making education more accessible to diverse student needs.
Data analytics	Universities have a powerful tool in these platforms to help them make data-driven decisions. Its data is like, they use data to examine student performance, enrollment patterns, and use of resources to enhance academic offerings and outcomes for students.
Automation and processs streamlining	The platforms help increase operational efficiency and lower costs. They use technology to automate processes such as registration, admissions, financial management, and even course scheduling
Collaboration and interaction	It fosters an engaged learning community by promoting better communication among staff, professors, and students through digital resources like social media, online forums, and virtual communication platforms.
Student support and services	The platform implements AI-powered chatbots, online advising, career services, and mental health support platforms to provide personalized assistance and enhance student well-being.

Source: Author

3. Team up with local partners to give digital learning and provide support with internet services.

Environmental sustainability
Even though digital transformation can be very helpful, it can also lead to some environmental concerns. The rise of data centers that power edtech platforms leads to a big increase in emissions. According to the IEA, data centers use about 1% of the world's electricity. What's more, the increasing amount of e-waste from electronics undergoing constant upgrades is a major problem for the environment.

Strategies for Green Edtech

Edtech platforms have to follow sustainability guidelines along with the set strategies:

- Moving to cloud solutions reduces energy use and makes businesses greener by removing the need for a lot of physical support structures. Both Google Cloud and Microsoft Azure are examples of companies trying to power their data centers with green energy rather than other resources.
- Promoting energy-efficient devices, such as low-consumption tablets and laptops, can lower the digital learning impact on the environment.
- Having digital literacy skills can lead to using less paper and save our natural resources while also reducing the amount of waste produced.

In addition, the principles of the circular economy can be adopted by edtech companies by recycling devices and refurbishing old ones. Thus, the sustainability of environmental concerns can be incorporated into the Edtech channels and can contribute to the formation of a sustainable future.

Economic business models for Edtech platforms
To be successful, Edtech platforms must develop sustainable business models that are good for students and work in economic aspects. The freemium model, which provides free essential services and paid premium features, has worked for TIMESPRO and Duolingo, balancing accessibility and revenue. The subscription-based model provides continuous access to new content and personalized learning. This model has been successfully implemented by platforms like Coursera and Udemy, using flexible pricing to cater to different income levels.

Literature Review

Digital transformation towards sustainability in higher education: state of the art and future research insights,' *Springer Nature B.V.*, published online Trevisan et al. [8]: This study explores how digital transformation (DT) contributes to sustainability in higher education institutions (HEIs) by conducting a bibliometric and content analysis of existing research. It identifies three key research areas, seven theoretical clusters, and five future research directions, offering theoretical insights and practical strategies to align HEIs with the United Nations Sustainable Development Goals (SDGs). How Does Digital Transformation Shape University Operations? – May 2022 (Think Beyond Cloud—Adam Czeczuk [7]): The article summarizes the areas in which DT has affected higher education. It covers both education and administrative aspects and how they affect learners, teachers, and support functions.

A Sustainable University: Digital Transformation and Beyond,' *Technology, Knowledge and Learning*, Ashmel et al. [2]. This study explores the need for sustainable digital transformation in universities to stay competitive amid global changes, including post-COVID implications, geopolitical shifts, and emerging technologies. Using a qualitative grounded theory approach, it proposes a conceptual model and sustainability blueprint for digital transformation, emphasizing strategic implementation, operational efficiency, and green technology adoption in higher education. Digital Transformation in Higher Education in Developing Countries to Promote Sustainable Development Aleryani [1]: This study examines the challenges that Arab universities face in adopting e-learning and digital transformation to enhance sustainability in higher education. It presents a strategic roadmap to integrate modern technologies, addressing resource depletion and administrative inefficiencies while aligning educational practices with sustainability goals. Multiple research papers covering the vast canvas of the subject are studied in detail. These papers contribute to synthesizing the challenges and looking for possible solutions to achieve sustainable digital transformation in higher education.

Indian and global examples

Several Indian edtech companies have set high standards of quality and personalized learning. For example, TIMESPRO provides video lessons, interactive quizzes, and tailored feedback to provide an all-around educational experience. On an international level, platforms like Khan Academy and Coursera have shown how AI-driven personalization can make high-quality education more accessible to everyone.

To maintain quality while scaling personalized learning, edtech platforms should:

1. Invest in teacher training.
2. In this rapidly evolving world, teachers must be equipped with the necessary abilities to handle digital tools and evaluate data.
3. Protect the privacy of your data: Create robust data security procedures to safeguard student information.
4. Focus on content quality: Review and revise the content regularly to ensure it is in sync with the current educational standards.

Indian case studies: digital transformation in higher education

The Indian higher education system has undergone a digital revolution in the past few years, thanks to innovative platforms that use technology to improve access, individualization, and environmental friendliness in learning. Figure 20.2 shows the trend of uptake of online programs shortly.

Three such example case studies from India are described below, and they show how these platforms are changing the revolution of higher education and sustainability.

SWAYAM: government-led initiative to provide free online courses

Overview

Study Webs of Active Learning for Young Aspiring Minds (SWAYAM) is an initiative by the Ministry of Education, India. It offers free courses from school to postgraduate level and provides everyone with a chance to learn.

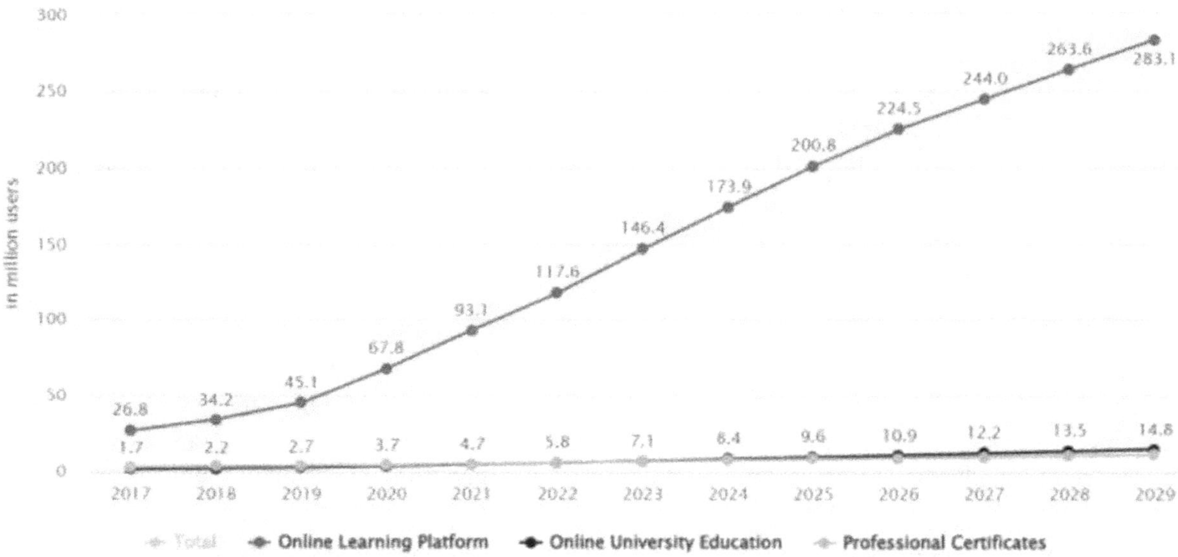

Figure 20.2 Trend of Registration for online programs
Source: Statista [6]

Contribution to digital transformation

- **Extensive access:** SWAYAM offers more than 2,000 courses in various fields, making it possible for students (30 million enrolled) in remote locations to obtain quality education from top institutions such as IITs, IIMs, and central universities.
- **Certification opportunities:** The courses students can get certificates for are recognized by universities and employers, and completed courses enhance their academic and professional credentials.
- **Hybrid learning:** Hybrid learning combines online education with conventional classroom instruction. Platforms like SWAYAM help institutions implement a blended approach that improves the overall learning experience.

Impact

SWAYAM has opened new doors to quality education for millions of learners, especially for the underserved segments of society. It has also encouraged institutions to adopt digital tools, encouraging innovation within the higher education system.

NPTEL: collaboration between IITs and IISC to offer certified online courses

Overview

The NPTEL was introduced by the Indian Institutes of Technology (IITs) in conjunction with the Indian Institute of Science (IISc). The university provides certified online classes in engineering science and humanities subjects.

Contribution to digital transformation

- **Quality content:** All the content comes from experienced instructors from major Indian universities through NPTEL.
- **Industry eelevance**: The courses are designed to meet industry needs; hence, the student learns from theory to practice that is useful in the workforce.
- **Flexibility:** The courses are also offered to learners at their own pace, which makes it easier for working.

Impact

More than 10 million learners have been certified by NPTEL, which has greatly enhanced the employability of the students as well as the professionals. Quality and sustainability are its commitments, which have made it a leading example of online education in India and beyond.

TimesPro, a leading Indian edtech company

TimesPro, a leading Indian edtech company, has changed the future of higher education by offering industry-oriented programs and degrees in association with leading universities. It provides technology-enabled learning solutions to working professionals and higher education students as its primary audience. Online education in India is growing in recognition and growth, and organizations like TimesPro are contributing significantly to it. In the digital learning environment, the work of edtech will be essential in defining the future of education and meeting the increasing needs of qualified specialists.

Contribution to digital transformation

- **Industry-focused learning:** TimesPro uses the latest technology and data analysis to create individual learning plans, where the learner can learn at their own pace and fill in the gaps in their knowledge.
- **Accessibility:** The platform provides management, technology, and data science programs to learners on both mobile and desktop devices. It ensures that students in urban and rural areas get globally recognized certifications and degrees because of its strong collaboration with universities.
- **Cost-effectiveness:** Thus, TimesPro provides high-quality education at relatively cheap prices, which makes it possible for more people to get higher education with flexible payment schedules.

Impact

Two million learners all over the world have been enabled by TimesPro to access high-quality, affordable, and specific education for working professionals. The commitment to lifelong learning and sustainability has helped it to set an example of a scalable, effective edtech solution in higher education.

To summarize

Online education services from India like TIMES PRO, Swayam, and NPTEL are transforming higher education to improve access while offering personalized and more economical options. Though these platforms initially face challenges, their growth will allow them to remove learning gaps and sustain higher education in India and its neighboring countries.

Global case studies: higher education's digital transformation

Globally, higher education undergoing digital transformation uses different software to make education easier to access, more engaging and better for the environment. According to these studies, these platforms support sustainability and improving education internationally.

Coursera: democratizing access to global education

With help from top universities and organizations across the world, Coursera provides access to many courses, certificates and degree programs online. The purpose of the law is to give access to good education to each individual.

Contribution to digital transformation

Global reach: There are more than 10,000 courses on Coursera available from distinguished professors at Stanford, Yale and the University of London. It helps provide outstanding education to people in more than 190 countries.

- Easy to use: Users can use the app on their schedule, and it suits those who have work or study responsibilities, or anyone else eager to learn.
- Industry-related learning: Because Coursera partners with leaders like Google and IBM, its courses stay current with what firm's need from candidates in the employment market.

Impact

Based on the Coursera Impact Report, as shown in Figure 20.3, over the years, Coursera has reached over 500 million learners and has made education more accessible. Through the platform, people have been able to improve themselves in a fast-paced job market. This is because the platform's commitment to sustainability has set a precedent for environmentally friendly digital education services.

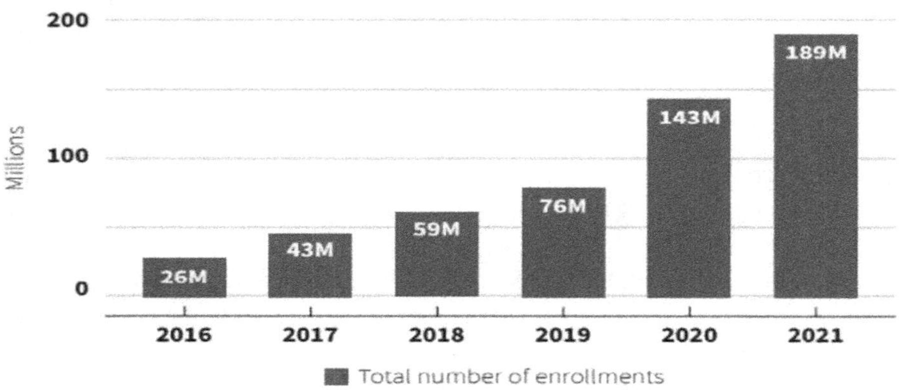

Figure 20.3 Number of enrollments on coursera
Source: Coursera [3]. 021 Coursera Impact Report

edX: Sustainable partnerships with universities and corporations

Founded by Harvard University and MIT, edX is a leading provider of massive open online courses (MOOCs) that offer a wide range of courses from esteemed universities and institutions around the globe. Its mission is to make education affordable and accessible to everyone.

Contribution to digital transformation

- **High-quality content:** The platform has over 3,000 courses from top institutions like Harvard, MIT, and Berkeley, and a learner is guaranteed high-quality education.
- **MicroMasters and degrees:** The platform provides MicroMasters programs and full online degrees so that learners can get advanced credentials at a fraction of the cost of traditional education.
- **Open-Source Platform:** Open edX, an open-source learning platform of edX, is used to build and disseminate the courses, promoting cooperation and creativity.

Impact

Because of edX, over 40 million people worldwide have had the chance to learn from excellent colleges at affordable prices, encouraging them to keep learning throughout life. This is the result of the organization's efforts to make education more affordable and more eco-friendly.

Duolingo

Millions use Duolingo to learn a new language because it's fun and easy, thanks to its gamified approach. Udemy offers classes in more than 40 languages, reaching people worldwide.

- **Making learning fun through gamification**: With features inspired by games, like Duolingo's points, levels and rewards, learning a language is made fun and effective.
- **Reachability**: Due to the free platform and affordable in-app fees, people all over the world can participate in language instruction.
- **Learning at anytime and anywhere**: Duolingo's mobile app helps people study whenever and wherever they like, making education more accessible.

Impact

With over 500 million users worldwide, Duolingo makes it fun and simple to learn languages, supporting more people in understanding and communicating with different cultures. It shows that learning online is effective and at the same time helps to save the environment.

To summarize

Online classes from Coursera, edX and Duolingo are making a big difference in the world of higher education. With technology, students can do more and stay more engaged during their education. What they do for the environment is an admirable model for teaching us about being responsible for nature. This means promoting digital alternatives, using less paper, and using less energy.

Comparative analysis: Indian and global EdTech platforms

Digitalization in higher education is a common aim for Indian and international edtech organizations. Even being in various types of markets, these platforms often take similar forms which give us a lot to learn. The following analysis compares the two groups by what they have in common and where they are different and explores how they could share knowledge.

Parallels between Indian and global EdTech platforms

Focus on accessibility and inclusivity

- **Indian platforms:** TimesPRO, SWAYAM and NPTEL have succeeded in extending their services to people in rural and semi-urban areas.

- **Global platforms:** By giving access to top university courses for little cost or at no charge, Coursera and edX have made education more attainable. Because of Duolingo's free language courses, millions across the globe can now learn languages for free.

Both Indian and global platforms strive to achieve the same goals in helping remove educational barriers.

Personalization and flexibility

- **Indian platforms:** Many Indian educational platforms are using adaptive learning to create learning plans suited for a wide variety of students.
- **Global platforms:** On Coursera and edX, users are allowed to learn whenever it suits them. Everyone learns differently, but Duolingo applications use games to give each person exactly the lessons they need.

Indian and international platforms are built to give each learner flexibility and adjust learning materials to their needs.

- **Indian platforms:** SWAYAM and NPTEL help learners avoid paper use by giving them digital certificates and open educational resources. Thanks to its digital-only setup, TIMESPRO can avoid most traditional bricks-and-mortar facilities.
- **Global platforms:** Coursera and edX issue digital credentials and promote OER, while Duolingo's mobile-first approach minimizes environmental impact.

The companies both lessen their environmental impact by reducing the number of paper documents, making the most out of resources and encouraging eco-friendly routines.

Lessons India can learn from global best practices

Industry-academia collaboration

- **Global example:** Coursera and partners Google and IBM test their courses to ensure they align with industry needs which helps improve finding a job.
- **Lesson for India:** NPTEL and SWAYAM could partner more with businesses to design courses that meet the required skills and ease students into work life.

Gamification and engagement

- **Example from around the world:** Using gamification, Duolingo ensures learning is enjoyable and keeps users committed and eager.
- **The lesson for India:** Gamification is a strategy that educational platforms in India can use to keep learning interactive and enjoyable, mainly for students in their early years.

Global reach and branding

Coursera and edX are popular around the world, receiving learners from 190 different countries.

By introducing their courses in many languages and forming alliances with international organizations, TIMESPRO and SWAYAM can reach a wider overseas audience.

Lessons global platforms can learn from India

Localization and regional focus

Indian examples: Indian companies provide educational resources in various regional languages. When learning is varied, diverse students feel supported and gain more from it.

Experience for global platforms: To increase their number of users, global platforms should share information in the languages spoken by non-English users in developing regions.

Government-led initiatives

Indian example: SWAYAM and NPTEL offer free or very affordable courses to millions of students and the government backs them.

Lesson for global platforms: Together with governments, global platforms can organize free or discounted educational programs to help people in underserved regions.

Cost-effective models

In India, educational platforms that offer subscriptions and SWAYAM's free courses show how quality education can be offered inexpensively.

Global platforms ought to create new pricing structures to provide access to education for those from financially challenged areas.

Framework for sustainable edtech integration

Education will be more effectively use technology when there is a solid and clear framework in place. Policy suggestions, steps for educational institutions, e-tech firm participation and support from the community should be part of these solutions. Ensuring these aspects enables stakeholders to improve how students learn and achieve other sustainability aims through digital tools.

Policy recommendations

Stronger backing and regulation from the government

As governments mainly set rules in education, they should clearly outline measures to protect students and teachers and draw up standards for data privacy, cyber defense and high-quality content.

- **Distribute funding**: Provide funding to support the development and upkeep of edtech infrastructure, especially in underserved areas.
- **Promote public-private partnerships (PPPs)**: Foster collaboration among governments, edtech companies, and educational institutions to create scalable, affordable, and inclusive solutions.

As an example, India's National Education Policy (NEP) 2020 stresses the use of technology in schools and plans to have a dedicated forum, the National Educational Technology Forum (NETF), that will supervise edtech efforts. Countries around the world may adopt these policies as an example.

Governments ought to motivate institutions and tech companies to support the environment by introducing special incentives for going green. The rewards you might receive could be

- Depending on how renewable energy is harnessed, use taxes to provide incentives for companies.
- Grants and subsidies are used to promote environmental research and technology growth. Besides, assist with funding solutions that inspire low-energy usage and cloud computing applications.
- Give recognition awards or certificates to leading organizations that are committed to environmental sustainability. As a result, economic reasons for focusing on sustainability can be applied in the edtech sector by governments.

Institutional strategies

Adoption of hybrid learning models

Now, educational institutions should introduce hybrid learning methods by mixing online and offline teaching. Students will therefore gain experience with online resources and learning in the classroom. Schools and universities may:

- Make sure that all classrooms are outfitted with technology such as smartboards, projectors and strong internet.
- Offer classes in two modes: Create courses that students can take online and also attend face-to face classes simultaneously.
- Assess data to see if the approach is working and make improvements if required. An example is other Indian universities, for instance the IITs which now hold hybrid classes, offering students additional online courses along with traditional learning.

- Technology becomes useful in teaching when teachers know how to use it in their lessons. Increasing the capacity of faculty should be a focus for educational institutions.
- **Workshops**: Offer workshops from time to time on digital technology, online teaching and data analysis.
- **Resources:** Provide a collection of different video tutorials and best practice guides on your online platform.
- Help faculty collaborate: Build an environment where sharing experiences and ideas is encouraged to find improved teaching ways. As a result, institutions can guarantee that technology enriches, instead of hinders, the education of teachers.

Role of edtech companies

Platforms from these companies should be simple to operate, consider how the users interact, be available to many and be priced affordably. This includes:

- **Researching users:** Making products that respond to user problems faced by students, teachers and parents.
- **Serving the many:** Building tools that work smoothly on all kinds of devices.
- **Adjustable price points:** Offering options so that different users can pay according to their means. Many people use e-tech platforms today because they offer personalized learning for a fair price. Because of these alternatives, many people have obtained a strong education.

Investment in R and D for sustainable technologies: Innovative solutions for sustainability can be produced through R and D investment, so it is important for edtech companies to focus on sustainable technology research and development. This includes:

- Growing energy-efficient devices by designing products that are both frugal and durable.
- Learning about Renewable Energy: Relying on solar or wind power to supply energy to data centers and different facilities.
- Set up systems for recycling electronic items so that we produce less e-waste.

With their Rand D work, educational technology companies are able to improve our environment and boost their profits by taking sustainability factors into account.

Community engagement

Involving students, parents, and local communities

As technology is used in multi-faceted ways in higher education, all the stakeholders must be involved to make it sustainable. Key stakeholders are students, parents, and the local communities. Strategies to engage the community include

- **Awareness campaign -** While highlighting the benefits of digital learning, it is crucial to consider screen time and data privacy. Thus, the focus should be on the benefits and not the technology used in digital learning.
- **Participation -** Engaging parents and community leaders in decision-making to implement edtech solutions that meet local needs and are easily implementable.
- **Trust**—Building effective communication through community-based initiatives such as digital literacy camps and integrating technology with education =to reduce resistance to innovations.

The community's engagement is necessary for the successful implementation of the decision made because they will be the ones who will directly or indirectly use the technology in the educational process.

Promoting digital literacy and awareness

Digital literacy is critical for the effective implementation of educational technology; thus, to improve digital literacy, stakeholders should:

- **Develop training programs**: Offer training and e-learning sessions that teach students and teachers how to use digital tools properly.
- **Create awareness campaigns**: Modes of mass communication like newspapers, TV, social media, etc., can be explored to impart digital skills.
- **Leveraging local networks**: Collaborate with NGOs and community organizations to implement digital literacy initiatives in rural and underserved regions. This way, communities can harness the power of educational technology to bring about real change by empowering individuals with digital skills.

To summarize

The sustainable ed-tech framework is an essential guide that can help various stakeholders in the process of digital transformation in education. Therefore, it is important to have solid policies, well-planned strategies, sustainable practices in edtech, and community involvement so that technology can improve learning, increase access and equality, and be environmentally friendly. Further collaboration between stakeholders is also crucial in order to fully harness the potential of sustainable edtech in the future.

Conclusion

The paper looks at the development of online learning platforms, virtual classrooms, and digital resources, which break geographical barriers and thus increase the accessibility of education. It mainly aims to cover the areas that have not been reached before. India is a key example of how technology is being used to address challenges like infrastructure gaps, teacher shortages, and demand for industry-specific courses. However, there are still challenges like the digital divide, systemic inequities, environmental concerns, etc. For marginalized groups, complex technological systems, costly devices and limited online access are extra barriers to using technology. E-tech solutions are said to cause concern by placing too much focus on growing big and making profits which can lead to more energy use, more e-trash and social problems.

Importance of sustainability in digital transformation

Sustainable growth in education through digital transformation depends on looking at technology, environment, society and the economy. Handling carbon footprints and e-waste depends mostly on using environmentally friendly practices and renewable energy. Learners should have no socioeconomic or geographical disadvantages when receiving the benefits of the educational program. Educational tools and systems should be easy on the budget and realistic, so that all students can access them without reducing their quality.

The article provides a detailed outline for achieving sustainable digital transformation in higher education. There are four key pillars:

- **Accessibility and Inclusion**: Mitigating the digital gap with local, multilingual, subsidized content and devices.
- **Environmental Sustainability**: Advancing energy-efficient technologies along with cloud computing and a circular economy in EdTech platforms.
- **Economic Viability**: Addressing cost-effective models like time-based subscriptions, public-private partnerships, and novel, scalable, inclusive financing.
- **Quality and Personalization**: Employing sophisticated AI and data analytics to produce supportive and relevant adaptive learning environments.

Call for collaborative action

The paper details the ne

- Necessity for an integrated effort from major players:
- Sustainable policies should be adopted, financial support provided, and collaboration between public and private entities facilitated by government policies.

- Professional development for teachers and improvement of the physical plant infrastructure will be the key elements of success for the adoption of hybrid teaching/learning methodologies in schools and universities, enhancing the physical infrastructure, and developing teachers' professional aptitude.
- Technology providers for education should design systems that are easy to use, accessible, and environmentally friendly and integrate artificial intelligence and data analysis to enhance learning.
- Learners and communities should be engaged through awareness campaigns, digital literacy education, and partnerships with organizations within the local community to ensure everyone's involvement.

A Vision for the Future: In the final section, the paper paints a positive picture of the future where, with the help of digital technologies, higher education can become the engine of sustainable development. As online platforms continue to spread their wings, they are sending a viable and equitable model. This enables the sharing of knowledge and supports the next generation to meet future challenges. In this way, by incorporating newer technologies that focus on justice and sustainability, colleges and universities can act as the Impetus for fostering and nurturing innovation, multi-faceted learners, and a robust society. This is because the combination of institutions, technology, and communities will be most important in making sure that the digital revolution not only improves learning but also improves the environment and thus makes the future better for the planet.

References

[1] Aleryani, A. Y. (2024). Digital Transformation in Higher Education in Developing Countries to Promote Sustainable Development. *International Journal of Scientific and Research Publications*, 14(2).

[2] Mohamed Hashim, M. A., Tlemsani, I., & Duncan Matthews, R. (2022). A sustainable university: Digital transformation and beyond. *Education and Information Technologies*, 27(7), 8961–8996.

[3] Yu, X., Karsten, E., Kenney, D., Sinha, A., & Brunamonti, C. (2021). Coursera impact report. *Coursera. Available online: https://about. coursera. org/press/wp-content/uploads/2021/11/2021-Coursera-Impact-Report. pdf (accessed on 23.1.25)*

[4] Pack, D. (2025, January 30). *Online Learning Statistics: The Ultimate List in 2025*. Retrieved from https://www.devlinpeck.com/content/online-learning-statistics

[5] Imed Bouchrika, P. (2025, January 20). research.com. Retrieved from https://research.com/education/online-education-statistics

[6] statista.com. (2024, December 22). Retrieved from https://www.statista.com/outlook/emo/ online-education/india.

[7] Czeczuk, A. (2025, January 12). https://thinkbeyond.cloud. Retrieved from https://thinkbeyond.cloud/blog/how-digital-transformation-shapes-university-operations/

[8] Trevisan, L. V., Eustachio, J. H. P. P., Dias, B. G., Leal Filho, W., & Pedrozo, E. Á. (2023). Digital transformation towards sustainability in higher education: state-of-the-art and future research insights. Environment, Development and Sustainability, 1.

21 From classroom to boardroom: industry 4.0 as a catalyst for sustainable business practices

Abeer Tadmori[a]

DBA Candidate, Switzerland, Rushford Business School, Switzerland

Abstract

This research paper explores the incorporation of Industry 4.0 with STEM education to aid students in sustainable business practices. Industry 4.0, which is based on advanced technologies such as the Internet of Things (IoT), artificial intelligence (AI), robotics, and big data analytics, has great transformative potential for both the education and business sectors. This research fills the gap in current educational practices by providing a full framework for integrating these technologies into STEM curricula. A qualitative research design was used, based on a systematic review of the explored literature. Peer-reviewed journal articles, books, and other scholarly publications will provide data. Few, if any, opportunities exist for visiting the actual government departments conducting their operations, leaving this method of data collection quite restrictive. Hence, to synthesize the findings and identify the common themes, patterns, and gaps, thematic, content, and comparative analyses will be conducted. This study develops a framework that suggests guidelines for educators to teach both the curriculum and sustainability education through hands-on learning or teacher training and assess the work. The study bridges the gap between education and industry better to equip students for future jobs in the tech world and to encourage sustained business practices. The study is designed to bring in a new generation of business leaders educated with the necessary skills and knowledge to be both technologically savvy and in support of sustainability. The findings are expected to play a role in educational reform, policy development, and more generally in the broader discourse of sustainable economic growth.

Keywords: Curricula, education, skills, sustainability, technology

Introduction

Another revolution, that of Industry 4.0, which is fueled using software and digital technologies like artificial intelligence (AI), big data analytics, and the Internet of Things (IoT), has impacted many areas of human and machine interactions, including manufacturing, healthcare, and finance. It's not only changing how businesses operate but also how they position themselves on sustainability. Concerns about the environment and resource depletion at the global level are intensifying, thus promoting sustainable business practices. The Industry 4.0 technologies bring new solutions to these challenges, including operational efficiency improvement, waste reduction, and the usage of renewable resources [10].

The field of education is also undergoing enormous changes, going on in parallel. As the job market keeps changing so rapidly, traditional educational models are being reevaluated in order to better teach students what they will be faced with. It is necessary to prepare students to develop in a technological environment. The idea is to integrate Industry 4.0 concepts into educational curricula, in particular in STEM (Science, Technology, Engineering, and Mathematics) education. Through this, educational institutions can fill the gap between theoretical knowledge and practical knowledge, so that students are ready for future careers [6].

Industry 4.0 technologies are advancing rapidly, and how they can lead to sustaining business is supported too; however, little is integrated into STEM education curricula. Educational programs today do not include teaching for the practical application of IoT, AI, robotics, and big data analytics from a sustainability perspective. It results in a workforce equipped with neither the tools for the use of the most modern technologies, nor the ability to build such environments to enable business.

Further, there is growing demand from businesses for people with the skills to use the latest technologies in order to help deliver sustainability goals. Additionally, there is no such integration in education, resulting in a yawning gap between what industry demands and what graduates possess in terms of skills. To address this

[a]abeertadmori@gmail.com

DOI: 10.4324/9781003739982-21

gap, this research explores ways in which the Industry 4.0 concept can be integrated into STEM education, so the students get experience in practicing sustainable business practices when they are engaged in their future careers; therefore, this research carries criticality.

Literature Review

Overview

During the past years, and particularly the context of promoting sustainable business practices, there has been a growing interest in integrating education with Industry 4.0 technologies. And Industry 4.0 is broadly speaking about the technologies, ranging from the IoT all the way to AI, robotics, and big data analytics [9]. Here is where these technologies have the potential to revolutionize multiple fields, such as education, with the ability to increase learning experiences and also help equip students with the remote jobs of the future in a tech-driven world.

Existing research and theories

Industry 4.0 and education

Importance of Education 4.0 with the concept Industry 4.0 is defined because the educational systems should respond to the requirements of the fourth industrial revolution [3]. Based on the above, the report contends that Education 4.0 refers to the process of infusing advanced technologies to provide educational services to foster 21st-century skills, including creative thinking and critical thinking, digital literacy, among others. This analytical method covers the gap and ensures students are ready for the dynamic labor market [1].

Sustainable business practices

In recent years, sustainability in business practices has received great importance, as a result of the global concerns about environmental degradation and resource depletion [13]. Industry 4.0 technologies provide innovative solutions to these challenges via increased operational efficiency and decreased waste and the promotion of the use of renewable resources [10]. As shown by Stock and Seliger [14], Industry 4.0 technologies and data analytics can both contribute to the emergence of sustainable manufacturing via smart technologies.

Integration of industry 4.0 in STEM education

Industry 4.0 technologies have been studied in several studies that seek to integrate technology in STEM education. As an example, Tortorella et al. [15] explain the need for the inclusion of IoT, AI, robotics into Science, Technology, Engineering, and Mathematics curricula to prepare students for future careers in high-tech companies. But they assert that involving students in hands-on experiences using these technologies can improve student technical abilities and a more complete understanding of their use in real-life circumstances [5]. This is further supported by Kumar and Mehra [8], who show how personalized learning technology can dramatically enhance educational outcomes consistent with a broader theme of using advanced technology in STEM education.

Educational frameworks and models

There have been many proposed educational frameworks and models on how Industry 4.0 technologies can be integrated into curricula. For example, the technological pedagogical content knowledge (TPACK) framework organizes these points and offers broad integration of technology in teaching, looking at the interactions among technology, pedagogy, and knowledge of content [11]. Why is the TPACK framework still important as teachers become more intentional about their integration of 21st-century skills into the instruction of their subject matter? Like the substitution, augmentation, modification, redefinition (SAMR) model, it provides structure for incorporating technology into education from basic substitution of traditional tools to totally redefining learning tasks using technology [12].

Critical Analysis

Strengths of previous studies

The strength of existing research is to recognize Industry 4.0 technologies' potential to transform education. The studies by González-Pérez and Ramírez-Montoya [6] and Tortorella et al. [15] are a great source of information for learning experience and practice for students in their future careers. In addition, experience learning and active learning are strengthened by the hands-on learning and real-world problem-solving aspects [18].

The focus on sustainability is another strength. Stock and Seliger [14] and Mian et al. [10] research point towards the potential for Industry 4.0 technologies to underpin sustainable business practice, thereby establishing a strong argument for integrating such technologies into teaching and learning. It is important now even more than ever before with the growing global commitment to sustainability and conservation of resources [16]. Find this interconnectedness in Figure 21.1.

Weaknesses of previous studies

However, the strengths of the existing literature are not free from weaknesses. A notable lack of empirical evidence on the long-term impact of Industry 4.0 technologies embedded in education. There is plenty of literature indicating the potential benefits of such initiatives, but surprisingly, little correspondence with what these initiatives have delivered in practice. Specifically, this gap is critical in the context of sustainable business practices where more longitudinal study is required for assessing how Industry 4.0 education can influence students' career readiness and competency for sustainability [4].

The other weakness is that the focus is limited to the challenges and barriers in integrating Industry 4.0 technologies in education [4]. Some studies have recognized these potential difficulties (for example, requiring teacher training and development of infrastructure) but none of them have carried out a comprehensive analysis of these problems. However, the proposed frameworks and models have not been genuinely applied due to this oversight.

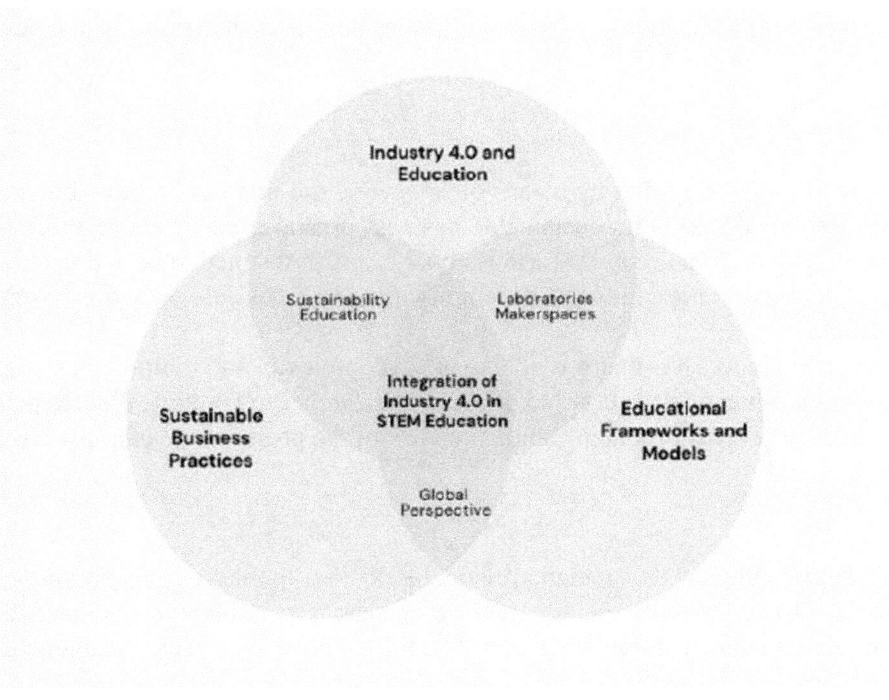

Figure 21.1 Conceptual Interconnectedness of Sustainable Business Practices and Educational Frameworks in Industry 4.0. This figure presents the overlap and relationship between sustainable business practices and educational frameworks and how their mutual synergy can lead to sustainability in education and work

Source: Author

Gap identification

A number of gaps in the current literature are introduced. The first step is to carry out additional empirical research into how Industry 4.0 technologies in education impact the long term. Assessing how these initiatives have improved technical skills and career readiness of students, as well as competencies in sustainability, is also part of what is included within this. Even without these longitudinal studies, Industry 4.0 education can provide invaluable insights of the outcomes should this be implemented across schools, as these studies would show.

The second is that literature has a gap to fill in terms of integrating Industry 4.0 technologies into education [17]. Some of the studies acknowledge these challenges but there is no in-depth analysis or solutions. Future research should explore what challenges educators and institutions face, and how they might be overcome.

Finally, a greater need for research in the interdisciplinary nature of Industry 4.0 education emerges. Whilst there are many studies of the integration of technologies, there is little study of the combination of different technologies in ways that generate holistic and interdisciplinary learning. Strictly speaking, it includes investigating how the different Industry 4.0 technologies and the different implementations of these are playing the interplay [17].

Justification

This research attempts to fill this gap and bring to the field a thorough analysis of Industry 4.0 technologies integration in STEM education for sustainable business practices. This study serves as empirical research of the long-term impacts of these initiatives and gives important insights into how these can improve students' technical skills, sustainability competencies, and career readiness. The research also explores the obstacles and barriers to integration to suggest practical solutions and strategies for educators and institutions [9].

Additionally, this research is also multidisciplinary, focusing on how different Industry 4.0 technologies interact and ascribe to different fields. This offers a more comprehensive view of how these technologies might be integrated into education to produce a more well-rounded, future ready workforce [9].

Finally, this research attempts to bridge the gap between education and industry by showing its role in applying Industry 4.0 technology to foster sustainable business practices. It prepares students to meet the challenges and receive the rewards of a tech-driven world and therefore its goal is to help contribute to a more sustainable and prosperous future for all.

Methodology

Qualitative research design is adopted in this study first by means of reviewing the literature on the integration of Industry 4.0 technologies in STEM education for sustainable business practices. Since the research is viewpoint-based and relies on secondary data from secondary articles/books, it is best suited to be approached qualitatively. An in-depth analysis of current theories, models, and empirical work is possible with this design, offering a view of the problem at hand.

The reason for choosing the qualitative approach is that it is able to grasp complexity and multidimensional nature integrating advanced technologies education. It serves to allow the researcher to combine diverse perspectives and gives insights from different sources producing a holistic view of the present state of knowledge and identify the gaps that have to be closed.

Data collection methods

Mainly, the data collection for this study included a systematic review of existing literature. This comprises peer-reviewed articles in journals, books, conference papers, and other scholarly publications related to (Industry 4.0, STEM education, and sustainable business practices). The following steps outline the data collection process:

1. Literature search: We systematically searched all academic databases, including "Google Scholar", "JSTOR", "ScienceDirect", and "Springer". To identify relevant sources, we used keywords and phrases

such as 'Industry 4.0 in education', 'STEM education', 'sustainable business practices', "IoT in education", "AI in education", and "Education 4.0".

2. Inclusion and exclusion criteria: To ensure only relevant and quality literature. The peer-reviewed articles, reputable academic publishers, and studies within the last ten years were included as inclusion criteria. We excluded non-peer-reviewed articles, academic sources, and studies published prior to 2014.
3. Data extraction: Information found within the selected literature was extracted and put together into themes and sub themes based on their relevancy. Specifically, it covered key findings; theoretical frameworks; methodologies; and conclusions regarding how Industry 4.0 technologies are implemented in education and their effects on sustainable business practices.
4. Synthesis of findings: To generate a synthesis from extracted data and create common themes, patterns, and gaps in the current literature. The critical analysis and discussion sections of the study were based on this synthesis.

Data Analysis

The process of data analysis had several steps done to do a critical and systematic review of the literature. The following techniques and tools were used:

1. Thematic analysis: The literature was analyzed and patterns and themes within the literature identified using thematic analysis. The coding of data, putting it into categories and then interpreting and understanding the findings. Thematic analysis is a good synthesis method for qualitative data and serves identifying the similarities and differences of the studies [2].
2. Content analysis: Quantification of presence of specific themes, concepts or keywords in the literature was achieved through content analysis. This technique provides a more objective look at the data and will help in identifying trends and patterns [7].
3. Comparative analysis: Comparison and contrast of the findings of different studies was made. It means reviewing the similarities and the differences between a methodology, a theoretical framework, and conclusions, in order to illuminate the topic.
4. Synthesis of findings: The thematic, content, and comparative analyses of the findings were synthesized into an overall overview of the state of knowledge. This synthesis reviewed the state of existing research on experienced issues, identified gaps, and recommended future research.

Ethical considerations

The study is based on secondary data, although ethical considerations must be addressed:

1. Intellectual property and copyright: All sources were attributed properly and cited to maintain respect for intellectual property rights and avoid plagiarism. Throughout the study, the same style (including Harvard) was used consistently.
2. Bias and objectivity: To avoid biases and maintain objectivity throughout the selection and analysis of literature, efforts were made. Such as a systematic and transparent method for literature search, and the extraction of information.
3. Confidentiality and privacy: As the study doesn't involve human participants therefore there are not many issues of confidentiality and privacy. Sensitive information encountered in the literature was handled with care and discretion, but no sensitive information was learned.
4. Transparency and accountability: The method used in the research process has been conducted transparently with full documentation of methods and procedures applied. This is accountability, and makes it possible for other researchers to replicate and verify the study.

This research methodology concludes a systematic and rigorous approach to integrating Industry 4.0 technologies into STEM education when implementing sustainable business practices. This study seeks to offer a comprehensive, yet insightful review of the current state of knowledge, elucidate knowledge gaps, and propose avenues for future research by means of reviewing a wide body of literature and using rigorous data analysis techniques. The research that is studied is undertaken with integrity and with ethical consideration for intellectual property.

Findings

The research finds that while Industry 4.0 technologies can integrate very well into STEM education, this substantially improves students' readiness for implementing sustainable business practices. So, these findings show how hands on experiences with technology like IoT, AI, and even robotics can help students get better technical skills and delve deeper in becoming more sustainable. Furthermore, the study pinpoints successful means of overcoming hurdles and obstacles to integration and offer guidelines for educators and institutes to overcome their challenges.

Impact
The results have significant implications for the field of study, policy, practice and society. The research offers a framework for blended learning and the marriage of advanced technologies into curricula, and for the field of education contributes to an ongoing discourse on educational reform and the future of work. The study provides some policy insights into the educational reforms necessary to support sustainable economic growth for policymakers. The research offers practical guidelines to practitioners engaged in implementing Industry 4.0 technologies in education, in order to achieve improved quality of STEM education.

On a larger societal level, the research seeks to nurture a new crop of leaders who not only have technological skills but moreover are committed to environmental values. The study aims to help set students up to 'deal with' and 'embrace,' the challenges and opportunities of a tech driven world in order to help secure a more sustainable and prosperous future.

Framework for Integrating Industry 4.0 Concepts into STEM Education

Introduction
This framework attempts to help educators figure out how to incorporate Industry 4.0 technologies into STEM education. It also helps educators to integrate advanced technologies like IoT, AI, robotics, and big data smart analytics to prepare students for future work in a tech-based world and to promote sustainable business practices. See Figure 21.2.

Key components of the framework

1. ***Curriculum development***
   - Identify core concepts: Identify the critical Industry 4.0 technologies and concepts specially related to the curriculum inclusive of IoT, AI, robotic, big data, etc.
   - Align with standards: Make sure that the curriculum matches historic and international educational standards and frameworks.
   - Interdisciplinary approach: Integrate Industry 4.0 concept in all STEM subjects to be able to provide holistic learning experience.
2. ***Teacher training and professional development***
   - Continuous training: Make provision for ongoing professional development of teachers to keep abreast of the current Industry 4.0 technologies and the ways of teaching.
   - Workshops and seminars: Have workshops and seminars with industry experts to help teachers understand and practice.
   - Collaborative learning: Requires collaboration between teachers to share good student work and ideas, for example.
3. ***Hands on learning and real-world application.***
   - Project-based learning: You can create project-based learning activities that use real-world examples of Industry 4.0 technologies.

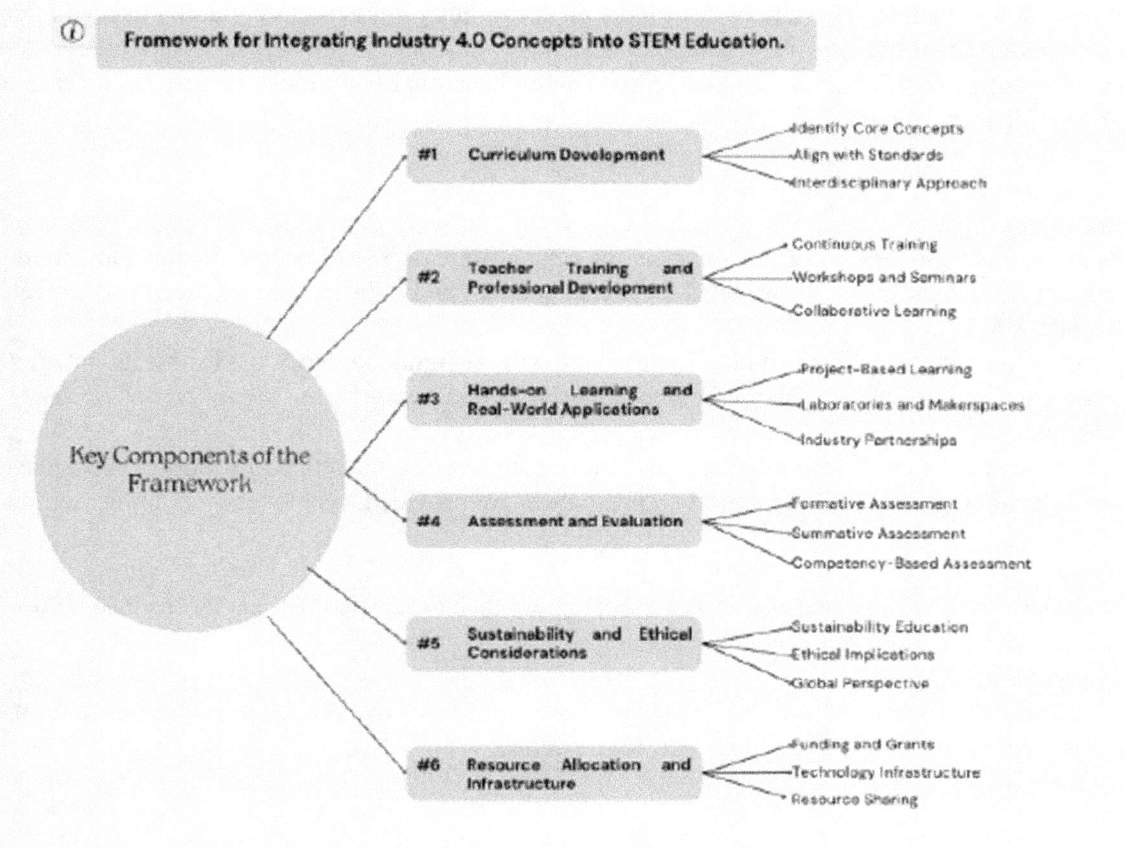

Figure 21.2 Framework for Integrating Industry 4.0 Concepts into STEM Education. This figure presents a comprehensive approach on embedding industry 4.0 technologies into STEM education as a guide to educators aimed at preparing students for tech-driven and sustainable business future
Source: Author

- Laboratories and makerspaces: Build laboratories and makerspaces teeming with Industry 4.0 tools and technology for students to take direct action.
- Industry partnerships: Work with local businesses and tech companies to offer students internships and real-world project chances.

4. ***Assessment and evaluation***
   - Formative assessment: Diagnosing errors during the learning process using formative assessments to identify problems.
   - Summative assessment: Use of summative assessments to assess what students understand and can do with Industry 4.0 concepts.
   - Competency-based assessment: Instead, assess students' competencies in technical skills, problem solving, and critical thinking.
5. ***Sustainability and ethics***
   - Sustainability Education: It is about integrating sustainability principles in the curriculum and valuing the relative role of Industry 4.0 technology in promoting more sustainable business practices.
   - Ethical Implications: Talk about the ethical issues related to using cutting edge technologies and asking students to ponder the social and environmental consequences of their work.
6. ***Infrastructure and resource allocation***
   - Funding and grants: Get funding or grants to help implement Industry 4.0 technology in your classroom.

- Technology infrastructure: The school must have the technology infrastructure, i.e. high-speed internet, computer and also Industry 4.0 tools.
- ResourcesSharing: Encourage top-ranked schools and educational institutions to help each other in using available technologies.

Implementation steps

1. ***Needs assessment***
   The needs assessment should conduct to ascertain the current state of STEM education, the gaps in integrating Industry 4.0 technologies. Learn what teachers, students, and industry partners need and expect.
2. ***Curriculum design***
   Come up with a full curriculum plan of how Industry 4.0 will be ingrained into STEM subjects. Integrate these technologies into your lesson plan, a project, an activity or activity.
3. ***Teacher training***
   Train teachers in Industry 4.0 technologies, teaching techniques, so that they are familiar with these industries 4.0 technologies. Ongoing support and resources are provided to help teachers implement the new curriculum.
4. ***Pilot Program***
   Run a pilot program among selected classes or school to pilot the new curriculum, gather feedback. Based on the feedback and the result of evaluation.
5. ***Full implementation***
   Make roll out of the curriculum for all STEM subjects at all grade levels. Yet, keep a close watch on the program to see whether it works and improve it when necessary.

Conclusion

Both business practice and preparation for future careers can be assisted by the integration of Industry 4.0 concepts into STEM education. This framework serves as a complete resource for educators on how to bring these technologies into their teaching in a mutually beneficial way. These guidelines help educators mold a dynamic and stimulating learning setting where students learn abilities and knowledge that are required to make it to a tech-driven society.

References

[1] Abdelmouli, D., Al-Amiri, D., Yahyani, D., Al-Maamari, D., & Al-Hajri, D. (2021). Objectives of current technical education between scientific knowledge and contemporary practices. *International Journal of Education and Learning Research*, 4(2), 128–144. https://doi.org/10.21608/ijelr.2023.215531.1008.

[2] Braun, V., & Clarke, V. (2006). Using thematic analysis in psychology. *Qualitative Research in Psychology*, 3(2), 77–101. https://doi.org/10.1191/1478088706qp063oa.

[3] Chakraborty, S., Gonzalez-Triana, Y., Mendoza, J., & Galatro, D. (2023). Insights on mapping industry 4.0 and education 4.0. Frontiers in Education, 8, 1–15. https://doi.org/10.3389/feduc.2023.1150190.

[4] Costan, E., Gonzales, G., Gonzales, R., Enriquez, L., Costan, F., Suladay, D., et al. (2021). Education 4.0 in developing economies: a systematic literature review of implementation barriers and future research agenda. *Sustainability*, 13(22), 12763. https://doi.org/10.3390/su132212763.

[5] Dominguez, A., Garza, J., Quezada-Espinoza, M., & Zavala, G. (2023). Integration of physics and mathematics in STEM education: use of modeling. *Education Sciences*, 14(1), 20. https://doi.org/10.3390/educsci14010020.

[6] González-Pérez, L. I., & Ramírez-Montoya, M. S. (2022). Components of education 4.0 in 21st century skills frameworks: systematic review. *Sustainability*, 14(3), 1493. https://doi.org/10.3390/su14031493.

[7] Krippendorff, K. (2018). Content Analysis: An Introduction to its Methodology. Sage Publications.

[8] Kumar, A., & Mehra, A. (2016). Remedying Education with Personalized Learning: Evidence from Randomized Field Experiment in India. *SSRN Electronic Journal*. https://doi.org/10.2139/ssrn.2756059.

[9] Malyzhenkov, P. V. (2023). The usage of industry 4.0 enabling technologies in the education. *Interactive Science*, 9 (85), 49–51. https://doi.org/10.21661/r-561087.

[10] Mian, S. H., Salah, B., Ameen, W., Moiduddin, K., & Alkhalefah, H. (2020). Adapting universities for sustainability education in industry 4.0: channel of challenges and opportunities. *Sustainability*, 12(15), 6100. https://doi.org/10.3390/su12156100.

[11] Mishra, P., & Koehler, M. J. (2006). Technological pedagogical content knowledge: a framework for teacher knowledge. *Teachers College Record*, 108(6), 1017–1054.

[12] Ruben R. Puentedura's Weblog: SAMR: Moving from Enhancement to Transformation. (n.d.). https://www.hippasus.com/rrpweblog/archives/000095.html

[13] Sheth, J., & Parvatiyar, A. (2020). Sustainable marketing: market-driving, not market-driven. *Journal of Macromarketing*, 41, 150–165. https://doi.org/10.1177/0276146720961836.

[14] Stock, T., & Seliger, G. (2016). Opportunities of sustainable manufacturing in industry 4.0. *Procedia CIRP*, 40, 536–541. https://doi.org/10.1016/j.procir.2016.01.129.

[15] Tortorella, G. L., Giglio, R., & van Dun, D. H. (2020). Industry 4.0 adoption as a moderator of the impact of lean production practices on operational performance improvement. *International Journal of Operations and Production Management*, 40(1), 1–29. https://doi.org/10.1108/IJOPM-01-2019-0005.

[16] Tsalis, T. A., Nikolaou, I. E., Konstantakopoulou, F., Zhang, Y., & Evangelinos, K. I. (2020). Evaluating the corporate environmental profile by analyzing corporate social responsibility reports. *Economic Analysis and Policy*, 66, 63–75. https://doi.org/10.1016/j.eap.2020.02.009.

[17] Vieira, M. C. C., Gouveia, R. C., & Dias, A. L. (2022). Interdisciplinary teaching activities for high school integrated to vocational education promoting reflections on industry 4.0 technologies and their implication in society. *Journal of Technical Education and Training*, 14(1). https://doi.org/10.30880/jtet.2022.14.01.007.

[18] Yao, J. (2023). Exploring experiential learning: enhancing secondary school chemistry education through practical engagement and innovation. *Journal of Education, Humanities and Social Sciences*, 22, 475–484. https://doi.org/10.54097/ehss.v22i.12508.

22 Exploring the environmental impact of global value chain participation: a case study of ASEAN countries

Nguyen Thi Phuong Linh[a], *Nguyen Ha Linh*[b], *Do Minh Anh*[c] *and Tran Chau Anh*[d]

Faculty of International Economics and Business, University of Economics and Business, Vietnam National University, Hanoi, Vietnam

Abstract

This study examines the impact of global value chain (GVC) participation on environmental issues (EI) in ASEAN countries from 2007 to 2021. Using a quantile regression model with panel data for 10 ASEAN countries, we analyze five key environmental indices: EI, air issues (AI), waste issues (WI), forest issues (FI), and land issues (LI). Our findings indicate a complex relationship between GVC participation and environmental outcomes. Specifically, we found that more GVC participation has detrimental impacts on overall environmental performance, and air quality, with increasing effects at higher quantiles, and waste management appears to be very negatively impacted, particularly in already poorly washed countries. We found no impact for forests, while GVC participation is an aid for land-based environmental issues, which was also unexpected. These findings highlight the need for clearer environmental policies in ASEAN countries that are increasingly engaged in GVCs to balance economic development and environmental stewardship.

Keywords: ASEAN countries, environmental issues, global value chain, participation

Introduction

In a globalized world, global value chains (GVCs) have reshaped the manner in which all goods are manufactured and exchanged internationally, turning a variety of actions - from conception to global distribution - into elaborate sequences of processes. This has been especially true for the Association of Southeast Asian Nations (ASEAN), where countries have only become progressively integrated into these complex networks of production and exchange. While GVCs have contributed to ASEAN economic growth and overall efficiencies - allowing for specialization and comparative advantages, this economic growth has been accompanied by serious environmental concerns [2].

Tracing and addressing the environmental implications associated with GVC activities may be problematic in ASEAN due to the diffuse and spread out nature of GVC activities, which also raises questions about the sustainability of such economic development practices [11]. The transnational dispersal of production means that it is often unclear who is responsible for any pollution, and it can be difficult to ascertain the areas or sustainable practices at all levels of focal geographic space [4]. Although there is an increasing amount of academic research on the environmental consequences of GVCs at the global level, a systematic assessment of the complex interactions between GVCs and air issues (EIs) within ASEAN is currently missing. Most other research on GVCs has approached EIs in isolation, focusing only on locations in ASEAN as opposed to capturing the broader, complex environmental dimensions of GVC integration across all of ASEAN. This research gap illustrates the mismatch between current studies' narrow perspectives and the complexity of environmental interactions related to GVCs within ASEAN.

This paper seeks to fill this critical gap by comprehensively investigating how participation in GVCs affects the environment in ASEAN countries. Specifically, we examine all ten ASEAN countries over a 15-year period (2007-2021), using advanced statistical methods, including a quantile quantitative model, to disentangle the complex relationship between GVC participation and environmental characteristics (air, waste, land and forest issues). By accounting for other influential factors like economic development (GDP), urbanization rate and population size, we aim to pinpoint the unique impact of GVCs on ASEAN countries' environmental performances.

[a]phuonglinhnt@vnu.edu.vn, [b]nguyenhalinh210404@gmail.com, [c]contact.dominhanh@gmail.com, [d]tranchauanh4217@gmail.com

DOI: 10.4324/9781003739982-22

The remainder of this paper is organized as follows. Section 2 provides a comprehensive review of the relevant literature, examining both the theoretical underpinnings and empirical evidence concerning the environmental implications of GVCs, with a focus on ASEAN countries. In Section 3 we analyze the data and methodologies we used in our paper. After this, we present the empirical results in Section 4. After that, in Section 5, we examine the implications of our findings for policy in ASEAN. In conclusion, in Section 6 we sum up the principal findings and outline areas for future research on GVCs and EIs related to ASEAN.

Literature Review

The GVCs are a complex and interconnected web of activities undertaken by firms and workers in many countries around the world that span the lifecycle of a product, from conception to end-user use and beyond [11]. GVCs include, but are not limited to, research and development, design, production, marketing, distribution, and consumer services reflecting a growing fragmentation and geographic dispersal of modern production systems, emphasizing the intricate interrelatedness in today's global economy. The degree with which a country is implicated in GVCs, GVC participation, is measured using a multi-dimensional measure of participating in vertically fragmented production processes across the global economy. There are two ways to consider GVC participation, backward participation where a country uses foreign inputs in exports, and forward participation where a country provides input for other countries' exports. These metrics, as prescribed by the Organization for Economic Co-operation and Development (OECD [23]), help us understand the depth and character of a country's economic interdependence in the global marketplace.

In this study, we adopt a holistic view of EIs and focus on four areas that relate to GVC participation and environmental sustainability. The first dimension is air quality, which includes the wide range of air pollution issues. Air pollution is described as "the contamination of the indoor or outdoor environment by any chemical, physical, or biological agent that modifies the characteristics of the atmosphere" [25]. This definition includes particulate matter, greenhouse gases, volatile organic compounds, and other airborne pollutants that can affect human health, ecosystems, and global weather patterns. The second dimension is waste management and resource efficiency which addresses the broader and more complex issues related to the management and disposal of waste, in all its forms, throughout the value chain; it includes a plethora of categories of waste (municipal solid waste, industrial byproducts, hazardous materials, electronic waste, etc.). According to UNEP [24], there is an essential connection between how waste is managed and environmental degradation, resource conservation, and the principles of a circular economy within the global production network. Third, forest ecosystems relate to a myriad of issues focused on forest values and biodiversity conservation. This includes the very real issue of deforestation, as well as forest degradation, given that the biodiversity loss associated with economic development and global trade has been alarming. The Food and Agriculture Organization, FAO [9] stress the importance of forests in ecological processes that sequester carbon and provide ecosystem services, and the necessity of sustainable management of forest resources, especially as the world becomes more economically integrated. Finally, land use dynamics, here we are talking about how economic activities make direct or indirect impacts to terrestrial ecosystems. This impact may include land use change (i.e., land conversion), unsustainable land use, and soil degradation, and desertification. The Intergovernmental Panel on Climate Change (IPCC) [14] links land use practices to climate change impacts and stresses the importance of sustainable land management in a time of expanding GVCs.

The association between involvement in GVCs and environmental consequences can be complicated and multifaceted. It is complicated and multifaceted as there are numerous feedback loops and context-dependent (social, political, and technological) relationships. For instance, Gamarra et al. [10] report that GVC linkages to concentrated solar power (CSP) plants in Europe were associated with an increase in greenhouse gas emissions; thus, emphasizing the potential for unintended consequences that may arise in the pursuit of sustainable energy. Additionally, Nawaz and Rahman [22] observed a positive relationship between GVC expansion and CO2 emissions in SAARC countries. This observation suggests that deeper integration into global production networks could worsen environmental degradation. Bo and Xu [8] also found environmental impacts, including energy use, increased greenhouse gas emissions from using respective extended transportation networks, and carbon leakage from transferring production to less-regulated countries.

There have been strides in understanding GVCs and the relationship of EIs with GVCs, particularly those issues related to air pollution and Greenhouse gas emissions. There are still substantial gaps in our knowledge of the broader implications for waste management and environmental impacts on forests and land use. The linkages and interactions of GVCs and environmental effects are rarely studied, especially as they relate to the various countries in the ASEAN region. The potential advantages of benefits of GVCs, like, for example, green technology transfer to long-term and short-term environmental implications are also completely overlooked in literature. Filling the gaps in existing literature can give a clearer perspective of environmental implications of GVC participation in ASEAN.

This research seeks to narrow these gaps via a multi-dimensional and thorough investigation of GVC involvement and its environmental influences across ASEAN countries. This study collectively aims to obtain a clearer picture of the complexity surrounding GVC economic development and environmental sustainability issues in the region. The aim of this study is to not only highlight possible environmental problems resulting from GVC involvement but to also identify opportunities in terms of sustainability and policies that will be able to support economic growth while positively impacting the local ecology.

Methodology

This research utilizes quantile regression to examine whether there exists a relationship between GVC participation and EIs in ASEAN countries. Quantile regression has several advantages over traditional mean regression, allowing for a more differentiated and robust analysis. Quantile regression provides a greater understanding of stochastic interactions between the dependent and independent variables by estimating the impact of the independent variable at different quantile levels [16]. Quantile regression is also effective in terms of accommodating outliers and the misspecification of an error distribution when the normality assumption fails [17]. Also, the risk of endogenous concerns caused by simultaneity of effects, for example, will not affect the results when we implement a panel quantile regression model [15, 1, 20]. In contrast to linear regression models that produce a single set of parameters, quantile regression produces parameters for every quantile with statistical tests that can be conducted at different levels of quantile [17]. These features contribute to making quantile regression an inclusive approach for analyzing and examining complex relationships in this study. The experimental model is defined as follows:

$$EI_{it} = \beta_0^p + \beta_1^p GVC_{it} + \mu . CONTROL_{it} + \varepsilon_i^p$$

Where EI_{it} represents the environmental index of country i at time t; GVC_{it} denotes GVC participation index of country i at time t; and ε_{it} is the error term of country i at time t and p is the number of quantiles. Control variables are represented by a variable called $CONTROL_{it}$ of country i at time t, including three factors: GDP, Population size, and Urbanization rate.

To assess participation in GVCs, we used the Asian Development Bank (ADB) input-output database, which provides extensive information regarding inter-industry relationships. The final GVC participation index is computed as a sum of the forward and backward indices. This approach facilitated a clearer understanding of how industries are effectively integrated into GVCs as suppliers (upstream) and users (downstream) of inputs. The complexity of GVC participation can be captured more thoroughly in this approach across sectors and countries, seeking to understand the extent of interconnectedness and reciprocity to global production networks.

- Forward GVC participation index = $\dfrac{DEVX_{i,s,t}}{GRE_{i,s,t}}$
- Backward GVC participation index = $\dfrac{FIVA_{i,s,t}}{GRE_{i,s,t}}$

- GVC participation index = $\frac{FIVA_{i,s,t} + DEVX_{i,s,t}}{GRE_{i,s,t}}$

Where $DEVX_{i,s,t}$ is domestic value-added of input in industry s of country i at time t; $FIVA_{i,s,t}$ is foreign value-added of output for exporting in industry s of country i at time t; $GRE_{i,s,t}$ is the total of exported products in industry s of country i at time t.

In assessing the environmental index, our method of analysis is through use of the Principal Component Analysis (PCA) method developed by Hotelling [13]. Firstly, PCA reduces the dimensionality of data while maintaining the most significant amount of information and statistical context by effectively transforming multiple variables into a composite variable by means of what we would describe as a statistical technique. Therefore, following Li et al. [18], we created a combination of steps to establish a comprehensive and statistically sound measure of industrial upgrading.

To begin our analysis, we must standardize the data. In this process, we will standardize the entire dataset by subtracting the mean variable for each dimension of industrial upgrading, creating a mean variable of 0 value prior to applying PCA. Thus, this gives consistency in scale across all the variables, so that one variable does not dominate the entire process simply because it has greater values. Once we complete the standardization, we can calculate the covariance matrix, denoted c, or the sample variance of the standardized dataset. The covariance matrix provides some insight regarding the covariation between the dimensions of industrial upgrading.

$$c = c_{11}\ c_{12}\ c_{13}\ c_{21}\ c_{22}\ c_{23}\ c_{31}\ c_{32}\ c_{33}$$

We then calculate eigenvectors and eigenvalues for each component of environmental index using the covariance matrix. With a covariance matrix, a non-zero eigenvector corresponds to an eigenvalue with a nontrivial solution [19]. Next, we selected the principal components for each aspect of the environmental index using the calculated eigenvectors and eigenvalues. The principal components are the most prominent features in the data, embodying the essential aspects of industrial upgrading while using fewer dimensions.

$$PCA_d = \frac{\sum_{k=1}^{j} F_{ki}\sqrt{\alpha_k}}{\sum_{k=1}^{j} \sqrt{\alpha_k}}, \ i=1,2,\ldots n;\ d = \underline{1,3}$$

Where F_{ki} represents the coordination of country i in component k with (j is the principal component retained, and its value is always lower than the total indices entered into PCA); α_k denotes the eigenvalue of component k and d represents the three aspects: air issues, waste issues, land issues and forest issues.

Finally, we calculate the composite index of environmental index using a matrix of the selected principal components from the various environmental aspects. This final step synthesizes all the information into a single, comprehensive measure of environmental index. By following this methodical approach, we create a measure that captures the multifaceted nature of industrial upgrading.

$$\text{Environmental index: } r_{i,t} = \left(\frac{EI_1}{EI_2 :: EI_n}\right), \ i=1,2,\ldots n$$

Where EI_n is the sample data of Environmental index; $r_{i,t}$ is the number of selected principal components in order to transform into a composite index of country i at time t.

The variables selected for use in the model are selectively inherited from previous studies related to the impact of GVC participation on environmental factors, including air issues, land issues, and forest issues. The descriptions of these three variables are presented specifically in Table 22.1.

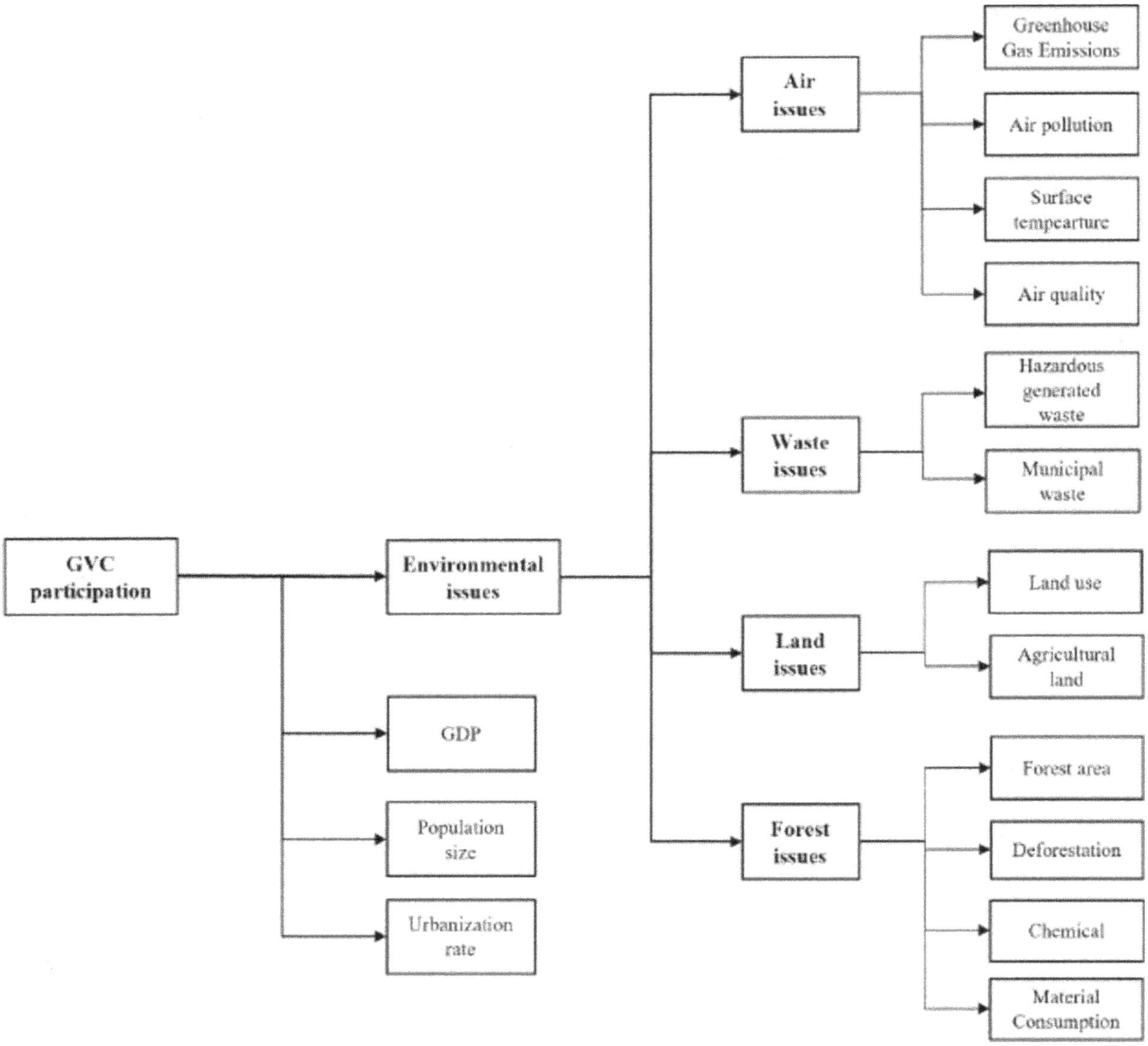

Figure 22.1 Conceptual framework
Source: Author

Results

This section presents the main research findings, demonstrating the impact of GVC participation on EIs in ASEAN countries from 2007 to 2021, as illustrated in Figure 22.1.

Table 22.2 presents the results of our regression analysis examining the impact of GVC participation on EIs in ASEAN countries. The table displays coefficients for various independent variables across different model specifications (columns 1–11), with EI as the dependent variable.

Table 22.3 presents the results of our regression analysis examining the impact of GVC participation on air issues (AI) in ASEAN countries. The table displays coefficients for various independent variables across different model specifications (columns 1–11), with AI as the dependent variable.

Table 22.4 presents the results of our regression analysis examining the impact of GVC participation on waste issues (WI) in ASEAN countries. The table displays coefficients for various independent variables across different model specifications (columns 1-11), with WI as the dependent variable.

Table 22.1 Variables used in the econometric model.

Variable type	Variable name	Variable description	Representative factor	Research time	Sources
Dependent variable	AI_{it}	Air issues of country i year t	Environmental issues	2007 - 2021	
	WI_{it}	Waste issues of country i year t	Environmental issues	2007 - 2021	
	LI_{it}	Land issues of country i year t	Environmental issues	2007 - 2021	
	FI_{it}	Forest issues of country i year t	Environmental issues	2007 - 2021	
Independent variable	$GVCs_{it}$	GVCs participation of country i year t		2007 - 2021	ADB database
	$Ln(GHG_{it})$	Greenhouse Gas Emissions of country i year t	Air issues	2007 - 2021	Climate Watch
	$Ln(AP_{it})$	Air pollution of country i year t	Air issues	2007 - 2021	OECD
	$Ln(ST_{it})$	Surface temperature of country i year t	Air issues	2007 - 2021	IMF
	$Ln(AQ_{it})$	Air quality of country i year t	Air issues	2007 - 2021	OECD
		Hazardous generated waste	Waste issues	2007 - 2021	UN Statistics Division
		Municipal waste	Waste issues	2007 - 2021	OECD
	$Ln(LU_{it})$	Land use of country i year t	Land issues	2007 - 2021	OECD
	$Ln(AL_{it})$	Agricultural land of country i year t	Land issues	2007 - 2021	World Bank
	$Ln(FA_{it})$	Forest area of country i year t	Forest issues	2007 - 2021	World Bank
	$Ln(Def_{it})$	Deforestation of country i year t	Forest issues	2007 - 2021	OECD
	$Ln(Chem_{it})$	Chemical of country i year t	Forest issues	2007 - 2021	World Bank
	$Ln(MC_{it})$	Domestic Material Consumption of country i year t	Forest issues	2007 - 2021	OECD
Control variables	GDP_{it}	GDP of country i year t		2007 - 2021	OECD
	PS_{it}	Population size of country i year t		2007 - 2021	World Bank
	UR_{it}	Urbanization rate of country i year t		2007 - 2021	World Bank
e_t	Error variance				

Source: Author

Table 22.5 presents the results of our regression analysis examining the impact of GVC participation on Land Issues (LI) in ASEAN countries. The table displays coefficients for various independent variables across different model specifications (columns 1-11), with Land Issues as the dependent variable.

Table 22.6 presents the results of our regression analysis examining the impact of GVC participation on forest issues (FI) in ASEAN countries. The table displays coefficients for various independent variables across different model specifications (columns 1–11), with Forest Issues as the dependent variable.

Discussion

The analysis of the effects of GVC participation on multiple environmental indicators within ASEAN countries has documented a complex and multifaceted relationship among economic integration, economic flows, and environmental outcomes. This analysis made use of five indicators: EI, AI, waste issues (WI) forest issues (FI), and land issues (LI). The findings are further substantiated by relevant scholarly literature, illustrating the breadth of the consequences arising from GVC participation with regards to the environment.

Table 22.2 Impact of GVC participation on environmental issues overall.

Variables	EI	EI	EI	EI	EI	EI	EI	EI	EI	EI	EI
	(1)	(2)	(3)	(4)	(5)	(6)	(7)	(8)	(9)	(10)	(11)
GVC	-0.584***	0.0238	-0.612***	-0.605***	-0.602***	-0.596***	-0.587***	-0.577***	-0.564***	-0.551**	-0.536**
	(0.165)	(0.0677)	(0.139)	(0.144)	(0.145)	(0.150)	(0.159)	(0.175)	(0.199)	(0.224)	(0.265)
GDPn	0.0370	-0.0350***	0.0796***	0.0688***	0.0637***	0.0556**	0.0426*	0.0271	0.00792	-0.0102	-0.0326
	(0.0241)	(0.00908)	(0.0190)	(0.0223)	(0.0221)	(0.0226)	(0.0246)	(0.0268)	(0.0301)	(0.0340)	(0.0369)
PSn	-0.640**	-0.205*	-0.390	-0.453*	-0.483*	-0.531**	-0.607**	-0.697***	-0.810***	-0.916***	-1.047***
	(0.253)	(0.109)	(0.281)	(0.253)	(0.251)	(0.250)	(0.254)	(0.267)	(0.292)	(0.331)	(0.336)
URn	-0.00257	-0.00175*	-0.000447	-0.000986	-0.00124	-0.00164	-0.00229	-0.00306	-0.00402	-0.00492	-0.00603
	(0.00241)	(0.000953)	(0.00183)	(0.00185)	(0.00193)	(0.00207)	(0.00233)	(0.00266)	(0.00310)	(0.00356)	(0.00392)
Year	0.0126***	0.00520***	0.00628	0.00788**	0.00863**	0.00984***	0.0118***	0.0141***	0.0169***	0.0196***	0.0229***
	(0.00388)	(0.00154)	(0.00386)	(0.00342)	(0.00347)	(0.00358)	(0.00394)	(0.00437)	(0.00498)	(0.00583)	(0.00520)
Constant	-15.31***	-6.046***	-7.960**	-9.829***	-10.70***	-12.10***	-14.35***	-17.02***	-20.32***	-23.46***	-27.31***
	(4.161)	(1.703)	(3.559)	(3.245)	(3.360)	(3.586)	(4.189)	(4.860)	(5.715)	(6.814)	(6.097)
Observations	150	150	150	150	150	150	150	150	150	150	150

Robust standard errors in parentheses, *** p < 0.01, ** p < 0.05, * p<0.1

Source: Author

Table 22.3 Impact of GVC participation on air issues.

	(1)	(2)	(3)	(4)	(5)	(6)	(7)	(8)	(9)	(10)	(11)
Variables	**AI**	**AI**	**AI**	**AI**	**AI**	**AI**	**AI**	**AI**	**AI**	**AI**	**AI**
GVC	-4.067*	-0.134	-3.825	-3.902	-3.975	-4.083*	-4.127**	-4.154***	-4.172***	-4.196***	-4.213***
	(2.307)	(1.779)	(5.206)	(4.236)	(3.353)	(2.149)	(1.759)	(1.578)	(1.500)	(1.445)	(1.451)
GDPn	2.287***	-0.389*	2.987***	2.765***	2.555***	2.242***	2.114***	2.034***	1.984***	1.913***	1.863***
	(0.354)	(0.233)	(0.693)	(0.581)	(0.481)	(0.349)	(0.307)	(0.285)	(0.279)	(0.274)	(0.279)
PSn	3.691	0.352	3.058	3.259	3.449	3.733	3.849	3.921	3.966	4.030	4.076
	(5.248)	(3.405)	(11.05)	(9.167)	(7.399)	(4.898)	(3.967)	(3.444)	(3.154)	(2.807)	(2.618)
URn	0.0454	-0.0276	0.0951	0.0793	0.0644	0.0422	0.0331	0.0274	0.0238	0.0188	0.0152
	(0.0333)	(0.0183)	(0.0616)	(0.0523)	(0.0443)	(0.0324)	(0.0282)	(0.0259)	(0.0248)	(0.0236)	(0.0234)
Year	-0.170**	0.0250	-0.215	-0.200*	-0.187**	-0.167***	-0.158***	-0.153***	-0.150***	-0.146***	-0.142***
	(0.0660)	(0.0402)	(0.135)	(0.112)	(0.0920)	(0.0621)	(0.0508)	(0.0441)	(0.0403)	(0.0357)	(0.0330)
Constant	221.2***	-45.42	303.0**	277.0***	252.5***	215.9***	200.9***	191.6***	185.8***	177.5***	171.6***
	(63.90)	(38.89)	(129.7)	(107.3)	(89.04)	(60.74)	(49.95)	(43.57)	(40.10)	(35.80)	(33.12)
Observations	150	150	150	150	150	150	150	150	150	150	150

Robust standard errors in parentheses, *** p < 0.01, ** p < 0.05, * p < 0.1

Source: Author

Table 22.4 Impact of GVC participation on water issues.

	(1)	(2)	(3)	(4)	(5)	(6)	(7)	(8)	(9)	(10)	(11)
Variables	**WI**	**WI**	**WI**	**WI**	**WI**	**WI**	**WI**	**WI**	**WI**	**WI**	**WI**
GVC	-3.309*	-1.698	-0.671	-1.390	-1.768	-2.239	-3.117*	-3.563*	-4.104*	-5.007*	-5.906*
	(1.921)	(1.078)	(1.951)	(1.690)	(1.667)	(1.680)	(1.842)	(1.973)	(2.192)	(2.594)	(3.554)
GDPn	0.584**	0.0997	0.429**	0.471***	0.494***	0.521***	0.573***	0.599**	0.631**	0.684**	0.736*
	(0.227)	(0.154)	(0.193)	(0.179)	(0.174)	(0.180)	(0.214)	(0.239)	(0.275)	(0.341)	(0.436)
PSn	-1.697	-0.909	-0.285	-0.670	-0.873	-1.125	-1.595	-1.833	-2.123	-2.606	-3.088
	(2.795)	(1.561)	(2.788)	(2.638)	(2.500)	(2.522)	(2.707)	(2.885)	(3.161)	(3.723)	(4.580)
URn	0.0314*	-0.0141*	0.0532**	0.0473**	0.0441**	0.0402**	0.0330*	0.0293	0.0248	0.0173	0.00984
	(0.0178)	(0.00762)	(0.0228)	(0.0202)	(0.0193)	(0.0189)	(0.0182)	(0.0182)	(0.0184)	(0.0192)	(0.0209)
Year	-0.0362	0.0105	-0.0526*	-0.0481*	-0.0458*	-0.0428*	-0.0374	-0.0346	-0.0313	-0.0257	-0.0201
	(0.0256)	(0.0135)	(0.0301)	(0.0276)	(0.0259)	(0.0253)	(0.0253)	(0.0261)	(0.0275)	(0.0313)	(0.0372)
Constant	87.27***	-7.550	99.00***	95.80***	94.12***	92.02***	88.12***	86.14***	83.73**	79.72**	75.72*
	(29.29)	(17.49)	(31.73)	(28.29)	(27.42)	(27.11)	(28.78)	(30.63)	(33.59)	(39.87)	(45.97)
Observations	150	150	150	150	150	150	150	150	150	150	150

Robust standard errors in parentheses, *** $p < 0.01$, ** $p < 0.05$, * $p < 0.1$

Source: Research by authors, 2024.

Table 22.5 Impact of GVC participation on land issues.

	(1)	(2)	(3)	(4)	(5)	(6)	(7)	(8)	(9)	(10)	(11)
Variables	**Li**	**LI**	**LI**	**LI**	**LI**	**LI**	**LI**	**LI**	**LI**	**LI**	**LI**
GVC	1.730***	-0.463	2.596*	2.142**	1.860***	1.613***	1.495***	1.429***	1.369***	1.251***	1.110***
	(0.576)	(0.441)	(1.377)	(0.930)	(0.689)	(0.508)	(0.440)	(0.408)	(0.397)	(0.396)	(0.414)
GDPn	0.0106	0.0622	-0.106	-0.0447	-0.00690	0.0263	0.0422	0.0511	0.0590	0.0749	0.0939*
	(0.120)	(0.0926)	(0.304)	(0.196)	(0.144)	(0.0999)	(0.0805)	(0.0699)	(0.0631)	(0.0539)	(0.0502)
PSn	2.419	-3.805***	9.530*	5.804	3.490	1.462	0.488	-0.0552	-0.540	-1.511	-2.668**
	(2.004)	(1.334)	(5.316)	(3.735)	(2.642)	(1.882)	(1.532)	(1.358)	(1.304)	(1.273)	(1.157)
URn	-0.0110	0.00642	-0.0230	-0.0167	-0.0128	-0.00937	-0.00772	-0.00681	-0.00599	-0.00435	-0.00240
	(0.00808)	(0.00644)	(0.0204)	(0.0138)	(0.00982)	(0.00698)	(0.00589)	(0.00546)	(0.00515)	(0.00496)	(0.00558)
Year	-0.0369	0.0540**	-0.138*	-0.0849	-0.0521	-0.0233	-0.00947	-0.00175	0.00513	0.0189	0.0353**
	(0.0296)	(0.0213)	(0.0784)	(0.0568)	(0.0394)	(0.0269)	(0.0211)	(0.0183)	(0.0170)	(0.0160)	(0.0153)
Constant	32.68	-45.55**	117.8	73.20	45.50	21.22	9.562	3.058	-2.747	-14.36	-28.22**
	(28.59)	(21.73)	(74.53)	(54.53)	(37.65)	(25.01)	(19.08)	(16.36)	(14.56)	(12.78)	(13.04)
Observations	150	150	150	150	150	150	150	150	150	150	150

Robust standard errors in parentheses, *** $p < 0.01$, ** $p < 0.05$, * $p < 0.1$

Source: Research by authors, 2024.

Table 22.6 Impact of GVC participation on forest issues.

	(1)	(2)	(3)	(4)	(5)	(6)	(7)	(8)	(9)	(10)	(11)
Variables	**FI**	**FI**	**FI**	**FI**	**FI**	**FI**	**FI**	**FI**	**FI**	**FI**	**FI**
GVC	0.237	-0.0252	0.270	0.264	0.257	0.247	0.234	0.221	0.216	0.209	0.198
	(0.269)	(0.0539)	(0.299)	(0.293)	(0.286)	(0.277)	(0.268)	(0.261)	(0.259)	(0.258)	(0.256)
GDPn	0.0131	-0.0278***	0.0499	0.0432	0.0351	0.0249	0.0101	-0.00385	-0.00937	-0.0171	-0.0299
	(0.0296)	(0.00809)	(0.0323)	(0.0310)	(0.0315)	(0.0308)	(0.0302)	(0.0301)	(0.0301)	(0.0315)	(0.0322)
PSn	0.810	-0.108	0.953	0.927	0.896	0.856	0.798	0.744	0.722	0.692	0.642
	(0.835)	(0.154)	(0.860)	(0.850)	(0.845)	(0.838)	(0.836)	(0.841)	(0.845)	(0.853)	(0.870)
URn	6.85e-05	-0.00135*	0.00185	0.00153	0.00113	0.000639	-7.88e-05	-0.000755	-0.00102	-0.00140	-0.00202
	(0.00191)	(0.000783)	(0.00239)	(0.00227)	(0.00214)	(0.00202)	(0.00191)	(0.00187)	(0.00188)	(0.00191)	(0.00201)
Year	-0.0186**	0.00273	-0.0222**	-0.0215**	-0.0207**	-0.0197**	-0.0183**	-0.0169*	-0.0164*	-0.0156	-0.0143
	(0.00919)	(0.00196)	(0.00936)	(0.00920)	(0.00925)	(0.00921)	(0.00924)	(0.00937)	(0.00943)	(0.00967)	(0.00998)
Constant	23.28***	-2.877*	27.09***	26.40***	25.56***	24.50***	22.97***	21.52***	20.95***	20.15***	18.82**
	(6.671)	(1.667)	(6.930)	(6.725)	(6.846)	(6.753)	(6.714)	(6.779)	(6.806)	(7.143)	(7.430)
Observations	150	150	150	150	150	150	150	150	150	150	150

Robust standard errors in parentheses, *** $p < 0.01$, ** $p < 0.05$, * $p < 0.1$

Source: Research by authors, 2024.

In general, it can be seen that GVC participation has a statistically significant negative effect on overall environmental performance at most (but not all) quantiles. A 1% increase in GVC participation correlates to an approximately 0.536–0.612% decrease in Environmental Index. The fact that this was consistent across quantiles means that there are still very likely common consequences of GVC participation regardless of a country's initial environmental performance, such as an increase in industrial activities, resource exploitation, or more relaxed regulatory requirements. These findings have similar conclusions to Baldwin and Lopez-Gonzalez [4] and Antweiler et al. [3] about trade, GVC participation and the environmental implications of participation in developing countries.

The adverse effect of participation in GVCs on air quality is enhanced at higher quantiles of air quality, with a 1% increase in GVC participation associated with an increase in air quality deterioration of between 4.067% and 4.213%. This generally implies that as countries become further engaged in GVCs and possibly worse air quality, it will be harder for them to control air quality deterioration, likely due to higher emissions and pollution from industry as transport activities with goods further contribute to transportation-related pollution or pollution relocation from certain industries to emerging economies. These findings are consistent with the findings of Copeland and Taylor [6] and Cole and Elliott [5] who examined the relationship between air pollution and international trade.

GVC participation has a negative effect on waste management, which becomes emphatic in the higher quantiles. For our result at the highest quantile a 1% increase in GVC participation is associated with 5.906% deterioration in waste quality. This shows that countries with waste management compromised are more sensitive to the negative impacts of GVC participation, possibly due to increased industrial waste volumes, imperfect disposal methods, and no recyclables collection methods. This supports an area of study by Duan et al. [7] and Sigman (2002) about GVC participation, its international spillovers on pollution, and waste.

GVC participation holds no statistically significant effect on forest-related EIs across all quantiles. However, GVCs could impact forests and associated EIs and still convey indirect effects via changes in land-use for agriculture or infrastructure based on supporting GVCs. The relationship among GVCs, forest, and environmental impacts is complex, and studies such as Hosonuma et al. [12] and Meyfroidt et al.'s [21] investigated drivers of deforestation and land-use displacement for international trade.

Contrary to expectations, GVC participation has a positive effect on land-related EIs of 0.237% - 0.270% for each 1% increase in participation. Following these findings, we can suggest that greater participation in GVCs will lead to greater pressure on land resources which may lead to land degradation, soil pollution or changes in land ensure how land was previously used. The positive relationship we discovered between GVC participation, and the environment strongly indicated the unexpected ways in which both the process of economic integration and GVC participation may lead to environmental signals. Any land policy that is to engage ASEAN member states that are involved in GVCs should take account of the complicated nature of land issues arising from participation in GVCs.

The current findings demonstrate the complicated nature of GVC participation's impact on environmental quality in ASEAN countries. It is worth noting the differentiated effects on the environmental indicators that were examined, which supports the need for a nuanced and complex approach to environmental quality management in ASEAN as global economic integration continues to deepen.

Conclusion

Global value chain involvement and environmental issues (Eis) are parts of broader EIs of concern across countries in the Association of Southeast Asian Nations (ASEAN) nations from 2007 to 2021. This study utilized a quantile regression model of panel data collected from 10 ASEAN countries. Our baseline information for each of the countries came from the 2020 database of input-output information of the Asian Development Bank (ADB), the World Bank (WB), and the United Nations Conference on Trade and Development (UNCTAD). Based on variables from these databases, the a-regression addresses the influence of involvement in GVCs second aggregate effect on EIs, air issues (AI), waste issues (WI), forest issues (FI), and land issues (LI).

The outcomes revealed a complex interplay between GVC involvement and environmental consequences. GVC participation invariably exhibited a negative impact on overall environmental performance; a 1% increase was linked to a 0.536–0.612% reduction in the Environmental Index. The adverse effect on air quality escalated with higher GVC engagement, with a 1% rise in participation corresponding to a 4.067–4.213% degradation. Likewise, GVC participation negatively affected waste management, especially at higher quantiles, showing a 5.906% decline at the uppermost quantile for a 1% increase. Interestingly, no statistically significant effect was found on forest-related issues. Contrary to expectations, GVC participation showed a positive effect on land-related environmental issues, with a 1% increase associated with a 0.237–0.270% increase in land problems.

These findings have significant implications for ASEAN policymakers, underscoring the need for a multifaceted approach to environmental management in the context of increasing global economic integration, highlighting the importance of targeted policies addressing specific challenges, particularly in air quality, waste management, and land use. As ASEAN countries continue to integrate into GVCs, implementing strategies that balance economic growth with environmental sustainability is crucial, potentially through stricter regulations, improved waste management infrastructure, and sustainable land use practices.

While this study offers valuable insights into the relationship between GVC participation and EIs in ASEAN, it has several limitations. The data, sourced from varying systems, may be inconsistent, especially in countries with weaker data collection. The 2007–2021 timeframe may not capture long-term trends, and country-level data can obscure local differences, leading to potential aggregation bias. Moreover, the study shows correlations without proving causality and treats GVC participation uniformly. Future research should focus on sub-national analyses, longer-term studies, and additional variables to better understand GVCs' environmental impacts.

References

[1] Aldieri, L., & Vinci, C. P. (2017). The Role of technology spillovers in the process of water pollution abatement for large international firms. *Sustainability*, 9(5), 868. https://doi.org/10.3390/su9050868.

[2] Ando, M., Kazunobu, H., & Fukunari, K. (2023). Supply chain decoupling: geopolitical debates and economic dynamism in East Asia. *Asian Economic Policy Review*, 19(1), 62–79. https://doi.org/10.1111/aepr.12439.

[3] Antweiler, W., Brian, R. C., & Taylor, M. S. (2001). Is free trade good for the environment? *American Economic Review*, 91(4), 877–908. https://doi.org/10.1257/aer.91.4.877.

[4] Baldwin, R., & Lopez-Gonzalez, J. (2015). Supply-chain trade: a portrait of global patterns and several testable hypotheses. *The World Economy*, 38(11), 1682–1721. https://doi.org/10.1111/twec.12189.

[5] Cole, M. A., & Elliott, R. J. R. (2003). Determining the trade–environment composition effect: the role of capital, labor and environmental regulations. *Journal of Environmental Economics and Management*, 46(3), 363–383. https://doi.org/10.1016/S0095-0696(03)00021-4.

[6] Copeland, B. R., & Taylor, M. S. (2004). Trade, growth, and the environment. *Journal of Economic Literature*, 42(1), 7–71. https://doi.org/10.1257/002205104773558047.

[7] Duan, Y., Ji, T., & Yu, T. (2021). Reassessing pollution haven effect in global value chains. *Journal of Cleaner Production*, 284(October), 124705. https://doi.org/10.1016/j.jclepro.2020.124705.

[8] Bo, M., & Xu, A. (2021). Rising risks to global value chains. In Global Value Chain Development Report: Beyond Production, (pp. 134–78). Asian Development Bank. http://dx.doi.org/10.22617/TCS210400-2.

[9] Food and Agriculture Organization of the United Nations (FAO). (2020). Global forest resources assessment 2020 – Key findings. FAO. https://doi.org/10.4060/ca8753en.

[10] Gamarra, A. R., Banacloche, S., Lechón, Y., & Rio, P. D. (2023). Assessing the sustainability impacts of concentrated solar power deployment in Europe in the context of global value chains. *Renewable and Sustainable Energy Reviews*, 171(January), 113004. https://doi.org/10.1016/j.rser.2022.113004.

[11] Gereffi, G., & Fernandez-Stark, K. (2016). Global value chain analysis: A primer (2nd ed.). Durham, NC: Duke Center on Globalization, Governance & Competitiveness. Duke University. https://dukespace.lib.duke.edu/items/e8010f4b-90c9-4835-bc54-16422bb7efb6.

[12] Hosonuma, N., Herold, M., De Sy, V., De Fries, R. S., Brockhaus, M., Verchot, L., et al. (2012). An assessment of deforestation and forest degradation drivers in developing countries. *Environmental Research Letters*, 7(4), 044009. https://doi.org/10.1088/1748-9326/7/4/044009.

[13] Hotelling, H. (1933). Analysis of a complex of statistical variables into principal components. *Journal of Educational Psychology*, 24(6), 417. https://doi.org/10.1037/h0071325.

[14] Intergovernmental Panel on Climate Change (IPCC). (2019). Climate change and land: An IPCC special report on climate change, desertification, land degradation, sustainable land management, food security, and greenhouse gas fluxes in terrestrial ecosystems. IPCC. https://www.ipcc.ch/srccl/.

[15] Kedir, Abbi. (2008). Health and Wages: Panel Evidence on Men and Women using IV Quantile Regression. Department of Economics, University of Leicester, Discussion Papers in Economics.

[16] Kong, E., & Xia, Y. (2012). A single-index quantile regression model and its estimation. *Econometric Theory*, 28(4), 730–768. https://doi.org/10.1017/S0266466611000788.

[17] Li, W. (2014). Risk Assessment of Power Systems: Models, Methods, and Applications. John Wiley & Sons. https://doi.org/10.1002/9781118849972.

[18] Liu, L., Johnson, H. L., Cousens, S., Perin, J., Scott, S., Lawn, J. E., et al. (2012). Global, regional, and national causes of child mortality: an updated systematic analysis for 2010 with time trends since 2000. *The Lancet*, 379(9832), 2151–2161. https://doi.org/10.1016/S0140-6736(12)60560-1.

[19] Margalit, D., Rabinoff, J., & Rolen, L. (2017). Interactive linear algebra, (p. 18). Georgia Institute of Technology.

[20] Martínez-Zarzoso, I. (2017). Gender Gap in Entrepreneurship and Firm Performance in Developing Countries (No. 2017/14).

[21] Meyfroidt, P., Rudel, T. K., & Lambin, E. F. (2010). Forest transitions, trade, and the global displacement of land use. *Proceedings of the National Academy of Sciences*, 107(49), 20917–20922. https://doi.org/10.1073/pnas.1014773107.

[22] Nawaz, A., & Rahman, M. M. (2024). Global value chains participation and environmental degradation in SAARC economies. *Environment, Development and Sustainability*, 26(6), 15595–15617. https://doi.org/10.1007/s10668-023-03265-2.

[23] Organization for Economic Cooperation and Development OECD (2013). Interconnected Economies: Benefiting from Global Value Chains. OECD Publishing. https://doi.org/10.1787/9789264189560-en.

[24] United Nations Environment Programme (2019). Global Chemicals Outlook II: From Legacies to Innovative Solutions. UNEP - UN Environment Programme. https://www.unep.org/resources/report/global-chemicals-outlook-ii-legacies-innovative-solutions. (Accessed September 22, 2024).

[25] WHO (2022). World Health Organisation. Retrieved from Air Pollution: https://www.who.int/health-topics/air-pollution#tab=tab_1.

23 Factors influencing the decision to apply green supply chain in Vietnam's fast moving consumer goods industry

Lan Anh Nguyen[a] and Quynh Anh Pham[b]

Faculty of International Business and Economics, University of Economics and Business, Vietnam National University, Vietnam

Abstract

Given the current state and strong growth prospects of the Fast Moving Consumer Goods (FMCG) sector in Vietnam, along with the present and future trend of greening supply chains (SC), this study identifies, analyzes, evaluates, and ranks four groups of factors and 15 key sub-factors driving the implementation of Green Supply Chains (GSC) in Vietnam's FMCG sector based on their levels of impact. Through the application of FAHP-based-scheme (fuzzy analytic hierarchy process), the findings reveal that the factors influencing the decision to adopt GSC ranked in descending order of impact are external pressures, sustainable performance, industry-specific factors, and internal pressures. Within the "external pressures" group, "consumer pressure" exerts the greatest influence; in the "sustainable performance" group, "operational performance" ranks highest. For "industry-specific factors", "green production" has the most significant impact, while "management commitment" is the most influential sub-factor under "internal pressures". Based on these findings and lessons from Sweden and China, the study proposes several solutions to drive the implementation of sustainable supply chain initiatives among FMCG enterprises in Vietnam.

Keywords: FMCG industry, fuzzy analytic hierarchy process, green supply chain

Introduction

The expansion of international trade has significantly heightened the role of supply chain (SC). However, the rapid development of global SCs presents substantial environmental challenges, as over 90% of a company's environmental impact originates from its SC (Kingsley, [42]). Notably, due to the ripple effect, SCs generate far greater environmental impacts than companies' direct activities. Specifically, SCs in the FMCG sector are responsible for impacts that are 11.5 times higher in retail, 19 times higher in personal and household consumer goods, and 24 times higher in food and beverage companies (McKinsey & Company, [47]). Moreover, pressures from governments, customers, businesses, NGOs, media, investors, and employees have driven supply chain management (SCM) to adopt eco-conscious sustainable practices. The FMCG sector in Vietnam is a dynamic and youthful industry that grows at an annual rate of 7-8%, significantly outpacing the global average of 3–5%. With its crucial role in national consumption, rapid development, and significant environmental impact, the development and management of green supply chains (GSC) in Vietnam's FMCG sector have become increasingly urgent. This is essential for achieving economic benefits while protecting the environment and national resources, contributing to Vietnam's commitment to net-zero emissions made at COP26. Given these reasons, GSC and GSCM (green supply chain management) have become a pressing need within the FMCG industry, warranting extensive research and application across various sectors and territories.

Previous studies have concentrated on GSC elements including green design, green production, managing product returns, and efficiently handling waste to reduce environmental harm. SCM researchers and experts, including Gilbert [11], Zhu et al. [26], Dey and Cheff [8], Mohanty [51]; Sharma et al. [18]; and H. Nozari, F.H. Lotfi, & E. Najafi [52], have all supported the adoption of GSC, asserting its effectiveness as an advanced management tool that benefits both businesses and the environment. However, there is a significant gap in research concerning green supply chains in the global FMCG sector, and no studies in Vietnam have explored this topic. This gap exists despite the significant prospects and importance of both GSC and FMCG for Vietnam's and the global economy.

[a]anhnl@vnu.edu.vn, [b]phamquynhanhtn2003@gmail.com

DOI: 10.4324/9781003739982-23

The study intends to investigate, identify, evaluate, and rank the critical variables affecting the decision to adopt GSC in the FMCG sector. To achieve this, the theoretical framework (presented in Section 2) forms the basis for formulating the model of inquiry. The FAHP method is employed to analyze, evaluate, and rank these factors based on their level of impact. The remaining sections of the study include Section 3 research methodology, Section 4 results and discussion, Section 5 recommendations for promoting GSC in Vietnam's FMCG sector, based on international experiences, and Section 6 conclusion.

Literature Review

Green supply chain

Since the early 1990s, research on GSC has gained momentum globally as the negative environmental impacts of economic activities have become increasingly severe (Mohanty and Prakash, 2013). GSC is defined as a SC that operates efficiently while remaining environmentally friendly and utilizing natural ecological resources effectively [28]. Traditional SCs have shown significant limitations in adapting to the agreed principles of the United Nations (e.g., land and ocean conservation, sustainable use, fair sharing of benefits) United Nations [21] and aligning with the goals of modern industries, which increasingly incorporate environmental protection initiatives. GSC helps mitigate negative impacts throughout the logistics chain to create a low-environmental-impact system [17]. GSC initiatives offer distinct competitive advantages, such as lower costs, greener products, and reduced environmental burdens. GSCM is instrumental in facilitating the transition from traditional procurement chains to GSCs within the economy. The term GSCM arose from incorporating environmental concerns into SCM to achieve sustainable competitive advantages with less waste, thereby reducing costs and enhancing the industry's reputation [19, 13]. The core of greening supply chains lies in generating demand for greener products (H. Nozari, F.H. Lotfi, and E. Najafi, [52]).

Green supply chains are fundamental components of sustainable development objectives within businesses. At the micro level, adopting GSC demonstrates an organization's obligation to safeguard the environment and uphold social ethics, enhancing brand image and creating a competitive advantage [24]. Additionally, it ensures compliance with environmental regulations, reducing risks associated with environmental liabilities [26]. Striking a balance between economic goals and social responsibility supports long-term stability and sustainable growth for businesses [4]. GSCM also drives companies to adopt new technologies and improve production processes, optimizing operational performance and responding flexibly to market demands [9]. Furthermore, GSC generates positive diffusion effects, encouraging small and medium-sized enterprises (SMEs) to enforce more effective environmental protection measures [11]. From a cost perspective, GSCM helps businesses save resources through strategies such as reuse and recycling [19]. It also strengthens partnerships to build a sustainable value chain, fostering long-term development (Ghobadian, [35]) [12]. At the macro level, GSCM assists governments in evaluating the overall international competitiveness of a country's industrial sectors [11]. From an environmental perspective, businesses adopting GSCM can implement strategies such as product life cycle analysis to identify and minimize environmental impacts throughout production cycles [25]. Shifting to renewable energy sources not only cuts carbon emissions but also strengthens supply chain sustainability [6]. From a social standpoint, GSCM adoption raises environmental awareness [23], protects public health (Porter & Van der Linde, [56]), and creates millions of new jobs in related fields [7].

FMCG industry

Fast-moving consumer goods (FMCG) are items that are purchased frequently marked by high turnover often yielding minimal profit margins (Kotler and Armstrong, [44]; Menidjel et al., [49]). These products contribute substantially to the international economy (Olutimehin et al., [53]). In an unpredictable environment marked by intense competition and low consumer loyalty to individual brands, businesses must continually adjust pricing and marketing strategies (Kotler & Keller, [45]).

Amid increasing environmental concerns and the expanding operations of FMCG companies, GSCM has emerged as a vital tool and an essential goal for the FMCG sector (Nozari, et al., [52]). Given the diverse range of products classified as essentials Aljunaidi and Ankrak [1], SCM poses significant challenges for FMCG companies [3]. Efficient SCM is a decisive factor for success in the industry, as it directly impacts timely delivery and product quality (Mentzer et al., [50]). Limited studies focus on key GSCM domains in the FMCG industry, including: inventory control, efficiency of distribution networks, and integration of technology (Olutimehin et al., [53]). Other studies further discuss factors like environmental management of organizations, pressures from competition and regulations, green design and purchasing, green manufacturing, cold storage facilities, performance metrics (economic, environmental, operational), eco-friendly transportation, and partnerships between suppliers and customers (Nozari, Lotfi, Najafi, [52]).

Factors influencing the decision to apply GSC in the FMCG industry in Vietnam

Regarding the factors influencing the decision to adopt GSC, green design, eco-friendly distribution, and environmental training constructively impact the capability to effectively implement GSC [10]. Zhu et al. [62] focus on three major components of GSCM in manufacturing enterprises in China, (a) external relationships, (b) investment recovery, and (c) wider engagements focused on sustainable design approaches. Mohanty (2014) developed a model comprising three groups of factors - external pressures, internal pressures, and firm-specific characteristics - that influence GSCM in MSMEs (micro, small, and medium enterprises) in India. Additionally, GSCM activities are impacted by internal supporting factors, including organizational environmental control systems and sustainable IT systems, alongside external components in the pharmaceutical sector in India [14]. Key GSCM KPIs, such as eco-friendly production, sustainable procurement, green logistics practices including distribution and reverse logistics, contributing to enhanced profits, improved quality assurance and delivery performance, and reduced transportation costs, ultimately improving profit margins (Imam, Rahman, and Ali, [37]).

Based on previous studies, the author proposes 15 factors influencing the decision to adopt GSC in the FMCG industry in Vietnam, including:

- Organizational cultural management regards the process by which members of the organization proactively consider environmental factors in business strategy and operations to minimize negative environmental impacts.
- Management commitment: demonstrates the positive attitude and dedication of leaders throughout the organization to promote green initiatives and environmental protection in the supply chain. When leadership shows strong commitment, it creates momentum throughout the organization to implement green strategies and uphold environmental standards.
- Competitive pressure: refers to the pressure from competitors, compelling companies to integrate green initiatives into their supply chains in order to maintain or enhance their market position.
- Regulatory pressure: refers to the pressures that organizations face from external sources, particularly from government agencies, legal frameworks, regulations, and authoritative organizations. These pressures force organizations to comply with specific rules, policies, or laws.
- Shareholder pressure: due to the increasing environmental awareness of stakeholders, including shareholders, companies are constantly under pressure to enhance their corporate image and improve their market competitiveness through the innovation of green products.
- Consumer pressure: The growing consumer interest in sustainability has forced companies to adjust their strategies to meet this demand, from selecting materials to managing production and transportation processes.
- Green marketing: refers to when companies focus on marketing strategies that help protect the environment, encouraging consumers to purchase green products with minimal negative impact on the ecosystem.
- Green design: This factor pertains to design aspects such as choosing sustainable materials, designing and redesigning packaging, saving resources, controlling pollution, and managing wastes.
- Eco-friendly manufacturing: denotes environmentally friendly manufacturing processes utilizing resources and energy efficiently, minimizing waste and pollution, while applying technologies and techniques to reduce negative environmental impacts.

Table 23.1 Factors influencing the decision to apply GSC in the FMCG industry in Vietnam.

Factor group	Factor	Sources
Internal pressures (IP)	Organizational cultural management (IP1)	Porter and Linde [56]; Christmann [31]; H.Nozari et al. [52]
	Management commitment (IP2)	Zhu and Sarkis [24]; Daily and Huang [32]
External pressures (EP)	Competitive pressure (EP1)	Porter and Linde [56]; Zhu and Sarkis [24]; Walker et al. [61]; Qu and Liu [41]
	Regulatory pressure (EP2)	Zhu and Sarkis [24]; Zhu and Sarkis [27]; Nozari et al. [52]
	Shareholder pressure (EP3)	L. Rivera, N. Ortiz, G. Moreno và I Páez-Gabriunas [58]
	Consumer pressure (EP4)	Peloza and Hassay [39]; McKinsey & Company [48]
Industry-specific factors (IsF)	Green marketing (IsF1)	Ottman et al. [55]
	Green design (IsF2)	Zhu and Sarkis [24]; Seuring and Müller [59]; Nozari et al. [52]
	Green manufacturing (IsF3)	Zhu and Sarkis [24]; Rao and Holt [57]; Deif [34]
	Cold storage (IsF4)	H.Nozari et al. [52]
	Green transportation (IsF5)	McKinnon [46]; DHL [33]; Wang et al. (2013)
Sustainable performance (SP)	Operational performance (SP1)	Beamon [29]; Sarkis (2001) Chiu et al. (2017)
	Economic performance (SP2)	The Economist (2018); Nozari et al. [52]
	Environmental performance (SP3)	Klassen et al. [43]; Nozari et al. [52]
	Social performance (SP4)	Seuring and Müller [59]; Cohen et al. (2012); Walker and Jones [40]; Chiu et al. (2017)

Source: Author

- Cold storage: refers to efficiently using energy, implementing green refrigerants, cutting down emissions, addressing leakage issues in cold storage infrastructure, logistics vehicles, and warehouses to support eco-conscious cold chain logistics.
- Sustainable transportation: denotes approaches aimed at reducing logistics and storage expenses meanwhile enhancing ecological effectiveness, considering multiple elements like emission origins coupled with the aim to reduce fossil fuel consumption and reliance on petroleum-based sources.
- Operational productivity: is the measure of the capacity of a business to efficiently produce as well as deliver products to customers through improvements in capacity utilization, thereby enhancing overall effectiveness.
- Economic performance: relates to the enhancement of profits through cost reductions in raw material procurement, the reduction of costs associated with environmental penalties, energy usage across GSCM activities coupled with the expenses to incur waste treatment and elimination. Additionally, it also investigates whether the adoption of GSC creates challenges for novelty and how GSCM contributes to increased financial gains for the business.
- Environmental productivity: measures a company's ability to minimize its environmental impact by comparing it with industry standards.
- Social performance: denotes a company's capability to handle its social responsibilities as well as impacts throughout the distribution network activities, while also promoting sustainability.

The 15 factors are divided into 4 groups to establish the AHP Table 23.1 as follows:

Methodology

With the goal of ranking the variables shaping the implementation of the adoption of green supply chain practices in the FMCG sector based on their level of impact, the FAHP method is applied because AHP has certain limitations in handling ambiguity and uncertainty in expert assessments. By applying fuzzy logic to AHP, it

Table 23.2 The value of the random consistency index.

n	3	4	5	6	7	8	9	10
RI	0,525	0,90	0,11	1.25	1,35	1,40	1,45	1,49

Source: Saaty and Vargas [16]

Table 23.3 Fuzzy scale conversion value.

Linguistic term	Velue	Fuzzy number
Equal importance	1	(1,1,1)
Moderate importance	3	(2,3,4)
Strong importance	5	(4,5,6)
Extremely strong importance	7	(6,7,8)
Absolute importance	9	(8,9,10)
Intermediate values	2	(1,2,3)
	4	(3,4,5)
	6	(5,6,7)
	8	(7,8,9)

Source: Author

allows the representation of imprecise and unclear judgments and the mathematical manipulation of them (S. Opricovic, G.H. Tzeng, [54]).

After reviewing the literature to determine the factors for constructing the AHP model, the data collection method through interviews with FMCG company experts and managers is implemented. They are asked to compare two factors in terms of their importance or priority across 19 levels of evaluation [16]. The quantitative research process continues as follows:

Step 1: The experts' opinions are synthesized into pairwise comparison matrices representing the relative importance between criteria through the comparison of criterion pairs. Each component's numeric value within the matrix represents the level of importance of criterion i relative to criterion j.

	Factor 1	**Factor 2**	**Factor j**	**Factor n**
Factor 1	1			
Factor 2		1		
Factor i				
Factor n				1

To ensure that the expert evaluations are reasonable, the consistency index (CI) is first calculated using the following formula:

$$CI = \frac{\lambda_{max} - n}{n - 1}$$

in which, λ_{max} is the largest eigenvalue of matrix A. Then, the consistency ratio (CR) is evaluated by dividing the consistency index (CI) by the corresponding random consistency index (RI) in Table 23.2:

If $CR < 0.1$, the matrix is considered to have a reasonable level of consistency. However, according to Saaty and Kearns [15], in some situations where it is difficult to collect information, with too many interpretations, and it is not common for the respondents, as in the case of this study, a $CR < 20\%$ may be accepted.

Step 2: Applying Fuzzy logic.

First, the actual values from the pairwise comparison matrix are converted into fuzzy numbers. The fuzzy quantity is symbolized as a triplet (l, m, u), corresponding to the lower bound, the average value and the upper bound, as per the formula $\tilde{a}_{ij} = (l_{ij}, m_{ij}, u_{ij})$ in Table 23.3:

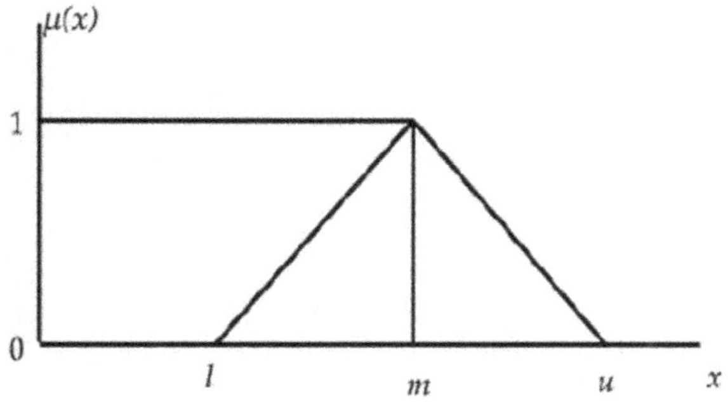

The pairwise comparison matrices are combined into one fuzzy reciprocal matrix with the form

$$\tilde{A} = \begin{bmatrix} \tilde{a}_{11} & \tilde{a}_{12} & \cdots & \tilde{a}_{1n} \\ \tilde{a}_{21} & \tilde{a}_{22} & \cdots & \tilde{a}_{2n} \\ \vdots & \vdots & \ddots & \vdots \\ \tilde{a}_{n1} & \tilde{a}_{n2} & \cdots & \tilde{a}_{nn} \end{bmatrix}$$

where each element $\tilde{a}_{ij}$ is a fuzzy triplet (l_{ij}, m_{ij}, u_{ij}) determined by the following formula (Huang et al. [36]):

$$\tilde{a}_{ij} = \left(\min_k (l_{ij}^k), \sqrt[k]{\prod_{k=1}^{k} m_{ij}^k}, \max_k (u_{ij}^k) \right)$$

Step 3: Evaluating the weights of the criteria

Utilizing the geometric mean technique, evaluate the fuzzy geometric mean value for each row i of the fuzzy comparison matrix Ã. For the fuzzy triangular number $\tilde{a}_{ij} = (l_{ij}, m_{ij}, u_{ij})$, the fuzzy geometric mean of row i is calculated using the following formula:

$$\tilde{G}_i = \left(\prod_{j=1}^{n} l_{ij}\right)^{\frac{1}{n}}, \left(\prod_{j=1}^{n} m_{ij}\right)^{\frac{1}{n}}, \left(\prod_{j=1}^{n} u_{ij}\right)^{\frac{1}{n}}$$

Next, after obtaining the fuzzy geometric mean $\tilde{G}_i = (l_{ij}, m_{ij}, u_{ij})$ for each row i the fuzzy weigh $\tilde{w}_i$ of criterion i is calculated by normalizing the geometric mean values:

$$\tilde{W}_i = \left(\frac{l_i}{\sum_{i=1}^{n} l_i}, \frac{m_i}{\sum_{i=1}^{n} m_i}, \frac{u_i}{\sum_{i=1}^{n} u_i} \right)$$

After calculating the fuzzy weights $\tilde{w}_i$, defuzzification is employed to compute the crisp weight for each evaluation factor using the weighted average method.

Table 23.4 Respondents characteristics.

	Characteristic	Frequency	Rate
Gender	Male	4	20
	Female	16	80
Age	25-30 years old	7	35
	31 – 40 years old	12	60
	41 – 50 years old	1	5
Educational level	Bachelor's degree (Engineer)	17	85
	Master's degree	3	15
Years of experience	2 – 11 years	12	60
	11 – 20 years	8	40
Position	Specialist	2	10
	Leader	5	25
	Manager	11	55
	Director	2	10

Source: Author

$$W_i = \frac{l_i + m_i + u_i}{3}$$

Finally, the normalization of weights helps bring all weights to the same scale, making comparison easier and ensuring that the sum of the normalized weights equals 1, using the following formula:

$$w_i = \frac{W_i}{\sum_{j=1}^{n} W_j}$$

Result and Discussion

Result

After sending the questionnaires to survey participants, the author collected 30 responses from managers at various levels in FMCG companies in Vietnam, as well as experts on supply chain operations in the FMCG sector. The surveys collected were carefully reviewed, and those of insufficient quality were excluded. As a result, 20 qualified responses were acquired for analysis. Table 23.4 describes the characteristics of the survey respondents:

After checking the consistency of the comparison matrices and removing the questionnaires with matrices that did not meet the CR < 20% requirement, 15 questionnaires remained with matrices that all met the consistency standard. These matrices will be converted into fuzzy scales and combined into corresponding reciprocal matrices. The author will proceed to calculate the weights for each criterion, reflecting the level of influence of each factor on the decision to adopt GSC in the FMCG industry in Vietnam. The findings are shown in Tables 23.5 and 23.6:

After normalizing the weights from the defuzzified weights, the ranking of the impact levels of key elements affecting the implementation of GSC within the FMCG industry is specifically presented in Table 23.7:

Discussion

The research outcomes shown in Table .4 reveal that when deciding to adopt GSC, FMCG companies are most influenced by "external pressures" (38%) and "sustainable performance" (29%). In contrast, "industry-specific factors" and "internal pressures" have less impact, accounting for 17% and 16% of the influence, respectively.

"External pressures" exerts the strongest influence, consistent with studies by Zhu and Sarkis [24], Mohanty and Prakash (2013), and Nozari et al. [52]. Among these, "consumer pressure" plays a vital role (Mohanty and Prakash, 2013) [14]. According to recent market research in Vietnam, consumers increasingly prioritize environmental issues and adopt sustainable consumption habits, encouraging companies to develop eco-friendly

Table 23.5 Reciprocal matrix at the factor level.

a. "Internal pressures" group

	IP1	IP2	Defuzzified weight
IP1	1	-	1.2
IP2	(0.17, 1.37, 7)	1	1.34

b. "External pressures" group

	EP1	EP2	EP3	EP4	Defuzzified weight
EP1	1	-	-	-	0.63
EP2	(0.25, 1.08, 5)	1	-	-	0.78
EP3	(0.14, 0.25, 0.5)	(0.125, 0.33, 2)	1	-	0.2
EP4	(0.5, 1.72, 10)	(0.25, 2.22, 7)	(2, 4.17, 10)	1	1.16

c. "Industry-specific factors" group

	IsF1	IsF2	IsF3	IsF4	IsF5	Defuzzified weight
IsF1	1	-	-	-	-	0.64
IsF2	(0.17, 2.1, 8)	1	-	-	-	0.75
IsF3	(0.5, 3.03 ,8)	(0.5, 1.86, 5)	1	-	-	0.99
IsF4	(0.2, 0.5, 4)	(0.14, 0.74, 4)	(0.14, 0,23, 0.5)	1	-	0.36
IsF5	(0.17, 0.88, 5)	(0.17, 0.62, 4)	(0.14, 0.3, 2)	(0.5, 1.32, 4)	1	0.55

d. "Sustainable performance" group

	SP1	SP2	SP3	SP4	Defuzzified weight
SP1	1	-	-	-	0.33
SP2	(0.5, 2.94, 6)	1	-	-	0.77
SP3	(0.5, 2.78, 6)	(0.17, 0.24, 0.5)	1	-	0.34
SP4	(0.5, 3.23, 8)	(0.25, 0.64, 2)	(0.5, 1.72, 4)	1	0.6

Source: Author

Table 23.6 Reciprocal matrix at the group factor level.

	IP	EP	IsF	SP	Defuzzified weight
IP	1	-	-	-	0.33
EP	(0.5, 2.94, 6)	1	-	-	0.77
IsF	(0.5, 2.78, 6)	(0.17, 0.24, 0.5)	1	-	0.34
SP	(0.5, 3.23, 8)	(0.25, 0.64, 2)	(0.5, 1.72, 4)	1	0.6

Source: Author

Table 23.7 Ranking of factors influencing the decision to apply GSC in the FMCG industry in Vietnam.

Factor group	Normalized weights	Factor	Internal normalized weights	Ranking
EP	0.38	EP1	0.23	3
		EP2	0.28	2
		EP3	0.07	4
		EP4	0.42	1
SP	0.29	SP1	0.3	1
		SP2	0.29	2
		SP3	0.15	4
		SP4	0.26	3
IsF	0.17	EF1	0.2	3
		EF2	0.23	2
		EF3	0.3	1
		EF4	0.11	5
		EF5	0.17	4
IP	0.16	IP1	0.47	2
		IP2	0.53	1

Source: Author

Table 23.8 Proposed solutions.

Factor	Measures			
	For the government		For enterprises	For other stakeholders
EP4	Consumer pressure	- Raise consumer awareness through communication and education.	- Raising consumer awareness through communication	*For consumers:* Actively seek information and practice green consumption.
EP2	Regulatory pressure	- Improve the environmental legal system. - Designe plans and development roadmaps focusing on the specific requirements and changes at each development stage.		
EP1	Competitive pressure	- Enact policies that support and offer incentives. - Create a level playing field, encouraging the participation of both domestic and foreign enterprises to drive innovation and the adoption of advanced GSC models.	- Competitive collaboration - Actively research and apply new technologies	
EP3	Shareholder pressure		- Attract strategic shareholders with a shared vision for green development - Encourage participation and contributions from shareholders	*For shareholders:* Actively learn about the role and necessity of transitioning to green business practices within companies

<table>
<tr><th>Factor</th><th colspan="4">Measures</th></tr>
<tr><th></th><th></th><th>For the government</th><th>For enterprises</th><th>For other stakeholders</th></tr>
<tr><td>SP1</td><td>Operational performance</td><td></td><td>Proactively research, implement, and evaluate GSC initiatives</td><td></td></tr>
<tr><td>SP2</td><td>Economic performance</td><td>Offer tax incentives and support packages for researching and implementing GSC.</td><td>Leverage tax benefits or financial support</td><td></td></tr>
<tr><td>SP4</td><td>Social performance</td><td>- Collaborate with businesses in social programs
- Honor leading businesses</td><td>Consider societal expectations and needs, such as contributions to the community, improving working conditions for employees, etc.</td><td>For consumers: Prioritize using products from brands that contribute to social projects.</td></tr>
<tr><td>SP3</td><td>Environmental performance</td><td colspan="2">Public-private partnership in environmental issues, promote technology transfer.</td><td></td></tr>
<tr><td>EF3</td><td>Green manufacturing</td><td rowspan="5">- Listen to the needs and initiatives from businesses
- Act as an intermediate to encourage stakeholders to collaborate on green initiatives
- Build infrastructure to support GSC.</td><td rowspan="5">- Collaborate and propose requirements and initiatives to improve each link in the chain.
- Encourage the direct participation of other stakeholders.
- Set internal goals aimed at greening various elements.</td><td rowspan="5">Actively participate in green initiatives</td></tr>
<tr><td>EF2</td><td>Green design</td></tr>
<tr><td>EF1</td><td>Green marketing</td></tr>
<tr><td>EF5</td><td>Green transportation</td></tr>
<tr><td>EF4</td><td>Cold storage</td></tr>
<tr><td>IP2</td><td>Management commitment</td><td></td><td>Leaders set specific green goals in the business plan.</td><td></td></tr>
<tr><td>IP1</td><td>Organizational cultural management</td><td></td><td>Organize training programs, raise awareness for employees, and create an environmentally friendly workplace.</td><td>For employees: Understand the role and necessity of a GSC in the company.</td></tr>
</table>

Source: Author

products and build a green image. "Regulatory pressure" is also significant, driven by regulations on waste management, the use of recycled materials, and emissions reduction from the government and international organizations. "Competitive pressure" ranks third. Practical evidence suggests that in Vietnam's highly competitive FMCG market, the GSC development policies of leading FMCG corporations during the same period show notable similarities. However, since GSC adoption requires long-term investment, not all companies can implement it immediately, resulting in a moderate level of influence. Finally, "shareholder pressure" is less impactful, as shareholders typically prioritize profits Straight [20], while green activities require significant investment and take time to yield clear economic benefits.

"Sustainable performance" ranks second, as it serves both as a goal and a benchmark for companies' green efforts, enhancing brand image, attracting customers and investors, and ensuring sustainable profits. Within this group, "operational performance" and "economic performance" are the most important, as they are directly linked to supply capacity, business expansion, and profit growth - fundamental corporate goals [22, 24]. In Vietnam, GSC adoption in the FMCG sector initially focuses on simple production processes as companies aim to cut costs and optimize operations. "Social performance" is also notable, as consumers increasingly favor businesses with strong social responsibility [2]. High social performance not only enhances brand reputation but also builds stakeholder trust, improves corporate culture, and boosts employee productivity. "Environmental performance" ranks lowest in this group, despite often being a priority in GSCM due to its role in enhancing competitiveness and regulatory compliance [24]. This result may reflect the specifics of Vietnam's FMCG market, where economic and social factors are prioritized.

"Industry-specific factors" ranks third due to their influence on each GSC link, with unique environmental management requirements for each link. Compared to "external pressure" and "sustainable performance", their impact is less comprehensive. Moreover, since most respondents are managers responsible for individual links, the average result tends to be neutral. Within this group, "green production" has the greatest impact. Since the early stages of GSC initiatives, Vietnamese FMCG companies have implemented GSCM starting with production, such as changing input materials, energy sources, and technologies in production lines. Additionally, the mass production requirements in FMCG mean that any process improvement can significantly reduce environmental impact. "Green design" ranks second, directly influencing product consumption, disposal, and customer purchasing decisions. "Green marketing" ranks third, as it communicates GSC goals and activities to customers, raising awareness and interest in sustainable products. "Cold storage" and "green transportation" have the least impact, likely because companies often outsource these services, reducing their focus on environmental processes and responsibilities [5].

"Internal pressures" rank last, as these factors primarily act as intermediaries, linking external pressures to GSCM practices, making their influence more indirect [14]. Within this group, "management commitment" has the greatest impact. In Vietnamese corporate culture, strategic decisions heavily depend on senior leadership. Strong commitment from leaders drives resource allocation and lays the foundation for green initiatives, which is particularly critical for SMEs - the majority in Vietnam's FMCG sector. Leadership commitment gradually fosters changes in corporate culture. Compared to "management commitment", "organizational cultural management" takes longer to develop.

Suggest Improvement Measures

Based on the factors influencing the decision to adopt GSC in Vietnam's FMCG industry (results presented in Section 4), combined with insights from sustainable initiatives and strong commitments by Swedish companies in utilizing recycled resources, as well as proactive transformations in China to enhance SC efficiency through technology adoption and process innovation, the proposed solutions for Vietnam are summarized as shown in Table 23.8:

Conclusion

This study aims to identify, analyze, evaluate, and rank the factors influencing the adoption of GSC in the FMCG industry in Vietnam based on their impact levels. Combining qualitative and quantitative methods, the research develops a theoretical model from literature and the industry's actual situation. The qualitative method is used to refine the measurement scale, while the quantitative survey targets 20 FMCG experts with a 19-point scale. The results show the factors in descending order of influence: external pressures, sustainable performance, industry-specific factors, and internal pressures. Among these, "consumer pressure" has the strongest impact (external pressures), "operational performance" is the most important (sustainable performances), "green manufacturing " leads (industry-specific factors), and "management commitment" has the most influence (internal pressures).

However, the study has limitations as it does not address other factors in the GSC of the FMCG industry, such as reverse logistics, green procurement or recycling. Furthermore, the survey focuses only on FMCG companies in three main sectors: food and beverages, personal and household care products, and healthcare products, and does not consider the specific influences of each sector. These limitations provide directions for future research.

References

[1] Aljunaidi, A., & Ankrak, S. (2014). The application of lean principles in the fast moving consumer goods (FMCG). *Journal of Operations and Supply Chain Management*, 2(2), 1–25. https://doi.org/10.22004/ag.econ.289410.

[2] Andalib Ardakani, D., Kiani, M., Saffari Darberazi, A., Zamzam, F., & Mofatehzadeh, E. (2024). An interval type-2 fuzzy AHP approach for success factors of green supply chain management. *International Journal of Research in Industrial Engineering*, 13(3), 237–256. https://doi.org/10.22105/riej.2024.441073.1416.

[3] Batra, R., & Sinha, I. (2000). Consumer-level factors moderating the success of private label brands. *Journal of Retailing*, 76(2), 175–191. https://doi.org/10.1016/S0022-4359(00)00027-0.

[4] Carter, C. R., & Rogers, D. S. (2008). A framework of sustainable supply chain management: moving toward new theory. *International Journal of Physical Distribution & Logistics Management*, 38(5), 360–387. http://dx.doi.org/10.1108/09600030810882816.

[5] Craggs, J. A. (2012). Maturity Assessment of Green Supply Chain Management in the South African FMCG industry. Thesis, University of Pretoria.

[6] Dahlmann, F., & Bullock, G. (2020). Nexus thinking in business: analyzing corporate responses to interconnected global sustainability challenges. *Environmental Science & Policy*, 114(4), 90–98. https://doi.org/10.1016/j.envsci.2020.02.022.

[7] Dahlmann, F., Branicki, L., & Brammer, S. (2019). Managing carbon aspirations: the influence of corporate climate change targets on environmental performance. *Journal of Business Ethics*, 158(1), 1–24. https://doi.org/10.1007/s10551-017-3731-z.

[8] Dey, P. K., & Cheff, W. (2012). Green supply chain performance measurement using the analytic hierarchy process: a comparative analysis of manufacturing organisations. *Production Planning & Control*, 24(8–9), 1–19. https://doi.org/10.1080/09537287.2012.666859.

[9] Dubey, R., Gunasekaran, A., Papadopoulos, T., & Wamba, S. F. (2017). Sustainable supply chain management: framework and further research directions. *Journal of Cleaner Production*, 142(5), 577–595. https://doi.org/10.1016/j.jclepro.2016.03.117.

[10] Epoh, R. L., Langton, I., & Mafini, C. (2024). A model for green supply chain management in the South African manufacturing sector. *Cogent Business & Management*, 11(1), 2390213. https://doi.org/10.1080/23311975.2024.2390213.

[11] Gilbert, S. (2001). Greening supply chain: Enhancing competitiveness through sustainable practices. *Environmental Quality Management*, 11(2), 13–21. https://doi.org/10.1002/tqem.1005.

[12] Govindan, K., & Bouzon, M. (2018). From a literature review to a multi-perspective framework for reverse logistics barriers and drivers. *Journal of Cleaner Production*, 187(2), 318–337. https://doi.org/10.1016/j.jclepro.2018.03.040.

[13] Sahoo, S., & Vijayvargy, L. (2021). Green supply chain management practices and sustainable performance in the Indian manufacturing industry: a structural equation modelling approach. *Journal of Manufacturing Technology Management*, 32(4), 862–886. https://doi.org/10.1108/JMTM-04-2020-0173.

[14] Sabat, K., Krishnamoorthy, B., & Bhattacharyya, S. S. (2023). Green drivers and green enablers in pharmaceuticals supply chain: in the context of an emerging economy. *The TQM Journal*, 35(6), 1349–1377. https://doi.org/10.1108/TQM-11-2021-0333.

[15] Saaty, T. L., & Kearns, K. P. (1985). The analytic hierarchy process. In Saaty, T. L., & Kearns, K. P. (Eds.), Analytical Planning, (pp. 19–62). Amsterdam: Elsevier.

[16] Saaty, T. L., & Vargas, L. G. (2012). Models, Methods, Concepts & Applications of the Analytic Hierarchy Process. New York: Springer Science & Business Media.

[17] Santos, C. C. R., Donato, V., Vianna, J. M. A., & Gomes, L. D. F. (2024). Green supply chain: the path to decarbonizing the supply chain. Preprints, no. 202406.0805.v1. https://doi.org/10.20944/preprints202406.0805.v1.

[18] Sharma, V. K., Chandna, P., & Bhardwaj, A. K. (2017). Green supply chain management related performance indicators in agro industry: a review. *Journal of Cleaner Production*, 141(9), 1194–1208. https://doi.org/10.1016/j.jclepro.2016.09.103.

[19] Srivastava, S. K. (2007). Green supply chain management: A stateoftheart literature review. *International Journal of Management Reviews*, 9(1), 53–80. https://doi.org/10.1111/j.1468-2370.2007.00202.x.

[20] Straight, B. (2024). Investor expectations influencing supply chain decisionmaking. Supply Chain Management Review. https://www.scmr.com/article/investor-expectations-influencing-supply-chain-decision-making (Accessed October 6, 2024).

[21] United Nations (2022). Report of the Conference of the Parties to the Convention on Biological Diversity on the Second Part of its Fifteenth Meeting (CBD/COP/15/7). United Nations. https://prod.drupal.www.infra.cbd.int/sites/default/files/2022-12/221222-CBD-PressRelease-COP15-Final.pdf (Accessed June 12, 2024).

[22] Van Hock, R. I., & Erasmus (2000). From reversed logistics to green supply chains. *Logistics Solutions*, 4(3), 129–135. https://doi.org/10.1108/13598549910279576.

[23] Zhu, Q., Sarkis, J., & Lai, K. H. (2013). Institutional-based antecedents and performance outcomes of internal and external green supply chain management practices. *Journal of Purchasing and Supply Management*, 19(2), 106–117. https://doi.org/10.1016/j.pursup.2012.12.001.

[24] Zhu, Q., & Sarkis, J. (2004). Relationships between operational practices and performance among early adopters of green supply chain management practices in Chinese manufacturing enterprises. *Journal of Operations Management*, 22(3), 265–289. https://doi.org/10.1016/j.jom.2004.01.005.

[25] Zhu, H., Duan, L., Guo, Y., & Yu, K. (2016). The effects of FDI, economic growth, and energy consumption on carbon emissions in ASEAN-5: evidence from panel quantile regression. *Economic Modelling*, 58(6), 237–248. https://doi.org/10.1016/j.econmod.2016.05.003.

[26] Zhu, Q., Geng, Y., Fujita, T., & Hashimoto, S. (2008). Firm-level correlates of green supply chain management practices in Chinese context. *Omega*, 36(4), 577–591. https://doi.org/10.1016/j.omega.2006.11.009.

[27] Zhu, Q., Sarkis, J., & Lai, K. H. (2007). Green supply chain management: pressures, practices and performance within the Chinese automobile industry. *Journal of Cleaner Production*, 15(11-12), 1041–1052. https://doi.org/10.1016/j.jclepro.2006.05.021.

[28] An Binh. 2021. Adapting Green Supply Chains to the Post-Covid-19 Context]. Vietnam Ministry of Industry and Trade. https://moit.gov.vn/phat-trien-ben-vung/ung-dung-chuoi-cung-ung-xanh-tich-ung-voi-boi-canh-hau-covid-19.html (accessed September 12, 2024).

[29] Beamon, B.M., 1999. "Measuring Supply Chain Performance" International Journal of Operations & Production Management 19, no. 3 (March): 275-292. https://doi.org/10.1108/01443579910249714

[30] Carter, C. R., and Rogers, D. S., 2008. "A framework of sustainable supply chain management: Moving toward new theory" International Journal of Physical Distribution & Logistics Management, no. 5 (June): 360–387. http://dx.doi.org/10.1108/09600030810882816

[31] Christmann, P., 2000. "Effects of Best Practices of Environmental Management on Cost Advantage: The Role of Complementary Assets" Academy of Management Journal 43, no. 4 (August): 663-680. http://dx.doi.org/10.2307/1556360

[32] Daily, B.F. and Huang, S., 2001. "Achieving Sustainability through Attention to Human Resource Factors in Environmental Management" International Journal of Operations & Production Management 21, no.12 (December): 1539-1552. http://dx.doi.org/10.1108/01443570110410892

[33] DHL. 2013. "Corporate Responsibility Report 2013" https://group.dhl.com/content/dam/deutschepostdhl/en/media-center/responsibility/dpdhl-corporate-responsibility-report-2013-complete.pdf (accessed June 2024)

[34] Dief, A. M., 2011. "A system model for green manufacturing" Advances in Production Engineering & Management 6, no. 1 (September): 27 - 36. https://doi.org/10.1016/J.JCLEPRO.2011.05.022

[35] Holt, D. and Ghobadian, A. (2009). "An Empirical Study of Green Supply Chain Management Practices Amongst UK Manufacturers" Journal of Manufacturing Technology Management 20, no 7 (September): 933-956. http://dx.doi.org/10.1108/17410380910984212

[36] Hsu, W. K. K., Lian, S. J. and Huang, S. H. S. (2020). "An assessment model based on a hybrid MCDM approach for the port choice of liner carriers" Research in Transportation Business & Management 34, (March): 100426. https://doi.org/10.1016/j.rtbm.2019.100426

[37] Imam, H., Rahman, H., and Ali, H. (2022). "Contributions of Green Supply Chain Management on perceived firm performance: An empirical investigation of the FMCG industry in Bangladesh" International Journal of Science and Business 11, no. 1 (April): 67–82. 10.5281/zenodo.6468354

[38] Irum, F., 2024. "Green supply chain management and sustainability: A proposed model of stakeholder pressure" Digital Management Sciences Journal 1, no. 2 (June): 132–42. 10.62854/dmsj.v1i2.25

[39] J. Peloza and D. N. Hassay, 2006. "Intra-Organizational Volunteerism: Good Soldiers, Good Deeds and Good Politics" Journal of Business Ethics 64, no. 4 (April): 357-379. http://dx.doi.org/10.1007/s10551-005-5496-z

[40] Jones, H., Jones, N., Shaxson, L. and Walker, D. 2012. Knowledge, Policy and Power in International Development: A Practical Guide. The Policy Press, Bristol.

[41] Kejin Qu and Zuoming Liu, 2022. "Green innovations, supply chain integration and green information system: A model of moderation" Journal of Cleaner Production 339, no.10 (March): 130557. http://dx.doi.org/10.1016/j.jclepro.2022.130557

[42] Kingsley, J. 2019. "Sustainability: The Missing Link." Economist Impact. https://impact.economist.com/sustainability/resilience-and-adaptation/sustainability-the-missing-link (accessed October 6, 2024).

[43] Klassen, R. D. and McLaughlin, C. P., 1996. "The Impact of Environmental Management on Firm Performance" Management Science 42, no. 8 (August): 1199-1214. https://doi.org/10.1287/mnsc.42.8.1199

[44] Kotler, P., and Armstrong, G. 2011. Principles of Marketing. 13th ed. Pearson Prentice Hall.

[45] Kotler, P., and Keller, K. L. 2016. Marketing Management. 14th ed. Shanghai: Shanghai People's Publishing House.

[46] McKinnon, A., Browne, M., Whiteing, A., and Piecyk, A. 2010. Green Logistics. Improving the Environmental Sustainability of Logistics. 3nd ed. Kogan Page.

[47] McKinsey & Company. 2016. Starting at the source: Sustainability in supply chains. McKinsey &Company. https://www.mckinsey.com/capabilities/sustainability/our-insights/starting-at-the-source-sustainability-in-supply-chains (accessed October 6, 2024)

[48] McKinsey & Company. 2022. The New B2B Growth Equation. https://www.mckinsey.com/capabilities/growth-marketing-and-sales/our-insights/the-new-b2b-growth-equation (accessed August 7, 2024).

[49] Menidjel, C., Benhabib, A., and Bilgihan, A. (2017). "Examining the moderating role of personality traits in the relationship between brand trust and brand loyalty" Journal of Product & Brand Management 26, no. 6 (August): 631–49. 10.1108/JPBM-05-2016-1163

[50] Mentzer, J. T. et al., 2001. "Defining supply chain management" Journal of Business Logistics 22, no. 2 (September): 1–25. 10.1002/j.2158-1592.2001.tb00001.x

[51] Mohanty, R. P. and Anand Prakash, 2014. "Green supply chain management practices in India: An empirical study" Production Planning & Control 25, no. 16 (December). 10.1080/09537287.2013.832822

[52] Nozari, H., Najafi, E., Fallah, M., and Hosseinzadeh Lotfi, F. (2019). "Quantitative analysis of key performance indicators of green supply chain in FMCG industries using non-linear fuzzy method" Mathematics 7, no. 11 (October): 1–19. 10.3390/math7111020

[53] Olutimehin D.O. et al., 2024. "Optimizing FMCG supply chain dynamics: A novel framework for integrating operational efficiency and customer satisfaction" International Journal of Management & Entrepreneurship Research, no. 3 (March): 770-779. 10.51594/ijmer.v6i3.934

[54] Opricovic, S. and Tzeng, G. H., 2003. "Defuzzification within a multicriteria decision model" International Journal of Uncertainty, Fuzziness and Knowledge-Based Systems 11, no. 5 (October): 635–52. 10.1142/S0218488503002387

[55] Ottman, J., Stafford, E. R. and Hartman, C. L. (2006). "Avoiding Green Marketing Myopia: Ways to Improve Consumer Appeal for Environmentally Preferable Products" Environment: Science and Policy for Sustainable Development 48, no. 5 (June): 22 - 36. http://dx.doi.org/10.3200/ENVT.48.5.22-36

[56] Porter, M. E. and van der Linde, C., 1995. "Toward a new conception of the environment-competitiveness relationship" Journal of Economic Perspectives 9, no. 4 (June): 97–118. http://dx.doi.org/10.1257/jep.9.4.97

[57] Rao, P. and Holt, D., 2005. "Do Green Supply Chains Lead to Competitiveness and Economic Performance?" International Journal of Operations & Production Management 25, no. 9 (September): 898-916. https://doi.org/10.1108/01443570510613956

[58] Rivera, L., Ortiz, N., Moreno, G., and Páez-Gabriunas, I. (2023). "The effect of company ownership on the environmental practices in the supply chain: An empirical approach" Sustainability 15, no. 16 (August): 1-24. https://doi.org/10.3390/su151612450

[59] Seuring, S. and Müller, M., 2008. "From a Literature Review to a Conceptual Framework for Sustainable Supply Chain Management" Journal of Cleaner Production 16, no. 15 (October): 1699-1710. http://dx.doi.org/10.1016/j.jclepro.2008.04.020

[60] Supply Chain Management Review. 2024. Investor Expectations Influencing Supply Chain Decision-Making. https://www.scmr.com/article/investor-expectations-influencing-supply-chain-decision-making (accessed October 6, 2024).

[61] Walker, H., Di Sisto, L. and McBain, D. (2008). "Drivers and Barriers to Environmental Supply Chain Management Practices: Lessons from the Public and Private Sectors" Journal of Purchasing and Supply Management 14, no. 1 (March) :69-85. http://dx.doi.org/10.1016/j.pursup.2008.01.007

[62] Zhu, et al., 2008. "Firm-level correlates of green supply chain management practices in Chinese context." Omega 36, no. 4 (August): 577–91. 10.1016/j.omega.2006.11.009

[63] Zhu, Q. and Sarkis, J., 2004. "Relationships between operational practices and performance among early adopters of green supply chain management practices in Chinese manufacturing enterprises" Journal of Operations Management 22, no. 3 (June): 265–89. 10.1016/j.jom.2004.01.005

24 The sustainability spectrum: AI meets global trade

Alaeddine Boubaker[1,a] *and Alok Satsangi*[2,b]

[1]DBA-Data Science, European School of Data Science and Technology, Switzerland

[2]NSHM Knowledge Campus, Durgapur, West Bengal, India

Abstract

The emerging intersection between artificial intelligence (AI) and sustainability in global trade is a subject that deserves attention, as AI technologies would be employed in the improvement of sustainable, efficient, and effective trade and business practices. Most industries, such as automotive, have global trade in all branches of industry, meaning every aspect from manufacturing a car to deciding where it is sold, and everything in between is global trade. The use of AI in international trade also helps to reduce waste, optimize transport routes, control and reduce the footprint of international trade operations, and improve resource allocation. This can be further leveraged into different areas including recycling optimization and smart logistics. Such integration can be carried on by artificial intelligence, as it has the redeeming quality to analyze real time data and use predictive analysis to make sustainable decisions about logistics, transportation, resource allocation, recycling and carbon footprint monitoring. The purpose of this research is to understand how AI-powered solutions through the application of collected real time data, the Internet of Things, machine learning algorithms and predictive analytics can aid in achieving environmentally sustainable trade practices.

Keywords: Artificial intelligence, carbon footprint, global trade, internet of things, machine learning algorithms, predictive analytics, smart logistics, sustainability

Introduction

The 4th Industrial Revolution is the shift of interconnection, digitization, automation of machines or systems, etc. Industry 4.0 is built on a range of sophisticated technologies such as artificial intelligence (AI), robotics, Internet of Things (IoT), and big data that industrial companies need to implement to significantly increase their profits. Technology has helped many sectors over the humanities, including logistics, reached significant advancements due to the gains in AI. With AI, more organizations have improved their smart logistics operations to achieve a better performance and lower costs involved in the process. It prepares for practices that look beyond competitive advantage to long-range positive consequences for the world and for future generations. Some of the most critical components that enable sustainable trade on a global scale are sustainability and supply chain responsibility; to be environmentally responsible (to do business in the least harmful way possible) and to ensure that the supply chain process serves a sustainable and ethical purpose. The question to solve is what role AI play in supporting sustainable decisions and monitoring adherence to sustainable standards through the supply chain.

Literature Review

Integration of AI solutions in supply chain management to reduce the carbon footprint

Research by Alali and Razuky [1] examines the impact of AI on improving foreign trade while considering sustainable development goals and concepts. It highlights the interaction of AI with the Paris Agreement concerning carbon reduction. The focus of this research is to investigate how AI can affect international trade and industrial transfer, by emphasizing the importance of resource allocation and strategic planning. Moreover, this study compares the performance of five machine learning algorithms for optimizing the supply chain, aiding making better decisions for more effective and efficient trade outcomes.

A study analysis by Hasan et al. [9] demonstrates several implications for organizations in the USA that aim to minimize their carbon footprint through the integration of AI and predictive analytics in supply chain management. The authors suggest various strategies for incorporating predictive analytics into existing supply

[a]ala.boubaker@gmail.com, [b]alok.satsangi@nshm.com

DOI: 10.4324/9781003739982-24

chain processes and showcase a predictive model that exhibits high accuracy in forecasting emissions related to the supply chain.

Integration of AI solutions to enhance smart logistics operations
Most research focusing on the impact of AI on global trade aims to investigate the primary roles in optimizing trade operations. According to Ozturk [12], various case studies have led to the conclusion that AI performs demand forecasting by using machine learning and predictive analytics, which allow businesses to adjust production levels based on market needs and requirements. The logistics and transportation industry uses machine-learning algorithms to optimize shipping routes based on weather, traffic patterns and geopolitical risk. Additionally, In the field of predictive maintenance, AI (via IoT-powered vehicles) monitors vehicles to help enhance logistics operations.

AI and achieving sustainable development goals in global trade
According to research done by Chaudhary [5] AI can influence various environmental sectors, including pollution control and clean energy. It talks about various AI applications in the context of environmental sustainability and discusses the environmental problems with which AI can assist in finding path towards attaining the sustainable development goals. There have been huge progresses at the interface of AI technologies and sustainability regarding global trade, but not much research exists on AI technologies targeting the environmental sustainability of international trade operations through the integration of machine algorithms and relevant data collected to lower the carbon footprint of global trade.

Research Objective

- The primary objective of this study is to explore the convergence between AI technology and global trade sustainability.
- It adds to the understanding of the potential of AI to enable sustainable trade practices with minimal environmental footprint.
- The goal of this study is to examine the role of AI-powered solutions in reducing the environmental impact of international trade operations through enabling smarter logistics, transport, and improving resource allocation.
- It helps in determining and analyzing the strengths, weaknesses, opportunities, and threats to incorporating AI into the sustainable supply chain.

Research Methodologies

The research approach of this paper employs a mixed-method strategy. It involves a critical examination of various literature regarding how AI is utilized in the supply chain process to optimize trade operations, reduce carbon emissions, and identify the most commonly used machine learning algorithms within this context. Examples from international companies will be provided to illustrate how they address these challenges and what they achieve.

AI and Global Trade Framework

The theoretical foundation for understanding the role of AI in global trade is based on three main areas. Below is a detailed overview of each component: Ozturk [12]

Trade operations
AI enables better decision making in supply chain management, including function predictions and improved levels of optimization that reduce costs relative to both overstock situations and out-of-stock situations. ML algorithms evaluate several factors, like traffic, geopolitical risks, weather conditions, etc., to optimize transportation routes and ensure prompt delivery as well as cut the shipping costs. For instance, AI can automate

customs workflows by evaluating shipping records and identifying compliance violations to maintain transparency as well as expedite the processes.

Trade finance
AI enhances risk estimation by evaluating large volumes of data, which helps in making better loan decisions. AI utilizes automation to process international trade documents, reducing the delays and errors associated with manual processing.

Market access
AI helps companies recognize consumer trends, enabling businesses to adapt their marketing strategies and address language and cultural barriers. Data analytics enhances customer satisfaction by analyzing consumer data to provide tailored recommendations and identify risks associated with targeting new markets by examining market, economic, and political conditions, thereby guiding strategic decision-making.

The Intersection of AI and Sustainable Trade Practices

AI plays diverse essential roles in reducing carbon footprints in supply chain management [3] and boosting trade efficiency, covering the following points [12].

Demand forecasting
AI uses ML algorithms and predictive analytics to analyze data and market trends, helping businesses predict demand. This helps prevent problems like overstock, as this allows vendor delivery levels to smoothly fall in line with market demand. It decreases overproduction, which saves resources and energy.

Optimizing shipping routes
AI algorithms evaluate several elements including traffic flow, weather patterns and worldwide political threats to optimize route efficiency. By optimizing the transportation routes, this leads to less fuel consumption and thus lower emissions. This leads to faster delivery times and cheaper delivery costs, which is beneficial for companies that handle time-sensitive products and just-in-time inventory systems.

Predictive maintenance
AI supports logistics operations by predicting maintenance of various vehicles monitored through IoT devices, which help sustain the long-lasting performance of equipment and accordingly make trade operations more efficient. Predictive maintenance helps organizations to run on a tight schedule by monitoring the equipment issues before they occur and avoid potential downtime. This targeted approach saves energy and emissions incurred through emergency work.

Risk management
AI technologies associated with risk management help to identify risks related to political and environmental uncertainties and disasters. Through the prevention signs, AI empowers organizations to create optional courses of action to maintain exchange consistency.

Environmental surveillance
Continue real-time tracking of environmental surveillance AI technologies help keep track of environmental metrics like air and water quality. This capability allows businesses to track their environmental impacts closely, ensuring their business is compliant with regulatory standards.

Waste management and recycling
Waste management and recycling artificial intelligence-based solutions would improve the waste management process since it will optimize the collection, transportation, processing, recycling, and disposal of waste. Durlik

et al. [6], particularly for enhanced pathfinding algorithms for electronic waste learners and also AI-based waste management [5].

Pollution management
AI technologies and ML algorithms, such as oil spill detection algorithms, are integrated into pollution control systems, assisting in the prevention and significant reduction of marine pollution while enhancing overall ecosystem health [5].

Energy efficiency enhancement
AI can help recognize where energy is wasted in factories and warehouses, so that companies can take actions to increase energy efficiency and decrease energy consumption.

Repetitive work automation
AI automates one-time things like customer service requests, stock control, order fulfillment, and more. It allows human resources to focus on more important things which makes them much more productive, hence lowering the operational cost.

The Impact of Using AI to Optimize Trade Operations

A study by Balfaqih [4] has shown that the classical approach to designing a logistics system with AI involves several key processes, including:

- Gathering real time data from different sources like warehousing and customer touchpoints.
- Analyzing the gathered data using AI algorithms to search for patterns, forecast demand, and optimize routes
- Using AI algorithms to optimize transport routes based on a variety of parameters like weather, traffic, and transportation conditions.
- Introducing automation in transport and storage on the use and coordination of autonomous systems like drones, and guided cars.
- Helping logistics managers to take appropriate decisions for resource distribution, vendor selection, and inventory management.
- Continuously improving the logistics system to recognize areas of change that increase efficiency and effectiveness.

Data collection relevant for a smart logistics system
The key task is to find, discover and gather relevant data to train and test the ML algorithms. It is a challenge to track shipments and inventory in real time with AI systems using IoT devices. This includes obtaining the real-time location and conditions of the goods traveling around the supply chain and using a cloud computing platform, like "OpenWeatherMap" Open Weather [11], which gathers relevant environmental data such as humidity and temperature, and the "Google Maps API" Google [8] to pull traffic data along the journey. A Logistic System Powered by AI Collects the following data to optimize logistics operations and support decision making. The tables below summarize the main data types relevant to smart logistics context.

Key performance indicators (KPIs), such as order shipping accuracy and order completion rates, are metrics that enable the evaluation of the effectiveness of logistics operations and lead to continuous improvement. The following tables provides an overview of the essential categories of data relevant to reducing the carbon footprint in smart logistics. An overview of the essential categories of data relevant to reducing the carbon footprint in smart logistics are presented in the Table 24.1.

Data collection relevant for diagnosing the carbon footprint
In a logistics system equipped with AI, various categories of data are collected to diagnose the carbon emissions related to supply chain operations and enhance decision-making regarding the reduction of the carbon

Table 24.1 Categories of collected data for a smart logistic system.

Customer data	Supplier data	Order data	Inventory data
Client preferences Feedback Purchase tendencies	Fulfillment times Charges Credibility	Requested quantities Shipping addresses Purchase history	Inventory levels item types Stock locations Stock turnover
Transportation data	**Environmental data**	**Operational data**	**Financial data**
Delivery routes transit duration Vehicle positions Delivery timelines	Climate conditions Road traffic patterns Roadway state	Storage operations Staff productivity Resource usage	Delivery expenses Storage costs inventory management expenses

Source: Balfaqih [4]

Table 24.2 Categories of data collected for diagnosing the carbon footprint.

Transportation emissions data	Route optimization data	Vehicle performance data	Supply chain data	Regulatory compliance data
Carbon emissions Fuel consumption rates Transport types Route distance	Previous shipping paths Road traffic patterns Road conditions Delivery times	Vehicle performance Fuel consumption Repair logs Load limit	Sustainable operations Shipping methods	Carbon emissions laws Sustainable development guidelines
Inventory data	**Packaging data**	**Customer demand data**	**Energy consumption data**	**Carbon footprint calculations**
Inventory levels Item types Stock locations Stock turnover	Packing materials Package dimensions	Customer purchasing trends	Energy consumption in logistics and storage	Total emissions from logistics transportation, warehousing, and packaging

Source: Balfaqih [4]

footprint. The following table provides an overview of the essential categories of data relevant to diagnosing carbon emissions. The essential categories of data relevant to diagnosing carbon emissions are presented in the Table 24.2.

Data analytics

Various algorithms are utilized in smart logistics systems powered by AI to analyze the collected data, optimize logistics operations, and reduce carbon emissions. Investigations and research such as Balfaqih [4] were conducted to identify which algorithms are suitable for optimizing each logistics operation.

Descriptive analytics

Utilize historical data to assess past performance and identify trend patterns, which help predict future demand, improve stock levels, and minimize the environmental cost. We apply machine learning algorithms (e.g., unsupervised learning methods such as K-means and hierarchical clustering) to ascertain and emulate behavior patterns of consumers, group the markets based on purchasing behavior and emissions while accommodating distance, transport mode, and load weight, and effectively enabling reduction emissions/travel distances. This creates a clear connection between operational drivers and emissions.

Demand forecasting can similarly be improved through using the K-means clustering algorithm by clustering customers, products, and geo-specific demand into customer segments using customer data (such as order history, shopping frequency, average cart size, and gender), product data (such as revenue history, sales volume, item category, selling price, and seasonal trends), and geo-specific data (such as geographical zones). K-means clustering is applied to cluster similar delivery routes that help to find more carbon-efficient routes [10].

Predictive analytics

Supervised learning algorithms (support vector machines, decision trees, and linear regression) are being used for predictive analytics based on the use of ML algorithms to predict future demand, identify potential disruptions, and improve routing and scheduling. These seek to enhance logistics efficacy across key variables, such as stock control, demand prediction, and reducing environmental impact. Graph neural networks (GNN) and deep reinforcement learning (DRL) are different components of neural networks and algorithms used in advanced data analytical methods such as for warehouse visual inspection tasks like image recognition. Moreover, anomaly detection algorithms include isolation forests allow identifying unusual patterns or anomalies in logistics or emissions data, which highlight potential threats in fraud or weaknesses and inefficiencies of operations, from which actions can be taken to lower emissions of carbon.

Furthermore, time series analysis, including the autoregressive integrated moving average (ARIMA) algorithm, is used to predict demand, inventory levels, and future emissions based on historical data patterns. Combining K-means as a clustering algorithm with a forecasting model like ARIMA for each cluster helps identify patterns within the data, such as grouping products that have similar demand trends and predicting future emissions based on historical performance trends [10]. Random Forest, on the other hand, is a machine learning algorithm that are applied for trade operations in multiple directions such as classification and regression which generates several decision trees during training. In classification tasks such as this, we treat inputs as feature categories contributing to the regression. In this configuration, each tree makes its own predictions based on the input features, and the average of all the trees predictors is taken to be the final class prediction. The algorithm is quite powerful for complex dataset.

Prescriptive analytics

Implement algorithms that recommend actions based on anticipated insights and assist in making informed decisions regarding resource allocation, inventory management, and route planning. The reinforcement learning algorithm is utilized to improve decision-making processes, such as dynamically adapting logistical routes and time allocations based on traffic conditions and emissions data to reduce the carbon footprint. It learns by analyzing the effects of actions taken within the logistics network to enhance future choices. Moreover, the genetic algorithm is a type of algorithm used to solve complex optimization problems, such as vehicle path planning and cargo management, leading to reduced fuel consumption and emissions, by replicating the process of natural selection to identify the optimal solutions. Furthermore, the linear programming algorithm is applied to optimize resource allocation and reduce costs in logistics operations while considering carbon emissions as a constraint.

AI-driven optimization

AI and route optimization algorithms reduce transportation time, costs, and carbon footprints by analyzing certain parameters such as weather, traffic conditions, delivery schedules, etc. to provide the fastest routes for delivery vehicles. Dijkstra's algorithm is one of the most popular route optimization algorithms. It finds the shortest static route between nodes in a graph of transportation networks and calculates the minimum distance from an initial point to all other nodes in the network.

Dijkstra's algorithm can be optimized by using heuristics to find the most direct route and evaluating potentially evaluated routes based on estimates on desired cost and distances to the destination. Dijkstra's algorithm can also be integrated with real-time information about roads and traffic and weather to recalculate routes dynamically. One other algorithm used here is Ant Colony Optimization (ACO), which mimics the way ants seek food, by discovering the best and most dynamic paths in a network and responding collectively, in real-time, to changes in traffic.

Discussion

After analyzing several machine learning algorithms and the contexts in which they were used to optimize trade operations, the question arises: Which machine learning algorithm performs best and is most suitable for optimizing trade operations? A critical examination of the studies below helps to answer this question.

A study conducted by Alali and Razuky [1] explores how machine learning can enhance decision-making processes throughout supply chains and lead to sustainability. Through the evaluation of five of the algorithms: Random Forest, XGBoost, Logistic Regression, KNN, SVM the study identifies the highest performing algorithm that could help in the prediction which can optimize the supply chain by using performance indicators like accuracy, precision, recall, F1 score, area under curve (AUC), the Random Forest model emerged as the top performer recording an accuracy of 92%, precision of 0.91, recall of 0.90, F1-score of 0.905, and AUC of 0.95.

The previous study was able to use a large dataset for their investigation, which included logistics, procurement, and inventory management data, which led to an explanation of the role of AI combining carbon footprint minimization efforts and global sustainability targets adopted in the Paris Agreement. Adopted in December 2015 at the 21st Conference of the Parties (COP 21), United Nations Framework Convention on Climate Change (UNFCCC), the Paris agreement is an international accord aimed at addressing climate change and fostering initiatives that support a sustainable, low-carbon world. Moreover, the impact of AI adoption to reduce carbon footprint among US Companies Hasan et al. [9] further explores findings related to the decrease of carbon footprints as AI models are developed. To investigate the carbon footprint a predictive model using the Random Forest algorithm was created. The model produced a 0.00141 mean square error, 0.9858 R-squared, indicating that it accurately captured approximately 99% of the variability in the real-world emissions across multiple industries.

SWOT Analysis

This SWOT analysis outlines the effects resulting from the convergence of AI and supply chain processes as well as the challenges companies may encounter when applying AI to optimize their trading processes. It aids in making strategic decisions concerning the transformation of businesses that can benefit from the potential of AI. The SWOT analysis in Table 24.3 provides an overview of how AI can transform supply chains, highlighting not only the potential for innovation and sustainability but also the issues of data security, ethical principles, and dependence on technology.

Case Studies

In this study, we investigate instances of international companies utilizing AI to optimize their supply chain operations. By examining these instances, we get comprehensive insights into the real-world uses of AI in streamlining supply chain activities.

Amazon

From small retailers to global giants like Amazon, businesses are leveraging a range of solutions powered by AI across their global supply chains. Data collected until October 2023 is used to train ML algorithms to understand historical sales trends, and analyze consumer preferences. Furthermore, artificial intelligence can automate logistics operations, speed up order processing and provide customers with status updates in real-time, leading to vast reductions in product unavailability and shorter delivery times [7].

Walmart

Walmart employs AI-powered solutions in its logistics operations, deploying ML to refine delivery routing, minimizing transportation expenses, and maintaining punctual deliveries. Moreover, AI examines extensive

Table 24.3 SWOT analysis of AI's role in enhancing supply chain efficiency.

Strengths	**Weakness**
Analysis of large datasets: AI can analyze massive analytics on social media, real-time data, and transport costs which could give a more holistic view of demand patterns and trends changes in market conditions. Improved strategic decision-making: AI improves the decision-making process by helping organizations to make data-driven decisions that contribute to optimizing supply chain operations. Automation of tasks: AI is one of the systems that can give a lot of certainty and serve to automate repetitive tasks that are needed in supply chain operations. Enhancing customer service: Order processing by AI can improve customer satisfaction. Cost minimization: AI technologies offer the potential for considerable savings in managing supply chain activities by optimizing routes, inventory levels, energy consumption, and reducing waste.	Reduction of Staff: With the automation of jobs with the assistance of artificial intelligence comes a need to reskill in different trades. Reliance on decision-making only by artificial intelligence, might miss the most precious asset in the supply chain management, critical human brains. Maintenance Costs: AI systems do not work independently; they require routine maintenance and diagnostics to continue to perform. Implementation Complexity: Companies may struggle with the inclusion of AI in transforming that supply chain processes, which can leave the company inefficient while those processes are being integrated. Ethics: The growth of the AI technology can pose challenges in meeting the requirements of laws, The laws giving respect to ethical principles. The lack of transparency may make compliance with the laws more difficult. Sensitive Data Protection: Many AI systems are using extensive datasets that include sensitive personal information. Data availability and accuracy: feeding biased dataset to AI models will produce it with inaccurate predictions and wrong decisions.
Opportunities	**Threats**
Product innovation: AI can enable product innovation by identifying market trends Entering new markets: AI can enable new market opportunities by locating untapped customer segments. Merging with innovative technologies: The fusion of AI technologies with IoT and Big data technologies significantly enhances supply chains' capacity to quickly respond to evolving market conditions. Improved collaboration: AI can enhance collaboration among supply chain participants by sharing data-backed best practices and involving them in decision loops. Staff development: AI diverts human-centric office tasks from employees to automated ones, which empowers them to focus on important business activities that achieve higher productivity from teams. Sustainability: AI tools help organizations in reducing and monitoring their environmental impact, validating compliance with sustainability goals. Continuous learning: AI systems can learn from new data over time leading to improved predictive capabilities.	Reliance on AI technology: Increased reliance on AI systems can lead to a decline in decision-making skills and potential vulnerabilities, including system breakdowns and cyberattacks. Continuous Improvement: If organizations cannot devote the necessary time and money to better the models, the AI models rate of advancement will decline resulting in inefficiency. Consideration of the environmental impact: AI can be resource-intensive upon use, as deploying and training AI models brings computational cost and thus the carbon emissions much higher. Transparency: Many AI models, particularly those based on deep learning algorithms, often lack transparency since they function like *black boxes* Making it hard to understand their decision-making processes. Ethical questions: The deployment of AI often sparks ethical concerns, especially when it comes to the confidentiality of data and the possibility of unethical or illegal decisions. Discrimination and unjust treatment: The presence of bias in training data can cause AI systems to perpetuate inequality, contributing to unfair outcomes in recruitment and decision-making in other domains.

Source: Alzoubi and Mishra [2]

customer datasets and demographic information to personalize product suggestions and enhance forecasting accuracy, leading to a 10% drop in transportation expenses and a 5% improvement in delivery timeliness [7].

Alibaba

Alibaba offers diverse AI services based on ML algorithms to analyze user preferences, buying history, and market trends, enabling customized product recommendations to predict demand and manage inventory effectively. Additionally, AI enhances the quality of logistics by optimizing shipping, delivery planning and scheduling to boost customer experience while cutting down on transportation costs, fuel consumption, and emissions [12].

DHL

DHL uses AI-based predictive analytics to support demand prediction, stock control, and logistics planning. The platform interprets a multitude of data, from traffic patterns to weather, to help the company optimize its operations. This ensures faster delivery times, savings in costs, and lower fuel consumption. DHL is using AI-controlled robots that sorts and packs products in its warehouses, providing significant breakthroughs and reaching 40% improvement in sorting capacity and 99% sorting accuracy by allowing 1,000 parcel sorting per hour [12].

Conclusion

Investment in artificial intelligence (AI) technologies contributes to the optimization of trade operations and maintains sustainable trade practices. AI-powered solutions play a crucial role in optimizing trade operations. Optimizing a single trade operation has a direct or indirect impact on the optimization of other trade operations and maintains sustainable practices. For example, forecasting demand indirectly affects inventory optimization by providing more accurate demand forecasts. Optimizing delivery routes influences transportation costs and customer satisfaction. This leads to reduced energy consumption and carbon emissions. Case studies confirm that the return on investment (ROI) yields measurable benefits. However, the SWOT analysis presents several challenges that organizations may face with the implementation of AI in their supply chain processes. This research could be further developed by investigating the potential of investing in AI to achieve environmentally sustainable trade practices and by analyzing the impact of the intersection of AI and global trade sustainability on stock prices.

References

[1] Alali, S., & Razuky, M. H. (2024). Intelligent system for enhancement of foreign trade depending on sustainable. *Journal of Positive Psychology*, 4(3).

[2] Alzoubi, Y. I., & Mishra, A. (2024). Green artificial intelligence initiatives: Potentials and challenges. *Journal of Cleaner Production*, 468, 143090.

[3] Anozie, U. C., Obafunsho, O. E., Toromade, R. O., & Adewumi, G. (2024). Harnessing big data for sustainable supply chain management (SSCM): Strategies to reduce carbon footprint. *International Journal of Scientific Research Archive*, 12(2), 1099–1104.

[4] Balfaqih, H. (2023). Artificial intelligence and smart logistics systems in industry 4.0. In Proceedings of the International Conference on Industrial Engineering and Operations Management. Manila, Philippines.

[5] Chaudhary, G. (2023). Environmental sustainability: Can artificial intelligence be an enabler for SDGs?. *Nature Environment and Pollution Technology*, 22(3), 1411–1420.

[6] Durlik, I., Miller, T., Kostecka E., Lobodzinska, A., & Kostecki, T. (2024). Harnessing AI for sustainable shipping and green ports: challenges and opportunities. *Applied Sciences*, 14(14), 5994.

[7] Gayam, S. R. (2019). AI for supply chain visibility in e-commerce: techniques for real-time tracking, inventory management, and demand forecasting. *Distributed Learning in Broadly Applied Sciences Research*, 5, 218–251.

[8] Google. (2018). Google Maps Platform. Available from: https://www.mapsplatform.google.com/. (Accessed January 10, 2025).

[9] Hasan, M. R., Islam, M. Z., Sumon, M. F. I., Osiujjaman, M., Debnath, P., & Pant, L. (2024). Integrating artificial intelligence and predictive analytics in supply chain management to minimize carbon footprint and enhance business growth in the USA. *Journal of Business and Management Studies*, 6(4), 195–212.
[10] Mediavilla, M. A., Dietrich, F., & Palm, D. (2022). Review and analysis of artificial intelligence methods for demand forecasting in supply chain management. *Procedia CIRP*, 107, 1126–1131.
[11] Open Weather (2014). Open weather. Available from: https://www.openweathermap.org/. (Accessed January 10, 2025).
[12] Ozturk, O. (2024). The impact of AI on international trade: opportunities and challenges. *Economies*, 12(11), 298.

25 Leveraging large language models in cybersecurity - a flip perspective

Vidhya Ashok[1,a], *Mamatha Balachandra*[2,b], *Sophia Rahaman*[3,c], *Nisha P. Shetty*[4,d] *and Madhumita Abhijeet Takalkar*[5,e]

[1]School of Engineering and IT, Manipal Academy of Higher Education, Dubai, United Arab Emirates

[2]Manipal Institute of Technology, Manipal Academy of Higher Education, Manipal, India

[3]School of Engineering and IT, Manipal Academy of Higher Education, Dubai, United Arab Emirates

[4]Manipal Institute of Technology, Manipal Academy of Higher Education, Manipal, India

[5]School of Information Technology, Crown Institute of Higher Education, North Sydney, NSW, Australia

Abstract

Large language models (LLMs) are advanced artificial intelligence systems meant to handle huge datasets and produce human-like text based on the given context. However, the advancement of LLMs has emerged out in different areas which include cybersecurity, where they pose both advantages as well as significant risks. This paper explores how LLMs are reshaping the cyber space environment acting positively in identifying the threat and responding to the same and intelligence harvesting and at the same time exploring the advancement in artificial intelligence (AI), attacking through machine generated phishing, malware. The paper focuses on the various ways of LLM usage in a destructive way and the significance of involving the regulatory authority and creating a framework to define the norms based on the ethical values to ensure the security of the system by reducing the risks associated in terms of emotional and economic aspects caused by the machine generated cyber-attacks.

Keywords: Large language models, malware, phishing, threats

Introduction

In today's digital era, artificial intelligence (AI) has seen remarkable advancements, with large language models (LLMs) exceeding out as a keystone of modern AI applications. These models are built to understand the context and produce the results in a way that human finds the solution in different domains. LLMs act like a foundational model which works on huge volume of unlabeled data and process to produce a valuable result in the form of text or as codelike structures. Typically, these are pre trained system on petabytes data with numerous parameters to deliver the accurate results. While their ability to increase productivity and efficiency is extraordinary, their integration into all areas has become evident. Incorporating the advancement of AI with cybersecurity presents a double-edged sword. LLMs provide the power for attackers as well as defenders in the cyberspace by redefining the traditional methods. This paper explores the way how disruption in the cyberspace exists, determines the risk associated with it and reaching out to a balance. By understanding how LLMs ground meaning, we can better explain their remarkable success and their ability to "understand" complex contexts [9].

A cyberattack is defined as a voluntarily attempt by cybercriminals or unauthorized individuals to penetrate a system, get their access rights, and copy, manipulate, delete, or expose confidential information [16]. These attacks can target individuals, businesses, or even government entities with the aim of accessing their critical resources such as intellectual property, client/customer data, or financial information. The development in Generative AI (GenAI) in cybersecurity contradicts the growth by enabling the high tech cyberattacks but also holds the potential to strengthen protective measures. For example, GenAI can improvise threat intelligence

[a]vidhya.ashok@manipaldubai.com, [b]mamtha.bc@manipal.edu, [c]sophia@manipaldubai.com, [d]nisha.pshetty@manipal.edu, [e]madhumita.takalkar@cihe.edu.au

DOI: 10.4324/9781003739982-25

and help to identify vulnerabilities in existing systems. However, the dual nature of LLMs in cybersecurity leads to the need for framing norms and innovative protective mechanisms. These challenges require deep understanding of interdisciplinary areas to ensure the effective usage of GenAI in cybersecurity [30].

A systematic literature review of LLMs in cybersecurity confirms their increasing adoption in use cases like vulnerability analysis, SOC automation, and phishing mitigation [29].

Literature Review

Cyberattacks can be classified based on various factors, including the nature of attack, method of attack, intent, target, and scope. This section focuses on how modern cyberattack methods such as malware-based attacks, phishing and social engineering, DDoS attacks, and injection attacks are evolving with and against advancements in LLMs.

Phishing and social engineering attacks

Phishing and social engineering attacks are among the most common threats in cybersecurity that explore human psychology to trap the individuals in revealing the sensitive information which in turn may lead to a dangerous action. Typically, cybercriminals send deceptive emails, messages, or phone calls that seem to be legitimate in attracting victims to share passwords, confidential information, or even transferring money. The advanced form of phishing is spear-phishing which crafts highly customized messages aimed at specific individuals or organizations. Social engineering can also extend to a level of impersonating like known sources such as colleagues or IT staff to gain access to confidential areas in physically as well as in digital mode. Cybercriminals target people's emotions like trust, curiosity, or fear to get the access often bypassing through the technical protection which makes them one of the most widespread and effective methods irrespective of geometric location used by cybercriminals.

Vulnerability exploitation is the key for attackers and the implementation of weak security protocols in newly implemented systems becomes the target which can lead to the theft of private data, identity theft in turn escalates to financial loss. For instance, attackers often use misleading URLs for the most prevalent website to trick users into giving up access to secure information like credit card details and one time passcode. The need for constant vigilance and staying informed about the latest cyber threats are the preventive measures. Adopting a "Trust but Verify" mindset can be an effective way to tackle with phishing attacks, encouraging the users to double-check the originality of requests before clicking [4].

Traditional detection methods will not suffice the counter measures for social engineering and phishing attacks. Cybercriminals use different tricks to get the relevant information from the users. We can analyze based on the characteristics of the attack and few warnings that are provided. In the real-world scenario, anti-phishing tools are used to counter these attacks; however, ever-evolving tactics pose a challenge. Hybrid algorithm that combines various machine learning techniques like decision trees (DT) and deep learning (DL) can be employed to improvise the phishing detection [12].

Cybersecurity landscape is growing as the same pace as AI introducing new techniques both for attackers and defenders. Hackers use AI to improvise their tactics in more customized way targeting a group of people in a faster manner. ChatGPT has demonstrated capabilities in detecting phishing sites, but it can also be misused to generate realistic phishing content, underlining the dual-use dilemma of LLMs in this domain [14]. It's time for us define a framework which collaborates the researchers and stakeholders to work together to predict these threats and design strategies to prevent and mitigate these attacks. PhishSim, a phishing simulation tool, enables feature-free training of both AI and humans for better preparedness against evolving phishing attacks [23]. A balance should be established between attackers and guards by investigating the attacks and providing a secure environment in all aspects such as digital, physical in future.

Malware-based attacks

Malicious software is set to penetrate which compromises the security of the individual system or organization is coined as Malware-based attacks. Malicious software is classified based on the mode of transmission such as viruses, worms, ransomware and trojans. Viruses attach themselves to the legitimate files and starts spreading when the host is activated. However, worms act independently across the network without the need for user interaction.

Ransomware attack locks or encrypts secure files and demanding a huge amount for their release, often causing substantial disruption to businesses. Trojans masquerade as a harmless software by tricking the users in downloading and executing them, which in turn grants attackers unauthorized access or control over the system. The intention of using this malicious code is meant to steal the confidential information and disrupting the operations or to take the control of the system. Malware attacks are considered as one of the most persistent and damaging threats in cybersecurity.

As a countermeasure, a new approach called heuristic analysis involves static and dynamic way of analyzing the code without executing it. Static analysis examines the code behavior and maps it to the existing malware codes whereas dynamic analysis runs the code in a secure environment and observes the behavioral pattern in real time. Dynamic analysis is effective in addressing the malware issues but comparatively slower than static method since it involves the real time execution environment [11, 5].

Cybersecurity landscape is targeted with the use of botnets which can be remotely controlled by attackers. The affected system will distribute malware, send spam content and perform a coordinated attack. Cybercriminals use botnets as a powerful tool to extract the user information without their knowledge and manipulate the infected system to carry out the same kind of attacks with those connected to it. LLMs can assist in malware de obfuscation, making it easier for attackers to modify or adapt real-world malicious code to evade detection systems [22].

Network-based attacks

Attackers exploit the vulnerabilities in network infrastructure to gain access control rights or to destroy the communication. These attacks range from sophisticated targeted intrusions to mass-scale automated cyber threats that leverage machine learning algorithms to bypass traditional security protocols. Denial-of-Service (DoS) and Distributed Denial-of-Service (DDoS) attacks are the most prevalent network-based attack in commercial domain which floods the server with unnecessary traffic, leading to service degradation and downtime. Recent AI-assisted DDoS attacks have demonstrated the ability to dynamically alter attack vectors in real-time, making mitigation increasingly difficult. These advancements highlight the importance of intelligent, adaptive security systems. Another common attack is man-in-the-middle (MITM) attack, where a third person is listening to the communication between two users and steals sensitive data like login details or financial data. AI-generated MITM strategies have become increasingly sophisticated, even evading encryption through real-time packet manipulation. Mainly network based attack targets the poorly configured systems such as no updating on latest patches to penetrate the network and access the secure data. These attacks clearly define the importance of strong network infrastructure which includes continuous monitoring and timely updates to address the flaws.

In the modern era, machine learning and deep learning models are deployed to network infrastructure effectively to counter all types of network related threats which are unpredictable and undefined in nature. Attackers are intelligent to identify the gaps in the intelligent-based systems and constantly changing their strategies thus leads to the attack [3]. AI-driven traffic analysis tools now detect anomalies and pattern deviations, enhancing the accuracy of intrusion detection systems. Studies show that hybrid AI models, particularly those combining deep learning and clustering techniques, significantly outperform traditional systems. Real-time Explainable AI frameworks can enhance transparency in intrusion detection, providing human analysts with reasoning behind threat classification [8].

This domain needs to be updated based on the adaptable and advanced approached to improvise the network security and be cautious of emerging threats.

Injection attacks

The major threat to web applications and databases is injection attacks, where attackers manipulate input fields to execute unauthorized commands or queries. The most common attack is SQL injection that involves sending errant SQL queries to manipulate databases which can lead to the exposure of sensitive information and granting the administrative rights to modify the data. Second common form is Cross-Site Scripting in which attackers inject malicious script in the websites. These scripts run on client's browsers which help hackers to gather information such as session id, login credentials or other sensitive data. There are certain vulnerabilities in input validation, it can be mitigated by practicing secure coding practices, proper input sanitization and the framework which includes built-in security features.

Detecting the SQL injection attack automatically or high accuracy remains as difficult task which is why research efforts focuses to develop more effective detection techniques in advanced attacks under complex conditions [27]. First order SQL injection is much easier to detect when compared to the second order SQL injection which poses high level of complexity with exclusive characteristics. A foundational classification of these attacks highlights different forms, such as tautology-based, union query, and piggy-backed queries, each requiring unique countermeasures [8, 2]. Additionally, modern detection strategies now leverage machine learning models to identify patterns in SQL payloads and predict malicious queries with high precision [2].

The primary goals of injection attacks are stealing personal or financial information or customer data or disrupting business operations. In more severe cases, hackers may target critical infrastructure, government systems, or national security, often as part of cyberespionage or state-sponsored campaigns.

Technologies driven cyber attacks

In the modern era, cyber attackers use technology to amplify their hacking strategies such as employing botnets for IoT systems, device hijacking and targeting the cloud infrastructure to perform information gathering. Figure 25.1 illustrates the various types of attacks categorized by technology.

IoT-based attacks

Internet of Things (IoT) systems are designed with group of networks of interconnected devices that in turn becomes the vulnerability for the hacker to perform the attacks defined as IoT-based attacks. IoT devices range from smart home gadgets to industrial sensors which have poor security settings such as default passwords or outdated software. Hackers exploit these flaws to grow the unauthorized access even employing botnets as part of the device for initiating DDoS attacks or other destructive activities. Second level is device hijacking where attackers take complete control of IoT devices which causes disruption in operations and causing major security issues. Securing IoT devices has become more important than ever as the industries employment of IoT devices has drastically increased. The key factors to keep IoT systems secured is by implementing strong security measures like encryption, regular software updates and robust authentication protocols.

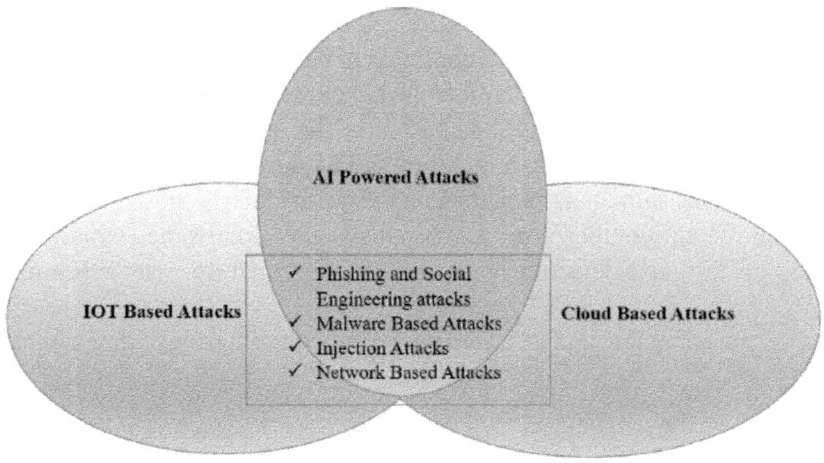

Figure 25.1 Tech based cyber-attack environment
Source: Author

Researchers and security experts design detection and prevention strategies because of the rapid rise of IoT-related threats present with major hurdles. Lack of awareness and training in handling IoT based devices is the real challenge which makes it difficult to create effective security solutions for IoT devices, highlighting the need for continued innovation and education in this area [26].

AI-powered attacks

AI is acting like a double-edged sword which helps for defenders as well as attackers to create more complex and efficient attacks and security strategies. By employing the advanced algorithms in machine learning and deep learning, attackers can automate tasks in identifying system weaknesses, crafting customized phishing emails, or producing deepfake content. For instance, Adaptive malware understands the ever-evolving change in the security tactics and generates accordingly. Another instance of deepfake phishing that uses synthetic audio or video to pretend to be famous personalities or trusted individuals in tricking the targets. This integration of artificial intelligence into cyberattacks poses a significant threat and harder to detect and defend against attacks.

AI-driven cyberattacks frequently occur during the access and penetration phase with 56% and 12% are seen in the exploitation and command-and-control phases. Another 11% take place during reconnaissance, and 9% during the delivery phase of the cybersecurity kill chain in the ethical hacking phases. These investigation reports focus on certain critical issues such as AI-driven cyber-attacks which operate at unprecedented speeds and use complex decision-making logic can easily bypass the traditional defense systems. To counter these attacks, organizations must integrate AI into their defensive strategies. This proactive approach can help in understanding and analyzing the attacks and providing the defending strategies before causing significant damage [6]. Generative AI, including LLMs, is now being leveraged to create adaptive malware, synthetic identity fraud, spoofed credentials, and deepfake videos, expanding the cyber threat landscape by making attacks harder to detect and easier to automate [7]. These mechanisms have been classified into transparent models specifically for cybersecurity automation and intelligence, ensuring AI-generated decisions are traceable and trusted [25].

Cloud-based attacks

Cloud infrastructure for data storage, processing and application hosting has increased drastically which leads to cloud-based attacks. The common vulnerabilities in cloud environments can be listed as misconfigured settings, weak access controls, or unpatched software, to gain unauthorized access or disrupt services. The primary challenge in securing cloud environments is the shared responsibility model in which users and cloud providers share equal responsibility. Few common threats include data breaches and account hijacking wherein the attackers extract the user credentials to control / alter cloud resources. DDoS attacks target cloud services with tremendous traffic and triggering downtime or degraded performance.

The cloud security is dependent on the cloud providers as well as the users. Both are accountable for keeping their data and application safely in shared responsibility model. Configuration issues and weak implementation of encryption in accessing the storage buckets are the gate way for the hackers. Threat detection and monitoring becomes complex with the use and dynamic nature of cloud environment. LLM-inspired architectures have shown promising results in identifying anomalies across distributed cloud systems. A transformer-based network intrusion detection model optimized for cloud environments demonstrates how AI techniques extend beyond text processing to cybersecurity defense [8].

The security practices like encryption of sensitive data to achieve confidentiality, regular audits and multi-factor authentication (MFA) are implemented in organization to eliminate the threats. Now-a days AI-driven monitoring systems are employed as advanced threat detection tools to identify and react to the suspicious activities.

Furthermore, creating awareness through proper training is the key role in mitigating phishing or social engineering attacks which primarily target the stake holders cloud credentials. As the technology advances in every field, the implementation of cloud environment continues to grow which gives the need for innovative and adaptive security solutions. Organizations can get the best benefit of cloud computing only by addressing the above-mentioned challenges and minimize the risks related to cloud based attacks.

LLMs in Cybersecurity

Cybersecurity defense and resilience

The tool for communication is language which assists humans to express themselves and enables them to interact with machines. In the recent era, large language models such as GPT -4 has implemented advanced natural language processing to make the machine understand and express like humans. On the other hand, LLMs carry its own challenges. The cost involved in computation, and interoperability are the major technical challenges in implementation. Such integration could drive proactive threat detection using multi-modal LLM Frameworks [18]. Additionally, these models are scaled up to solve most complex task or to operate in the complex dynamic environment with various challenges such as scalability, privacy and real-time processing [21].

LLMs hold enormous transformative potential in the cyberspace in defensive mode which offers innovative tools that can automate threat detection and response. The LLMs such as OpenHermes-2.5-Mistral-7B in penetration testing introduces a fundamental shift in terms of security audits and response. LLM-based models work on a huge amount of data with complex numerous parameters using advanced learning algorithms to generate intelligent report that can help the system to response in an effective way. The system is fast enough to handle the threats and make out the detailed security assessment just within hours. Threat intelligence system can handle the threat in fraction of seconds and reducing the false positive cases. Furthermore, LLMs excel in understanding and learning the cyber space threats that traditional tools cannot identify. Their ability to mimic the human intelligence allows them to evaluate the intricate network configurations and detect the security threats that many times human miss. Recent studies further emphasize that LLMs have evolved into state-of-the-art tools capable of learning, adapting, and defending against highly dynamic cyber threats across enterprise environment [20]. On the other hand, LLM evaluation system requires a human expert's intuition to get the better results in threat response. This advanced analytical way results in high efficiency in detecting both known and novel vulnerabilities, thereby improving the overall security of the organizations [28]. For example, GPT-based systems have shown efficacy in generating Governance, risk, and compliance (GRC) policies tailored for ransomware mitigation moving LLMs from detection to strategic defense [19].

LLMs can be trained with vast real time data and thus it can easily identify the anomalies in this evolving cyberspace enabling the organizations to react to attacks and threats more quickly and efficiently. Adversarial test cases may be provided to the LLM to effectively improvise the decision capacity. Large Language Models based cybersecurity solutions can provide better decisions based on large training sets and be more predictive in understanding the nature of cyberthreats. However, this advancement poses significant challenges such as data protection and privacy, managing biases, transparency of the model and addressing the infrastructure and integration issues [24]. For instance, these trained models can analyze the email patterns to successfully identify phishing attempts and raise the flag in case of malicious content, thus by reducing the risk of attacks. Additionally, LLMs uses threat intelligence feeds, analyze the common pattern and summarize the vulnerabilities which can be helpful in predicting the attack vectors, thus providing cybersecurity teams to take the necessary actions/ response and to stay ahead with the adversaries.

LLMs uses data from diverse cybersecurity forums which contains reports and information about recent attacks. These summarization reports allow the cybersecurity profession to be aware of various threat mechanisms employed to make the decision in threat response. Cybersecurity professionals stay ahead in threat response not just with help of volume of data, but it plays a major role in security awareness and training. In current scenario, phishing and social engineering attacks stands at top in cyberattacks, LLMs can help the employees recognize and response to this potential threat which can lead to major financial stains in the individual or in the organization.

By leveraging these capabilities, organizations can improvise the cyberspace environment with better threat response and be more resilient against evolving threats. The integration of LLMs into cybersecurity strategies proves to be a significant step forward to create a more digital landscape combining technology with human expertise.

LLMs for threat detection and SOC automation
LLMs are increasingly being integrated into security operations centers (SOCs) for tasks such as threat triage, log summarization, and anomaly flagging. Trained on cybersecurity-specific corpora, LLMs can:

- Parse and summarize system logs (e.g., firewall, SIEM)
- Identify indicators of compromise (IOCs) from threat intel feeds
- Generate context-aware alerts by correlating events
- Assist in phishing URL analysis and payload decoding

For example, a fine-tuned GPT model on MITRE ATT&CK patterns can identify command-and-control attempts by analyzing suspicious process chains and obfuscated scripts. Unlike traditional systems that rely on fixed signatures, LLMs generalize and reason over previously unseen threats [29, 20].

Negative Impact: Escalating Cybersecurity Threats and Risks

The LLM) gives defensive advantages but poses serious risk that can disrupt the cybersecurity landscape. LLMs can amplify the phishing and social engineering attack by designing highly convincing phishing emails or customized messages which make individuals very difficult to differentiate between legitimate and illegitimate communication. Attackers can use LLMs to automate the creation of targeted spear-phishing campaigns, leveraging personal data scraped from social media to make their attacks more effective. The performance of phishing emails created automatically by GPT-4 and manually using the V-Triad are compared. They also combine GPT-4 with the V-Triad to assess their combined potential and a different set of people exposed to generic phishing emails. The control group emails received a click-through rate between 19-28%, the GPT-generated emails 30–44%, emails generated by the V-Triad 69–79%, and emails generated by GPT and the V-Triad 43-81%. Each participant was asked to explain why they pressed or did not press a link in the email. These answers often contradict each other, highlighting the importance of personal differences [10].

Cybercriminals can exploit LLMs to develop advanced malware and exploits that bypass traditional security measures. For instance, polymorphic malware which constantly changes its code to evade detection by anti-malware tools. LLMs are used to craft the adversarial inputs or poisoned training data to produce harmful results thus reducing the reliability of the system.

Prompt injection attacks represent a critical vulnerability, where cleverly crafted inputs manipulate LLMs into executing unintended commands or leaking sensitive information [17].

Generative AI generates huge volumes of fake content which seems to be realistic and enables the communication on a massive scale creating a chaotic situation. Generally malicious software is identified by the payload and LLMs automate the payload making it harder to identify the malicious code. For example, LLMs can rewrite malicious scripts to avoid keyword-based detection or generate obfuscated code that slips past endpoint protection systems. Several password cracking tools can be automated to steal the credential datasets and by analyzing the pattern leads to future data breaches.

A notable example is DarkBERT, a large language model trained specifically on dark web data, which highlights the potential misuse of LLMs in automating illegal cyber activities like ransomware communication, illicit trade, and phishing kits [13].

LLMs can be used to design unique ransomware strains tailored to specific systems or industries. This customization increases the likelihood of successful attacks and maximizes the impact on targeted victims. These risks highlight the dual-edged nature of LLMs in cybersecurity. While they can enhance defense mechanisms, they also empower attackers with tools to launch more sophisticated and damaging attacks. Addressing these challenges requires proactive measures, including robust security protocols, continuous monitoring, and ethical guidelines for the use of LLMs.

Problem Statement

Challenges of LLM in disrupting cybersecurity

The wide use of Large Language Models (LLMs) in this digital era poses challenges in cybersecurity landscape. To ensure the safety of the confidential data it is important to have a collaborative approach. The critical issue posed by LLM is their dual-use nature. LLMs can improvise the threat detection and mitigation effectively at the same time cybercriminals exploit the advantage of LLMs which can be used for generating the deceptive messages to trick the users. This dual nature raises few important concern a) how should we make use of technology, b) who should have the access. There is a need to strike the balance between development and implementation process which involves regulatory bodies to define the limit.

Another significant concern is the opacity of LLMs. LLM s act as “black boxes”, which means their outcome is known to all but how to derive is not easily explainable. In cybersecurity, analysis of threat will lead to the prompt response but with black box approach of LLM it’s a major drawback in high-stakes scenario. At the same time, the threat landscape is constantly evolving, with attackers quickly adapting to new defenses. By leveraging LLMs, they can develop more advanced and harder-to-detect attack methods, keeping cybersecurity professionals on constant alert.

In addition to these challenges, there is no regulatory framework worldwide. The rapid pace of LLM development has surpassed the creation of governance mechanisms creating significant gaps in accountability. LLMs are also vulnerable to adversarial inputs, and in the absence of appropriate access control, they can be exploited with ease. Researchers propose countermeasures such as output filtering, developer responsibility, and LLM sandboxing to reduce misuse in high-risk scenarios [1]. Without a proper framework to define the clear guidelines, it is difficult to prevent the misuse of the technology which in turn increases the risks associated with LLMs in cybersecurity. It’s a delicate balancing act, but one that is critical for the future of cybersecurity.

Key Challenges:

Four major challenges of LLMs use which can be highlighted are

1) Dual use of technology- Defenders use LLMs to craft the threat modelling to identify the threats and provide a proactive approach. On the other hand, Attackers use LLMs to create malicious content dynamically to trick and trap the users with the motive to steal the sensitive data.
2) Black box approach of LLM makes it very difficult to understand and generate the decisions. This transparency issue limits their reliability in cybersecurity applications as the decision may be false positive.
3) LLMs are ever evolving technology which poses challenges to the traditional threat defense mechanism.
4) Lack of regulation framework- The development of LLMs outpaced the development in regulatory frameworks creating huge gaps between the governance and accountability.

Addressing these challenges requires a proactive approach, combining technological innovation, ethical considerations, and regulatory oversight to ensure LLMs are used responsibly in cybersecurity.

Proposed Solution

Opportunities for mitigation and advancement

The LLMs are misused in cyberattacks such as phishing, misinformation campaigns, and malware generation which evades the mitigation strategy. To address these challenges effectively, we propose a five-part framework techno-ethics model. Figure 25.2 depicts the Techno-Ethical Solution Framework, which is designed to minimize risks and promote the responsible use of LLMs.

Figure 25.2 Techno-Ethics Model
Source: Author

Access control restriction by developers

Dual nature of technology can be solved by introducing the secure development practices and strict access control. Developers may employ the role-based access control (RBAC) and multi-factor authentication (MFA) to ensure that only legitimate individuals can interact with LLMs. APIs must be developed with rate-limiting features to provide secure environment and can prevent automated misuse. Regular audits of access logs can help in identifying and address suspicious activities.

Model training and testing

The models which are designed should be subjected to adversarial scenarios in the development to make sure that the model is trained to recognize and respond to the threats such as phishing or fake/illegitimate code. Dynamic defensive algorithm which can adapt to the ever- changing environment in identifying the patterns and responding to the threat. By analyzing the latest threat updates from communities or forums, intelligence reports and red-team exercises will strengthen the models against evolving attack techniques.

Stakeholders collaboration

A unified approach such as Techno- ethics model is critical to mitigate LLMs posed threats by collaborating the researchers, developers, policymakers, and industry leaders to establish a vulnerability disclosure and promote ethical AI practices. Governments and AI governance bodies should play a key role in regulating and monitoring LLM development to ensure accountability. Partnerships between global and regional stakeholders can enhance threat intelligence sharing and improve overall defense mechanisms.

Ethical guidelines and governance

The use of LLMs should be well-defined based on ethical guidelines and governance frameworks. It is the responsibility of the governance to ensure that the technology is not misused. Policies should explicitly prohibit the generation of harmful or deceptive content and be strictly enforced. Regular audits, compliance with international cybersecurity standards, and the integration of ethics-by-design principles into development processes are crucial. Certification programs can also help verify that LLMs are deployed in an ethical and secure manner.

Public awareness and training

Educating the public and training professionals are vital components of this strategy. Awareness campaigns can inform users about the risks of LLM-generated threats, such as AI-enhanced phishing or fraud. Security professionals need specialized training to detect and counter LLM-related attacks effectively. Workshops on AI ethics and cybersecurity can also empower businesses, government agencies, and the public to recognize and respond to these emerging threats.

This comprehensive framework combines secure development practices, rigorous testing, collaborative governance, ethical standards, and public education to reduce the risks associated with LLM misuse. By implementing these measures, we can ensure the safe and responsible use of LLMs, fostering trust and security in an increasingly digital world.

Future Work

In future, researchers and policy makers should collaborate to create a framework which is acceptable worldwide that can tackle the challenges posed by LLMs in cybersecurity domain. Explainable AI techniques should be employed to make these models more transparent and reliable by improvising the defenses against threats.

A comprehensive regulation to be framed to ensure their ethical use and deployment from adversarial attack. Developing GPT-based policies for GRC has shown promise in automating ransomware mitigation strategies across enterprise networks [19]. Equally important is encouraging collaboration across different fields, bringing together AI experts, cybersecurity professionals, and policymakers to come up with practical and effective solutions. A robust adversarial training framework is needed to secure LLMs against evolving manipulation techniques, especially in autonomous security systems [15].

By working on these areas, we can responsibly and securely integrate LLMs into our increasingly connected digital world.

Conclusion

In summary, the advancement of LLMs has transformed the cybersecurity landscape providing improvements in the threat detection and mitigation, threat response and proactive approach based on the intelligence information gathering and analysis. At the same time, the potential of misuse cannot be ignored. LLMs are faster in creating the customized content to automate phishing attacks, generate the dynamic malware codes, and communicating the fake information as real, posing serious threat to the cybersecurity. To counter these threats, we need a balanced and cooperative strategy which includes strengthening defenses through measures like adversarial training and access controls, setting clear ethical standards to promote responsible use, and crafting thorough regulatory frameworks to guide their deployment.

Collaborative work which includes researchers, developers, policymakers, and industry leaders on a global scale to define the consistent standards and reduce the dangers of LLM misuse. Creating public awareness and providing specialized training for cybersecurity professionals will help build stronger defenses against evolving threats. By combining these efforts, we can harness the benefits of LLMs while minimizing their potential to harm cybersecurity. This thoughtful approach can lay a foundation for more innovative digital landscape.

References

[1] Sara Abdali, Richard Anarfi, C. J. Barberan, Jia He, and Erfan Shayegani. 2025. Securing Large Language Models: Threats, Vulnerabilities and Responsible Practices. arXiv preprint arXiv:2403.12503. https://arxiv.org/abs/2403.12503

[2] Alghawazi, M., Alghazzawi, D., & Alarifi, S. S. (2022). Detection of SQL injection attack using machine learning techniques: A systematic literature review. *Journal of Cybersecurity and Privacy,* 2(4), 764–777. https://doi.org/10.3390/jcp2040039.

[3] Aljabri, M., Aljameel, S. S., Mohammad, R. M. A., Almotiri, S. H., Mirza, S., Anis, F. M., et al. (2021). Intelligent techniques for detecting network attacks: review and research directions. *Sensors (Basel)*, 21(21), 7070. https://doi.org/10.3390/s21217070.

[4] Andaluri, N., Srivastava, A., & Andaluri, R. (2023). A critical study of social engineering vis-a-vis phishing attacks. *International Journal of Innovative Research in Technology, Basic and Applied Sciences,* 10, 19–31.

[5] Ansari, M. F., Dash, B., Sharma, P., & Yathiraju, N. (2022). The impact and limitations of artificial intelligence in cybersecurity: a literature review. *International Journal of Advanced Research in Computer and Communication Engineering,* 11, 81–90. https://doi.org/10.17148/IJARCCE.2022.11912.

[6] Blessing, G., Azeta, E., Misra, S., Osamor, V., Fernandez-Sanz, L., & Pospelova, V. (2022). The emerging threat of AI-driven cyber attacks: a review. *Applied Artificial Intelligence*, 36, 1–34. https://doi.org/10.1080/08839514.2022.2037254.

[7] Ferrag, M., Alwahedi, F., Battah, A., Cherif, B., Mechri, A., Tihanyi, N., et al. (2025). Generative AI in cybersecurity: A comprehensive review of LLM applications and vulnerabilities. *Internet of Things and Cyber-Physical Systems.* 5, 1–46. ISSN 2667-3452, https://doi.org/10.1016/j.iotcps.2025.01.001.

[8] Halfond, W. G. J., Viegas, J., & Orso, A. (2006). A classification of SQL injection attacks and countermeasures. In International Symposium on Signals, Systems, and Electronics.

[9] Havlík, V. (2025). Meaning and understanding in large language models. *Synthese*, 205(1), 9. https://doi.org/10.1007/s11229-024-04878-4.

[10] Heiding, F., Schneier, B., Vishwanath, A., Bernstein, J., & Park, P. (2024). Devising and detecting phishing emails using large language models. *IEEE Access*, 12, 42131–42146. https://doi.org/10.1109/ACCESS.2024.3375882.

[11] Hossain Faruk, M. J., Shahriar, H., Valero, M., Barsha, F., Sobhan, S., Khan, A., et al. (2021). Malware detection and prevention using artificial intelligence techniques. In IEEE International Conference on Big Data, 10.1109/BigData52589.2021.9671434.

[12] Jazyah, Y., & Shalabi, L. (2024). Phishing detection using clustering and machine learning. *IAES International Journal of Artificial Intelligence (IJ-AI)*, 13(4), 4526–4536. https://doi.org/10.11591/ijai.v13.i4.pp4526-4536.

[13] Youngjin Jin, Eugene Jang, Jian Cui, Jin-Woo Chung, Yongjae Lee, and Seungwon Shin. 2023. DarkBERT: A Language Model for the Dark Side of the Internet. In Proceedings of the 61st Annual Meeting of the Association for Computational Linguistics (Volume 1: Long Papers), pages 7515–7533, Toronto, Canada. Association for Computational Linguistics.

[14] Koide, T., Nakano, H., and Chiba, D. 2024. ChatPhishDetector: Detecting Phishing Sites Using Large Language Models. IEEE Access, 12:154381–154400. https://doi.org/10.1109/ACCESS.2024.3483905

[15] Kumar, P. (2024). Adversarial attacks and defenses for large language models (LLMs): methods, frameworks & challenges. *International Journal of Multimedia Information Retrieval*, 13(3), 26. https://doi.org/10.1007/s13735-024-00334-8.

[16] Li, Y., & Liu, Q. (2021). A comprehensive review study of cyber-attacks and cybersecurity; emerging trends and recent developments. *Energy Reports*, 7, 8176–8186. https://doi.org/10.1016/j.egyr.2021.08.126.

[17] Liu, Yi, Gelei Deng, Yuekang Li, Kailong Wang, Tianwei Zhang, Yepang Liu, Haoyu Wang, Yanhong Zheng and Yang Liu. "Prompt Injection attack against LLM-integrated Applications." ArXiv abs/2306.05499 (2023) https://doi.org/10.48550/arxiv.2306.05499.

[18] Long, Z., Yan, H., Shen, G., Zhang, X., He, H., & Cheng, L. (2024). A transformer-based network intrusion detection approach for cloud security. *Journal of Cloud Computing*, 13(1), 5. https://doi.org/10.1186/s13677-023-00574-9.

[19] McIntosh, T. R., Liu, T., Susnjak, T., Alavizadeh, H., Ng, A., Nowrozy, R., et al. (2023). Harnessing GPT-4 for generation of cybersecurity GRC policies: a focus on ransomware attack mitigation. *Computers and Security*, 134, 103424. https://doi.org/10.1016/j.cose.2023.103424.

[20] Motlagh, Farzad Nourmohammadzadeh, Mehrdad Hajizadeh, Mehryar Majd, Pejman Najafi, Feng Cheng and Christoph Meinel. "Large Language Models in Cybersecurity: State-of-the-Art." International Conference on Information Systems Security and Privacy (2024). https://doi.org/10.48550/arxiv.2402.00891.

[21] Humza Naveed, Asad Ullah Khan, Shi Qiu, Muhammad Saqib, Saeed Anwar, Muhammad Usman, Naveed Akhtar, Nick Barnes, and Ajmal Mian. 2025. A Comprehensive Overview of Large Language Models. ACM Trans. Intell. Syst. Technol. 16, 5, Article 106 (October 2025), 72 pages. https://doi.org/10.1145/3744746

[22] Constantinos Patsakis, Fran Casino, Nikolaos Lykousas, Assessing LLMs in malicious code deobfuscation of real-world malware campaigns, Expert Systems with Applications, Volume 256, 2024,124912,ISSN 0957-4174,https://doi.org/10.1016/j.eswa.2024.124912. (https://www.sciencedirect.com/science/article/pii/S0957417424017792)

[23] Purwanto, R., Pal, A., Blair, A., & Jha, S. (2022). PhishSim: Aiding phishing website detection with a feature-free tool. *IEEE Transactions on Information Forensics and Security*, 17, 1497–1512. https://doi.org/10.1109/TIFS.2022.3164212.

[24] Kaur, R., Klobučar, T., & Gabrijelčič, D. (2025). Harnessing the power of language models in cybersecurity: a comprehensive review. *International Journal of Information Management Data Insights*, 5(1), 100315. https://doi.org/10.1016/j.jjimei.2024.100315.

[25] Sarker, I. H., Janicke, H., Mohsin, A., Gill, A., & Maglaras, L. A. (2024). Explainable AI for cybersecurity automation, intelligence and trustworthiness in digital twin: methods, taxonomy, challenges and prospects. *ICT Express*, 10(4), 935–958. https://doi.org/10.1016/j.icte.2024.05.007.

[26] Sasi, T., Lashkari, A. H., Lu, R., Xiong, P., & Iqbal, S. (2024). A comprehensive survey on IoT attacks: taxonomy, detection mechanisms and challenges. *Journal of Information and Intelligence*, 2(6), 455–513. https://doi.org/10.1016/j.jiixd.2023.12.001.

[27] Sun, H., Du, Y., & Li, Q. (2023). Deep learning-based detection technology for SQL injection: research and implementation. *Applied Sciences*, 13(16), 9466. https://doi.org/10.3390/app13169466.

[28] Verma, D. (2024). Automated penetration testing using large language models. *International Journal of Scientific Research (IJSR)*, 13, 1826–1831. https://doi.org/10.21275/SR24427043741.

[29] Xu, Hanxiang & Wang, Shenao & Li, Ningke & Wang, Kailong & Zhao, Yanjie & Chen, Kai & Yu, Ting & Liu, Yang & Wang, Haoyu. (2024). Large Language Models for Cyber Security: A Systematic Literature Review. 10.13140/RG.2.2.10132.92800

[30] Yagmur Yigit, William J. Buchanan, Madjid G. Tehrani, and Leandros Maglaras. 2024. Review of Generative AI Methods in Cybersecurity. arXiv preprint arXiv:2403.08701. https://arxiv.org/abs/2403.08701.

For Product Safety Concerns and Information please contact our EU representative GPSR@taylorandfrancis.com
Taylor & Francis Verlag GmbH, Kaufingerstraße 24, 80331 München, Germany

www.ingramcontent.com/pod-product-compliance
Lightning Source LLC
LaVergne TN
LVHW080809011026
849160LV00015B/1574

9781041240785